Dr. Lama has made a careful study of tl [barcode: MW00332437]
Psalter. He has recovered the importance of the kingdom of God as the hope
of the Psalter. David submits himself and the future of his dynasty to God's
universal rule. This study follows the compositional and canonical approach.
It is a good read!

Willem A. VanGemeren

Professor of Old Testament and Semitic Languages

Trinity Evangelical Divinity School, IL, USA

Reading Psalm 145 with the Sages: A Compositional Analysis

A. K. Lama

Langham

MONOGRAPHS

© 2013 by A. K. Lama.

Published 2013 by Langham Monographs
an imprint of Langham Creative Projects

Langham Partnership
PO Box 296, Carlisle, Cumbria CA3 9WZ, UK
www.langham.org

ISBNs:
978-1907713-35-4 Print
978-1907713-36-1 Mobi
978-1907713-37-8 ePub

British Library Cataloguing in Publication Data
Langham Monographs
A. K. Lama
Reading Psalm 145 with the Sages
   1. Bible. O.T. Psalms CXLV--Criticism, interpretation, etc.
   I. Title
   223.2'06-dc23
   ISBN-13: 9781907713354

Cover & Book Design: projectluz.com

Contents

Abstract ix

Acknowledgments xi

Chapter 1 1

Introduction

    The Significance of Psalm 145 2

    History of Interpretation 7

        Pre-Form-Critical Interpretation 7

        Form-Critical Interpretation 9

    Compositional Critical Interpretation 14

        Brevard S. Childs 15

        Gerald H. Wilson 16

    The Turning Point 17

        Composition of Book V 19

        Composition of the 11QPSa 21

        Composition of the LXX 24

    Criticism of the Compositional Critical Interpretation 26

        Different Compositional Readings of Book V 30

    Conclusion 31

Chapter 2 35

Methodological Considerations

    Theological Assumptions 35

    Hermeneutical Assumption 38

        Canonical-Linguistic Approach 42

        Discourse Analysis 45

        Seven Standards of Textuality 46

    The Exegetical Assumption 49

        Historical Context 49

        Democratization of David 54

        Thematic Patterning 55

        The Acrostic Structure 57

        Textual Critical Theory 58

        The Absence of Nun Line 60

    Conclusion 69

Chapter 3 73

A Discourse Analysis of Psalm 145

 Translation...74

 The Literary Genre...78

 The Literary Structure..80

  Traditional Literary Division....................................83

  Thematic Considerations 84

 Rhetorical Literary Division...87

  Key Words 87

  Concentric Structure 90

  Literary Symmetry...91

  Reuven Kimelman 93

  Conclusion 99

 Linguistic Analysis 102

  The Anticipating Praise of David 102

  The Kingship of YHWH 105

  The Phenomena of the Blessing 113

  The Language of Universalism and Particularism 116

  The Language of Hope..119

 Conclusion 121

Chapter 4... 125

The Last Davidic Psalm and
the Final Hallel Psalms

 The Editorial Purpose 125

  The Final Wisdom Frame 126

  The Climax of Book V..131

 The Final Hallel Psalms...153

  Psalm 146..154

  Psalm 147..156

  Psalm 148..158

  Psalm 149..160

  Psalm 150..162

  Conclusion 163

 The Last Place 164

 Conclusion 170

Chapter 5... 173

David in the Kingdom of God

 The Davidic Psalms..174

  The Paradigm of David..175

Psalm 108..177
Psalm 109..181
Psalm 110..184
Psalm 138..189
Psalm 139..192
Psalm 140..195
Psalm 141..199
Psalm 142..202
Psalm 143..205
Psalm 144..209
Conclusion...213
YHWH Kingship Psalms in Book IV.....................................216
Psalm 93..218
Psalm 95..219
Psalm 96..219
Psalm 97..220
Psalm 98..221
Psalm 99..222
Psalm 103..223
The Motif of the Kingdom of God...228
Conclusion 237

Chapter 6...241
    Conclusion

Appendix 1...249
    The Order of Qumran Psalms

Appendix 2...253
    Canonization of the Psalter

Appendix 3...255
    Concentric Structure of Psalm 145

Appendix 4...257
    Different Usage of מלך *in the Psalter*

Appendix 5...259
    The Use of YHWH in Psalm 145

Appendix 6...261
    Lexical Connections Between Psalms 103 and 145

Bibliography..263

Abstract

This study analyzes the placement of Psalm 145 in the MT in relation to the final *hallel* (Psalms 146-50), the two groups of Davidic psalms (Psalms 108-10 and 138-44), and the YHWH Kingship psalms in Book IV (Psalms 93, 95, 96, 97, 98, 99 and 103). The methodology applied for this study underscores the use of discourse analysis for the compositional critical study of the above-mentioned psalms. In this study, the psalms are considered both at the level of their lexemes, syntagmemes, themes, and their individual discourse meanings.

Reading Psalm 145 as a single discourse provides a useful lesson for our meditation; however, reading it in relation with the discourse meaning of other psalms (*Sitz in der Literatur*) in sequence makes the didactic lesson more comprehensive. Such reading enables one to observe and analyze thematic patterning and the intratextual dialogue of individual psalms with other adjacent psalms, thereby broadening the didactic lesson in the context of the whole Psalter.

Psalm 145 is a unique Davidic psalm. The psalm is Janus-like, looking backward to the group of Davidic psalms and forward to the final *hallel* psalms. The central theme of the psalm is universal Kingdom of God—a Kingdom in which the providential care of YHWH is available to all creation. The placement of such a unique theme in the mouth of David at the end of the Psalter is purposeful.

The study shows numerous editorial reasons for the placement of Psalm 145 in the fifth book of the Psalter (MT). It provides information about the socio-historical, the theological, and the hermeneutical perspectives of the redactor (s) and the community of sages who compiled the Psalter in its final shape.

To God, my King, and to my prudent wife Asangla
and to our three godly children: Sonam, Neema, and Joshua

Acknowledgments

First, I thank God for granting me health, guidance, prayer support, finance, and friends during my Ph. D. studies. In a miraculous way, he brought godly men and women on my path to provide help that I needed to complete my academic journey at Trinity International University.

I am grateful to Dr. Willem A. VanGemeren, whose scholarly insight and pastoral demeanor impressed me from the day I first met him. His academic mentoring has pushed me to excellence for the language skill, research, and writing. His pastoral care and encouragement has been like manna in the desert to me.

I also owe gratitude to John Stott Ministries and Christian International Scholarship Fundation for their scholarships that enabled a smooth academic and family life at Trinity. Men and women from these two organizations provided us continuous moral support and encouragement. I am particularly grateful to Mrs. Sheri Woodruff who diligently edited all my writings.

There are others who also deserve mention in this acknowledgement for their enormous trust and confidence in me: the Pastor and the members of Providence Baptist Church (Lanett, AL), the leaders of the Transforming Leaders in Asia (TLA), the Dean and the faculty of Beeson Divinity School (Birmingham, AL), Yohanna and Dina Katanacho, Dali and Ling Luo, Earle and Ginny Combs, Evona VanGemeren, and my beloved family. They all stood beside me unconditionally.

CHAPTER 1

Introduction

The purposeful placement of psalms within the collection seems to have given the final form of the whole Psalter a function and message greater than the sum of its parts.

— J. Clinton McCann[1]

Current psalms scholarship lays emphasis on the final form of the Psalter with an interest to explore the significance of the whole as a canon.[2] This new approach calls attention to the literary setting (*Sitz in der Literatur*), the shape and the shaping of the Psalter as a literary collection, and the intent of the editor(s) that shaped the Psalter as a book. In this new perspective, the Psalter is not only a collection of man's word to God, but it has become God's word to humanity at the level of individual psalms as well as

---

1. J. Clinton McCagn, preface to *The Shape and Shaping of the Psalter* (ed. J. Clinton McCann; JSOTSup 159, Sheffield: JSOT Press, 1993a), 7.

2. The following publications capture the shift in emphasis on the methodological approach in psalms scholarship in detail: David M. Howard, Jr., "Recent Trends in Psalm Study," in *The Face of Old Testament Studies: A Survey of Contemporary Approaches* (ed. David W. Baker et al.; Grand Rapids: Baker, 1999): 413-20; David M. Howard, Jr., "The Psalms and Current Study," in *Interpreting the Psalms: Issues and Approaches* (ed. David G. Firth et al.; Downers Grove: InterVarsity, 2005), 23-40; David G. Firth, "The Teaching of the Psalms," in *Interpreting the Psalms: Issues and Approaches* (ed. David G. Firth et al.; Downers Grove: InterVarsity, 2005), 159-74. James Luther Mays, "Past, Present, and Prospect in Psalm Study," in *Old Testament Interpretation: Past, Present, and Future: Essays in Honor of Gene M. Tucker* (ed. Gene M. Tucker et al.; Nashville: Abingdon, 1995), 147-56; Erich Zenger, "New Approaches to the Study of the Psalms," *PIBA* 17 (1994b): 37-54; Brevard S. Childs, "Reflections on the Modern Study of the Psalms," in *Magnalia Dei: The Mighty Acts of God: Essays on the Bible and Archaeology in Memory of G. Ernest Wright* (ed. George Ernest Wright et al.; Garden City: Doubleday, 1976), 375-88.

at the level of their editorial placement in the Psalter. Recent scholars have argued for unequivocal patterns in the arrangements of the Masoretic Text (MT), the Septuagint (LXX), and the Qumran text of the Psalter for editorial intent and theological motive.

On the one hand, the new approach has raised questions and skepticism concerning the placement of certain psalms in certain locations in the Psalter. On the other hand, it has invigorated modern psalms scholarship.[3] A number of psalms scholars have begun reading the psalms in relation to other psalms compositionally. In the context of such advancement, this dissertation will investigate the placement of Psalm 145 in the Masoretic Text (MT), especially in the context of Book V, and examine how such a methodological reading enriches the understanding of Psalm 145.[4]

The Significance of Psalm 145

Investigating the placement of Psalm 145 in Book V is important for four reasons. First, the location of Psalm 145 in the MT is uniquely different from the Septuagint text (the LXX), and the Qumran *Psalms scroll* (11QPsᵃ).[5] In the LXX, Psalm 151 is the last Davidic psalm, while in the 11QPsᵃ the order of the psalms is entirely different.[6] In fact, Psalm 145 is placed between Pss 118:29 and 154:3, close to the middle of the scroll.[7]

---

3. Howard writes, "The question of literary unity within the Psalter is a more complicated one than it is for most biblical books—owing to discrete nature of each psalm and their early functions in liturgical settings—and it has been ignored for the most part in the history of Psalm study." David M. Howard, Jr., "A Contextual Reading of Psalms 90-94," in *The Shape and Shaping of the Psalter* (ed. J. Clinton McCann; JSOTSup 159, Sheffield: JSOT Press, 1993), 108.

4. All references to the biblical texts [including chapter(s) and verse(s)] and the Books of the Psalter [I (Psalms 1-40); II (Psalms 41-72); III (Psalm 73-89); IV (Psalms 90-106); and V (Psalms 107-150)] are taken from the Masoretic Text (MT), unless otherwise mentioned. Hereafter the Masoretic Text is cited as the MT. The MT used in this dissertation is based on the codex Leningrad B19ᵃ (L).

5. Hereafter the Septuagint Text is cited as the LXX. The 11QPsᵃ refers to the largest Qumran *Psalms Scroll* discovered in Cave 11 (1956).

6. Gerald Henry Wilson, "The Qumran Psalms Scroll (11QPsa) and the Canonical Psalter: Comparison of Editorial Shaping," *CBQ* 59 (1997): 450.

7. James A. Sanders, *The Psalms Scroll of Qumran Cave 11 (11QPsᵃ)* (Oxford: Clarendon, 1965), 226; Wilson, "The Qumran Psalms Scroll," 448-64.

But in the MT, Psalm 145 is the last Davidic psalm,[8] uniquely placed at the end of the last Davidic collection (Psalms 138-45).[9] It is also the only psalm with תהלה in its superscript, placed before the final הלל psalms (Psalms 146-50). This specific location in the MT poses several questions. Why is Psalm 145 placed in between Psalms 144 and 146? Why is this psalm placed as the last Davidic psalm in the MT but not in the LXX or in the 11QPs^a? Does this placement indicate a unique role in the MT, different from the LXX and the 11QPs^a? Is there any implicit or explicit literary evidence within the MT that may indicate why Psalm 145 is uniquely placed? How does Psalm 145 connect lexically, syntactically and thematically with other Davidic psalms in Book V? Is there any theological motive that is tacit in its literary context for its purposeful placement? Does this placement indicate any new role for this Davidic psalm? How does it connect with the final הלל psalms (Psalms 146-50)?

Second, the Talmudic tradition records the reading of Psalm 145 in combination with its adjacent psalm (Psalm 144). Although Psalm 145 does not have the word אשרי in the MT, it is commonly known as the אשרי psalm in the Synagogue liturgy.[10] In its liturgical reading Psalm 145 is preceded by Ps 84:5 (אשרי אדם עוז־לו בך מסלות בלבבם) and Ps 144:15 (אשרי העם שככה לו אשרי העם שיהוה אלהיו) by way of introduction, and is concluded by Ps 115:18 (ואנחנו נברך יה מעתה ועד־עולם הללו־יה).[11] Thus,

---

8. The MT text of Psalm 145 has לדוד in its superscript. Hereafter, all chapter and verse citation of the Hebrew text refer to the 5th diplomatic edition of *Biblia Hebraica Stuttgartensia*, edited by K. Elliger and W. Rudolph (1967-77), unless otherwise specified. The 5th edition of *Biblia Hebraica Stuttgartensia* is cited as BHS.

9. Davidic collections are the groups of psalms that have לדוד in their superscripts, or the psalms that are attributed as Davidic by implied relation with the predecessors (such as Psalms 10 and 33). There are five Davidic collections (Psalms 3-41, 51-65, 68-70, 108-110, 138-145) and eight individual Davidic psalms (Psalms 86, 101, 103, 122, 124, 131, 132, and 133) in the Psalter.

10. There are psalms that are distinctly recognized as אשרי psalms (see Pss 1:1; 32:1, 2; 84:5, 6; 119:1, 2; 128:1, 2; and 137:8, 9.), but not Psalm 145. However, in the Prayer Book of the Synagogue, the opening word of this psalm is אשרי. See Chaim Pearle, "The Theology of Psalm 145: Part I," *JBQ* 20/1 (1991): 3.

11. Both Pearle and Z. Adar point out that in Jewish liturgy this psalm was prefixed with Ps 84:5 and Ps 144:5 and suffixed by Ps 115:8. Ibid., 3. See also Adele Berlin, "The Rhetoric of Psalm 145," in *Biblical and Related Studies Presented to Samuel Iwry* (ed. Ann Kort and Scott Morschauser; Winona Lake: Eisenbrauns, 1985), 17-22.

the word אשרי is repeated three times before Psalm 145 is read.[12] This tradition does not have continuity in the Christian tradition. We wonder if the traditional reading of Psalm 145 as an אשרי psalm in connection with Ps 144:15 is editorially intended. Why is Psalm 145 placed between the two אשרי psalms (Pss 144:15; 146:5, a total of three אשרי)? Is there any tacit or explicit literary evidence in its unique placement for its usage as an אשרי psalm?

Third, we notice that Ps 145:8 reverses the Exodus imagery (Exod 34:6) from חנון ורחם to רחום וחנון, conforming uniquely to other similar occurrences in Book V (Pss 111:4, 112:4, 116:5) in the MT. This is unique because the Exodus imagery in Book III (Pss 86:15) and Book IV (Ps 103:8) appears in the same order as in Exod 34:6 (רחם וחנון). It may be suggested that this reversal in Pss 111:4, 112:4, and 145:8 is for the purpose of an acrostic arrangement; however, the same cannot be true for the non-acrostic Psalm 116. In Ps 116:5, יהוה is introduced first as חנון and then as the one who has רחם. The consistency in the reversed order is most unlikely accidental. Perhaps it indicates an editorial shaping of the language of Book V. Furthermore, we notice that the clause (ארך אפים ורב־חסד) that follows the Exodus imagery (רחם וחנון) in Exod 34:6 is retained in the psalms (Pss 86:15; 103:8) in Book III and Book IV, but in the psalms in Book V, it is changed.

Additionally, Pss 112:4 and 116:5 has the phrase וצדיק, while in Ps 145:8 ורב is replaced with וגדל. These changes in the language of Exodus arouse our interest in this psalm. Do these changes in the Exodus language in Book V suggest its purposeful editorial shaping? Are there any other

---

12. This triple reading of אשרי has traditionally supported the Talmudic notion that Psalm 145 is worthy enough to be recited three times a day. In the liturgical use of the Synagogue, this psalm was recited twice in the morning and once in the evening service. See A. F. Kirkpatrick, ed., *The Book of Psalms* (Cambridge Bible for Schools and Colleges; Cambridge: Cambridge University Press, 1902), 813; Willem A. VanGemeren, "Psalms," in *Psalms, Proverbs, Ecclesiastes, Song of Songs* (ed. Frank E. Gæbelein; EBC 5, Grand Rapids: Zondervan, 1991), 860. In *B. Berakhoth* 4b, this psalm is introduced by an apophthegm: "Every one who repeats the תהלה לדוד three time a day may be sure that he is a child of the world to come (בן העולם הבא)." See Franz Delitzsch, *Biblical Commentary on the Psalms* (trans. Francis Bolton; 3 vols.; Grand Rapids: Eerdmans, 1955), 387; Pearle, "Psalm 145: Part I," 3-4. In the liturgical use of Synagogue, this psalm was recited twice in the morning and once in the evening service. See Kirkpatrick, ed., *The Book of Psalms*, 813; VanGemeren, "Psalms," 860.

characteristics of the language of Book V that can be distinguished? If yes, what are they and what may be the editorial motive? If not, does the use of Exodus imagery (רחם וחנון) in Psalm 145 have any specific significance? Is Psalm 145 editorially designed with specific language to be placed in Book V?

Fourth, it appears that the theme of Psalm 145 is in tension with the themes of the adjacent psalms in the MT. Psalm 145 is thematically unique in Book V because it is the only psalm, which explicitly presents YHWH's Kingdom as universal and eternal.[13] Scholars agree with the centrality of the theme of the Kingdom of God and an added emphasis on universalism in this psalm. Wilfred G. E. Watson highlights the ingenious work of the poet in the internal structure of this psalm by pointing out the "miniacrostic," and the reverse root play in verses 11-13 (notice the first letter of each verse: v. 11 כבוד, v. 12 להודיע, v. 13 מלכותך).[14] The reversing phenomenon of the letters כ, ל, and מ from the root word מלך, the chiasm in verses 11-12 (v. 11 כבוד, גבורתיו; v. 12 גבורתיו, כבוד), and the four-fold repetitions of the root word מלך lead Watson to suggest that the basic theme of Psalm 145 is "God's eternal and universal kingship."[15] The eternal aspect is emphasized by the repetition of the phrase לעולם ועד (Ps 145:1, 2, 21), and the cosmic reign is underscored by the inclusive language of כל (Ps 145:9, 14, 16, 18), and ברך (Ps 145:21, ויברך כל-בשר). The beneficiaries of this cosmic reign are stated to be "all flesh" (Ps 145:21) and all those who love and fear YHWH (Ps 145:18-20). No ethnic group, nation, or geography is mentioned in this psalm.

On the contrary, the neighboring psalms (Pss 137:7-9; 147:20; 148:14; and 149:2-9) in the MT contain the language of particularism that projects Israel as a favored nation, set against all other nations. In Ps 137:7-9, the psalmist anticipates a cruel retribution against the enemy nations: Edom and Babylon. In Ps 147:20, the psalmist proclaims that YHWH has favored the nation of Israel by revealing to them the word, the ordinance, and the law, but he did not reveal these to other nations. In Ps 148:14,

---

13. VanGemeren entitles Psalm 145 "Great is Yahweh's Universal Kingdom." See VanGemeren, "Psalms," 860. See also Kirkpatrick, ed., *The Book of Psalms*, 813.

14. W. G. E. Watson, "Reversed Rootplay in Ps 145," *RB* 62 (1981): 101-2.

15. Ibid.

Israel is mentioned as YHWH's people (לעמו), as the one close to him (עם־
קרבו). And in Ps 149:2-9, Israel rejoices in YHWH their King (במלכם),
and praises him because he inflicts vengeance against other nations. The
kings and the noblemen of other nations are put in chains. In the context
of this aforementioned language of particularism, the language of Psalm
145 seems to be in contradiction. In other words, the universal Kingdom
of YHWH seems to be in tension with Israel's particular eschatological
expectation of the Davidic kingdom.

Furthermore, Psalm 145 would have belonged more appropriately to
the YHWH Kingship psalms (Psalms 93, 96-99) in Book IV. Why then
is Psalm 145 placed purposefully in a place of tension? Why does the language of universality (Ps 145:8-12, 14-17) and the language of the universal kingdom (Ps 145:13, 21) include only those who love and fear Yahweh
(Ps 145:18-20) rather than any particular ethnic group in the last Davidic
psalm? Is it because the editor(s)/sages intended a certain theological shift
or emphasis? Does the reading of Psalm 145 in its new canonical context
imply any change in sociological, theological, and eschatological thinking?
Does this psalm affirm the eschatological expectation of a Davidic kingdom or redefine the Davidic kingdom in light of the Kingdom of God?
What does the psalmist have to say about the Kingdom of God through
the mouth of David?

The answers to these questions would not only complement and enhance the ongoing psalms research on compositional reading of the Psalter,
but also improve our understanding of the theological message embedded
in the final shape of the Psalter. Additionally, there is a contextual and
contemporary reason for the author to consider this project. The compositional reading of Psalm 145 may help improve the general perception of
the God of the Bible in India. The author of this project hails from the
Asian subcontinent of India, where Christianity is perceived as a foreign
religion and the God of the Bible as the deity of the Jews and the Western
nations. However, the compositional reading of Psalm 145 underscores the
emphasis on the message of universal Kingdom of God. It counters such
false social, cultural, and religious thinking. In fact, the twenty-first century
churches in India are comprised of people who have embraced Christianity
from diverse ethnic and religious backgrounds. They have become a living

example of the inclusive and universal domain of the God of the Bible, which Psalm 145 boldly proclaims.

History of Interpretation

A literary review of the history of the interpretation of Psalm 145 reveals that many questions concerning the compositional placement of the psalm, especially at the micro level, have not been considered.[16] The following survey on the history of interpretation of the psalm affirms this.

The history of interpretation of Psalm 145 can be classified broadly into three major methodological criteria of interpretation: pre-form-critical interpretation, form critical interpretation, compositional critical interpretation. A comprehensive survey of the history of interpretation of this psalm is outside the purview of this section. However, we will discuss the subject adequately enough to highlight how this project complements methodologically the body of knowledge concerning the interpretation of this psalm.

Pre-Form-Critical Interpretation

Prior to the rise of the modern critical scholarship, most psalms scholars of Jewish and Christian traditions showed interest in the inter-link between consecutive psalms. In the Jewish tradition, the reading of Psalm 145 is preceded by Ps 84:5 and Ps 144:15, and is followed by Ps 115:8.[17] In Christian tradition, authorship, key words, motifs, and theological themes were used to establish the connection between the psalms.[18] For instance, John Calvin

---

16. The recent work of Frank-Lothar Hossfeld and Erich Zenger does analyze psalms with the compositional approach; however, at the writing of this chapter, a comprehensive analysis of Psalms 1-50 and 101-150 are still anticipated. Frank-Lothar Hossfeld et al., *Psalmen 51-100* (Freiburg im Breisgau: Herder, 2000); Frank-Lothar Hossfeld et al., *Psalms 2: A Commentary on Psalms 51-100* (ed. Klaus Baltzer; trans. Linda M. Maloney; Minneapolis: Fortress, 2005). See also VanGemeren, "Psalms," 1-880; Leslie C. Allen, *Psalms 101-50* (WBC 21; Nashville: Nelson, 2002); Samuel L. Terrien, *The Psalms: Strophic Structure and Theological Commentary* (Grand Rapids: Eerdmans, 2003).

17. Pearle, "Psalm 145: Part I," 3. See also Berlin, "The Rhetoric of Psalm 145," 17-22.

18. Howard's brief analytical survey of pre-1970s Christian psalm scholars illustrates these phenomena. David M. Howard, Jr., "Editorial Activity in the Psalter: A State-of-the-Field

(1509-1564) believed Psalm 145 to be the original composition of David and therefore he interprets it in relation to the adjacent Davidic psalm (Ps 144:9).[19] He claims that Psalm 145 is David's personal response to the desire for singing a "new song" expressed in Ps 144:9.[20] Several years later, Joseph A. Alexander (1809-1860) interpreted this psalm exactly as Calvin.[21] Franz Delitzsch (1813-1890) also read this psalm in relation to other adjacent psalms. He notices Psalm 144 as the psalm that closes the collection doxologically, while Psalm 145 initiates a new beginning with the language of blessing and benediction.[22] A. F. Kirkpatrick alleges this psalm as the head of a series of psalms of praise.[23] According to him, Psalms 140-50 must have been composed together for a liturgical purpose, for they are connected by many similar thoughts and language. E. W. Hengstenberg also notices this psalm as a parallel to Psalm 103. Both Psalms 103 and 145 are about the greatness, goodness, and righteousness of YHWH.[24]

In general, pre-form-critical psalm scholars do not grapple with the historical critical issues related to the Psalter's composition, transmission, and compilation.[25] The primary interest, as reflected in their method, is to make the received text of the Psalter relevant to their daily spiritual needs. Their

---

Survey," in *The Shape and Shaping of the Psalter* (ed. J. Clinton McCann; JSOTSup 159, Sheffield: JSOT Press, 1993), 54.

19. John Calvin, *Commentary on the Book of Psalms* (trans. James Anderson; 5 vols.; Grand Rapids: Eerdmans, 1949), 271-72.

20. Ibid., 271-2. See also Joseph A. Alexander, *The Psalms: Translated and Explained* (Philadelphia: Presbyterian Board of Publication, 1850), 292.

21. Alexander, *The Psalms: Translated and Explained*, 292.

22. Delitzsch, *Biblical Commentary on the Psalms*, 387.

23. Kirkpatrick, ed., *The Book of Psalms*, 813.

24. Ernst Wilhelm Hengstenberg, *Commentary on the Psalms* (Cherry Hill: Mack Publishing, 1845), 534-35.

25. A number of psalm study show pre-form-critical approaches. See J. M. Neale et al., *A Commentary on the Psalms: From Primitive and Mediaeval Writers and from the Various Office-Books and Hymns of the Roman, Mozarabic, Ambrosian, Gallican, Greek, Coptic, Armenian, and Syriac Rites* (2d ed.; London: Joseph Masters, 1976); William Holladay, *The Psalms through Three Thousand Years: Prayerbook of a Cloud of Witnesses* (Minneapolis: Fortress, 1993); Martin McNamara, *The Psalm in the Early Irish Church* (ed. David Clines et al.; JSOTSup 155; Sheffield: Sheffield Academic Press, 2000); Mayer Guber, *Rashi's Commentary on Psalms (Books I-III): With English Translation, Introduction and Notes* (ed. Jacob Neusner et al.; Atlanta: Scholars, 1998); Bishop of Cyrus Theodoret, *Theodoret of Cyrus: Commentary on the Psalms, Psalm 1-72* (ed. Thomas Halton et al.; trans. Robert Hill; Washington, D.C.: Catholic University of America, 2000).

method majors on key words and theological themes in the psalms rather than their historical context or genre, much less the shape and the shaping of the Psalter.

Form-Critical Interpretation

In the beginning of the late nineteenth and early twentieth centuries, psalms studies emphasized on the reconstruction of the history of Israel and its religion.[26] Among many scholarly works, Hermann Gunkel's work on the literary genre (*Gattung*) and life setting (*Sitz im Leben*), as the two parallel historical criteria for interpreting psalms, inaugurated a new approach in psalms' studies.[27] In his approach, the history of provenance continued

---

26. A number of psalm studies published from the nineteenth to the twenty-first centuries represent this phenomenon. For reference see Wilhelm and Theodore Parker De Wette, *A Critical and Historical Introduction to the Canonical Scriptures of the Old Testament* (trans. Theodore Parker; 2d ed.; Boston: Little, Brown, and Company, 1858); John De Witt, *The Psalms: A New Translation with Introductory Essay and Notes* (New York: Anson D. F. Randolph, 1891); Julius Wellhousen, *The Book of Psalms: A New English Translation with Explanatory Notes and Appendix on the Music of the Ancient Hebrews* (ed. Paul Haupt and Horace Furness; trans. John Taylor Horace Furness, and J. A. Paterson; The Sacred Books of the Old and New Testaments 14; New York: Dodd, Mead, 1898); Von Max Haller, "Ein Jahrzehnt Psalmenforschung," *Tru* 1 (1929): 377-402; Ovid Sellers, "The Status and Progress of Research Concerning the Psalms," in *The Study of the Bible Today and Tomorrow* (Chicago: University of Chicago Press, 1947), 129-43; A. R. Johnson, "The Psalms," in *The Old Testament and Modern Study: A Generation of Discovery and Research; Essays by Members of The Society for Old Testament Study* (ed. Harold Rowley; Oxford: Clarendon, 1951): 162-209; Johann Stamm, "Ein Vierteljahrhudert Psalmenforschung," *TRu* 23 (1955): 1-68; David Clines, "Psalm Research 1955: I. The Psalms and the Cult," *TynBul* 18 (1967): 103-26; David Clines, "Psalm Research 1955: II. The Psalms and the Cult," *TynBul* 20 (1969): 105-25; Childs, "Reflections on the Modern Study," 377-88; John Haralson Hayes, *An Introduction to Old Testament Study* (Nashville: Abingdon, 1979), 238-73; J. H. Eaton, "The Psalms and Israelite Worship," in *Tradition and Interpretation: Essays by Members of the Society for Old Testament Study* (ed. George Anderson; Oxford: Clarendon, 1979); J. Kenneth Kuntz, "Engaging the Psalms: Gains and Trends in Recent Research," *CurBS* 2 (1994): 77-106; Erich Zenger, "New Approaches to the Study of the Psalms," *PIBA* 17 (1994a): 37-54; Mays, "Past, Present, and Prospect," 147-56; Howard, "Recent Trends in Psalm Study," 329-68; James Crenshaw, introduction to *The Psalms in Israel's Worship*, by Sigmund Mowinckel (Grand Rapids: Eerdmans, 2004), xix-xxxii.

27. Although Gunkel is popularly known as the father of Form Criticism (*Formgeschichte*), the term Form Criticism (*Formgeschichte*) first appeared in the title of Martin Dibelius's work. See Martin Dibelius, *Die Formgeschichte des Evangeliums* (Tübingen: Mohr, 1919); Martin Dibelius, *From Tradition to Gospel* (trans. Bertram Lee Woolf; London: Ivor Nicholson and Watson, 1934). See also Hayes, *An Introduction to Old Testament Study*, 127. The popular writings of Gunkel are: Hermann Gunkel, *Die Psalmen* (Göttingen: Vandenhoeck & Ruprecht, 1926); Hermann Gunkel, *Einleitung in Die Psalmen: Die Gattungen der Religiösen Lyrik Israels* (Göttingen: Vandenhoeck and Ruprecht, 1933);

to be the key to the meaning of the psalms.[28] Based on the literary genre (*Gattung*) and life setting (*Sitz im Leben*), Gunkel classifies the Psalter into five major categories: individual laments, individual thanksgiving psalms, hymns, community laments, and royal psalms.[29] He places Psalm 145 in the category of hymns (Psalms 145-50). He separates it from the last group of Davidic psalms (Psalms 138-144).[30] Based on the linguistic forms, he notices different hymn-like features in the psalm (Ps 145:1f-2, 3, 4-7, 8f, 10-12, 13, 14, 17, and 21).[31] His method results in the fragmentation of the psalm. For example, Gunkel notices that the phrase אהללה in Ps 145:2 links the psalm with Pss 22:23; 69:31; 109:30; and 146:2, while the phrase אברכה and אברכך in Ps 145:1-2 links the psalm with Pss 16:7; 26:12; 34:2; 63:5.[32] Gunkel's classification is so preoccupied with atomized language forms that the discourse meaning of the psalm in relation with the adjacent

---

Hermann Gunkel et al., *Introduction to Psalms: The Genres of the Religious Lyric of Israel* (trans. James D. Nogalski; Macon: Mercer University Press, 1998); Hermann Gunkel, *The Psalms: A Form-Critical Introduction* (trans. Thomas M. Horner; Philadelphia: Fortress Press, 1967); Hermann Gunkel et al., *Israel and Babylon the Influence of Babylon on the Religion of Israel: A Reply to Delitzsch* (Philadelphia: John Jos, 1904).

28. Other psalms scholars explored Ancient Near Eastern (ANE) literature, history, culture, and archeological findings that might elicit the life setting (*Sitz im Leben*) of the text and the history of the literary genre (*Gattung*). The following works reflect the emphasis on the ANE context in the psalms studies. Godfrey Driver, "The Psalms in the Light of Babylonian Research," in *The Psalmists: Essays on Their Religious Experience and Teaching, Their Social Background, and Their Place in the Development of Hebrew Psalmody* (ed. D.C. Simpson; London: Oxford University Press, 1926), 109-75; Aylward Blackman, "The Psalms in the Light of Egyptian Research," in *The Psalmists: Essays on Their Religious Experience and Teaching, Their Social Background, and Their Place in the Development of Hebrew Psalmody* (ed. D.C. Simpson; London: Oxford University Press, 1926), 177-97.

29. For more information on Hermann Gunkel's work see Martin Buss, *Biblical Form Criticism in Its Context* (ed. David Clines and Phillip Davis; JSOTSup 274; Sheffield: Sheffield Academic Press, 1999), 209-62; M. J. Buss, "Gunkel, Hermann (1862-1932)," in *Historical Handbook of Major Biblical Interpreters* (ed. Donald McKim; Downers Grove: InterVarsity, 1998), 487-91.

30. Gunkel et al., *Introduction to Psalms*, 22.

31. Ibid., 23-28.

32. Ibid., 26.

psalms is entirely ignored.[33] He does not inquire about the editorial placement of Psalm 145 in the Psalter.[34]

Following Gunkel, Sigmund Mowinckel uses Israel's cult setting as the criterion for the interpretation of psalms.[35] He writes, "A true interpretation of the psalm must try to form as complete and vivid a picture as possible of the old Israelite and Jewish cult and its many situations and acts."[36] In his classification, he places Psalms 90-150 into four smaller collections: (1) the Enthronement psalms (Psalms 93; 95-99); (2) the Egyptian *hallel* psalms (Psalms 113-118); (3) songs of the procession (Psalms 120-34); and (4) the final *hallel* psalms (Psalms 146-50). He does not comment on the cult of several psalms (Psalms 90-92; 94; 111-112; 119; and 135-144), including Psalm 145, because he fails to see that some psalms (like Psalm 145) present the enthroned king (Pss 93:1; 96:5) as well as the eschatological king whose kingdom is universal and eternal. Like Gunkel, Mowinckel ignores any editorial link between Psalm 145 and the rest of the Psalter because he sees the shaping of the Psalter as a long and gradual process.[37]

Continuing under the framework of *Sitz im Leben*, Artur Weiser introduces a new hypothetical perspective. The new life setting is the Covenant Festival of Yahweh observed in autumn in order to renew the Sinai covenant and the promise of salvation.[38] This life setting was greatly influenced

---

33. Concerning Gunkel's method that ignored adjacent psalms, Goulder comments, "Gunkel's method in practice treated the order of the Psalms as nugatory. The key to understanding a psalm was to classify it; what shed light on 47 was not its relation to 46 or 48 as its neighbouring psalms in the tradition, but to 93, 97 and 98 as fellow songs of Yahweh's throne-ascent." M. D. Goulder, *The Psalms of the Sons of Korah* (JSOTSup 20; Sheffield: JSOT Press, 1982), 8.

34. Gunkel et al., *Introduction to Psalms*, 2.

35. Sigmund Mowinckel, *The Psalms in Israel's Worship* (trans. D. R. Ap-Thomas; Grand Rapids: Eerdmans, 2004). [Hereafter first volume is cited as *PIW (1)* and the second volume as *PIW (2)*]. For more information on Mowinckel's work see Ronald Clements, "Mowinckel, Sigmund," in *Historical Handbook of Major Biblical Interpreters* (ed. Donald McKim; Downers Grove: InterVarsity, 1998); Ernest C. Lucas, *Exploring the Old Testament: A Guide to the Psalms and Wisdom Literature* (Downers Grove: Inter Varsity Press, 2003), 11-16; J. J. M. Roberts, "Mowinckel's Enthronement Festival: A Review," in *The Book of Psalms: Composition and Reception* (ed. Peter W. Flint et al.; VTSup 99, Leiden: Boston, 2005), 97-115.

36. Mowinckel, *PIW (2)*, 35.

37. Ibid., 195-97.

38. Artur Weiser, *The Psalms: A Commentary* (Philadelphia: Westminster, 1962), 35-52.

by the unique theology of Israel and the revelation of Yahweh, rather than by the Ancient Near East (ANE) context. According to Weiser, Psalm 145 was recited during the feast of the covenant in autumn because the idea of the Kingship of Yahweh played an important role during this festival.[39] But according to Hans-Joachim Kraus, the *Sitz im Leben* of Psalm 145 is not a festival but regular worship in the temple.[40] Mowinckel, Weiser, and Kraus's discussions on the hypothetical "life setting" of Psalm 145 fail to derive a consensus. Additionally, form criticism as a method does not answer the questions concerning the setting for the shape and shaping of the Psalter. In fact, it entirely ignores the inter-link of individual psalms and the internal structures of the Psalter.[41]

However, James Muilenberg, noticing the inadequacy in the exclusive practice of form criticism,[42] draws psalms scholars' attention to the rhetorical phenomena in the literary style, the structure, and the aesthetic of the psalms. According to him, understanding the rhetorical phenomena involves "the understanding of the nature of Hebrew literary composition, in exhibiting the structural patterns that are employed for the fashioning of a literary unity, whether in poetry or prose, and in discerning the many and various devices by which the predications are formulated and ordered into a unified whole."[43] He calls this approach Rhetorical Criticism. Although Muilenberg popularized the method in 1969, Leon J. Liebreich noticed the literary structure, style, and aesthetics of Psalm 145 extensively in 1956.[44]

---

39. Ibid., 827.

40. Hans-Joachim Kraus, *Psalms 60-150: A Continental Commentary* (trans. Hilton C. Oswald; Minneapolis: Fortress, 1989), 547.

41. Howard, "Editorial Activity," 52-53.

42. James Muilenberg writes, "[F]orm criticism by its very nature is bound to generalize because it is concerned with what is common to all the representatives of genre, and therefore applies an external measure to the individual pericopes. It does not focus sufficient attention upon what is unique and unrepeatable, upon the particularity of the formulation. Moreover, form and content are inextricably related. They form an integral whole. The two are one. Exclusive attention to the *Gattung* may actually obscure the thought and intention of the writer or speaker." See James Muilenburg, "Form Criticism and Beyond," in *Hearing and Speaking the Word: Selections from the Works of James Muilenburg* (ed. Thomas F. Best; Chico: Scholars Press, 1984), 31.

43. Ibid., 34.

44. Leon J. Liebreich, "Psalms 34 and 145 in the Light of Their Key Words," *HUCA* 27 (1956): 181-92.

Indeed, Liebreich did not consider the use of these rhetorical devices in Psalm 145 in relation to the composition of the fifth book of the Psalter.

Claus Westermann, who advanced form critical interpretation beyond its traditional approach, was the first who observed connections between the psalms in the overall shape of the Psalter.[45] He categorizes psalms in the Psalter into just two groups: Lament and Praise. Additionally, since the word for thanksgiving תודה is just another Hebrew word for "praise," Westermann names the "thanksgiving psalms" as "psalms of descriptive praise," and the "praise hymns" as "declarative praise."[46] In his classification, Psalm 145 is not a declarative praise (praise hymn) but a "descriptive psalm of praise" (thanksgiving psalm) because in this psalm praise is given to YHWH, whose majestic work is revealed in history.[47] With such an understanding, Westermann groups this psalm along with Pss 33:10-19; 65:5, 7; 66: 5-7, 8-12; (68); 89:10-14; 15-18; 100; 111; 135:8-12; 136:10-24; (146); 147:10-14; and 149:4-9. But his classification is questionable, because the genre of Psalm 145 also has the literary feature of a declarative praise. Psalm 145 does not begin with any imperative calls, but a vow or resolution to praise YHWH.[48] It has a unique language and its connection with Psalms 146-50 or Psalm 144 is undeniable.[49]

By the late twentieth century, the form critical method, which primarily engages in an analysis of the form, genre, and social setting of the individual

---

45. According to Westermann, the psalms of lament and the psalms of praise shaped the corporate worship of Israel. These two groups of psalms are the only distinct categories that characterize the Psalter as a whole. He brought a new perspective in the reading of the Psalter by making a seven-fold observation: (1) Lament psalms are concentrated in the first half of the Psalter. (2) Praise psalms are located in larger numbers in the second segment of the Psalter. (3) The superscripts of the psalms and their groupings reflect that at a certain stage in the history of the tradition of the Psalter, the psalms existed in smaller collections. (4) Among the smaller collections, the collection of praise psalms had the function of closing. (5) The collection of royal psalms was gradually scattered into other smaller collections because at a certain point in time they lost their significance for cultic use. (6) The Psalter has no discernible collection that signifies its liturgical usage. (7) Individual psalms were separated from community psalms and the lament psalms were separated from praise psalms. See Claus Westermann, *Praise and Lament in the Psalms* (trans. Keith R. Crim and Richard N. Soulen; Atlanta: John Knox, 1981), 11, 257-58.

46. Ibid., 25-35.

47. Ibid., 236.

48. Ibid., 131.

49. Ibid., 131, 256.

psalm, became the subject of critical evaluation. Modern psalms scholarship began to incorporate new critical approaches.[50] They proposed different "postcritical" readings of the Psalter. Walter Brueggemann, who proposed a sociological reading of the Psalter, classified the Psalter into three categories: "psalms of orientation," "psalms of disorientation," and "psalms of reorientation."[51] He categorized Psalm 145 as a "psalm of orientation."[52] Others approached the Psalter with Rabbinic and Patristic reading,[53] liturgical reading,[54] and feminist reading.[55] However, the questions concerning the shaping of the whole Psalter remained unrequited, as was the question of the placement of Psalm 145 in the fifth book.

Compositional Critical Interpretation

Beginning in the 1960s some psalms scholars started to notice unequivocal shape and structure of the Psalter in the MT as well as in the LXX.[56]

---

50. For a fuller analysis of form criticism see Marvin A. Sweeney et al., eds., *The Changing Face of Form Criticism for the Twenty-First Century* (Grand Rapids: Eerdmans, 2003). For a detailed survey on the historical critical approaches see Leo G. Perdue, *The Collapse of History: Reconstructing Old Testament Theology* (Minneapolis: Fortress, 1994).

51. Walter Brueggemann, *The Message of the Psalm* (Minneapolis: Augsberg, 1984), 18-19; Walter Brueggemann, *Abiding Astonishment: Psalms, Modernity, and the Making of History* (Louisville: Westminster/John Knox, 1991); Walter Brueggemann, *The Psalms and the Life of Faith* (Minneapolis: Fortress, 1995).

52. Brueggemann, *The Message*, 28.

53. Uriel Simon, *Four Approaches to the Book of Psalms: From Saadiah Gaon to Abraham Ibn Ezra* (Albany: State University of New York Press, 1991).

54. A renewed interest in such reading is represented in the following works: Anton Arens, *Die Psalmen im Gottesdienst des Alten Bundes: Eine Untersuchung zur Vorgeschichte des christlichen Psalmengesanges* (Trier: Paulinus, 1961); Anton Arens, "Hat der Psalter seinen 'Sitz im Leben' in der synagogalen Lesung des Pentateuch?" in *Les Psautiers, ses origines, ses problèmes littéraires, son influence* (ed. Robert de Langhe; Louvain: Publication Universitaires, 1962); M. D. Goulder, *The Psalms of Asaph and the Pentateuch* (Sheffield: Sheffield Academic Press, 1996); Aileen Guilding, "Some Obscured Rubrics and Lectionary Allusion in the Psalter," *JTS* 3 (1952): 41-55.

55. Ulrike Bail, *Gegen das Schweigen klagen: eine intertextuelle Studie zu den Klagepsalmen Ps 6 und Ps 55 und der Erzählung von der Vergewaltigung Tamars* (Gütersloh: Chr. Kaiser/Gütersloher Verlagshaus, 1998); Marchiene Vroon Rienstra, *Swallow's Nest: A Feminine Reading of the Psalms* (Grand Rapids: New York, 1992).

56. David M. Howard, Jr. has traced the history of psalms scholarship in detail, developed from Form Criticism to Compositional Method. See Howard, "Recent Trends in Psalm

Westermann and J. P. Brennan were the first among them;[57] however, it was Brevard S. Childs and his student, Gerhard H. Wilson, who brought the compositional reading of the Psalter to the vanguard of psalms scholarship.

Brevard S. Childs

Brevard S. Childs, in his magnum opus *Introduction to the Old Testament as Scripture*, points out definite editorial work in the placement of Psalms 1 and 2 as the introduction to the book of the Psalter.[58] According to him, the absence of a cluster of royal psalms in the Psalter implies an editorial arrangement.[59] Some psalms are purposefully taken out of their cultic context and historicized with the help of historical superscripts.[60] This is because the new historical situation in Israel promoted a new theological thinking among the pious, resulting in certain types of preferences in both the editorial composition and the literary setting of the final form of the Psalter. This, in turn, allows its readers to understand it as the Word of God speaking to their need.[61] Childs' hermeneutical framework is appealing, because it encourages the reader to interpret the Psalter canonically as a relevant book of instructions.[62]

Study," 329-68; Howard, "Editorial Activity," 52-70. See also Mays, "Past, Present, and Prospect," 147-56.

57. Westermann, *Praise and Lament*, 256-58; Joseph P. Brennan, "Some Hidden Harmonies in the Fifth Book of Psalms," in *Essays in Honor of Joseph P. Brennan* (ed. Robert F. McNamara; New York: Saint Bernard's Seminary, 1976), 126.

58. Brevard S. Childs, *Introduction to the Old Testament as Scripture* (Philadelphia: Fortress, 1979), 513. G. T. Sheppard, a student of Childs, explains how Psalms 1-2 together form the preface of the Psalter. See Gerald T. Sheppard, *Wisdom as a Hermeneutical Construct: A Study in the Sapientializing of the Old Testament* (BZAW 151; Berlin: de Gruyter, 1980), 136-44.

59. Childs, *Introduction*, 156.

60. For Childs, the historical superscripts are a literary continuity rather than historical, a midrashic exegesis that connected the individual psalm with the canonical narrative in order to enhance the personal appropriation of the Psalter in a new historical context. See Brevard S. Childs, "Psalm Titles and Midrashic Exegesis," *JSS* 16 (1971): 137-50.

61. According to Childs, the Psalter in its final form must be read canonically and in the community for which it had become canon. See Childs, *Introduction*, 511-13.

62. Lindbeck regards Childs' canonical approach to be a "renewed" form of the classical scriptural interpretation without ignoring the contribution of other critical approaches. See George A. Lindbeck, "Postcritical Canonical Interpretation: Three Modes of Retrieval," in *Theological Exegesis: Essays in Honor of Brevard Childs* (ed. K.G. McCreight; Grand Rapids: Eerdmans, 1999), 26-51.

Gerald H. Wilson

Wilson's Yale dissertation and several of his articles assert that the final form of the Psalter displays tacit and explicit evidences of its purposeful editorial organization.[63] His work introduces a new paradigm for understanding the psalm titles,[64] doxologies,[65] and the five-book division of the Psalter. In his view, the arrangement of the first three books of the Psalter (Psalms 2-89) exhibits its concern with the Davidic Covenant; Psalm 2 introduces the Davidic Covenant while Psalm 89 remembers the covenant to indicate its failure (Ps 89:38-39).[66] The arrangement of Book IV (Psalms 90-106), which Wilson claims as the "editorial heart of the Psalter," is intended to

---

63. In his ground-breaking dissertation, *The Editing of the Psalter*, Wilson argues for the editorial nature of the Psalter. First, he analyzes Sumerian Temple Hymns and the Catalogue of Hymnic Incipit. Second, he analyzes the Qumran Psalms and the Hebrew Psalter in the MT. Third, he compares both findings to prove his thesis. In his analysis, he explores both tacit and explicit evidence for the editorial arrangement of the final form of the Psalter. See Gerald Henry Wilson, *The Editing of the Hebrew Psalter* (Chico: Scholars Press, 1985). McCann has given a good précis of his work. See J. Clinton McCann, "The Books I-III and the Editorial Purpose of the Psalter," in *The Shape and Shaping of the Psalter* (ed. J. Clinton McCann; JSOTSup 159, Sheffield: JSOT Press, 1993), 94-95. Wilson's other writings are: Gerald Henry Wilson, "Evidence of Editorial Division in the Hebrew Psalter," *VT* 3 (1984): 337-52; Wilson, *The Editing*; Gerald Henry Wilson, "The Use of 'Untitled' Psalms in the Hebrew Psalter," *ZAW* 97 (1985): 404-13; Gerald Henry Wilson, "The Use of Royal Psalms at the 'Seams' of the Hebrew Psalter," *JSOT* 35 (1986): 85-94; Gerald Henry Wilson, "The Shape of the Book of Psalms," *Int* 46 (1992): 129-42; Gerald Henry Wilson, "Shaping the Psalter: A Consideration of Editorial Linkage in the Book of Psalms," in *The Shape and Shaping of the Psalter* (ed. J. Clinton McCann; JSOTSup 159, Sheffield: JSOT Press, 1993): 72-82; Gerald Henry Wilson, "Understanding the Purposeful Arrangement of Psalms in the Psalter: Pitfalls and Promise," in *The Shape and Shaping of the Psalter* (ed. J. Clinton McCann; JSOTSup 159, Sheffield: JSOT Press, 1993): 42-51; Wilson, "The Qumran Psalms Scroll," 448-64; Gerald Henry Wilson, *Psalms: From Biblical Text to Contemporary Life* (Grand Rapids: Zondervan, 2002); Gerald Henry Wilson, "King, Messiah, and the Reign of God: Revisiting the Royal Psalms and the Shape of the Psalter," in *The Book of Psalms: Composition and Reception* (ed. Peter W. Flint et al.; Leiden: Boston, 2005): 391-06.

64. According to Wilson, editorial concerns in the Psalter are evidenced by the fact that the superscripts in the Psalter were used to bind the psalms together, or soften the transition between the groups of psalms, or to loosen the psalms from their original cultic setting to a didactic role by introducing them to the life situation of David (as David, so every man!). The presence of large numbers of untitled psalms in Books IV and V, their juxtaposition, and their various combinations and divisions indicate a programmatic structure of the Psalter. See Wilson, *The Editing*, 167-73.

65. Wilson believes the placement of the doxologies in Pss 41:14; 72:19; 89:53; and 106:48 is "not fortuitous, but represent editorially induced methods of giving 'shape'" to the Psalter. Ibid., 185-86.

66. Ibid., 213.

say that YHWH was, is, and will be the King forever.[67] YHWH was there before David in the time of Moses (למושה; Ps 90:1) and he is present now. Finally, Book V (Psalms 107-150) is editorially placed at the end of the Psalter as "an answer to the plea of the exiles."[68] It stresses the fact that deliverance of Israel can be effected by trust in YHWH alone (Psalm 107), by obedience to God's law (Psalm 119), and by recognizing that YHWH is the ideal King of all humanity (Psalms 145-46).

Wilson claims that the editorial composition of Book V is distinct from the four previous books of the Psalter. It is distinct in the placement of הודו and הלל psalms.[69] The הודו psalms are placed as "the opening psalms," while הלל psalms are placed as "the closing psalms." This arrangement results in three subgroups (Psalms 107-17, 118-35, 136-45), which reflect certain shaping and linking of the second segment to the final הלל psalms.[70] The placement of the largest psalm on the תורה, Psalm 119, at the beginning of Book V underscores the primacy of the תורה of God.[71] Through this distinct organizational techniques and genres, Book V presents David "modeling an attitude of reliance and dependence on YHWH" in accordance with the תורה of God.[72]

The Turning Point

In 1989, Wilson's persuasive work received acceptance among psalms scholars. In that year, the Society of Biblical Literature (SBL) initiated a special session to discuss the shape and the shaping of the Psalter.[73] Since then, a number of commentaries have shown some inter-link between the psalms.[74]

---

67. Ibid., 215.

68. Ibid., 227.

69. Ibid., 189-90. Erich Zenger, "The Composition and Theology of the Fifth Book of Psalms, Psalms 107-145," *JSOT* 80 (1998): 78.

70. Wilson, *The Editing*, 188.

71. Ibid., 223.

72. Ibid., 227.

73. J. Clinton McCann, ed., *The Shape and Shaping of the Psalter* (Journal for the Study of the Old Testament Supplement Series 159; Sheffield: JSOT Press, 1993b), 7.

74. VanGemeren, "Psalms," 1-880; James Luther Mays, *Psalms* (Louisville: Westminster

Several writings emerged, presenting a plurality of perspectives on the compositional method.[75] James Luther Mays gives five reasons for reading the Psalter as a book: (a) an interpretive ordering of the psalms; (b) a shift in the conception and use of the genres; (c) the use of psalms for the purpose of ritual accompaniment to instruction; (d) the combination and consolidation of genres, topics, and motifs; and (e) the place of the Psalter in reference to other books of the Scripture.[76] Mathias Millard employs form criticism to claim that there are enough internal evidences to support the unity of the Psalter.[77] According to him, the change of *Gattung* neither proves random juxtaposition of psalms, nor their literary disunity; rather, it indicates that they are deliberately arranged to underscore the progressive movement in the Psalter.[78] Developing Wilson's work, Nancy L. DeClaissé-Walford's dissertation explores clues to the shape and the shaping of the Psalter in the chronological arrangement of the individual psalms.[79] She reads the Psalter as a story line that addresses post-exilic Israel's questions—"Who are we?" and "What are we to do?" The way forward for the post-exilic community is to trust and hope in the Kingship of Yahweh. Finally, two remarkable compositional works, which lay more emphasis on the micro-level analysis of the Psalter, are David M. Howard, Jr.'s analysis of Psalms 93-100,[80] and

---

John Knox, 1994); J. Clinton McCann, *The Book of Psalms* (NIB 4; 12 vols.; Nashville: Abingdon, 1996); Peter C. Craigie, *Psalms 1-50* (2d ed.; WBC 19; Nashville: Thomas Nelson, 2004); Marvin E. Tate, *Psalms 51-100* (WBC 20; Dallas: Word Books, 1990); Allen, *Psalms 101-50*; Terrien, *The Psalms*.

75. The entire volume of *JSOT* supplement series 159 and the second issue of April 1992 of *Interpretation* were dedicated to studies in psalms. See McCann, ed., *The Shape and Shaping.*

76. James Luther Mays, "The Question of Context in Psalm Interpretation," in *The Shape and Shaping of the Psalter* (ed. J. Clinton McCann; JSOTSup 159, Sheffield: JSOT Press, 1993), 16.

77. Matthias Millard, *Die Komposition des Psalters: Ein formgeschichtlicher Ansatz* (FAT, 9; Tübingen: Mohr, 1994), 19-47, 162-67.

78. According to Millard, just as a single psalm, in spite of the change of *Gattung* (namely from singular to plural) within, maintains its unity, so does the Psalter, in spite of the abrupt changes of *Gattung*, which points to a deliberate arrangement for progressive movement. Ibid., 162-67.

79. Nancy L. DeClaissé-Walford, *Reading from the Beginning: The Shaping of the Hebrew Psalter* (Macon: Mercer University Press, 1997). See also Nancy L. DeClaissé-Walford, *Introduction to the Psalms: A Song from Ancient Israel* (St. Louis: Chalice, 2004).

80. David M. Howard, Jr., *The Structure of Psalms 93-100* (Winona Lake: Eisenbrauns, 1997).

Frank-Lothar Hossfeld and Erich Zenger's recent commentary on Psalms 51-100.[81] However, a comprehensive compositional analysis of Book V is not available at the time of this writing, except for some macro-level observations by Wilson and Zenger.

Composition of Book V

Zenger claims that the editorial composition of Book V is distinct for its linguistic and theological profiles for five reasons.[82] First, the phrase הללו־ יה sets the book apart in decisive way, semantically as well as conceptually from the previous four books. Besides the fifth book, the only occurrence of the phrase הללו־יה is noticed in Psalms 104, 105, and 106. Zenger thinks that this might be in order to provide a transition to the fifth book. Second, the frequent occurrence of the two verbs ידה and הלל is another characteristic of the fifth book. Except for Psalms 110, 119, 134, 137, 143, and 144, at least one of the two lexemes are found in each of the psalms in the fifth book. This feature is not noticed in the previous four books. Third, unlike the previous four books which has the two-fold doxological formula (Pss 41:14; 72:18-19; 89:53; and 106:48), Book V has none. Zenger concludes that the phrase הללו־יה was not part of the original system of closing doxologies but was added later when the fifth book was appended to the Psalter. Fourth, the underlying concept of the fifth book is different from the previous four books. In Book IV, the vision of the universal Kingdom of God develops from the lament on the demise of the Davidic kingdom in Psalm 89. The vision appears almost as a counter concept to the Davidic kingdom. However, in the fifth book, the psalms revive the Davidic—messianic idea for a theocratic message by including the two groups of Davidic psalms (Psalms 108-110 and 138-145). This is distinct from the fourth book. Finally, the fifth book is distinct for the specific technique used in its

---

81. Frank-Lothar Hossfeld and Erich Zenger begin their commentary with the premise that the Psalter is "a successively developed, but nevertheless compositionally structured entity whose form gives an additional dimension of meaning to each individual psalm." For this reason, they intend to write the "introduction" (Psalm 1-50) after they have analyzed Psalms 51-150. Their compositional method majors on *Stichwort* that connects individual psalms not only with other psalms in the Psalter, but also with the other books in the Canon. See Hossfeld et al., *Psalm 2* , xi.

82. Zenger, "The Composition and Theology," 77-102.

composition. Similar to Wilson, Zenger points out the specific technique is the placement of הודו and הלל psalms in the fifth book.

According to Wilson, Book V is distinct because David is not portrayed as a king but as a servant, who will inaugurate the universal Kingdom of God.[83] He sees this happening editorially at two levels. First, he sees two distinct segments in the Psalter—the segment of royal concerns (Psalms 2-89) and the segment of the wisdom concerns (Psalms 90-150). These two segments are "editorially bound together into a whole."[84] At the macro level, he also sees two frames: the Royal Covenant Frame (Psalms 2, 72, 89, and 144) and the "Final Wisdom Frame" (Psalms 1, 73, 90, and 145). He suggests that the "Final Wisdom Frame" (Psalms 1, 73, 90, and 145) "subsumes" the "Royal Covenant Frame" (Psalms 2, 72, 89, and 144) in order to present the wisdom frame as a solution to the problems posed in Books I-III.[85] The solution comprises the need of "an attitude of dependence and trust in YHWH alone (Ps 107:12-13, 19, 28)."[86] Second, he sees David in the last two Davidic groups of psalms (Psalms 108-110 and 138-145) as the one who is presented modeling "the attitude of reliance and dependence."[87] David is characterized as the "wise man" (in response to Ps 107:43), who depends absolutely on the חסד of YHWH.[88] He is portrayed as God's anointed servant, who will inaugurate the Kingdom of God over all humanity (Ps 145:21).[89]

However, these aforementioned claims are confined to the editorial arrangement in the MT alone. There are no such claims for the psalms' placement in the 11QPs^a and the LXX. In fact, scholars suggest a different editorial arrangement of the psalms in the 11QPs^a and the LXX than that of the MT. In the following paragraphs, we will briefly discuss the composition of the 11QPs^a and the LXX.

---

83. Wilson, "King, Messiah," 402-05.

84. Wilson, "Shaping the Psalter," 80.

85. According to Wilson, the answer to the problems that are faced in Books I-III lies in the Wisdom frame. YHWH alone is the solution. See Wilson, "King, Messiah," 392-93; See also Wilson, "Shaping the Psalter," 80-81.

86. Wilson, *The Editing*, 227.

87. Ibid.

88. Ibid., 221.

89. Wilson, "King, Messiah," 404-05.

Composition of the 11QPSa

The purpose of the editorial composition of the Qumran Psalms scroll seems to be different from the MT. The placement of the 51 psalms in the 11QPs[a] is arranged in an entirely different order than the MT (see appendix 1).[90] Of the 51 Qumran psalms, 40 are masoretic psalms and 11 are non-masoretic; of the 11 non-masoretic psalms, seven belong to familiar texts (such as 2 Sam 23:1-7; Catena; Sir 51:13-20, 30; Syriac Psalms 151A, 151B, 154, and 155), while the four (Plea for Deliverance; Apostrophe to Zion, Hymn to the Creator; and David's composition) are entirely new. Interestingly, all the masoretic psalms in the 11QPs[a] correspond to the psalms of Books IV and V.[91] However, unlike the MT, these psalms are interspersed with other non-masoretic psalms (apocryphal psalms). Wilson notices that some masoretic psalms are included, others are purposefully dropped out in the 11QPs[a].[92] These phenomena of inclusion and exclusion of the masoretic psalms suggest plausibility of different editorial purposes in the 11QPs[a] and the MT. The following three observations support this.

---

90. According to Wilson, the different arrangement of the psalms in the 11QPs[a], as well as the inclusion of 'apocryphal' psalms, has raised more controversy regarding the nature and authority of the Qumran texts and its relationship to the history of the transmission of the canonical text. In his analysis, he demonstrates that there are both supporting and conflicting evidences for the canonical order. He concludes, "The appearance of supportive evidence is somewhat deceptive since much is derived from MSS which elsewhere vary considerably from the canonical arrangement (e.g. the supportive series of Pss 120 through 132 in the extremely variant 11QPs[a]). As a result, it is impossible to determine absolutely whether this opposition of conflicting and supportive evidence indicates: (a) deviation from a prior fixed canonical Psalter form; (b) a more fluid 'proto-canonical' stage prior to final fixation; or (c) an independent competing Psalter tradition, which parallels the transmission of the canonical arrangement. Gerald H. Wilson, "The Qumran Psalms Manuscripts and the Consecutive Arrangement of Psalms in the Hebrew Psalter," *CBQ* 45 (1983): 377-88. See also Gerald Henry Wilson, "The Qumran Psalms Scroll Reconsidered: Analysis of the Debate," *CBQ* 47 (1985): 624-42; Wilson, "The Qumran Psalms Scroll," 448-64.

91. Sanders interprets this correspondence as an evidence for the late and gradual fixation of the Psalter. According to him, it indicates that the first three books (Psalms 1-89) were the first to be fixed while Books IV and V were still in a state of flux in the first century B.C. Thus, the 11QPs[a] may be considered a prior stage to the MT in the sequence. But Wilson has shown that the 11QPs[a] may also be a "parallel edition" or a "library edition" (dependent on the MT as proposed by Skehan). See appendix 2. Wilson, *The Editing*, 63-91. See also James A. Sanders, *The Dead Sea Psalms Scroll* (Ithaca: Cornell University Press, 1967), 13-14.

92. Wilson, "The Qumran Psalms Scroll," 452.

First, Psalms 90-92 and 106-8, which fall at the "seams" of Books IV and V, are missing in the 11QPs[a]. In the MT, these psalms are employed to give a certain editorial shape to the Psalter by providing a transition from Book III to Book IV and from Book IV to Book V.[93] The absence of these psalms suggest that the editorial purpose in the ordering of the psalms in the 11QPs[a] is different from the MT.

Second, Psalms 94-100 are missing in the 11QPs[a]. According to Wilson, these psalms form the central and thematic core of "the YHWH kingship psalms," as well as constitute the "editorial heart" of the Psalter in the MT. He writes,

> In my opinion, Pss 90-106 function as the editorial "center" of the final form of the Hebrew Psalter. As such, this group-ing stands as the "answer" to the problem posed in Ps 89 as to the apparent failure of the Davidic covenant with which Book One –Three are primarily concerned. Briefly summarized the answer given is: (1) YHWH is king; (2) He has been our "ref-uge" in the past, long before the monarchy existed (i.e., in the Mosaic period); (3) He will continue to be our refuge now that the monarchy is gone; (4) Blessed are they that trust in him![94]

Howard has also shown how these psalms are interwoven together to present a coherent theme.[95] Absence of Psalms 94-100 implies different thematic emphasis in the 11QPs[a] scroll than the MT.

Third, Psalms 110-17 in the MT, with the exception of Psalm 110, are הלל psalms. Psalms 113-17 are considered Egyptian Hallel psalms. Earlier, we have seen that the הלל psalms in the MT are editorially placed to close a section while הודו psalms open a section. The absence of such a section distinguishes the 11QPs[a] from the MT in its editorial arrangement.[96]

---

93. Wilson, *The Editing*, 207. See also Wilson, "The Use of Royal Psalms," 85-94.
94. Wilson, *The Editing*, 215.
95. Howard, *The Structure of Psalms*.
96. Wilson, "The Qumran Psalms Scroll," 453.

The most noteworthy difference in the 11QPsᵃ is the emphasis on the role of David.[97] In the MT, the kingship of David yields to the Kingship of YHWH (in Books IV and V, and especially in Psalms 145 and 146), but in the 11QPsᵃ the concentration of Davidic psalms seems to reaffirm the divine and kingly role of David.[98] This is postulated from the following fact.

In contrast to the MT, where the concentration of the הלל psalms increases toward the end, the last segment of the 11QPsᵃ has more psalms that have reference to David (2 Sam 23, David's composition, Psalm 151A and 151 B). A total 16 psalms that are ascribed to David appear in the 11QPsᵃ. Psalms 104 and 123, which are not Davidic in the MT, are provided with Davidic superscriptions. As a whole, the Davidic composition of the 11QPsᵃ is 31.1% (out of 51 psalms) in contrast to 27.8% (out of 61 psalms in Books IV and V) of the last segment of the MT. Hence, Wilson asserts:

> In contrast to the masoretic Psalter, where we see David yielding finally to the kingship of Yhwh (Psalms 145; 146), and where the concluding focus (in Psalms 146-50) is clearly on the kingly rule of Yhwh grounded firmly in his creative power, the Qumran *Psalms Scroll* concludes with its vision and hopes firmly focused on the Davidic king. He is divinely selected and gifted, and he remains the sure foundation of Israel's hope for restoration.[99]

Moreover, specific to the composition and the placement of Psalm 145 in the 11QPsᵃ, six distinctions differentiate it from the MT. First, the placement of Psalm 145 in the 11QPsᵃ is close to the center of the whole collection: 27 psalms before and 21 psalms after. Second, the order of the placement is entirely different. It is placed between Pss 118:29 and 154:3. Third, Psalm 145 in the 11QPsᵃ begins with a superscript תפלה in contrast to תהלה in the MT. This indicates a unique editorial insertion in the 11QPsᵃ, because its appearance is not supported in rest of the psalm. The

---

97. Ibid., 454.
98. Ibid., 464.
99. Ibid.

word תהלה in the MT is more obvious because the root word הלל occurs three times [verses 2 (ואהללה, cohortative); 3 (ויהולל, participle, perhaps מ is omitted); 21 (תהלה, noun construct)] in the rest of the psalm. Also, the word תהלה forms an inclusion by reappearing in verse 21 and also connects it compositionally to the הלל group of hymns (Psalms 146-50).

Fourth, Psalm 145 in the 11QPsᵃ has a postscript זאת לזכרן, which Wilson suggests to be a closing remark for the section.[100] Fifth, Psalm 145 in the 11QPsᵃ has a nun clause with אלהים as the subject, which is different from the MT (missing) and the LXX (יהוה). Sixth, Psalm 145 is expanded throughout by the addition of a refrain (ברוך יהוהוברוך שמו לעולם ועד) which is repeated 16 times. This refrain suggests a liturgical use of Psalm 145 in the 11QPsᵃ. These observations clearly indicate that the editorial arrangement of the 11QPsᵃ is different.

Composition of the LXX

Likewise, the editorial composition of the LXX seems to enhance the importance of David and the Davidic covenant.[101] Although the composition of the LXX has great similarity with that of the MT with regard to its contents and the arrangement of the psalms,[102] a number of variants suggest a different editorial purpose for the LXX. Three observations would suffice our brief discussion here. First, the LXX contains fourteen Davidic psalms that do not have any reference to David in the MT.[103] Of these fourteen, nine are from Book IV (Psalms 90-106). This is especially significant because six (Psalms 93; 95; 96; 97; 98; and 99) of these nine in the MT are actually "YHWH kingship" psalms. Hence, the number of Davidic psalms

---

100. Ibid., 457-58.

101. Gerald Henry Wilson, "The Structure of the Psalter," in *Interpreting the Psalms: Issues and Approaches* (ed. David G. Firth et al.; Downers Grove: InterVarsity, 2005), 241.

102. In the LXX, some psalms of the MT are merged to make one psalm (Psalms 9+10=LXX 9; 114+115=LXX 113) while others are split into two (Psalms 116=LXX 114 + LXX 115; 147= LXX 146 + LXX 147). Except for a few textual variants most of Psalm 145 is the same as the MT. For the LXX textual variants, see the footnotes on the translation of Psalm 145 in chapter 3.

103. The 14 LXX Psalms are 32 (MT 33); 42 (MT 43); 70 (MT 71); 90 (MT 91); 92 (MT 93); 93 (MT 94); 94 (MT 95); 95 (MT 96); 96 (MT 97); 97 (MT 98); 98 (MT 99); 103 (MT 104); 136 (MT 137); and 151. However, the name "David" appears 100 times in the whole of the LXX while it appears only 89 times in the MT.

in Book IV is greater in the LXX than the MT. This would imply a different characterization of Book IV in the LXX. In the MT, after the rejection in Psalm 89, the kingship of David is overshadowed by the "YHWH kingship" in Book IV, but "the LXX heightens the profile and importance of David and the Davidic collection."[104] Second, the LXX has ten historical ascriptions to David in the superscripts of the Psalms while only four of these have specific reference to David's life (LXX 26; 96; 142; 143). Third, the LXX has one additional psalm, Psalm 151, which is missing in the MT. This additional psalm has a superscript which reads οὗτος ὁ ψαλμὸς ἰδιό-γραφος εἰς Δαυιδ καὶ ἔξωθεν τοῦ ἀριθμου, meaning *This Psalm is the original writing of David, though outside of the number* (my translation). This implies a clear assertion of Davidic presence at the end of the LXX, while at the end of the MT (Psalm 150) the focus is on the praise of YHWH.

Now, specific to Psalm 145 (LXX 144) in the LXX, it is important to note that Psalm 145 (LXX 144) is not the last Davidic psalm. Unlike the MT, the adjacent Psalms 146, 147, 148 (LXX 145, 146, 147, and 148) have a superscript strangely ascribed to "Aggaeus and Zacharias." Finally, the addition of Psalm 151 as the final Davidic psalm in LXX suggests different thematic emphasis. The theme of the Kingship of YHWH is no longer the final proclamation in the mouth of David. It rather projects David and his kingly rule.

Since the focus of this dissertation is the placement of Psalm 145 in the MT, a comprehensive discussion on the placement of Psalm 145 in the 11QPs[a] and the LXX is not intended here. The brief discussions on different editorial composition of the 11QPs[a] and the LXX above, however, help us to put the rest of our research in perspective.

Thus far, we have seen how the history of interpretation of psalms has unfolded, ending in a compositional critical interpretation, contributing new and significant information on the composition of the Psalter. We have also considered how the editorial purposes in the arrangement of the 11QPs[a] and the LXX are different from that of the MT. In the following paragraphs, we will now discuss some scholars, who have expressed their

---

104. Wilson, "The Structure," 241.

reservation and skepticism against the compositional critical interpretation of the psalms. A response to their views is appropriate in this chapter.

Criticism of the Compositional Critical Interpretation

Some psalms scholars believe that the compositional critical interpretation not only undermines the importance of the historical-critical interpretation, but also that it results in a subjective and arbitrary reading of the Psalter.[105] Roland E. Murphy, Walter Brueggemann, Erhard Gerstenberger, and Roger Norman Whybray are prominent among them. Others such as J. Clinton McCann Jr., Rolf Rendtorff, and B. W. Anderson disagree with Wilson's reading of Book V.[106] In this section, we will discuss their cautions in order to be aware of the pitfalls that this research may encounter.

First, Roland E. Murphy presents six theses to caution us against the reading of the psalms in the context of the Psalter.[107] They are as follows:

(i) The contextual reading is no more objective than the historical reading because in either case the hypothetical reconstruction is "inescapable";

(ii) The "usefulness" of reading psalms in the context of the Psalter is "relatively limited" in contrast to the reading of psalms in the context of *Sitz im Leben*;

(iii) There is a "relationship between worship and teaching," which was already implicit in the tradition;

---

105. John Barton, "Intertextuality and the 'Final Form' of the Text," in *Congress Volume: Oslo 1998* (ed. André Lamaire and Magne Sæbø; VTSup 80, Leiden: Brill, 2000), 33-37; Roland E. Murphy, "Reflections on Contextual Interpretation of Psalms," in *The Shape and Shaping of the Psalter* (ed. J. Clinton McCann; JSOT Sup 159, Sheffield: JSOT Press, 1993); Walter Brueggemann, "Response to James L. Mays, 'The Question of Context'," in *The Shape and Shaping of the Psalter* (ed. J. Clinton McCann; JSOTSup 159, Sheffield: JSOT Press, 1993); Roger Norman Whybray, *Reading the Psalms as a Book* (JSOTSup 222; Sheffield: Sheffield Academic, 1996).

106. McCann, "The Book I-III," Rolf Rendtorff, "The Psalms of David: David in the Psalms," in *The Book of Psalms: Composition and Reception* (ed. Peter W. Flint et al.; VTSup 29, Leiden: Boston, 2005); Bernhard W. Anderson et al., *Out of the Depths: The Psalms Speak for Us Today* (3d ed.; Louisville: Westminster John Knox, 2000).

107. Murphy, "Reflections on Contextual," 21-28.

(iv) "A theological or emotive context engendered by the Psalms" may lead one to "reader-response" reading;

(v) Some criteria are needed against forging "an unprofitable or even erroneous contextualization";

(vi) There must be continuity between "the literal historical sense and the various meanings," so as to eliminate arbitrary proposals.

Murphy's six theses above are helpful warnings concerning a contextual reading of psalms. Nevertheless, they fail to bring forth the advantages that contextual reading offer in the interpretation of the psalms. In his first thesis, Murphy fails to notice that the new approach, unlike the form critical approach, underscores the literary context (*Sitz in der Literatur*) of the text. The emphasis is not only on the diachronic reading, but also on the synchronic reading of the Psalter. In his second thesis, he presupposes the elimination of the old reading by the new. Yet, the two methods are not mutually exclusive; one can benefit from the others. The plausibility of the new *Sitz im Leben* of the *textus receptus* of the Psalter must not be ignored. Murphy's third thesis, which asserts the "relationship between worship and teaching" implicit in the tradition, is well received; however, the new contextual reading which underscores the Psalter's canonical role in the exilic and post-exilic community cannot be undermined. In the fourth, fifth and sixth theses, Murphy cautions against subjectivity and an arbitrary interpretation. Since subjectivity is subtle and often unavoidable, outlining our prejudices and presuppositions explicitly at the very outset is the best approach to a method. This is a valid reminder for all methods. The important distinction that gives the contextual reading its advantage is its focus on the literary context of the text (*Sitz in der Literatur*) rather than a hypothetical context, which Murphy fails to acknowledge in his theses.

Second, Brueggemann believes that without addressing the "historical reality" of the psalms, reading them in the context of a book is not desirable.[108] In his view, the way to address the questions related to "canonical shape" [context of the Psalter] is to first address the questions concerning the "canonical process," [the process of movement toward the formation

---

108. Brueggemann, "Response to James," 29-41.

of the Psalter],[109] and the questions related to the "developmental process" are connected to historical-critical issues. Thus, the constructs and
categories of historical criticism of the Israelite religion are inescapable.[110]
Brueggemann's criticism assumes the certainty of a definite "historical reality" and the plausibility of a provable answer to the questions concerning
the canonical process. However, decades of psalms scholarship, based on
overwhelmingly hypothetical theories, has proven otherwise. The complexity of the history of the composition, transmission, and the compilation of
the Psalter should be taken into consideration. Brueggemann admits that
his preference for a theological and thematic approach [orientation, disorientation, and reorientation] to the Psalter may be the reason for his "sober
attention to the editorial details."[111]

Third, Erhard Gerstenberger points out three significant problems associated with compositional reading:[112]

(i)   The emphasis put on the final form of the text and its
      unchangeable authority undermines the importance of the
      beginning of the faith, tradition, and the places;

(ii) The meaning of the word is related to human communication in
      a certain social situation; and

(iii) The final form of the Psalter is the product of a long process;
      therefore, any sense of a uniform theological alignment in the
      book should be ruled out.

Gerstenberger insists on the primacy of the historical background of
each psalm and the indispensability of the historical-critical approach in
psalms studies, but the question may arise: which historical background of
the psalms? Do we have consensus on the historicity of each psalm? Since
the psalms have undergone constant redaction from one historical context
to another, it is difficult to determine which diachronic reading we should
consider for the meaning of the word.

---

109. Ibid., 30.

110. Ibid., 33.

111. Ibid., 41.

112. Erhard S. Gerstenberger, "Der Psalter als Buch und als Sammlung," in *Neue Wege der
Psalmenforschung: für Walter Beyerlin* (ed. Klaus Seybold et al.; HBS 1, Freiburg: Herder,
1994), 3-4.

Although Gerstenberger's criticism sounds theoretically legitimate, pragmatically it is too simplistic in its assumptions. Gerstenberger's concern for connecting modern psalms studies to the valuable contributions made by historical-critical studies is understandable; however, his skepticism against the compositional method is unconvincing.

Fourth, Roger Norman Whybray vehemently denies the existence of any evidence that may support "a systematic and purposeful redaction of the whole Psalter" in order to editorially present "a single comprehensive message in any of the suggested ways."[113] He discards Wilson's idea of seeing Psalm 1 as the "hermeneutical spectacle" for reading the Psalter. He asserts that if such an intention for editorial arrangement ever existed it would be evident from the placement of the "pure" *torah* psalms (Psalms 1, 19, and 119), the wisdom psalms, and their interpolation in other psalms.[114] He also fails to find any systematic editing of the "royal psalms" either by their position or by their interpolations.[115] According to him, the only thing that can be said with certainty is that the redactional process of the Psalter was "extremely complex, took place over a considerable time, and was influenced at its various stages by different editorial policies."[116] In other words, Whybray is not against the idea of editorial activity in the Psalter, but the idea of "a comprehensive editing" for the purpose of one "single theological tone." Another skepticism he emphasizes concerns 'concatenation' (a method that links adjacent psalms by theme or by 'catchwords' or by repeated identical poetical lines). He writes, "[M]any if not most of these supposed links can probably be put down to coincidence or are for other reasons devoid of editorial significance."[117] Although Whybray is against the idea of one distinctive editorially intended theological tone in the Psalter, he does not deny the plausibility of a single and a consistent theological progression in its synchronic/canonical reading.[118] He wants us to understand that the Psalter is a complex collection of divergent songs and prayers and the

---

113. Whybray, *Reading the Psalms*, 119. See also Lucas, *Exploring the Old Testament*, 33.
114. Whybray, *Reading the Psalms*, 120-21.
115. Ibid., 122-24.
116. Ibid., 119.
117. Ibid., 121.
118. Ibid., 122.

diachronic process of its composition is much more complex than Wilson's proposal seems to assume. On the one hand, Whybray seems to negate the possibility of any symmetrical pattern in the Psalter, which underwent a complex process of composition, transmission, and compilation. On the other hand, he expects a distinct thematic pattern in the Psalter in order to approve of an editorial arrangement in the Psalter—more than what Wilson claims. This calls for a comprehensive analysis—a "thick reading" of the psalm in relation to other psalms.[119]

Different Compositional Readings of Book V

Psalms scholars vary in their compositional reading of Book V.[120] Unlike Wilson, J. Clinton McCann suggests that the problem of the apparent failure of the traditional Davidic/Zion covenant theology is not only addressed in Books IV and V, but also in Books I-III.[121] In other words, Book V is not necessarily unique in its theological arrangement, as Wilson asserts. Rolf Rendtorff, in his recent article "David in the Psalms," argues that Books I-III portray David as righteous, law abiding, lamenting, and a

---

119. According to Vanhoozer, "thick reading" of the text is canonical reading, which is reiterating the reformers' commitment to the idea of *sola scriptura* and *tota scriptura*. The interpreter is supposed to read the Bible as "unified communicative act, that is, as the complex, multi-leveled speech act of a single divine author." The "thick description" of text goes beyond the level of words, concepts, genres, human speech or acts. It intends to capture the ultimate divine communicative act where authors, human, and the divine are considered together. See Kevin J. Vanhoozer, "Exegesis and Hermeneutics," in *New Dictionary of Biblical Theology* (ed. T. Desmond Alexander et al.; Downers Grove: Inter-Varsity Press, 2000), 61. We will discuss this in detail in chapter two.

120. Most psalms scholars accept the significance of the psalms' arrangement in the final shape of the Psalter, but their methodological approaches to the compositional criticism differ. Goulder regards the arrangement of the psalms significant. He writes, "The instinct that the order of the psalms may be important is not however naïve, and far from irrational." Goulder, *The Psalms of the Sons of Korah*, 8. However, in his treatment to the psalms, unlike Wilson, he assumes the historical settings of the psalms as their primary category of linking. For him, the Psalter is a rationally ordered liturgical collection, but he does not raise the question of the editorial purpose. See M. D. Goulder, "The Social Setting of the Book II of the Psalter," in *The Book of Psalms: Composition and Reception* (ed. Peter W. Flint et al.; Leiden: Boston, 2005); M. D. Goulder, *The Psalms of the Return (Book V, Psalms 107-150): Studies in the Psalter IV* (JSOTSup 258; Sheffield, Eng.: Sheffield Academic Press, 1998); M. D. Goulder, *The Prayers of David (Psalms 51-72)* (JSOTSup 102; London: New York, 2004).

121. McCann, "The Book I-III," 104.

helpless fugitive who is dependent on God.[122] Put differently, there are no significant differences in the image of David portrayed in the two segments (Books I-III and Books IV-V) of the Psalter. Likewise, quoting Psalms 110 and 132 as examples, B. W. Anderson disagrees with Wilson: "The truth is that Israelite interpreters, even in the face of harsh realities of history, never surrendered the hope for a coming monarch of the Davidic line who would rule as God's vicegerent."[123] Thus, McCann, Rendtorff, and Anderson differ from Wilson in their theological reading of the purposeful placement of the first three books of the Psalter, casting a shadow of doubt on Wilson's interpretation of Book V's role in the Psalter.

Investigating the placement of Psalm 145 may not answer all the theological questions concerning the uniqueness of Book V in the Psalter. However, it may be a litmus test for Wilson's claims concerning Psalm 145, which he uses to support the uniqueness of Book V. Wilson suggests that Psalm 145 forms a "Final Wisdom Frame" in the final shape of the Psalter. It stands as the "climax" of the second segment, editorially placed before the final הלל psalms.[124] It is purposefully "set in the mouth of David (Ps 145:1)," and strategically placed to recall some of the major themes of the Psalter."[125] Wilson's claim faces challenge on two fronts: the difference of opinion of his critics concerning the uniqueness of Book V; and the deficiency of a micro-level analysis of the purposeful placement of Psalm 145 in Book V. This dissertation intends to provide the latter.

Conclusion

Five conclusions are noteworthy to mention at the end of this chapter. First, a compositional analysis of Psalm 145 is significant from its textual, contextual, and social perspective. The following five observations support this: (1) the placement of Psalm 145, the last Davidic psalm, in MT is distinct

---

122. Rendtorff, "The Psalms of David," 63.
123. Anderson et al., *Out of the Depths*, 209. Wilson has responded to Anderson in a recent article. See Wilson, "King, Messiah," 396-99.
124. Wilson, *The Editing*, 225-26.
125. Ibid.

from its placement in the Septuagint (the LXX), and the Qumran *Psalms scroll* (11QPsᵃ); (2) in the Talmudic tradition, Psalm 145 has always been read in combination with Pss 84:5, 144:15 and 115:18, but such practice does not have continuity in the Christian tradition; (3) Ps 145:8 reverses the Exodus imagery (Exod 34:6) from רחם וחנון to חנון ורחם, conforming to all the psalms in Book V (Pss 111:4, 112:4, 116:5), but not to the psalms in Book III (Ps 86:15) and Book IV (Ps 103:8) in the MT; (4) Psalm 145 is thematically unique in Book V because it is the only psalm that explicitly presents YHWH's Kingdom as universal and eternal—it seems to be thematically in tension with the adjacent psalms in the MT (for example, Pss 137:7-9; 147:20; 148:14; and 149:2-9 in the MT have the language of particularism, projecting Israel as a favored nation, set against all other nations); and (5) a compositional reading of Psalm 145 emphasizes the universal Kingdom of God, which the churches in India must proclaim. Christians are drawn from diverse ethnic and religious backgrounds; however, Christianity in India is still perceived as foreign religion. The message of the universal Kingdom of God is an appropriate proclamation.

Second, a survey of the history of interpretation of Psalm 145 suggests that the questions concerning its placement in the final shape of the Psalter have not been considered either by pre-from-critical scholars, or by form-critical scholars. Reading psalms in context of the whole Psalter is an acceptable historical development in psalms studies. Psalms scholars have begun to engage compositional critical interpretation.

Third, the compositional critical interpretation as a method supplements the pre-form-critical and form-critical approaches that failed to consider the placement of psalms in the final shape of the Psalter. Numerous works concerning the *Sitz im Leben* of individual psalms have been published, but the works about the *Sitz in der Literatur* of the psalms are rare. The diachronic history of psalms' composition, transmission, and compilation is a complex historical phenomenon. It is difficult to pinpoint the different layers of the historical settings of the individual psalms in their long redactional process. In the absence of specific data, this will continue to be the Achilles' heel for the psalms scholars. However, investigating the *Sitz in der Literature* of the psalms in the *textus receptus* is a possible task. It provides hints to the plausible editorial intent, which may in turn provide information concerning *Sitz im Leben* of the redactor(s) who were involved in the final shape of the Psalter. Although the compositional critical interpretation is not free from the subjectivity and postulation of hypotheses, at least it requires a "thick reading" of the text. This will become clearer when we discuss the methodological considerations in chapter two.

Fourth, the editorial composition of the MT is distinct from the editorial composition of the Septuagint (the LXX), and the Qumran *Psalms scroll* (11QPs[a]). Since Wilson has considered the MT for compositional-critical criticism, we will investigate the placement of Psalm 145 in the MT in particular.

Fifth, Wilson's claim concerning the unique compositional reading of Book V faces challenges on two fronts. On the one hand, some scholars contradict him. On the other hand, his claims lack an adequate micro-level analysis of the psalms in Book V. Since a micro-level analysis of all the psalms in Book V is too large a project for a dissertation, we will investigate the placement of Psalm 145 in Book V.

CHAPTER 2

Methodological Considerations

The goal of this chapter is to delineate our approach to the compositional analysis of Psalm 145 in Book V.[1] We will first discuss our theological assumptions that form the basis for a compositional analysis of Psalm 145. Second, we will consider the hermeneutical assumptions that influence our preference for "discourse analysis" as the hermeneutical tool for this project. Third, we will examine our exegetical assumptions concerning the historical context, David in the superscript, the thematic patterning, the acrostic structure, the textual critical theory, and the absence of the *nun* line in Psalm 145 in the MT. These discussions are important because they will provide us the methodological framework for the rest of our dissertation.

Theological Assumptions

We begin with an important assumption that the final form of the Old Testament as Scripture is intrinsically theological and divinely authoritative for the believing community that receives it.[2] As discussed in the first

---

1. Steven L. McKenzie and Stephen R. Haynes' book *To Each Its Own Meaning* identifies as many as 13 distinct methodological approaches in biblical criticism. See Stephen R. Haynes et al., *To Each Its Own Meaning: An Introduction to Biblical Criticisms and Their Applications* (rev. ed.; Louisville: Westminster John Knox, 1999).

2. This does not necessarily mean a preference of the MT over the LXX. The believing communities were guided in their understanding of the books and their divine authority over their lives. Since the arrangement of the Psalms in the MT has found its continuity in the protestant Christian community, we are sensitive to the preserved tradition for this dissertation. For more details see Brevard S. Childs, *Introduction to the Old Testament as Scripture* (Philadelphia: Fortress, 1979), 74-79; Leo G. Perdue, *The Collapse of History:*

chapter, Childs named this assumption the "Canonical approach." In this approach, the goal a hermeneutical question is not of the history-of-religion, but of the theological function of the Scripture to the interpretive community that shaped the Psalter as a canon.[3]

The emphasis on the final form of Scripture in the canonical approach is reasonable for three reasons. First, the final form of Scripture is the only witness to "the full history of revelation."[4] It gives the shape and scope of the history of the encounter between God and Israel. Second, the final form of the text does not necessarily undermine the historical dimension. It rather brings historical process under critical and theological judgment.[5] It bridges the existing gaps between pure "historical," "literary," and "theological" readings of the Bible. Third, the fact that ancient Israel preserved the final form of Scripture, not the underlying layers of tradition, suggests, "[T]he witness to Israel's experience with God lies not in recovering such historical process, but is testified to in the effect on the biblical text itself."[6] In fact, scribes and editors purposefully obscured the history of the "shaping" of the texts by a process of "actualization" (*Vergegenwärtigung*), in which the scribes and editors not only updated or transmitted the past traditions, but also purposefully prevented them from being moored in the past.[7] This is why the attempt to describe the historical backgrounds of the biblical texts has been largely speculative and unproductive.[8]

The canonical approach is the essential methodological assumption to this dissertation because it is historically seminal to the compositional reading of the Psalter. This approach considers the canonical order of the psalms beyond the form-critical approach and cult-functional approaches, facilitating questions related to the specific order of the psalms in the final form of the Psalter, which comes under the purview of this research. It seeks to

---

Reconstructing Old Testament Theology (Minneapolis: Fortress, 1994), 153-96.

3. Childs, *Introduction*, 511-13.

4. Ibid., 75-76.

5. Ibid., 76.

6. Ibid.

7. Ibid., 79.

8. Brevard S. Childs, "Response to Reviews of Introduction to the Old Testament as Scripture," *JSOT* 16 (1980): 54.

interpret the text from the vantage point of its theological and authoritative role in shaping the faith and practice of the community, rather than the *Sitz im Leben* of the individual composer, or even recovering "an original literary or aesthetic unit."[9] Thus, we begin with an assumption that the final form of the Old Testament as Scripture is intrinsically theological and divinely authoritative for the believing community that receives it.

We also assume that the final form of the Psalter not only contains the theological message for the community of faith for whom it was compiled but also information concerning their historical settings. Childs' perspective of the final form of the biblical texts as fixed entities, which excludes the historical settings of the communities that shaped the final form, needs James A. Sanders' perspective on the canonical process.[10] Contrary to Childs, Sanders sees biblical texts encoded with the historical information that testifies to us not only the final story, but also a story about the underlying traditions of the communities of faith who preserved the text from generation to generation.[11] If communities had not found the biblical texts valuable and meaningful, meeting their existential needs, then the transmission and compilation of the biblical text for the benefit of the successive generations would not have taken place. The community of faith is the foundation of canon, where through the process of selection and use, certain texts are repeated, adopted, and preserved while others are dropped out. It is in these settings the preserved texts gradually become authoritative, as they prove relevant for the existence of the community. Thus, the biblical text informs us not only about the historical setting of the individual scribe or editor, which was the preoccupation of the historical critical scholarship, but also of the communities of faith for whom it is compiled. For example, historical superscriptions in the psalms that describe David

---

9. Childs, *Introduction*, 74.

10. James A. Sanders, *Canon and Community: A Guide to Canonical Criticism* (GBS; Philadelphia: Fortress, 1984); James A. Sanders, *From Sacred Story to Sacred Text: Canon as Paradigm* (Philadelphia: Fortress, 1987a).

11. Sanders writes, "There has been a relationship between tradition, written and oral, and community, a constant, ongoing dialogue, a historical memory passed on from generation to generation, in which the special relationship between canon and community resided." Sanders, *From Sacred Story to Sacred Text: Canon as Paradigm*, 166.

implicitly inform us about knowledge of the community concerning the story of David.[12]

Therefore, improving on Childs' canonical approach by integrating Sanders' views on the canonical process, this dissertation assumes that, along with the theological message, the Psalter is also encoded with the historical information concerning the life situation of the editor(s) and the community for whom it was compiled. In other words, we assume here that the purposeful arrangement of the Psalter tells us a story, which reflects both the editor(s)' and the communities' historical setting and their hope for the future.[13] DeClaissé-Walford writes, "The Psalter is deeply imprinted with hermeneutical underpinnings from the community that shaped the text into final form."[14] Thus, the hermeneutical question is not only what any individual psalm means to its reader, but also what it means by its placement in the book. How did the editors of the Psalter shape the book we call the Psalter? What were the hermeneutical underpinnings of the process that resulted in the final shape of the Psalter? What does it tell us about the community that received it? More precisely, what did they read when they read Psalm 145 between Psalms 144 and 146? With these theological assumptions, we will now discuss our hermeneutical assumptions concerning the problem of meaning and our preference for discourse analysis.

Hermeneutical Assumption

The study of linguistics in the twentieth century has illumined the great complexity of the problems of meaning.[15] In general, we understand

---

12. Ibid., 170.

13. McCann states that the purposeful placement of psalms in the collections has given the final form of the Psalter "a function and a message greater than the sum of its parts." J. Clinton McCann, preface to *The Shape and Shaping of the Psalter* (ed. J. Clinton McCann; JSOTSup 159, Sheffield: JSOT Press, 1993), 7.

14. Nancy L. DeClaissé-Walford, *Reading from the Beginning: The Shaping of the Hebrew Psalter* (Macon: Mercer University Press, 1997), 103.

15. C. K. Ogden and I. A. Richards' book *The Meaning of Meaning*, published in 1923, demonstrates how a word can have as many as 22 definitions. See C. K. Ogden et al., *The Meaning of Meaning* (8th ed.; London: Routledge, 1946), 186-87.

language by discerning the minimal unit of sound (phonemes), the minimal grammatical unit (lexeme), and the minimal syntactical unit (syntagmeme). Nevertheless, at the next level, the discerning of the minimal unit of the semantic, which is a sememe, is difficult.[16] One faces the challenge of discerning the semantic range both at the level of its denotation and connotation. Similarly, the discerning of pragmatics in linguistics (the historical and cultural reasonableness of a text in a cotext), which is also essential for knowing the meaning of a text, is also difficult. These difficulties are furthermore convoluted in biblical interpretation because we neither have access to the speakers, nor the recipients, nor its referents. It is precisely because of these reasons that the problem of polysemy—the wide range of meanings of the biblical text—continues to challenge the exegetes of Biblical Hebrew. Ascertaining meaning, therefore, is not as simplistic as it is traditionally assumed.

Meaning is more than just knowing the grammar and lexicons. Cotterell points out five myths about meaning.[17] First, the myth of a point meaning—the supposition that there is a "basic" or "fundamental" meaning assigned to each word is not true in every usage. Second, the myth of finding a meaning through etymology—the assumption that the original usage of the word embodies the meaning fails to consider the dynamic phenomena in a language that prescribes meaning to a word. Third, the myth of aggregated meaning—the concept the meaning can simply be determined by aggregating the meanings assigned independently to the constituents of a text is not accurate. Fourth, the myth of a unique denotation—the supposition that meaning is fixed does not recognize the phenomena of cultural connotation that varies so greatly. Fifth, the myth of a totality transfer—the assumption that a word can communicate all its meaning fails to recognize the impossibility of importing the polysemy of a particular word into a single occurrence. Cotterell also reminds us of the problem of diachrony. In fact, diachronically all living language undergo changes in the semantic values of the lexical stock. Hence, meaning also has to do with

---

16. Robert De Beaugrande et al., *Introduction to Text Linguistics* (London: Longman, 1981), 20-21.

17. Peter Cotterell, "Linguistics, Meaning, Semantics, and Discourse Analysis," *NIDOTTE* 1: 148-53.

the function of language in a particular culture and time. Barr's seminal work *The Semantics of Biblical Hebrew*, which points out the inadequacy of the study of grammar, the study of the words (philology) and their meanings, their etymologies, and their cognates in related languages, underscores the importance of understanding how the Hebrew language functions to communicate meaning.[18] Cotterell prefers to look at the text as an *utterance*, rather than a mere sentence.[19] An *utterance* has both a socio-linguistic context and a cotext. The meaning of an utterance, therefore, "cannot be determined merely by reference to dictionary, lexicon, the thesaurus, and grammar."[20] Geoffrey Leech's book *Semantics*, published in 1974, proposes seven types of meaning: Conceptual meaning (sense), Connotative meaning, Stylistic meaning, Affective meaning, Reflective meaning, Collocative meaning, and Thematic meaning in the text.[21] Put differently, the text has more than one meaning and the source of meaning is more than just the text, grammar, and lexicons.

Linguists have long debated the location of meaning. Broadly speaking, three sources are considered by interpreters: the mind of the author, the text, and the mind of the reader. Since it is practically impossible to know the mind of the author,[22] the debate on the source of meaning is polarized on the two extreme ends—one that emphasizes the text as the only source of meaning and the other that focuses on the readers' mind alone.[23] But Peter Cotterell proposes a better balance in this discussion. He critically examines the three hermeneutical approaches (meaning in the text, meaning in the intention of the author of the text, and meaning in the reader of the text) and then proposes a fourth approach. In his approach, the

---

18. James Barr, *The Semantics of Biblical Language* (London: Oxford University Press, 1961). See also James Barr, *Comparative Philology and the Text of the Old Testament* (Oxford: Clarendon, 1968).

19. Cotterell, "Linguistics," 136.

20. Ibid., 136.

21. Geoffrey Leech, *Semantics* (Harmondsworth: Penguin Books, 1974), 10–27.

22. W. K. Wimsatt and Monroe Beardsley's famous essay "The Intentional Fallacy," published in 1946, claimed the irrelevancy of the author's intention in the interpretation.

23. E. D. Hirsch, H. P. Grice, and Wayne Booth believe that the meaning lies in the text, while Jacques Derrida, Paul De Man, and Stanley Fish argue the case for a Reader-response theory, where the meaning lies with the reader. See Cotterell, "Linguistics," 139.

interpretation of the text is not merely dependent on an idea of an objective text alone, nor the author's intention, or the text, cotext, and context, but rather it is "moderated through the subjectivity of the reader and reader's culture and context."[24] Cotterell writes,

> On the one hand, we seek to avoid the notion of the seman-
> tic autonomy of the text. A text cannot carry any meaning,
> but it does carry a meaning intended by the original speaker
> or author, related to the context within which it was gener-
> ated and the cotext of which it is a part. On the other hand,
> we avoid also the complete relativity of meaning inevitable
> when meaning is no more than that meaning perceived by the
> reader, however much that meaning might appear to others to
> be inimical to the objective text.[25]

With these understandings of the text, Cotterell proposes the concept of the *discourse meaning*, which is different from the *significance*, the meaning perceived by the reader. According to him, a text is a communicative oc-currence that meets seven standards of textuality: cohesion of grammar and syntax, coherence, intentionality, acceptability, informativity, situationality, and intertextuality.[26] Of these, the first three have particular importance in identifying the *discourse meaning* of the text. This is important because it claims, against the postmodern denial of any meaning in the text, a de-terminate meaning embedded in the text.[27] We will discuss the *discourse meaning* in more detail in the section on discourse analysis. At this point, it is appropriate to discuss Kevin J. Vanhoozer's canonical linguistic approach in which he develops a robust and persuasive understanding of the biblical

---

24. Ibid., 143.

25. Ibid., 144.

26. De Beaugrande et al., *Introduction to Text Linguistics*, 3.

27. Kevin J. Vanhoozer writes, "If the author's intention is embodied in the text, then the ultimate criterion for right or wrong interpretation will be the text itself, considered as a literary act." See Kevin J. Vanhoozer, *Is There a Meaning in This Text? The Bible, the Reader, and the Morality of Literary Knowledge* (Grand Rapids: Zondervan, 1998), 303.

text linguistically to emphasize the importance of the meaning of a text at the canonical level.

Canonical-Linguistic Approach

Developed from Childs' canonical approach, Vanhoozer's theological and hermeneutical theory called the "Canonical-Linguistic Approach" underscores the importance of canon, linguistics, literary, and sapiential insights.[28] He is aware of the complexity of the text, in terms of its compositional prehistory, its genre, and the process of canonization, yet he believes that reading the Bible as "unified scripture" is the best "interpretive strategy" because it "corresponds to the nature of the text itself."[29] Reiterating the reformers' commitment to the idea of *sola scriptura* and *tota scriptura*, he equates canonical reading as the "thick description" of the text, in which the interpreter is supposed "to read the Bible as unified communicative act, that is, as the complex, multi-leveled speech act of a single divine author."[30] The "thick description" of a text goes beyond the level of words, concepts, genres, human speech or acts. It intends to capture the ultimate divine communicative act where authors, human, and the divine are considered together.[31]

Vanhoozer advocates a fuller meaning (*a sensus plenior*), intended by the divine author, which emerges only at the level of whole canon.[32] He wants to read a text in light of its intentional context. According to him, both the human authors as well as the divine author "intended the readers to receive their words not merely as human words but as the Word of God."[33] He writes, "*If we are reading the Bible as the Word of God, therefore, I suggest that the context that yields his maximal sense is the canon, taken as a unified*

---

28. Kevin J. Vanhoozer, *The Drama of Doctrine: A Canonical-Linguistic Approach to Christian Theology* (Louisville: Westminster John Knox, 2005).

29. Kevin J. Vanhoozer, "Exegesis and Hermeneutics," in *New Dictionary of Biblical Theology* (ed. T. Desmond Alexander et al.; Downers Grove: Inter-Varsity Press, 2000), 61.

30. Ibid.

31. Ibid., 61-62.

32. Vanhoozer, *Is There a Meaning*, 263-65.

33. Ibid., 264.

communicative act. The books of Scripture, taken individually, may antici-pate the whole, but the canon alone is its *instantiation*."[34]

The language of canon as a divine communicative act must be discerned at more than one level of action. Developing the idea from J. L. Austin, Vanhoozer introduces three kinds of linguistic actions: locutionary act (actual utterance), illocutionary act (what the communicator does in ut-terance), and perlocutionary act (what the communicator bring about by uttering).[35] While the locution has to do with a sign system or *langue*, the illocutions and perlocutions have to do with sentences, with the languages in action or *parole*. In this way, the speech act emerging from texts is not merely understood at a basic semiotic level, but also, at the level of dis-course, which embodies in itself the propositional content (e.g., the matter) as well as illocutionary force (e.g., the energy) and the perlocutionary effect (the purpose).[36]

Ascertaining the illocutionary intent in the discourse, for Vanhoozer, is critical to the theological interpretation of the text. He writes:

> To interpret a text is thus to ascribe a particular illocution-ary act, or set of acts, to its author. To interpret a text is to answer the question, what is the author doing in the text? Interpretation involves coming up with appropriately "thick" descriptions of what an author is doing that get beyond the locutionary level (e.g., "he uttered a sentence" or "he spoke with a French accent") to descriptions of relevant communica-tive, which is to say illocutionary, action ("he confessed Jesus is Lord").[37]

A good interpretation, therefore, demands the inference of a just and exact illocutionary intent from the textual and the contextual evidence. However,

---

34. Ibid., 265.

35. Ibid., 208, 18, 427-28.

36. Ibid., 228; Kevin J. Vanhoozer, "Language, Literature, Hermeneutics, and Biblical Theology: What's Theological About a Theological Dictionary?" *NIDOTTE* 1: 34.

37. Kevin J. Vanhoozer, *First Theology: God, Scripture and Hermeneutics* (Downers Grove: InterVarsity: 2002), 182.

the illocutionary intent comes at different levels: sentential, generic (literary whole), and canonical level.[38] Vanhoozer asserts that our theological conviction on the divine authorship of the Scripture, in which human and divine authors are brought together and where various genres and intentionality are ensembled as a canon, compels us to consider the canonical level of illocutionary intent as the higher level. This higher level of illocutionary intent is the ultimate divine intent, which "supervenes" all lower levels of illocutionary intent.[39] Although the lower level illocutions are important for understanding "what the text meant" to its author and its intended receiver, the higher-level illocution is the ultimate historical binding that enables us to discern the original intention of the divine author for the community that received it.

For Vanhoozer, the final form of Scripture is a *theo-drama* of God, through which the God of the Bible draws others into his communicative action at many levels.[40] He writes, "Canonical-linguistic theology attends both to the drama in the text—what God is doing in the world through Christ—and to the drama that continues in the Church as God uses Scripture to address, edify, and confront its readers."[41] This theology affirms the plurality of voices in the Scripture and their theological significance.[42] These pluralities indicate the different levels of complexity and different aspects of reality.[43] Together they represent the theo-dramatic reality of the canon, which is independent of our perspectives, constructs, speech, thought, or silence. Reading Scripture, therefore, involves more than summarizing a set of propositional statements, but "the ability to see, feel, and taste the world as disclosed in the diverse biblical text."[44] It is not merely lexical, historical, and grammatical exercises that involve the interpreter's

---

38. Ibid., 191-94.
39. Ibid., 194.
40. Vanhoozer, *The Drama of Doctrine*, 48-56.
41. Ibid., 17.
42. Ibid., 272.
43. Ibid., 289.
44. Ibid., 285.

intellectual, spiritual, and imaginative discipline, but most of all, the "sapiential ability to participate fittingly in the theo-drama."[45]

Vanhoozer's profound and robust understanding of the biblical text as the communicative act of God calls attention to discourse analysis as the appropriate hermeneutical tool for compositional analysis of the Psalter.

Discourse Analysis

Discourse analysis, which some scholars word it as the text-linguistic analysis, is an appropriate hermeneutical tool in the hands of a biblical exegete.[46] It focuses on the discourse meaning of a text by examining the forms and functions of language used in communication. Since language is structured and not random, understanding its forms and functions is significant. Discourse analysis focuses on the lexical, syntagmatical, and paradigmatical forms, their functions, and their relations at the discourse level. It studies the functions of language—what it does and how it does. While it focuses on the text and the cotext, it also considers the pragmatic situation (historical or cultural) that prompted the text.[47] Put differently, discourse analysis considers the lexical, syntagmatic, and paradigmatic semantics in relation to its textual context, but also it draws our attention to the extra-linguistic context (the pragmatics of a language system) where it is intended to make sense. Thus, discourse analysis is a comprehensive and useful tool for examining a text in its cotext and the extra-linguistic context.

The term discourse represents "any coherent sequence of strings, any coherent stretch of language."[48] Therefore, the discourse meaning involves the meaning of a text "determined by the words from which it is constructed and the manner of their incorporation in the text syntactically and paradigmatically."[49] It also involves "the meaning of any pericope deter-

---

45. Ibid.

46. The text-linguistic analysis and discourse analysis are the same. However, it is important to note that there is no consensus on the definition of discourse analysis, as its practice is diverse and broad. Susan Anne Groom, *Linguistic Analysis of Biblical Hebrew* (Carlisle: Waynesboro, 2003), 131.

47. Ibid., xii.

48. Peter Cotterell et al., *Linguistics and Biblical Interpretation* (Downers Grove: InterVarsity, 1989), 230.

49. Cotterell, "Linguistics," 154.

mined also by the larger text of which it is part."[50] In other words, discourse analysis treats the text as a coherent whole.

For analyzing a discourse, Cotterell follows Robert de Beaugrande and Wolfgang Dressler's seven standards of textuality: cohesion of grammar and syntax, coherence, intentionality, acceptability, informativity, situationality, and intertextuality.[51]

Seven Standards of Textuality

The first standard is the "cohesion" of grammar and syntax in which the actual words are mutually connected to each other in a set of sequence of grammatical forms and conventions.[52] The sequence is indicative of inter-action taking place in the sentence structure to communicate meaning. In the Hebrew language, the pattern would greatly vary from poetry to prose. For example, poetry does not necessary follows the verb subject order. On the one hand, a hymnic sentence, void of any verb, may be used to intensify the content. On the other hand, a verb may be called to perform double duty for an anticipated action.

The second standard of textuality is "coherence" at the semantic level. In coherence, "concepts" and "relations" that underlie the surface of the text are "mutually accessible and relevant."[53] He defines concept as "a configura-tion of knowledge (cognitive content) which can be recovered or activated with more or less unity and consistency in the mind," while the relations are the "links between 'concepts' which appear together in a textual world."[54] Cotterell explains "coherence" as the meaningful relation between *constitu-ent theme* to produce a *thematic net*.[55]

The third standard of textuality is "intentionality." What does the text reveal about the writer's attitude and intention through the cohesion of the grammar and the coherence in the communication? For example, the

---

50. Ibid., 154.

51. De Beaugrande et al., *Introduction to Text Linguistics*, 3-13. See also Groom, *Linguistic Analysis*, 131-35.

52. De Beaugrande et al., *Introduction to Text Linguistics*, 3.

53. Ibid., 4.

54. Ibid.

55. Cotterell, "Linguistics," 155.

intention of the poet in Psalm 119, which majors on the *torah*, is clearly distinguishable from the group of *hallel* psalms (Psalms 146-150) at the end of the Psalter.

The fourth standard of textuality is "acceptability." This is about the relevance of the text to the receiver. In other words, a communicative occurrence is not only cohesive and coherent but also sensible to the recipient. The text achieves a desirable goal and meaningful dialogue when it makes meaningful sense to the receiver. The response often depends on the text type, the social and cultural settings, and the desirability of the goal. A relevant example would be the difference observed in the language of the first segment of the Psalter (Books I-III) to that of the second segment (Books IV and V). Buttenwieser claims Psalm 145 as the post-exilic psalm because of its theme the universal Kingdom of God with special emphasis on "broad universalism."[56] Wilson and DeClaissé-Walford have argued that the compilation of Books IV and V meets the acceptability of the post-exilic community.[57]

The fifth standard of textuality is "informativity." This concerns the extent to which the discourse is presenting a known or unknown fact. Too much of new information can be overloading the audience, while the absence of any new information can be boring. In some instances, building on the previously known is easier than presenting something completely new. In the Psalter, we see this phenomenon being used by the editor(s) artistically. The post-exilic community read the familiar name *Moses* at the seam of Book IV (Psalm 90) and the memory of the exilic experience at the seam of Book V (Psalm 107). These pieces of information are historical and thus familiar to the recipient; however, an emphasis on the continuity of YHWH's loving-kindness by repetition of the phrase "for his loving kindness endures forever" (כי לעולם חסדו) is completely new in Books IV and V.[58]

---

56. Moses Buttenwieser, *The Psalms: Chronologically Treated with a New Translation* (Chicago: University of Chicago Press, 1938), 848.

57. Gerald Henry Wilson, *The Editing of the Hebrew Psalter* (Chico: Scholars Press, 1985), 227; DeClaissé-Walford, *Reading from the Beginning*, 29.

58. See Pss 100:5; 106:1; 107:1; 117:2; 118:1ff, 29; 136:1f, 4ff.

The sixth standard of textuality is "situationality." This concerns the factors that make the discourse relevant to the situation. The situationality may affect the means of cohesion—the situationality of psalms with refrains differs from the narrative. Scholars agree that the situationality of the *hallel* psalms suggest a crescendo of praise for YHWH.

The seventh standard of textuality is "intertextuality." This refers to the factors that make the use of one text dependent on the knowledge of one or more previously known texts in a discourse. Intertextuality causes "text types" with typical patterns of characteristics efficiently used to connect events, actions, cause, reason, purpose, enablement, and time proximity in discourse.[59] We will name this as "thematic pattern." We will discuss this later in detail. Several examples of intertextuality or thematic patterns in the Psalter are evident. For example, Ps 107:1 begins with Ps 106:1 (הדו כי לעולם חסדו) (ליהוה כי־טוב כי לעולם חסדו) and the second part of Ps 107:1 (כי לעולם חסדו) links Psalms 106 and 107 with Psalms. 100; 117; 118; and 136.

Sue Groom points out that De Beaugrande's last five standards of textuality have certain fundamental limitations for biblical Hebrew.[60] First, the complex history of transmission, redaction, and the compilation of the biblical text has complicated the question of intentionality. Second, what was inferentially obvious to the ancient readers is no longer obvious to modern readers. Third, the problem of determining the original situation or the historical context of the text still lingers. The modern reader, who may not be the intended one, is facing the challenge of not only studying "the linguistic properties of the text but also the pragmatic context of the original communicative act and the mental process involved in its production."[61] Therefore, determination of discourse meaning "with respect to the situation of the original author and intended receiver" of the individual psalm, as well as the editor's intentionality for the final form of the Psalter, is subject to some amount of speculation.[62] Therefore, our goal is not historical accuracy, but

---

59. Groom, *Linguistic Analysis*, 134.
60. Ibid., 136-37.
61. Ibid., 137.
62. Ibid.

a reasonably plausible answer to the question: what does the placement of Psalm 145 possibly mean in the Psalter?

With this caveat, the objective of the discourse analysis in this dissertation is first to understand the discourse meaning of Psalm 145 as an individual psalm and then analyze its plausible discourse meaning in relations to its placement in the Psalter. The aim here is to allow the discourse to speak to us at multiple-levels and in its own literary context.[63] This will demand from us to engage in a meticulous text-linguistic analysis of all important lexical, syntactical, and thematic connections of Psalm 145 with other psalms in the Psalter, and especially in Book V, and then to consider their semantics and pragmatics in the discourse. We will clarify this task in chapters four and five.

The Exegetical Assumption

We will now turn to certain exegetical assumptions that must be clarified before we exegete Psalm 145 in the next chapter. We will explain our exegetical positions on the possible historical context of Psalm 145, the reading of "David" in the superscript, the acrostic structure of Psalm 145, the phenomena of the thematic patterning, the textual critical theory, and on the absence of *nun* line in Psalm 145.

Historical Context

Psalms scholars do not agree on the early dating of Psalm 145.[64] In absence of explicit textual evidence, many conjectures are made. The great reformer John Calvin believed that this psalm was composed when David's kingdom was at the peak of prosperity.[65] According to him, David called YHWH the King in order to give YHWH the glory due to him. Leupold also agrees

---

63. Gerald Henry Wilson, "Understanding the Purposeful Arrangement of Psalms in the Psalter: Pitfalls and Promise," in *The Shape and Shaping of the Psalter* (ed. J. Clinton McCann; JSOTSup 159, Sheffield: JSOT Press, 1993), 48.

64. Allen writes, "The setting of the psalm has been a controversial issue." Leslie C. Allen, *Psalms 101-50* (WBC 21; Nashville: Nelson, 2002), 371.

65. John Calvin, *Commentary on the Book of Psalms* (trans. James Anderson; 5 vols.; Grand Rapids: Eerdmans, 1949), 272.

with Calvin.[66] However, there is no scholarly consensus for such a belief. Although Gunkel defended the plausibility of this psalm being part of the Israel's cult prior to the Chronicler, he identified this psalm as part of "the latest" poetry.[67] P. A. Munch, Crüsemann, and J. Becker suggested that this psalm belonged to a non-cultic educational setting because of its acrostic nature.[68] At the same time, others like Wieser, H. Schmidt, and Anderson supported its cultic function because of its hymnic form and language.[69] Still others suggested its composition for liturgical purposes in the second temple period.[70] Thus, there is lack of consensus on the early dating of this psalm.

A majority of psalms scholars suggest that Psalm 145 may have been composed during post-exilic times.[71] Referring to the final verse of Psalm 145, Oesterly suggests, "A special feature is the earnestly expressed wish

---

66. Leupold writes, "The claim that the mere fact of the mention of the kingdom of God indicates a rather late date in Old Testament thinking is not warranted. Already in David's day the subject was broached (cf. I Chron 17:14; Ps. 2, etc.). Broader aspects of truth may flush upon certain generations without entering fully into the thinking of the men of that age. David could well have uttered thoughts such as these." H. C. Leupold, *Exposition of the Psalms* (Grand Rapids: Baker, 1969), 979.

67. Hermann Gunkel et al., *Introduction to Psalms: The Genres of the Religious Lyric of Israel* (trans. James D. Nogalski; Macon: Mercer University Press, 1998), 64.

68. P. A. Munch, "Die alphabetische Akrostichie in der judischen Psalmendichtung," *ZDMG* 90 (1936): 703-10; Frank Crüsemann, *Studien zur Formgeschichte von Hymnus und Danklied in Israel* (Neukirchen: Neukirchener, 1969), 297-98; Joachim Becker, *Israel deutet seine Psalmen: Urform und Neuinterpretation in den Psalmen* (SBS 18; Stuttgart: Verlag Katholisches Bibelwerk, 1967), 74-75.

69. Weiser suggests that Psalm 145 was recited at the feast of the covenant, which was celebrated in autumn, as this psalm has strong emphasis laid on the Kingship of YHWH (vv. 1, 11ff) and the mighty acts of God in the *Heilsgeschichte* (v. 5f). Artur Weiser, *The Psalms: A Commentary* (Philadelphia: Westminster, 1962), 827; Anderson, who agrees with Wieser, adds "[T]he cultic setting o the Psalm was the great Autumn Festival or the Feast of Tabernacles." Bernhard W. Anderson, *The Book of Psalms* (NCBC; 2 vols.; Grand Rapids: Eerdmans, 1981), 936. But noteworthy is Kraus' comment. Referring to Schmidt, who assigns this psalm to the festival of the enthronement of Yahweh, Kraus writes, "One can only ask what significance the festival of enthronement still has at all if the process of renewal that has otherwise so prominently been emphasized in the cultic-mythical interpretation now suddenly is not to play a role any longer—on 'understandable' grounds." See Hans-Joachim Kraus, *Psalms 60-150: A Continental Commentary* (trans. Hilton C. Oswald; Minneapolis: Fortress, 1989), 547.

70. A. F. Kirkpatrick, ed., *The Book of Psalms* (Cambridge Bible for Schools and Colleges; Cambridge: Cambridge University Press, 1902), 813.

71. Buttenwieser, *The Psalms*, 848.

that the knowledge of Yahweh may become world-wide; this universalistic outlook was by no means always prominent among the Jews in *post-exilic times* [emphasis added], as witnessed by [*sic*] the polemic in the book of Jonah."[72] He considers this psalm to be one of the latest in the Psalter because of its numerous points of affinity with psalms of both early and late dates as well as the use of Aramaisms.[73] Kraus places acrostic writings in the Bronze Age by establishing the dating of the acrostics on the Ugaritic tablet.[74] According to him, "the singer of the psalm is an individual" and "it may have been sung as a temple song."[75] George Arthur Buttrick dates this psalm late for two reasons: the use of late language [Aramaisms and late Hebrews (v. 14 has זקף and כפופים; v. 15 has ישבר)] and the use of other late psalms.[76] In other words, most psalms scholars have preferred to date this psalm late, but the question remains unresolved: how late was it? Some dates it to the period of Ezra and Nehemiah, others to the Maccabaean age. But the arguments in favor of the Maccabean age are weakened after the discovery of the Hebrew text of Ecclesiasticus, which contains a hymn of thanksgiving largely composed of phrases taken from psalms in Book V (Psalms 121; 132; 142; and 143).[77] Although the psalm may be placed in the period of Simon ben Johannan [Simon I (B.C. 310-291), or Simon II (B.C. 219-199)], the textual evidence supports the preference for the period of Ezra and Nehemiah. Kirkpatrick believes that Psalm 145 was composed during same period for the same liturgical purpose as last

---

72. W. O. E. Oesterley, *The Psalms: Translated with Text-Critical and Exegetical Notes* (London: SPCK, 1939), 572.

73. Ibid.

74. Kraus, *Psalms 60-150*, 336.

75. Ibid., 547.

76. George Arthur Buttrick, *The Interpreter's Bible: The Holy Scriptures in the King James and Revised Standard Versions with General Articles and Introduction, Exegesis, Exposition for Each Book of the Bible* (New York: Abingdon, 1951), 740.

77. Kirkpatrick writes, "The Maccabean age to which Ps cxlix has very commonly been referred is excluded by the fact that, according to the newly discovered Hebrew text of Ecclesiasticus, Pss cxlvii and cxlviii were known to the author, and must at the latest be older than B.C. 180. The clearest indications of date seem to be furnished by Ps cxlvii, which may have been written for Dedication of the walls of Jerusalem under Nehemiah; an allusion in Ps cxlvi may also be explained from the circumstances of that period. To this date then the whole group may best be referred." See Kirkpatrick, ed., *The Book of Psalms*, 776, 813.

hymnic group of psalms (Psalms 145-50). Since Psalms 147 and 148, after the discovery of the Hebrew text of Ecclesiasticus, can be dated prior to 180 B.C.E. and both Psalms 146 and 147 allude to Nehemiah's time, it is reasonable to suggest the composition of Psalm 145 might have taken place sometime during the second temple period.[78] This does not deny the possibility that some portions of Psalm 145 might have been composed before and then reused in constituting the whole discourse in Psalm 145.

Dating the placement of Psalm 145 in the MT is another difficult proposition. Wilson suggests the fixation of the Psalter in the first century.[79] He derives his arguments from the analysis of the Qumran psalms scrolls. According to him, the first segment of the Psalter (Psalms 2-89) was fixed in the 4th century B.C.E., while the second segment (Psalms 90-150) of the Psalter was in flux until the first century C.E.[80] Wilson proposes three plausible processes of fixation of the Psalter (see appendix 2): (1) Direct-Sequential Linkage [11QPs^a prior]; (2) Parallel collection; (3) Library Edition [MT150 prior-11QPs^a].[81] He sees the first two as more plausible. He then goes on to propose the mid-first century C.E. as the most probable date for the final fixation of the Psalter.[82] To support his claim, he presents four evidences: (i) the correspondences between the 11QPs^a and the editorial shaping of the Psalter; (ii) the activities of Johanan ben Zakkkai, and the Academy of Yavneh (Jamnia), (iii) the absence of manuscript evidence for variation in psalms manuscripts in the first century C.E., and (iv) the co-relation between the socio-historical setting and the setting of

---

78. Ibid., 813.

79. Gerald Henry Wilson, "A First Century C. E. Date for the Closing of the Book of Psalms?" *JBQ* 28 (2000): 102-10.

80. Considering the presence of Levitical names only in Book II and III, Louis S. Jonker argues for Levitical influence in the formation and closing of Book I-III. Thus, he suggests that although the psalms may have existed in the pre-exilic era their superscription might have taken place in early post-exilic period. See Louis C. Jonker, ed., *Revisiting the Psalm Headings: Second Temple Levitical Propaganda?* (ed. Dirk J. Human et al., Psalms and Liturgy; New York: T & T Clark, 2004), 111-13.

81. Wilson engages Sanders, Skehan, Shemaryahu Talmon and M.H. Goshen-Gottstein on the issues of canonicity in his dissertation *Editing of the Hebrew Psalter*, and then he proposes three possible processes of compositions. Wilson, *The Editing*, 63-92.

82. Wilson, "A First Century," 102-3.

Psalms 90-150.[83] DeClaissé-Walford also posits the fixation of the Psalter at Yavneh. She writes,

> Yavneh's role in stabilizing the Hebrew "canon" was probably that of finally laying to rest questions about the status of any books that, though accepted as scripture, had been the subject of discussion in Pharisaic circles before 70 CE, including any questions about different "editions" of scriptural books, including the Psalter. At this time the community addressed any remaining questions about the shaping of the Psalter—especially in Books Four and Five—and determined a "final" form of the text.[84]

However, Wilson and DeClaissé-Walford arguments in favor of the first century date is heavily dependant on probability rather than historical facts. They do not take into account the historical tradition of the antiquity of the LXX translation and composition.[85] The LXX places Psalm 145 exactly as the MT except with a few minor changes. Although their arguments support the existence of a canonical order they do not qualify its date of fixation. Since the fixation of the Psalter was a complex and gradual process, narrowly locating a date for final placement of Psalm 145 in the Psalter is unreasonable. However, it is possible that the fixation of the Psalter could have taken place in a post-exilic period during or prior to

---

83. Commenting on the historical setting, Wilson writes, "We have seen that in Psalms 90-150 concern is deflected away from the restoration of the David monarchy to Isarel's need for total reliance on God as King. . . . The post-war program of Johanan and the Academy follows a similar pattern of distancing hope from military opposition to Rome." Ibid.: 108-9.

84. DeClaissé-Walford, *Reading from the Beginning*, 116.

85. Tov writes, "According to the generally accepted explanation of the testimony of the Epistle of Aristeas, the translation of the Torah was carried out in Egypt in the third century BCE. This assumption is compatible with the early date of several papyrus and leather fragments of the Torah from Qumran and Egypt, some of which has been ascribed to the middle or end of the second century BCE (4QLXXLev[a], 4QLXXNum, Pap. Fouad 266, Pap Rylands Gk. 458)." Emanuel Tov, *Textual Criticism of the Hebrew Bible* (2d rev. ed.; Minneapolis: Fortress, 2001), 136.

the probable date of the LXX translation (200-250 B.C.E.),[86] rather than the first century C.E.

Democratization of David

We suggest that David in the superscript of Psalm 145 is presented as a pedagogical human type who models a lifestyle and attitude for its readers.[87] There is a wide consensus among the psalms scholars that the superscripts are secondary additions. They are not intended to be authentic historical data for the life situation of the individual psalms; however, they do inform us "how the psalms as a collection of sacred literature were understood and how this secondary setting becomes normative for the canonical tradition."[88] David in the superscript is a literary device through which an allusion is made to the familiar history, or an image is created for a pedagogical purposes. According to Childs, the psalms from their ancient cultic context are placed in a new canonical context.[89] Some psalms are purposefully placed in the mouth of David because he is a common person's representative. These psalms, in their new canonical context, became the sacred words of God, in which every generation of suffering and persecuted Israel finds an example in the person of David, as a glimmer of hope—"As David, so every man!"[90]

David is no longer merely a distant historical figure of remembrance but a role model to emulate. He is democratized for the present and the future of the post-exilic community of Israel. His inner spiritual life is exposed as the new criteria to which the post-exilic community was expected to

---

86. According to Wurthwein, "the Letter of Aristeas places the origin of the Pentateuch in the first half of the third century B.C." Ernst Würthwein, *The Text of the Old Testament: An Introduction to the Biblia Hebraica* (trans. Erroll F. Rhodes; Grand Rapids: Eerdmans, 1995), 51-54.

87. Wilson, *The Editing*, 172-73.

88. Brevard S. Childs, "Reflections on the Modern Study of the Psalms," in *Magnalia Dei: The Mighty Acts of God: Essays on the Bible and Archaeology in Memory of G. Ernest Wright* (ed. George Ernest Wright et al.; Garden City: Doubleday, 1976), 383-84.

89. Ibid., 384.

90. Wilson, *The Editing*, 173. Susanne Gilmayer-Bucher writes, "The reading of the psalms in light of generally acknowledged texts and the recollection of David and his life assures the readers of their own way and raises their hopes." Susanne Gillmayer-Bucher, "The Psalm Headings. A Canonical Relectur of the Psalms," in *The Biblical Canons* (ed. J. M. Auwers et al.; BETL 163, Leuven: Leuven University Press, 2003), 253-54.

respond appropriately. Speaking about what happens in democratization, Jamie A. Grant writes, "The circumstance differ, but the spiritual truths do not. This is called democratization—the words written by a *specific* individual grounded in the *specific* circumstances can be appropriated by *all* people in a *wide variety* of circumstances as they adopt the expression of the psalmist's thoughts and emotions to reflect their own."[91] Perhaps for this reason, Psalm 145 was used as a Jewish traditional table-blessing psalm in which every Jew identifies oneself singing with David. Martin Luther commended the psalm in the *Small Catechism* to be read before every mealtime. David's praise became the praise of the people of faith.[92] The compositional reading of psalms with such assumptions concerning David in the superscript has exegetical implications. This will become more evident as we revisit the subject in chapters 4 and 5.

Thematic Patterning

According to David G. Firth, psalms have an "intentional teaching function" when read compositionally in the final shape of the Psalter.[93] He suggests two strategies are visible at the canonical level: "thematic modeling" and "intratextual dialogue." In the thematic modeling, psalms interact with each other at the level of themes. The editors of the Psalter placed certain selection of psalms in certain location with similar themes to provide theological consistency. Through their compositional reading, certain theological instructions are inculcated indirectly by way of repetition. For example, the complaint psalms when read individually do not have a teaching function but when read together they provide a model to the reader attitudes and response. Regarding intratextual dialogue, Firth observes that certain psalms provide both "commentary and specification of the application of other psalms." For example, Psalm 1, which according to Brueggemann, provides orientation in the Psalter, is soon counteracted

---

91. Jamie A. Grant, "The Psalms and the King," in *Interpreting the Psalms: Issues and Approaches* (ed. David G. Firth et al.; Downers Grove: InterVarsity, 2005), 110.

92. James Limburg, *Psalms* (ed. Patrick D. Miller et al.; Louisville: Westminster John Knox, 2000), 490.

93. David G. Firth, "The Teaching of the Psalms," in *Interpreting the Psalms: Issues and Approaches* (ed. David G. Firth et al.; Downers Grove: InterVarsity, 2005), 172-74.

by the disorientation in Psalm 3. Such an intratextual dialogue has the pedagogical function of informing us that blessing is not the absence of struggle, nor does the presence of struggle mean the absence of blessings. In this way the intratextual dialogue between the psalms form "its own model of teaching within the Psalter."[94]

David G. Firth's insight on thematic modeling and intratextual dialogue is very helpful; however, it needs explanation and clarity. His definition fails to capture the complex phenomena that are seen in the compositional reading of the psalms. In actual practice, thematic modeling and the intratextual dialogue are difficult to discern as two separate phenomena. The two phenomena may be the same and perform more than one function. We suggest a broader term "thematic patterning" to be appropriate. In "thematic patterning," we see both the continuity of theme as well as the development of theme.[95] Certain themes find continuity through synonymous repetition and allusion, while others show development by expanding their semantic range with its new usage, context, and the associated "rhemes."[96] Such readings augment our theological understanding of the themes under considerations. The hermeneutical implications of such phenomena in the compositional reading of psalms depend on the discourse analysis of the psalms involved. This will become clearer as we engage this in chapters 4 and 5.

---

94. Ibid., 174.

95. The idea is indebted to Willem A. VanGemeren, whose insight on the subject has facilitated the approach. Nancy L. deClaissé-Walford does not use the term thematic patterning, but an "intertextual reading." In her analysis of Psalms 22, 23, and 24, she observes connectedness of these psalms in which the individual poetic and theological character is retained. However, when read together they create "a powerful statement of trust in the Lord God of the Israelites." Nancy L. deClaissé-Walford, "An Intertextual Reading of Psalms 22, 23, and 24," in *The Book of Psalms: Composition and Reception* (ed. Peter W. Flint et al.; VTSup 99, Leiden: Boston, 2005), 139-52.

96. The starting point of the communication is theme, while the "rheme" is the new element added in the communication. The theme-rheme structure is the platform of the communication in which one may see the thematic progression unique to the discourse. See for more details. Luise Lutz, *Zum Tema 'Thema': Einfüruing in die Thema-Rhema-Theorie* (Hamburg: Hamburger Buchagentur, 1981), 74.

The Acrostic Structure

Psalm 145 is one of the most regular acrostics in the MT.[97] One may ask why did the psalmist choose to present the message by an acrostic. What significance does this have for exegesis? We suggest that the acrostic structure of Psalm 145 is an artistic literary tool in the hands of the poet used to communicate its message effectively. Traditionally, acrostics are viewed as a mnemonic or didactic device.[98] However, psalms scholars have noticed that it is also a literary device used for an effective communication. According to Lindars, an acrostic structure in the psalms is an artistic literary tool through which the poet communicate their message more effectively.[99] A. R. Ceresko's study on Psalm 34 suggests the poet omits the *waw* line and adds the *pe* line in order to present the *lamed* line as the hinge, to form פ ל א (אלף, the first letter of Hebrew alphabet) and emphasize the message by visual effect.[100] Commenting on Psalm 119, which consists of twenty-two stanzas of eight verses each in acrostic arrangement, Allen observes that the number of verses for each Hebrew letter might have been determined by the use of eight synonymous expressions for the word תורה.[101] He sees in it a purposeful creation of "a randomness or kaleidoscopic patterning of certain number of motifs."[102] Thus, we suggest that the acrostic nature of Psalm 145 is a literary device used in harmony with its content by an expert poet to make the message persuasive and effective.

The acrostic structure of the psalm emphasizes the "all inclusive" nature of praise that YHWH deserves.[103] Psalm 145 is a unique acrostic psalm because it combines both an acrostic and "praise of YHWH" beautifully.[104]

---

97. Other acrostics psalms are Psalms 9, 10, 25, 34, 37, 111, 112, and 119.

98. Norman Gottwald, *Studies in the Book of Lamentation* (Chicago: Alec R. Allenson, 1954).

99. Barnabas Lindars, "The Structure of Psalm CXLV," *VT* 29 (1989): 23-30.

100. Anthony R. Ceresko, "The ABCs of Wisdom in Psalm XXXIV," *VT* 35 (1985): 99-104.

101. Allen, *Psalms 101-50*, 180.

102. Ibid., 180-81.

103. Adele Berlin, "The Rhetoric of Psalm 145," in *Biblical and Related Studies Presented to Samuel Iwry* (ed. Ann Kort and Scott Morschauser; Winona Lake: Eisenbrauns, 1985), 18.

104. Franz Delitzsch, *Biblical Commentary on the Psalms* (trans. Francis Bolton; 3 vols.; Grand Rapids: Eerdmans, 1955), 387.

The intended visual effect in the alphabetic arrangement (א to ת) emphasizes the "all-inclusive" nature of praise of YHWH, which includes, namely:
(a) the praise by the use of all of the Hebrew letters (א to ת) symbolically
representing all potential words in the language; (b) praise by all created
things which are YHWH's handiwork (Ps 145:10); (c) praise by all his covenant people (Ps 145:10); and finally (d) praise by all humanity (Ps 145:21).
Thus, Psalm 145, with the help of an acrostic, underscores the "all inclusive" nature of praise that YHWH deserves. According to Brueggemann,
the implicit intent in the acrostic structure is "to assert the fullness and
comprehensiveness of creation, to praise God for a world well arranged and
oriented from A to Z."[105] This will become clearer in our discourse analysis
of Psalm 145 in the next chapter.

Textual Critical Theory

For the most part, Psalm 145 in the MT is without any major textual critical problem, except for the missing *nun* line. The questions may arise here:
Why Psalm 145 of the MT does not have the *nun* line? Is it a transmissional
error or editorially intended? In order to deal with this important issue in
the rest of this chapter, we will first establish our methodological assumptions concerning the textual critical theory and then discuss our theological
and methodological position on the missing *nun* line.

Recent textual critics have come to the consensus that aim of the textual
criticism is not the recovery of the "original text," but the final hypothetical form of the text before transmission. The evidence from the discovery of Qumran scrolls and the multiple textual witnesses [the Samaritan
Pentateuch (SP), the LXX, Philo, Josephus, the New Testament, Rabbinic
Quotations, and the MT] indicate that until at least 70 C.E. the biblical
text existed in pluriform (multiple literary editions of many of the books).[106]
The text of each of these books was produced organically in multiple layers.
Thus, the task to determine which of these multiple layers is the "original
text" is insurmountably complex. Tov replaces the idea of "original text"

---

105. Walter Brueggemann, *The Message of the Psalm* (Minneapolis: Augsberg, 1984), 29.
W. S. Prinsloo, "Psalm 145: Loof Jahweh Van A tot Z," *IDS* 25 (1991): 457-70.
106. Eugene Charles Ulrich, *The Dead Sea Scrolls and the Origins of the Bible* (Grand
Rapids: Leiden, 1999), 9-12, 31.

with the Urtext (a hypothetical final literary text at the beginning of textual transmission); however, he admits that the task to reconstruct even an element of Urtext is "a presumptuous and precarious undertaking."[107] Therefore, we do not intend to reconstruct the so-called "original," but rather suggest a final plausible form of Psalm 145.

Likewise, the task of textual criticism is also complex.[108] Traditionally, the textual critics followed textual rules such as: (1) *Utrum in alterum abiturum erat?* (Which would have changed into the other?); (2) *Difficilior lectio potior* (The more difficult reading is to be preferable); and (3) *Brevior lectio potior* (The shorter reading is preferable).[109] However, the modern textual critics agree that their wooden application is problematic. Emmanuel Tov rightly asserts, "Relying on textual rules does not imply that one's conclusions are correct, nor does avoidance of them imply that they are incorrect."[110] Textual criticism, according to him, "is an art in the full sense of the word, a faculty which can be developed, guided by intuition based on experience."[111] In other words, the more experience one has, the better the results one may achieve. There is no mathematical formula for its accuracy.

Textual criticism is a complex task because it involves interdisciplinary skill. It involves not only language skills but also an understanding of the complex history of the development of the biblical text, "its copying and transmission" over a long period.[112] It involves discernment of the different stages of development of the biblical books—from the literary growth of the biblical books to their final form with respect to their content; from their copying and textual transmission to its final composition. It also involves discerning between the two possible variants—one caused by the textual transmission, other by the literary growth. Both of these variants need a different scientific approach for their evaluation. The former needs

---

107. Emanuel Tov, "Criteria for Evaluating Textual Readings: The Limitations of Textual Rules," *HTR* 75 (1983), 431.

108. Ibid. See also Tov, *Textual Criticism*; Ulrich, *The Dead Sea Scrolls*.

109. P. Kyle McCarter, *Textual Criticism: Recovering the Text of the Hebrew Bible* (Philadelphia: Fortress, 1986), 72-74.

110. Tov, "Criteria for Evaluating," 444.

111. Tov, *Textual Criticism*, 309.

112. Ibid., 289-90.

textual criticism, which "deals with all matters pertaining to the biblical text, the nature, copying, and transmission of the biblical text."[113] While the latter needs literary criticism, which "deals with various matters relating to the literary composition as a whole."[114] In other words, textual criticism not only involves the knowledge of the plausible transmissional errors, but also a wider spectrum of other disciplines.[115] Thus, a textual critic needs to be aware of his/her many limitations.

The Absence of Nun Line

Psalm 145 in the MT has 21 bicolons each beginning with a fresh acrostic alphabet, but the *nun* bicolon is absent. However, in the LXX (but not Aquila, Symmachus, and Theodotion), the 11QPs[a], Syriac (P), Aethiopic, Vulgate, and the Kennicott Medieval Hebrew manuscript 142 (hereafter, we will call these versions as the *nun* versions), as well as in the Scottish Gaelic, the *nun* bicolon is present. BHS emendation suggests בכל־דבריו וחסיד בכל־מעשׂיו נאמן יהוה , meaning "The Lord is faithful in his words, and holy in all his works." In the following paragraphs, we claim that the re-instatement of the missing *nun* line in Psalm 145 of the MT is appropriate.

Some scholars think that the omission of the *nun* bicolon is just a transmission error. They agree with the LXX and the 11QPs[a] and restore the *nun* bicolon. Most modern translations (NIV, RSV, NIB, and NLT) are in agreement with them. However, others reject the authenticity of the *nun* bicolon. They warrant their claim with the following six reasons.

(1) The Talmudic rabbis of the third century accepted the absence of the *nun* bicolon as originally intended. According to them, the letter *nun* was not included in the original composition because it would remind them of a negative prophecy on Israel's destruction in Amos 5:2 (נפלה לא־תוסיף קום בתולת ישראל, "Fallen is Virgin Israel, never to rise again . . .") which starts

---

113. Ibid., 315.

114. Ibid.

115. Tov writes, "Since the 'context' is taken in a wide sense, he [the critic] has to refer to data and arguments bearing on different aspects of the text, hence to different disciplines: the language and vocabulary of the Bible as a whole as well as of individual literary units, the exegesis of individual verses, chapters, and books and the general content and ideas of a given unit or book, including areas such as biblical history and geography." See Tov, "Criteria for Evaluating," 445.

with the Hebrew letter *nun*.[116] If this is true, one may wonder why then the *nun* bicolon is not dropped in other acrostic psalms. In fact, other acrostic psalms lack *qof* (Psalm 25), *waw* (Psalm 34), and *ayin* (Psalm 37) lines, rather than the *nun* bicolon. Why is the *nun* bicolon missing in Psalm 145 in particular? Why is it missing in the MT only, not in the *nun* versions?

Additionally, there are several negative prophecies that begin with other letters of the alphabets in the book of Amos [6:1 (ה); 6:14 (כ); 7:9 (ו); and 7:17 (ל)]. Why then is the letter *nun* in particular selected for omission in the MT? Chaim Pearl gives the following plausible explanations. (i) Psalm 145 is considered as an *ashre* Psalm and is used more often than other acrostic psalms in the Synagogue liturgy. The absence of the *nun* bicolon might have been noticed more often.[117] (ii) The second phrase of Amos 5:2, which proclaims Israel is never to rise again, is one of the most frightening prophecies. (iii) Psalm 145 presents YHWH as all-powerful and all- merciful. A frightening reminder of Amos 5:2 ("Israel never to rise again") would be theologically contradictory.[118] These arguments explain why the Talmudic rabbis justified the absence of the *nun* bicolon in their transmitted text. It does not disqualify the presence of the *nun* bicolon in the *nun* versions. If we agree with Talmudic rabbis and consider the absence of the *nun* bicolon as authentic, then we may have to either place the composition of Psalm 145 later than Amos, or believe that David, the composer of Psalm 145, was divinely inspired to drop the *nun* bicolon around 200 years prior to the prophecy of Amos. However, that would not explain the reason for the extant of the *nun* bicolon in the *nun* versions.

(2) According to Ernst Wilhelm Hengstenberg the *nun* bicolon is absent because the psalmist intended to compose Psalm 145 with three strophes only, each with seven verses only.[119] He emphasizes the priority of the literary structure and the sense over continuity of the acrostic in the poetry. He

---

116. Chaim Pearle, "The Theology of Psalm 145: Part II," *JBQ* 20/2 (1991/92): 75-78.

117. Chaim Pearle, "The Theology of Psalm 145: Part I," *JBQ* 20/1 (1991), 3.

118. Pearle, "Psalm 145: Part II," 77.

119. Ernst Wilhelm Hengstenberg, *Commentary on the Psalms* (Cherry Hill: Mack Publishing, 1845), 535. See also J. M. Neale et al., *A Commentary on the Psalms: From Primitive and Mediaeval Writers and from the Various Office-Books and Hymns of the Roman, Mozarabic, Ambrosian, Gallican, Greek, Coptic, Armenian, and Syriac Rites* (2d ed.; London: Joseph Masters, 1976), 378.

gives similar reasoning for the missing *qof* (Psalm 25), *waw* (Psalm 34), and *ayin* (Psalm 37) line in other acrostic psalms.[120] It is not clear why Psalm 145 has the *nun* bicolon missing, while other acrostic psalms have different alphabetic lines. In fact, scholars even vary concerning the division of the strophe in Psalm 145. This is clearer in our discussions on the literary structure of the psalm in the next chapter.

(3) Reuven Kimmelman, along with Dahood, rejects the authenticity of the *nun* bicolon because they see missing alphabetic bicolons in acrostic Psalms 25, 34, and 37.[121] Kimmelman gives three reasons for its rejection. First, the phrase וחסיד בכל־מעשׂיו in *nun* bicolon is identical to the second colon of verse 17 (בכל־מעשׂיו וחסיד) in Psalm 145. It is more likely that the *nun* bicolon is a reproduction. Second, the *nun* bicolon in the 11QPsᵃ has אלהים instead of יהוה. Since יהוה occurs 23 times while אלהים occurs only once in the 11QPsᵃ, it is more appropriate to anticipate יהוה rather than אלהים. Therefore, the originality of the *nun* bicolon is doubtful. Third, the first colon on the *nun* bicolon reads similarly to "the peroration of the post-*haftarah* blessing" (האל הנאמן בכל דבריו, meaning 'the God who is faithful in all his words'). Therefore, it may be a liturgical *topos* interpolated to complete the acrostic of this psalm.[122]

Kimmelman's three arguments above are weak. He fails to consider the fact that unlike the *nun* bicolon, the missing bicolons of other acrostic psalms are not preserved in other versions. Against his first objection about the repetition of a colon from verse 17, B. Lindars suggests that

---

120. Ernst Wilhelm Hengstenberg, *Commentary on the Psalms* (Edinburgh: T & T Clark, 1876), 154, 427-28; Ernst Wilhelm Hengstenberg, *Commentary on the Psalms* (Edinburgh: T. &. T. Clark, 1846), 24.

121. In Psalm 25, the ו and ק lines are missing and the acrostic pattern is interrupted by an additional ר bicolon and the פ bicolon at the end. In Psalm 34, the ו bicolon is wanting and the acrostic is interrupted by the פ bicolon at the end. See Mitchell Dahood, *Psalm III: 101-150* (AB 17A; 3 vols.; New York: Doubleday, 1970), 335. Reuven Kimmelman also observes that all acrostic psalms ascribed to David (Psalms 25, 34, and 37) have such lacking, but the acrostic psalms without any ascription (Psalms 111, 112, and 119) are all perfect acrostics. See Reuven Kimmelman, "Psalm 145: Theme, Structure, and Impact," *JBL* 113 (1994): 49-50.

122. The *haftarah* is a text selected from "the Prophets" for reading publicly in the synagogue after the reading of the torah on each Sabbath, as well as on Jewish festivals and fast days. The post-*haftarah* blessing is a blessing pronounced after the reading of the *haftarah* text. See Kimmelman, "Psalm 145," 50.

such phenomenon is artistically acceptable.[123] In fact, the phrase כל־מעשיו of verse 9 is also repeated at the end of verse 17. Kirkpatrick writes, "It is not likely that the נ verse was originally omitted: it was not necessary for the LXX to supply it [נ bicolon]: and the psalm contains many imitations and is not free from repetitions."[124] For example, Ps 144:7b repeats in verse 11a; Ps 144:7d in verse 11b; Ps 144:8 in verse 11bc; Ps 140:2b in verse 5b; Ps 119:149b in verse 156b; and so on.

The irregular use of אלהים in the *nun* bicolon of the 11QPs[a] text has parallels in the MT. There are several psalms (Pss 14:2; 47:6; 48:9; 58:7; 68:17, 27; 69:14; 70:2, 6; 73:28) where both אלהים and יהוה are used side by side to capture the poetic intention. In fact, it would be more obvious for the scribe(s) intending to harmonize the acrostic to insert יהוה rather than אלהים.

Again, a mere resemblance of the *nun* bicolon with that of the post-*haftarah* blessing cannot be treated as a valid warrant for a liturgical *topos*. Logically a mere resemblance of documents does not prove one being the source of the other, especially when we are not sure if we could date the *haftarah* blessing prior to the LXX. Resemblance may be considered as a plausible mutual correspondence, but not necessarily a proof for its provenance.

(4) Roy Kong Low accepts the absence of the *nun* line as an intentional rhetorical device; however his arguments are not convincing. He claims that the *nun* line is dropped to highlight the theme of the "Kingdom of God."[125] He presents three arguments. First, in Ps 145:11-13, the three Hebrew letters ד, ל, and מ, the reverse of the root word מלך (king), appear together. Second, the root word מלך (king) is repeated four times in the psalm. Third, the dropping *nun* line is creates an 'anacoluthon'—a literary device for breaking off the sequence of thought. This literary device is used to emphasize the theme of the Kingdom of God.[126] Furthermore, Low prefers to read the MT reading because it is shorter and more difficult reading. Low's argument in favor of the absence of *nun* line is not convincing.

---

123. B. Lindars, "The Structure of Psalm cxlv," *VT* 29 (1979): 24.

124. Kirkpatrick, ed., *The Book of Psalms*, 817.

125. Roy Kong Low, "An Exegetical and Theological Study of Psalm 145," (Th.M. thesis, Dallas Theological Seminary, 1984), 19-20.

126. Ibid., 20.

In fact, 'anacoluthon' is a grammatical literary device, which represents an interruption of thought, idea or decision rather than emphasis. The break in the continuity of an acrostic psalm underscores the missing Hebrew letter rather than what is already there. The emphasis on the theme of the Kingdom of God is overt even after the inclusion of the *nun* line.

(5) Others reject the inclusion of the *nun* bicolon because they see a unique lexical and syntactical feature in the *nun* line. The participle נאמן qualifying YHWH does not occur in the Hebrew Bible (MT). The only reference that comes close is Isa. 49:7 (יהוהאשר נאמן). YHWH is never designated as חסיד. In Jer 3:12, YHWH claims himself to be חסיד (כי־חסיד אני) and in 2 Sam 22:26 and Ps 18:26 he is introduced as the one who shows חסד (תתחסיד). Both these features are unique to the *nun* bicolon. However, this is not a valid argument for exclusion of the *nun* bicolon. Several other unique lexical and syntactical feature in the Hebrew Bible stand by itself.

(6) Some scholars, who prefer the MT to other witnesses, suggest that the MT represents a different tradition of scripture, different from the LXX and the 11QPs^a. Therefore, it must be retained as it is. For an example, Psalm 145 in the 11QPs^a has an additional bicolon of refrain (ברוך יהוה ובֿרוך שמו לעולם ועד) and the subject in the *nun* bicolon is אלהים not יהוה. Thus, the 11QPs^a represents a unique tradition. Likewise, the absence of the *nun* bicolon in the MT represents a different tradition. In this tradition, the break in the continuity from א to ת by the absence of the *nun* bicolon may be purposefully intended to suggest that the praise of YHWH by "all flesh" is incomplete and inadequate. The argument however may seem be attractive, but crumbles when they fail to answer the question: why drop the *nun* line only, and not different alphabetic line?

Having considered in detail all the arguments against the inclusion of the *nun* bicolon, we will now present two views in favor of restoring the *nun* bicolon in the MT. First, we have six textual witnesses [the LXX (but not Aquila, Symmachus, and Theodotion), 11QPs^a, Syriac (P), Aethiopic, Vulgate, and Kennicott Medieval Hebrew manuscript 142] that have the *nun* bicolon. It is remarkable to note that except for the *nun* bicolon these witnesses have great correspondence with the MT. Furthermore, the witness of the LXX is significant. Numerous references to the LXX in the New

Testament underscore the important role of the LXX in the shaping the theology of the early Church. Therefore, the witness of the LXX cannot be ignored in this case.

Second, there are sufficient literary correspondences between the *nun* bicolon and the overall literary features and the thematic emphasis of Psalm 145. In other words, the presence of the *nun* bicolon substantiates the thematic continuity in the strophe as well as the overall theological message of the poem in the MT. According to John I. Durham, the *nun* bicolon must be reinstated because it "moves the thought from Yahweh's reign to his provision for his creatures." The emphasis in the text here is on the *consistency* of YHWH's faithfulness in what he does.[127]

Jacob Chinitz observes two fascinating features in Psalm 145 when the *nun* bicolon is included.[128] First, he notices two types of verses in Psalm 145: proclamation and action. In proclamation verses one reads the psalmist's desire to proclaim and praise God, but in action verses one reads God's action. When the *nun* line is included, the number of proclamation verses match with the action verses (see the Table below):

א	ארוממך אלוהי המלך ואברכה שמך לעולם ועד:	(1) Proclamation
ב	בכל־יום אברכך ואהללה שמך לעולם ועד:	(2) Proclamation
ג	גדול יהוה ומהלל מאד ולגדלתו אין חקר:	(3) Proclamation
ד	דור לדור ישבח מעשיך וגבורתיך יגידו:	(4) Proclamation
ה	הדר כבוד הודך ודברי נפלאותיך אשיחה:	(5) Proclamation
ו	ועזוז נוראתיך יאמרו וגדולתיך אספרנה:	(6) Proclamation
ז	זכר רב־טובך יביעו וצדקתך ירננו:	(7) Proclamation
ש	חנון ורחום יהוה ארך אפים וגדל־חסד:	(1) Action
ט	טוב־יהוה לכל ורחמיו על־כל־מעשיו:	(2) Action
י	יודוך יהוה כל־מעשיך וחסידיך יברכוכה:	(8) Proclamation
כ	כבוד מלכותך יאמרו וגבורתך ידברו:	(9) Proclamation
ל	להודיע ׀ לבני האדם גבורתיו וכבוד הדר מלכותך:	(10) Proclamation

---

127. John I. Durham, *Esther-Psalms* (ed. Clifton J. Allen; The Broadman Bible Commentary; 12 vols.; Nashville: Broadman, 1969), 456-57.
128. Jacob Chinitz, "Psalm 145: Its Two Faces," *JBQ* 24 (1996): 229.

(3) Action	מלכותך מלכות כל־עלמים וממשלתך בכל־דור ודור:	מ
(4) Action	נאמן יהוה בכל־דבריו וחסיד בכל־מעשיו	נ
(5) Action	סומך יהוה לכל־הנפלים וזוקף לכל־הכפופים:	ס
(6) Action	עיני־כל אליך ישברו ואתה נותן־להם את־אכלם בעתו:	ע
(7) Action	פותח את־ידך ומשביע לכל־חי רצון:	פ
(8) Action	צדיק יהוה בכל־דרכיו וחסיד בכל־מעשיו:	צ
(9) Action	קרוב יהוה לכל־קראיו לכל אשר יקראו באמת:	ק
(10) Action	רצון־יראיו יעשה ואת־שועתם ישמע ויושיעם:	ר
(11) Action	שומר יהוה את־כל־אהביו ואת כל־הרשעים ישמיד:	ש
(11) Proclamation	תהלת יהוה ידבר־פי ויברך כל־בשר שם קדשו לעולם ועד:	ת

In the table above, we notice 11 proclamation verses and 11 action verses, forming a perfect symmetry and balance between the psalmist's desire to proclaim and his description of God's action. Chinitz does not claim this balance to be originally intended by the psalmist, but he draws our attention to the fascinating structure that emerges by the inclusion of the *nun* bicolon. Second, Chinitz points out that the inclusion of the *nun* bicolon in Psalm 145 balances the two categories of the Hebrew letters—namely the letters that are roots (*otiot shorshiyot*) and the letters that serve as servant letters (*otiot shimushiot*)—in perfect equilibrium.[129] The former is the group of the Hebrew letters that form the root of Hebrew word (for an example דבר), while the latter is the group of those used as prefixes or suffixes to supply the subject, object and the tense to the verb (for an example the letter י in ידבר). Thus, the inclusion of *nun* bicolon in Psalm 145 balances the 11 *otiot shorshiyot* (ג, ד, ז, ח, ט, ס, ע, פ, צ, ק, ר) with 11 *otiot shimushiot* (א, ב, ה, ו, י, כ, ל, מ, נ, ש, ת).

Chinitz's observations do not necessarily prove the originality of the *nun* bicolon in Psalm 145, but they show how the inclusion of the *nun* bicolon helps reveal a fascinating symmetry and balance in the poetic artistry of Psalm 145.

---

129. Ibid., 232.

Barnabas Lindars presents a structural and thematic analysis to support the inclusion of the *nun* bicolon.[130] He demonstrates how the inclusion of the *nun* bicolon helps one to see a reasonable symmetry and a chiastic structure that supports a central theme in the artistry of the poem. In this structure, verse 1 is set apart because it is similar to verse 2. Verse 2 is shown forming an inclusion with verse 21 with the help of a similar theme of praise (הלל) of Yahweh and his name (שם). Lindars sees verses 10-13b, ending with the *nun* bicolon, as the central strophe of the whole poem, around which two other strophes [quatrain (vv. 3-6), triad (vv. 7-9) X penta (vv. 10-13b) X triad (vv. 14-16), and quatrain (vv. 17-20)] are arranged in a chiastic pattern.[131] Notice the structure below.

ארוממך אלוהי המלך ואברכה שמך לעולם ועד:	א	verse 1
בכל־יום אברכך ואהללה שמך לעולם ועד:	ב	verse 2
גדול יהוה ומהלל מאד ולגדלתו אין חקר:	ג	verse 3
דור לדור ישבח מעשיך וגבורתיך יגידו:	ד	verse 4
הדר כבוד הודך ודברי נפלאותיך אשיחה:	ה	verse 5
ועזוז נוראתיך יאמרו וגדולתיך אספרנה:	ו	verse 6
זכר רב־טובך יביעו וצדקתך ירננו:	ז	verse 7
חנון ורחום יהוה ארך אפים וגדל־חסד:	ש	verse 8
טוב־יהוה לכל ורחמיו על־כל־מעשיו:	ט	verse 9
יודוך יהוה כל־מעשיך וחסידיך יברכוכה:	י	verse 10
כבוד מלכותך יאמרו וגבורתך ידברו:	כ	verse 11
להודיע | לבני האדם גבורתך וכבוד הדר מלכותך:	ל	verse 12
מלכותך מלכות כל־עלמים וממשלתך בכל־דור ודור:	מ	verse 13
נאמן יהוה בכל־דבריו וחסיד בכל־מעשיו:	(נ)	verse 13b
סומך יהוה לכל־הנפלים וזוקף לכל־הכפופים:	ס	verse 14
עיני־כל אליך ישברו ואתה נותן־להם את־אכלם בעתו:	ע	verse 15
פותח את־ידך ומשביע לכל־חי רצון:	פ	verse 16
צדיק יהוה בכל־דרכיו וחסיד בכל־מעשיו:	צ	verse 17

130. Lindars, "The Structure of Psalm cxlv," 24.
131. Ibid., 26.

קָרוֹב יהוה לכל־קֹראיו לכל אשר יקראו באמת:	ק	verse 18
רצון־יראיו יעשה ואת־שועתם ישמע ויושיעם:	ר	verse 19
שומר יהוה את־כל־אהביו ואת כל־הרשעים ישמיד:	שׁ	verse 20
תהלת יהוה ידבר־פי ויברך כל־בשר שם קדשו לעולם	ת	verse 21
וָעֶד:		

These two chiastic structures surround the central strophe of the poem (vv. 10-13b) to emphasize the YHWH Kingship theme. This is also made explicit by the central arrangement of the "three letters [מלך] as a group in the middle,"[132] in which the alphabet ל is the center of the word מלך in reverse form (vv. 11-13).[133] Notice also verse 10, which revisits the theme of the previous two stanzas: YHWH's great works (vv. 3-6) will praise YHWH and his faithful ones who are the recipients of his goodness and mercy (vv. 7-9) will bless YHWH. When verse 10 is compared with verse 13b, Lindars suggests, the theme of the *nun* bicolon [YHWH's faithfulness in his words (probably referring to the covenant promises) and his own character as the חסיד)] chiastically balances the themes picked up in verse 10. Hence, the *nun* bicolon could not be an after thought.

The aptness of the *nun* bicolon is also evident by its semantic and pragmatic link with its two neighboring verses: the מbicolon (מלכותך מלכות בכל־דור ודור כל־עלמים וממשלתך, "Your kingdom is an everlasting kingdom, and your dominion is throughout all generations") and ס bicolon (סומך יהוה לכל־הנפלים וזוקף לכל־הכפופים, "The Lord sustains all who fall, and he raises up all who are bowed down"). Both these verses represent

---

132. Ibid., 28.

133. Two other features support the centrality of the ל bicolon in the central penta strophe (vv. 10-13b) which Lindars fails to notice. First, the ל bicolon serves as the transition between the themes of verses 10-11 and 13-14. Notice that verses 10-11 are concerned with YHWH's praise, but verses 13-14 are concerned about his kingdom and faithfulness. But in verse 12 (the ל bicolon) the sons of men will praise not only his might (notice וגבורתך in verse 11 and גבורתיו in verse 12) but also the glory of his kingdom (notice מלכותו in verse 12 and מלכותך in verse 13). By joining the two themes, the psalmist gives a smooth transition to the two themes. Second, there is a grammatical pattern in this structure, which also centers the ל bicolon. Notice the parts of speech of the beginning letter of verse 10 (verb; יודוך) and verse 11 (masculine noun; כבוד) which reverses in verse 13 (feminine noun; מלכותך) and verse 13b (participle, a verbal noun; נאמן), but the beginning word in verse 12 (infinitive; להודיע) is centered by its unique grammatical role as infinitive.

affirmative and optimistic ideas about what YHWH does. But the *nun* bicolon (בכל־דבריו וחסיד בכל־מעשיו נאמן יהוה) meaning "The Lord is faithful in his words, and holy in all his works") links the two optimistic ideas of what YHWH does by stating who YHWH is. It focuses on YHWH's virtues (faithfulness and holiness), which is the basis of what YHWH does. The מ bicolon introduces YHWH as the King who has dominion over all, the *nun* bicolon explains how his rule is carried out in faithfulness and loving-kindness, and the ס bicolon explicates how his faithfulness and holiness are effected upon the fallen and the down-trodden. According to Clifton J. Allen, the *nun* bicolon provides a thematic transition "from Yahweh's reign to his provision for his creature."[134] Thus, the three consecutive bicolons provide more clarity and a smooth thematic transition.

In light of the above structural and thematic movements, a majority of psalms scholars prefer to include the *nun* bicolon.[135] In 1979, Barthélemy and his conservative team of text-critics adopted the *nun* bicolon.[136] Their work persuade us to include the *nun* bicolon in the MT.

Conclusion

In this chapter, we set forth our methodological considerations for the compositional analysis of Psalm 145 under three categories of assumptions:

---

134. Durham, *Esther-Psalms*, 456.

135. Psalms scholars such as Weiser, Anderson, Kraus, VanGemeren, Mays, James Montgomery Boice, James Limburg, Allen, and Terrien include the emendation. See Weiser, *The Psalms*, 826; Anderson, *The Book of Psalms*, 939; Kraus, *Psalms 60-150*, 546; Willem A. VanGemeren, "Psalms," in *Psalms, Proverbs, Ecclesiastes, Song of Songs* (ed. Frank E. Gæbelein; EBC 5, Grand Rapids: Zondervan, 1991), 862; James Luther Mays, *Psalms* (Louisville: Westminster John Knox, 1994), 438; James Montgomery Boice, *Psalms* (3 vols.; Grand Rapids: Baker, 1994), 1249; Limburg, *Psalms*, 489; Allen, *Psalms 101-50*, 366; Samuel L. Terrien, *The Psalms: Strophic Structure and Theological Commentary* (Grand Rapids: Eerdmans, 2003), 903; P. Auffret, "Essai sur la structure littéraire du Psaume 145," in *Melanges bibliques et orientaux. FS H Cazelles* (ed. A. Caquot and M. Delcor; Neukirchen-Vluyn: Neukirchener, 1981), 15. Since the literary structure of Psalm 145 is intended to be beautifully regular acrostic psalm, it is appropriate to include the *nun* bicolon.

136. Dominique Barthélemy et al., *Preliminary and Interim Report on the Hebrew Old Testament Text Project: Compte rendu préliminaire et provisoire sur le travail d'analyse textuelle de l'Ancien Testament hébreu* (2d rev. ed.; New York: United Bible Societies, 1979), 439.

theological, hermeneutical, and exegetical. Our discussions led us to make the following conclusions:

(1) Concerning theological assumptions, our primary hermeneutical question in understanding the final form of the Psalter is not of the history of religion, but of the theological function that the psalm has in instructing the community that receives it. However, the Psalter is not silent about history. It tells a story that reflects both the redactor(s) and the receiving communities' historical setting and their hope for the future. This theological assumption is essential to this dissertation because it is historically seminal to the compositional reading of the Psalter.

(2) Regarding hermeneutical assumption, we arrived at three conclusions. First, locating meaning is a complex process in which interpretation is not solely dependent on finding the meaning in the text, in the intention of the author, or in the mind of the reader, but in all of these. Second , the speech act emerging from the psalms is not merely understood at a basic semiotic level, but at the level of discourse, which embodies in itself the propositional content (e.g., the matter) as well as illocutionary force (e.g., the energy), and the perlocutionary effect (the purpose of the text as a communicative act). Third, discourse analysis is the best available methodological tool because it considers not only lexical, syntagmatic, and paradigmatic semantics in relation to its textual context, but also it draws our attention to the extra-linguistic context (the pragmatics of a language system) where it is intended to make sense.

(3) Under exegetical assumptions, we stated the following four assumptions. First, it is impossible to determine the historical date or the settings for the composition and the placement of Psalm 145 in the Psalter. However, it is possible that the final shaping of the Psalter could have taken place in the post-exilic period during or prior to the probable date of the LXX translation (200-250 B.C.E.). Second, David in the superscript is democratized. He is no longer a distant historical figure of remembrance but a role model for the readers of the Psalter. Third, the compositional reading of psalms enables us to notice "thematic patterning," in which themes find continuity and development in other psalms. Such reading enhances our understanding of the theme and the related theology. Fourth, we decided

that the *nun* line should be included in the psalm because it fits in the literary structure and the message the psalm intends to convey.

With these conclusions, we will now proceed to the next chapter to perform a discourse analysis of Psalm 145.

CHAPTER 3

A Discourse Analysis of Psalm 145

It [Psalm 145] is certainly one of the most interesting and beautiful of the compositions of the sweet singer of Israel; and so high an opinion did the ancient Hebrews form of it that they were wont to say—"Whoever utters this Psalm thrice each day with the heart and tongue is a happy man, and shall infallibly enjoy the blessings of the world to come."

– John Calvin[1]

Psalm 145 is a noteworthy liturgical psalm in the Psalter. It was extensively read in the Synagogue and the early Church. An apophthegm in *B. Berakhoth* (4b) claims, "Every one who repeats תהלה לדוד [Psalm 145] three times a day may be sure that he is a child of the world to come (בן העולם הבא)."[2] In the liturgical use of the Synagogue, this psalm was recited twice in the morning and once in the evening service.[3] In the early Church, it was used as part of the grace spoken at the midday meal.[4] The

---

1. John Calvin, *Commentary on the Book of Psalms* (trans. James Anderson; 5 vols.; Grand Rapids: Eerdmans, 1949), 271.

2. Franz Delitzsch, *Biblical Commentary on the Psalms* (trans. Francis Bolton; 3 vols.; Grand Rapids: Eerdmans, 1955), 387. See also A. F. Kirkpatrick, ed., *The Book of Psalms* (Cambridge Bible for Schools and Colleges; Cambridge: Cambridge University Press, 1902), 813-14. Eaton sees an interesting parallel between the Talmudic statement and the Lord's prayers. He writes, "In the same tradition the Church's prayer is both 'Thy Kingdom come,' and 'Thine is the Kingdom, the Power, and the Glory for even and ever.'" J. H. Eaton, *Psalms: Introduction and Commentary* (London: S.C.M. Press, 1967), 310.

3. Chaim Pearle, "The Theology of Psalm 145: Part I," *JBQ* 20/1 (1991): 3-4.

4. Delitzsch, *Biblical Commentary on the Psalms*, 387.

early church father Chrysostom records that this psalm was read in every Eucharist service.[5] It is no surprise that numerous commentaries on the psalm, dating from antiquity to modern time, are available. Nonetheless, we are not aware of any discourse analysis on the psalm.

In this chapter, our goal is to present a fresh look on Psalm 145 with the help of discourse analysis. We will first translate the BHS text of Psalm 145, taking into consideration all the significant textual critical issues in the footnotes. Second, we will examine the literary genre of the psalm and demonstrate how the traditional view on the literary genre of the psalm is restricted. Third, we will analyze different literary structures to explain how the current use of rhetorical and linguistic tools in understanding the literary structure of Psalm 145 produces convincing results. Finally, in light of our findings we will perform lexical, syntagmatic, paradigmatic, semantic, and pragmatic analysis to understand the discourse meaning of the psalm. Our aim is to understand the whole message of the psalm on its own terms.

Translation

1. A song of praise,[6] of David.

(א)   I will exalt you my God, the King,[7]
       and I will bless your name forever and ever.

(ב)   2. Every day I will bless you,
       and I will praise your name forever and ever.

---

5. Kirkpatrick, ed., *The Book of Psalms*, 814.

6. It is the only psalm that has תהלה (praise) in its superscription. This is remarkable because the plural of תהלה makes the title of the Psalter (ספר תהלם).

7. Some commentators translated המלך as an appositional vocative *O King* (NAS; Delitzsch, 386; Briggs, 525; Dahood, 334; Allen, 366), others *who art King* (Buttenwieser, 847), still others as *the King* (NIV; Alexander, 292; Oesterley, 573; VenGemeren, 860; Terrien, 902). In reference to Ps 144:10, where YHWH is compared with other earthly kings and in the context of the thematic emphasis on the kingdom of YHWH in Ps 145:13, the rendering of המלך as *theKing* is plausible. A lexical study of מלך in Pss 5:3; 20:10; 24:8, 10; 29:10; 93:1; 95:3; 96:10; 99:1 supports this. See Joseph A. Alexander, *The Psalms: Translated and Explained* (Philadelphia: Presbyterian Board of Publication, 1850), 293.

(ג)   3. The Lord is great and he is to be praised highly;
          and his greatness is unsearchable.

(ד)   4. One generation will[8] acclaim your works to another,
          and they will declare your mighty acts.[9]

(ה)   5. They will speak[10] of the glorious splendor[11] of your majesty,
          I will ponder[12] *over* your wonderful works,

(ו)   6. They will speak of the power of your awesome works,
          and I will give an account[13] of your great acts.[14]

---

8. Based on the form critical considerations, Allen prefers to read it as jussive (contra NAS, NIV, and RSV); however, the emphatic language of verses 1-3 favors an affirmative language here.

9. The MT has the plural construct וגבורתיך, but according to the BHS emendation 4a the LXX, Syriac, and the Targum has the singular. The difference is not of significant exegetical importance. It is preferable to retain the MT here because וגבורתיך has grammatical parallelism with the preceding word מעשיך.

10. The BHS emendation suggests the phrase ודברי in the MT to be read with Qumran text as ידברו (Jussive imperfect third masculine plural). This reading establishes parallelism with the phrase יאמרו in the first colon of verse 6. It will also match the similar metrical count (4+3) in verse 4. The LXX reading (λαλήσουσιν, "let them declare") and the general meaning of the Syriac version supports this emendation. The haplography between the letters *waw* and *yod* is "probable". Anderson, VanGemeren, and Allen rightly prefer this emendation. See Bernhard W. Anderson, *The Book of Psalms* (NCBC; 2 vols.; Grand Rapids: Eerdmans, 1981), 937; Willem A. VanGemeren, "Psalms," in *Psalms, Proverbs, Ecclesiastes, Song of Songs* (ed. Frank E. Gæbelein; EBC 5, Grand Rapids: Zondervan, 1991), 861; Leslie C. Allen, *Psalms 101-50* (WBC 21; Nashville: Nelson, 2002), 367.

11. The BHS emendation suggests the word הדר or כבוד be deleted. The Syriac version supports this emendation. Although this may balance the metrical count from 4+3 to 3+3, the metrical counts in Hebrew poetry are often uneven. For example, the metrical count in verses 3 and 4 is 4+3, but in verses 1 and 2 it is 3+4. In addition, the LXX version contains similar grammatical construction (τὴν μεγαλοπρέπειαν τῆς δόξης τῆς ἁγιωσύνης σου) as that of Hebrew phrase (הדר כבוד הודך).

12. The BHS emendation suggests that the phrase אשׂיחה of the MT texts should be read as ישׂיחו (Jussive, third person plural). The LXX reading and the general meaning of the Syriac are also in agreement. However, the haplography between the two letters *alef* and *yod* is less probable. Moreover, the LXX alteration violates the parallelism with the phrase אספרנה in verse 6. A. F. Kirkpatrick notices this alteration as "unnecessary." See Kirkpatrick, ed., *The Book of Psalms*, 815.

13. The BHS emendation יספרו (Jussive, third person plural), supported by the LXX and the Targum reading, may be ignored. The MT phrase אספרנה has external parallelism with the phrase אשׂיחה in verse 5. Furthermore, the 11QPsᵃ also has אספר (first person).

14. The MT has וגדולתיך (plural construct); however, according to the BHS emendation 6a several of the medieval Hebrew manuscripts, the LXX, the Theodotion Greek translation, the Syriac, and the Targum support the Qere reading וגדולתך (singular construct). The plural construct form of the MT וגדולתיך has both external and internal parallelism with the phrase נפלאותיך in verse 5. The Kethib reading of the Hieronymus

(ז)   7. They will evoke out loud[15] the memory of your
          abundant[16] goodness,
          and they shall sing out loud of your righteousness.[17]

(ח)   8. The Lord is gracious and merciful,
          Slow to anger and great in loving kindness.

(ט)   9. The Lord is good to all,[18]
          and his mercies are upon all he has made.[19]

(י)   10. All you have made shall give thanks to you, O Lord,
          and your godly ones shall bless you.

(כ)   11. They shall speak *about* the glory of your kingdom,
          and they will talk *about* your mighty acts;

---

text also has a plural construct.

15. Most commentators translate נבע literally as *pour forth* (Alexander, 294; Oesterley, 573; Leslie, 52; Dahood, 334), others interpret it as *utter* (KJV, NAS; Allen, 366), *celebrate* (NIV; VanGemeren, 861), and *recall* (Terrien, 902). Considering נבע (*pour forth*) as the metaphor parallel to רנן (sing out loud), the word may be interpreted as *evoke out loud*.

16. According to the BHS editors, the vowel *patah* is either to be replaced with *qames hatuf* or *holem*, meaning "abundant" instead of "many." This is supported by the LXX translation (τοῦ πλήθους, "abundant/multitude"). In the context of the word נבע (gush forth), the use of word "abundant' fits semantically better. Hence, some commentators (VanGemeren, 861; Allen, 367) prefer this emendation.

17. The phrase וצדקתך (singular construct form) is translated as plural in the Symmachus and Hieronymus versions; however, the LXX has the singular (τῇ δικαιοσύνῃ). Notice, its parallelism with טובך (singular construct) in the first colon.

18. The phrase לכל is missing in Syriac (P); however the LXX (τοῖς σύμπασιν) agrees with the MT.

19. The literal translation "all his works" (NAS) cannot mean the very act of YHWH, but the end result of his works upon whom his mercies are poured. Hence, the translation "all he has made" (NIV; Allen, 366; VanGemeren, 861) is appropriate.

(ל)   12. To declare your[20] mighty acts[21] to the sons of men
         and the glorious majesty[22] of your[23] kingdom.

(מ)   13. Your kingdom is an everlasting kingdom,
         and your dominion is throughout all generations.

(נ)[24]   The Lord is faithful in his words,
         and faithful in all his works

(ס)   14. The Lord sustains all who fall,
         and he raises up all who are bowed down.

(ע)   15. The eyes of all look up to you with hope,
         and you will give to them[25] their food in due time.

(פ)   16. You[26] open your hand
         and satisfy the desire of every living being.

---

20. Notice the second person in verses 10, 11 and 13. The sudden switch to third person in verse 12 breaks the poetical flow in the reading. The LXX and the Syriac version have rendered it as second person. Some Commentators (KJV, Kirkpatrick, 816; Dahood, 334; and Allen, 366) prefer to retain the MT because the change in the person is common in the Hebrew poetry. Others (NAS, NRS, NIV, Anderson, 938; Kraus, 546; Limbaugh, 489; and VanGemeren, 863) prefer the LXX and the Syriac reading.

21. The phrase גבורתיו (plural construct) is a *hapaxlegomenon*; however, the phrase גבורתו (singular construct) occurs six times (Judg 8:21; 1 Kgs 15:23; 2 Kgs 10:34; 20:20; Job 26:14; and Ps 106:8) It appears in the marginal note for Job 26 14 as the Qere reading. The phrase could be translated as "the mighty acts" or "the might." Semantically, the former fits in the context of verse 6b (וגדולתיך אספרנה).

22. The BHS emendation 12b informs us that the word הדר is missing in the Hebrew fragments of the Cairo Geniza and in the Syriac version. Metrically, verse 12 is parallel to verse 13 (4+3) in the MT. The LXX renders the phrase וכבוד הדר as τὴν δόξαν τῆς μεγαλοπρεπείας. Watson notices chiastic repetition of the two words כבוד and גבר in verses 11 and 12. See W. G. E. Watson, "Reversed Rootplay in Ps 145," *RB* 62 (1981): 101-2. Hence, the BHS emendation may be ignored.

23. The last phrase מלכותו with suffix third person singular has been translated with second person singular person in the LXX and in the Syriac version. As discussed earlier in the footnote 14, the literary context favors the LXX and the Syriac rendering here.

24. See our discussion on the missing nun line in chapter two.

25. Although the phrase להם (to them) is deleted in the Septuagint, the object (3mp) is implied here. Also in Ps 104:27, a thematically similar verse, the phrase is להם (to them) is wanting.

26. The 11QPs[a], the LXX, the Syriac, and the Hier versions suggest the word את (direct object) to be read as אתה (*you*, second person masculine singular). The chiastic order in verses 15 and 16 support this.

(צ)   17. The Lord is righteous in all his ways,
        and kind in all[27] his works.[28]

(ק)   18. The Lord is near to all who call upon him,
        to all who call upon him in truth.

(ר)   19. He will fulfill the desire of those who fear him,
        He will also hear their cry and will save them.

(שׁ) 20. The Lord guards all those who love him,
        but all the wicked, he will destroy.

(ת)   21. My mouth will speak the praise of the Lord,
        and all flesh will bless his holy name forever and ever.[29]

The Literary Genre

Psalm 145 combines different literary genres to communicate the intended message. Although Psalm 145 is traditionally classified as a hymn of
"praise," modern psalms scholars see more than one type of literary genre in
it. On the one hand, there are hymn-like features such as praise, laudation
and hymnic participles affirming its hymnic genre.[30] On the other hand,
it also has features of the תודה "thanksgiving" form.[31] This is why some

---

27. The Hebrew fragment of Cairo Geniza has לכל; however, the LXX and its syntactical
parallelism with the phrase בכל־דרכיו in the first cola support the MT.

28. The inseparable preposition ב in the phrase בכל־מעשׂיו and its parallel phrase דרכיו בכל
(in all his ways) in the first cola distinguish it from its earlier translation in verses 9 and 10
as *all he has made.*

29. The phrase לעולם ועד is added. Many medieval Hebrew manuscripts add the same verb
as in Ps 115:18.

30. See our discussion under the section "Form Critical Interpretation" in the first
chapter. Gunkel saw hymn-like features in Ps 145:1f-2, 3, 4-7, 8f, 10-12, 13, 14, 17, 21.
Crüsemann and Kraus point out the three hymnic participles in verses 14, 16, and 20.
Kraus also claims the strong hymnic elements such as laudations in verses 4-7 and 10-
12. See Hermann Gunkel et al., *Introduction to Psalms: The Genres of the Religious Lyric of
Israel* (trans. James D. Nogalski; Macon: Mercer University Press, 1998), 23-28. Frank
Crüsemann, *Studien zur Formgeschichte von Hymnus und Danklied in Israel* (Neukirchen:
Neukirchener, 1969), 198, 269-70, 98; Hans-Joachim Kraus, *Psalms 60-150: A
Continental Commentary* (trans. Hilton C. Oswald; Minneapolis: Fortress, 1989), 547.

31. Kraus, *Psalms 60-150*, 547.

scholars (such as Kraus, Crüseman, Allen, and Low) place this psalm into Westermann's broad category of descriptive psalms of praise.[32]

However, Westermann's classification of the descriptive psalms of praise, which does not have the unity of a literary structure, is too broad a classification to be precise.[33] Furthermore, a close observation of Psalm 145 reveals that, unlike other descriptive psalms of praise (Psalms 92, 113, 117, 135, and 147), this psalm neither begins with an imperative nor does it have the כי causal clause in the subsequent verses. In fact, Psalm 145 has features of the declarative psalms of praise, because the introduction of such psalms, according to Westermann, is usually voluntative.[34] And Psalm 145 begins with a voluntative vow or proclamation (ארוממך אלוהי המלך, "I will exalt you my God the King") in verses 1-2. Although the voluntative language is interrupted by a descriptive language in verse 3 (גדול יהוה ומהלל מאד, "The Lord is great and he is to be praised highly"), it resumes with a change in the subject (from singular to plural) in verses 4-7.

On the one hand, some scholars see Psalm 145 switching from declarations to description without any כי causal clause, affirming the features of both declarative and descriptive psalms of praise. On the other hand, some scholars read wisdom language in this psalm. Berlin informs us that S. Holm-Nielsen considered this psalm to be a wisdom psalm.[35] Additionally, Wilson, in his macro-level classification of certain roles of the psalms in the

---

32. According to Westermann, the structure of a descriptive psalms of praise constitutes six distinct features: (1) an imperatival call to praise in the beginning; (2) imperative calls following with the reason for praise; (3) the theme of God's majesty, grace and love is further developed; (4) the praise of the Creator; (5) praise of the Lord of history; (5) praise of Yahweh for his preserving grace; (6) a tendency to supplement the praise; and (7) no single concluding formula. See Claus Westermann, *Praise and Lament in the Psalms* (trans. Keith R. Crim and Richard N. Soulen; Atlanta: John Knox, 1981), 123-32; Crüsemann, *Studien zur Formgeschichte von Hymnus und Danklied in Israel*, 269; Roy Kong Low, "An Exegetical and Theological Study of Psalm 145," (Th.M. thesis, Dallas Theological Seminary, 1984), 21; Allen, *Psalms 101-50*, 368.

33. Westermann notices the complexity of his classification. He observes the imperatives in Psalms 100, 148, 150, but cohortative in Psalm 95, and voluntative and jussive forms of verbs in Psalm 145. See Westermann, *Praise and Lament*, 122, 32.

34. Ibid., 105.

35. Adele Berlin, "The Rhetoric of Psalm 145," in *Biblical and Related Studies Presented to Samuel Iwry* (ed. Ann Kort and Scott Morschauser; Winona Lake: Eisenbrauns, 1985), 18; S. Holm-Nielsen, "The Importance of Late Jewish Psalmody for the Understanding of Old Testament Psalmodic Tradition," *ST* 14 (1960): 1-53.

Psalter, has identified this psalm as on par with Psalms 107, 117 and 136, forming the "wisdom frame" in Book V, and with Psalms 1, 73, 90 and 107 as the "Final Wisdom Frame" of the entire Psalter.[36] It is clear from the above observations that the literary composition of Psalm 145 combines different literary genres.

The Literary Structure

Some scholars underplayed the literary structure of the psalm; others considered it a literary gem. Gunkel regarded it as a *Kunstlei* (artefact) rather than *Kunstwerk* (work of art).[37] Buttenwieser rejected it as poetically "worthless" and "a product of the time of literary decadence."[38] However, W. O. E. Oesterley saw it as "harmoniously interwoven together" with "no sign of mechanical construction."[39]

Psalms scholars differ on the literary shape and structure of the psalm. They suggest literary structures, which are highly arbitrary. The following chart presents their strophic divisions.

---

36. Wilson comments, "At the other end of the book [the Psalter], Psalm 145 presents a further wisdom challenge. This acrostic psalm extols the kingship of YHWH and God's love, and it concludes in 145.19-20 with the wisdom admonition." See Gerald Henry Wilson, "Shaping the Psalter: A Consideration of Editorial Linkage in the Book of Psalms," in *The Shape and Shaping of the Psalter* (ed. J. Clinton McCann; JSOTSup 159, Sheffield: JSOT Press, 1993), 79.

37. Hermann Gunkel, *Die Psalmen* (Göttingen: Vandenhoeck & Ruprecht, 1926), 610.

38. Moses Buttenwieser, *The Psalms: Chronologically Treated with a New Translation* (Chicago: University of Chicago Press, 1938), 849.

39. W. O. E. Oesterley, *The Psalms: Translated with Text-Critical and Exegetical Notes* (London: SPCK, 1939), 572.

Scholar (Year)	Strophic divisions →							
Hengstenberg (1845)	1-7	8-14	15-21					
Delitzsch (1861)	1-7	8-13	14-21					
Briggs (1906)	1-7	8-13	14-21					
Buttrick (1951)	1-3	4-7	8-9	10-13a	13b-20	21		
Liebreich (1956)	1-2	3-6	7-9	10	11-13	14-20	21	
Weiser (1962)	1-3	4-7	8-9	10-13a	13b-17	18-19	20	21
Scroggie (1965)	1-6	7-10	11-13	14-21				
Eaton (1967)	1-12	12-20	21					
Leupold (1969)	1-2	3-7	8-9	10-16	17-21			
Durham (1969)	1-7	8-21						
Anderson (1972)	1-3	4-9	10-20	21				
Kidner (1975)	1-3	4-7	8-9	10-13a	13b-20	21		
Magonet (1982)	1-3	4-7 +10	8-9 +17	11-13	14-16 +18-20	21		
Kraus (1989)	1-3	4-9	10-20	21				
Lindars (1989)	1	2	3-6	7-9	10-13b	14-16	17-20	21
VanGemeren (1991)	1-3	4-9	10-13a	13b-21				

Harman (1998)	1-2	3-7	8-13a	13b-16	17-20	21		
Mays (1994)	1-2 +3	4-7 +8-9	10-13a +13b	14-20 +21				
McCann (1994)	1-6	7-9	10-13	14-20	21			
Kimelman (1994)	1-2	3-6	7-9	10	11-20	21		
Broyles (1999)	1-3	4-9	10-14	15-21				
Limburg (2000)	1-6	7-10	11-20	21				
Allen (2002)	1-2 +3	4-7 +8-9	10-12 +13a	13b-20 +21				
Terrien (2003)	1-3	4-6	7-9	10-12	13a-15	16-18	19-21	

Some scholars (such as Delitzsch, Briggs, Eaton, and Durham) do not give any explicit reason for their choice of literary division.[40] Hence, it is difficult to analyze their literary structures. However, others claim certain reason(s) for the literary structure of the psalm as the see it, but they are arbitrary. For example, Hengstenberg, who divides this psalm into three strophes, suggests that the division had to be of three heptastichs because Psalm 145 has a three-fold appearance of YHWH's name and the three fold attributes of YHWH: greatness, goodness, and righteousness.[41] He also points out that the psalmist mentions seven times the purpose of praising God's glory. Although Hengstenberg's observation of a literary phenomenon in Psalm 145 is partly correct, there is no good warrant for his conclusion. For instance, Psalm 149 has only one occurrence of YHWH while Psalm 150 has none. In these psalms, the number of occurrences of YHWH could

---

40. Delitzsch, *Biblical Commentary on the Psalms*, 388-91; Charles A. Briggs et al., *A Critical and Exegetical Commentary on the Book of Psalms* (Edinburgh: T. & T. Clark, 1906), 526-28; Eaton, *Psalms*, 309-10.

41. Ernst Wilhelm Hengstenberg, *Commentary on the Psalms* (Cherry Hill: Mack Publishing, 1845), 535.

not be the criteria for the number of strophes they have. Moreover, besides the three attributes of YHWH in Psalm 145, YHWH is also introduced as gracious and compassionate (חנון ורחום; v. 8), faithful (נאמן; v. 13b), and loving (חסיד; v. 17).

Broadly speaking, we can discuss the above literary divisions under three categories of approaches: traditional, thematic, and rhetorical. These categories are based on the preference of emphasis.

Traditional Literary Division

Traditional literary division focuses on the hymnic features of the psalms. Some scholars (such as Kraus, Anderson, Weiser, Kidner, Mays, McCann, and Allen) follow Gunkel's form-critical classification of Psalm 145.[42] They commonly agree that Psalm 145 is a hymn, composed of four literary divisions: verses 1-3, 4-9, 10-13a, and 14-21. Each of the first three sections opens with a call to praise and then closes with the grounds of praise. However, the fourth section has a reverse pattern. Allen explains this more explicitly in the following table.[43]

Divisions	Calls to Praise	Grounds for Praise
I	verses 1-2	verse 3
II	verses 4-7	verses 8-9
III	verses 10-12	verse 13a
IV	verse 21	verses 13b-20

This literary division recognizes the alternation between the "calls to praise" and the "grounds for praise," as well as it underscores the expansion of praise: from an individual to the praise of "all your works," (v. 10) and then to "all flesh" (v. 21). However, an overloaded focus on the form-critical hymnic features blurs other literary features of the psalm. For example, this division undermines the hymnic bicolons (vv. 3, 8-9, 13, and 17) and the cluster of participles (מהלל in v. 3; סומך and זוקף in v. 14; נותן in v. 15; פותח in v. 16; and שומר in v. 20), which form a certain pattern, emphasizing the

---

42. Kraus, *Psalms 60-150*, 547-49.
43. Allen, *Psalms 101-50*, 368.

attributed of God. Thus, imposition of the category of "Calls to Praise" and "Grounds for Praise" of the so-called "hymnic structure" on the whole psalm undermines some of these remarkable features. Furthermore, the identification of certain hymnic features in the psalm is arbitrary. Unlike Allen, David Dickson divides the psalm into two sections.[44] In the first section, verses 1-7, David is stirring himself for praise, while in the second section, verses 8-21, David gives ten arguments for praise.

Thematic Considerations

Thematic division of the psalm is based on an emphasis of a theological theme over other themes. Psalms scholars such as Buttrick, Scroggie, Anderson, Kidner, VanGemeren, and Harman divide this psalm based on different theological themes.[45] On the one hand, such thematic considerations underscore certain themes that were ignored in the past. On the other hand, they may be restrictive, perspectival, and arbitrary in their results. While one theme is underscored, others are undermined. The following table illustrates this.

44. David Dickson, *A Commentary on the Psalms* (Edinburgh: Banner of Truth, 1985), 508-16.

45. George Arthur Buttrick, *The Interpreter's Bible: The Holy Scriptures in the King James and Revised Standard Versions with General Articles and Introduction, Exegesis, Exposition for Each Book of the Bible* (New York: Abingdon, 1951), 740-44; Anderson, *The Book of Psalms*, 936-40; Derek Kidner, *Psalms 73-150: A Commentary on Books III-V of the Psalms* (London: Inter-Varsity Press, 1975), 480-82; VanGemeren, "Psalms," 860-62; Allan M. Harman, *Commentary on the Psalms* (Fearn: Mentor, 1998), 444-46.

Scholars	Main Theme	(I) sub-themes	(II) sub-themes	(III) sub-themes	(IV) sub-themes
Buttrick	A Hymn of Praise	The psalmist's purpose (vv. 1-3)	God's mighty acts (vv. 4-7)	The Lord's compassion (vv. 8-9)	The Lord's justice and kindness (vv. 13b-20
Scroggie	The God Whom Men Should Praise	The greatness of God (vv. 1-6)	The goodness of God (vv. 7-10)	The glory of God (vv. 11-13)	The grace of God (vv. 14-21)
Anderson	Yahweh's Dominion Endures Forever	The praise of Yahweh' greatness (vv. 1-3)	Yahweh's wondrous works and graciousness (vv. 4-9)	The praise of Yahweh's rule (vv. 10-20)	
Kidner	An Alphabet of Praise	An opening doxology (vv. 1-3)	A theme for all men (vv. 4-7)	God the compassionate (vv. 8-9)	King for ever (vv. 10-13a) God the provider (vv. 13b-20)
Van-Gemeren	Great is Yahweh's Universal Kingdom	In praise of the Lord's Kingship (vv. 1-3)	In praise of the Lord's faithfulness to the covenant (vv. 4-9)	In praise of the Lord's Kingship (vv. 10-13a)	In praise of the Lord's covenant fidelity (vv. 13b-21)
Harman	A psalm of Praise	Praise to the king (vv. 1-2)	The splendor of God's majesty (vv. 3-7)	The glory of God's Kingdom (vv. 8-13a)	The gracious care of the Lord (vv. 13b-16) The Lord's providence (vv. 17-20)

As shown in the table above, Buttrick emphasizes the mighty acts of the Lord, and his compassion, justice and kindness in the psalm, while Scroggie sees YHWH's greatness, goodness, glory, and his grace. Anderson begins with the main theme "Yahweh's Dominion Endures For Ever," so he divides the psalm into three sub-themes: (i) the praise of Yahweh's greatness (vv. 1-3); (ii) Yahweh's wondrous works and graciousness (vv. 4-9); and (iii) the praise of Yahweh's royal rule (vv. 10-20).[46] However, VanGemeren's main theme is "Great is Yahweh's Universal Kingdom," so he divides this psalm into four sub-themes: (i) in praise of the Lord's Kingship (vv. 1-3), (ii) in praise of the Lord's faithfulness to the covenant (vv. 4-9), (iii) in praise of the Lord's Kingship (vv. 10-13a), and (iv) in praise of the Lord's covenant fidelity (vv. 13b-21). In his literary structure, he also sees a thematic pattern repeated.

> A In Praise of the Lord's Kingship (vv. 1-3)
>> B. In Praise of the Lord's Faithfulness to the Covenant (vv. 4-9)
> A′ In Praise of the Lord's Kingship (vv. 10-13a)
>> B′ In Praise of the Lord's Covenant Fidelity (vv. 13b-21).[47]

VanGemeren's emphasis on the theme of the covenant fidelity in the psalm is unique and different from all other scholars.

On the one hand, the thematic divisions of the psalm augment our perspectives of the psalm. On the other hand, it limits the literary division of the psalm to certain theological perspective or theological presuppositions. Instead of a progression, our reading of the psalm moves in concentric circles around a preferred theme. Such reading may artificially impose certain literary structures at the expense of others. Therefore, caution is necessary.

---

46. Anderson, *The Book of Psalms*, 936-40.

47. VanGemeren, "Psalms," 860-62.

Rhetorical Literary Division

The rhetorical literary division pays more attention to literary features, drawing our attention to plausible poetic artistries of the poet. It applies sophisticated linguistic tools to analyze the literary structures and other literary phenomena, uncovering complex literary proposals. In this section, we will examine the literary structure of Leon J. Liebreich, Jonathan Magonet, Adele Berlin, Barnabas Lindars, and Reuven Kimelman to establish a better understanding of the literary structure of the psalm.

Key Words

Liebreich's literary division highlights unity as well as a linear development of themes ("progression") in the psalm. He uses the *leitwörter* (key words) to demonstrate it.[48] He focuses on the three strategic placements of the key verb ברך, each one in the second half of the verse, which constitutes a "progression."[49]

verse 1   ואברכה שמך לעולם ועד

verse 10   וחסידיך יברכוכה

verse 21   ויברך כל־בשר שם קדשו לעולם ועד

In verse 1, the poet begins to bless the Lord all alone, but in verse 10 he is joined by God's saints, and in verse 21, the climax is attained by anticipating "all flesh" may bless the Lord. The literary progression from individual psalmist to all humanity is also seen in the alteration of a first person verb to third person verbs in verses 3-6: יאמרו, אשיחה, יגידו, ישבח, אספרנה. Based on this assumption, Liebreich divides the psalm into two equal parts.[50]

---

48. Leon J. Liebreich, "Psalms 34 and 145 in the Light of Their Key Words," *HUCA* 27 (1956): 187-92.

49. Ibid., 187.

50. Ibid. Like Liebreich, Adele Berlin also divides this psalm into two equal halves. According to her, the first half predominates by the verbs of speaking or uttering praise and the second half is full of "the actions of God toward his creatures." Berlin's division fails to capture the movement that Liebreich intends to show. See Berlin, "The Rhetoric of Psalm 145," 19.

Prelude	*: verses 1-2*
I	*: verses 3-6*
II	*: verses 7-9*
Interlude	*: verse 10*
III	*: verses 11-13*
IV	*: verses 14-20*
Postlude	*: verse 21*

Since the divisions of the component parts are based on "key words," Liebreich claims that the above literary division of the psalm is more objective.[51] In each of the above component parts, he points out the stylistic device of opening and closing the unit with similar key words. The prelude opens with "praise" and closes with "and I will praise." Likewise, Unit I commence with "great is the Lord" and "his greatness" and conclude with "and I will tell of your greatness." Unit II starts with "your great goodness" and ends with "the Lord is good to all." Unit III opens with "the glory of your kingdom" and closes with "your kingdom is a kingdom of all ages." Thus, the entire division is based on the repetition of the key words.

However, Unit IV, which is the biggest unit in Liebreich's division, uses a different stylistic device to achieve a different role in this psalm.[52] Notice the middle verse of this section, verse 17, where the root word צדק of verse 7 (Unit II) and חסד of verse 8 (Unit II) reappears, expressing its continuity and dependence on Unit II. Unit IV also applies the literary device of repeating the key word כל 8 times to emphasize the theme of universalism, broadening the categories of beneficiaries from individual to all.

Leibreich sees a programmatic movement of themes in the psalm.[53] In the prelude, the psalmist begins by expressing his desire to praise God as the King. In Unit I, he goes on to specify the content of his praise—the greatness of God. In Unit II, he informs us how the greatness of God is expressed in his nature (such as his justice, his righteousness, his goodness and mercy). Then in the interlude, in view of God's nature, he anticipates

51. Liebreich, "Psalms 34 and 145," 187.
52. Ibid., 189.
53. Ibid., 187.

all creatures and saints will join him to bless God. In Unit III, the theme of "King" from the prelude is picked up and made the primary theme by repeating its root word (מלך) three times. Ideologically, according to Liebreich, the theme of the "divine kingdom" progresses from Unit II. In Unit II God's nature (such as his justice, righteousness, his goodness and mercy) is introduced to make the theme in Unit III persuasive and known world-wide. Likewise, Unit IV explicates the subject of Unit II (the nature of God), so that "all flesh" might be inspired to bless him.

Liebreich's claim concerning the "interconnectedness" of the four units lack symmetry and balance. He points out two evidences in favor of his claim. First, they are interconnected by the *inclusion* formed by the phrase דור לדור of verses 4a and 13b.[54] Second, they are interconnected explicitly through a rhetorical feature in which the same words are repeated in anadiplosis.[55] However, he has no comment on Unit IV and the postlude. Notice how this interconnectedness is incomplete in the following table.[56]

Prelude	*verse 1*	ואברכה שמך לעולם ועד
	verse 2	<u>ואהללה</u> שמך לעולם ועד
Unit I	*verse 3*	גדול יהוה <u>ומהלל</u> מאד
Unit II	*verse 9*	על־כל־<u>מעשיו</u>
Interlude	*verse 10*	יודוך יהוה כל־<u>מעשיך</u>
Unit III	*verse 11*	<u>וגבורתך</u> ידברו
	verse 12a	להודיע ׀ לבני האדם <u>גבורתיו</u>
	verse 12b	וכבוד הדר <u>מלכותו</u>
	verse 13	<u>מלכותך</u> מלכות כל־עלמים

In the table above, verse 2 of the prelude flows into Unit I with the repetition of the root word הלל (praise). The root word עשה (works) of Unit II reoccurs in the interlude. However, there is no connection between Unit

---

54. Ibid., 188.

55. Anadiplosis is a rhetorical figure of speech that means to "double back" and repeat a word or phrase that appears at the end of sentence or clause at the beginning of the next sentence or clause.

56. Liebreich, "Psalms 34 and 145," 188.

I and II, the interlude and Unit III, Unit III and IV, and Unit IV and the postlude. The absence of symmetry and balance in the literary divisions of each unit needs insights from other literary proposals.

Concentric Structure

Jonathan Magonet, who considers both literary symmetry and asymmetry as equally significant tools in the poetics in this psalm, proposes a concentric structure[57] (see appendix 3). According to him, Verses 11-13 are both the geographical and thematic center of the poem. Since the root word מלך repeats three times in this section, he names this section "God the King." Around this section, the two groups of seven verses (vv. 4-10 and 14-20) form the next concentric structure on either side. The first group (vv. 4-10) is composed of two sub-sections (vv. 4-7+10 and verses 8-9). He sees similar patterns of praise addressed to God in verses 4-7+10, but in verses 8-9 he finds attributes of God described in third person. He calls the former subsection "Man to God" and the latter "Attributes of God." Likewise, the second group (vv. 14-20) is also composed of two subsections (vv. 14-16+18-20 and 17). Here the former section, he calls "God to Man" and the latter section "Attributes of God." In this section, Magonet applies different criteria for division. According to him, verse 17 is different from the rest because it is the only verse that talks about the attributes of God. This verse divides this section into two equal parts [three verses (vv. 14-16+18-20) on either sides], forming a mirror image of each other. This forms a literary symmetry (three verses on each side); however, there is also a case of asymmetry in the previous section because it has four verses against one (vv. 4-7+10 around 8-9).

Magonet's proposal for concentric structure exposes the following four facts. First, grammatical structure may not support the concentric literary structure. The poet has the freedom to switch from first person to second or to the third person plural. Second, the concentric structure of Magonet is based on the assumption that verses 11-13 are the central piece of the psalm. This assumption undermines the continuity of the third person plural subject in verse 10 (יודוך) into verse 11 (יאמרו and ידברו) and the

---

purpose clause להודיע in verse 12. Third, Magonet's concentric structure fails to capture Liebreich's thematic continuity and progression. Fourth, Magonet resorts to asymmetry as a tool for the poetic effect when he fails to prove symmetry. This is inconsistent with the acrostic design of the psalm.

Literary Symmetry

Lindars, unlike Magonet, claims a literary symmetry in the psalm.[58] Noticing the poet's inclination for a symmetry expressed in the acrostic as well as between the first and the last line of the psalm, he proposes a chiastic structure to the psalm (notice the chiastic structure on the next page). In his chiastic structure, Lindars separates verse 1 from verse 2 because verse 1 has the word מלך but verse 2 does not. He sees verse 2 forming an *inclusion* with verse 21 even though (as noted by Liebreich) the key word ברך in verse 1 connects with verse 21.

> verse 1
> verse 2 (*inclusion*)
>   verses 3-6 (Quatrain)
>   verses 8-9 (Triad)
>   verses 10-13b (Penta)
>   verses 14-16 (Triad)
>   verses 17-20 (Quatrain)
> verse 21 (*inclusion*)

Lindars' concern through this symmetry is to show the ל line as the hinge point of the psalm. It is significant to him for two reasons: (i) first, the Hebrew letter ל is the middle of the acrostic מ ל ך (king) in reverse (vv. 13, 12, and 11); (ii) second, he believes that the Kingship of Yahweh is "the apex of the meaning of this psalm."[59] Pictorially, he sees the three occurrences of the root word מלך in the three verses (11, 12, and 13), forming a triangle and pointing its apex to the left, which Liebreich failed to notice.

---

58. Barnabas Lindars, "The Structure of Psalm CXLV," *VT* 29 (1989): 23-30.
59. Ibid., 26.

כבוד מלכותך יאמרו וגבורתך ידברו   verse 11

להודיע | לבני האדם גבורתך וכבוד הדר מלכותך   verse 12

מלכותך מלכות כל־עלמים וממשלתך בכל־דור ודור   verse 13

Lindars claims that the above chiastic division of stanzas shows thematic correspondence. The theme of the second division (both quatrain/triad) corresponds with the theme of the first division (both quatrain/triad). For example, the first quatrain (vv. 3-6) focuses on the theme of YHWH's greatness (v. 3 has גדול and ולגדלתו; v. 6 has וגדולתיך), and the second quatrain (vv. 17-20) revisits YHWH's greatness expressed in the acts of his righteousness (צדיק יהוה; v. 17), kindness (חסיד; v. 17), nearness (קרב; v. 18), deliverance (ישע; v. 19), and protection (שמר; v. 20), and in his destruction of the wicked (שמד; v. 20).[60] The first triad (vv. 7-9) underscores the goodness (notice טובך in v. 7 and טוב in v. 9) and mercy (notice חנון ורחום in v. 8 and ורחמיו in v. 9) of Yahweh, while the second triad (vv. 14-16) revisits YHWH's goodness expressed in YHWH's action. YHWH sustains (סמך; v. 14) the fallen, strengthens (זקף; v. 14) the weak, gives food (נתן; v. 15) on time, and satisfies (שבע; v. 16) the desires of all living beings. Thus, there are thematic correspondences between the two-chiastic sections.

Lindars also sees the interconnectedness between the six distinct chiastic sections of this psalm through what he calls "overlap."[61] For example, verse 6 (יאמרו) overlaps in verse 7 (יביעו). Likewise verse 10 continues the thought (כל־מעשיך) initiated in verse 9 and the theme of verse 16b (רצון) finds continuity in verse 19, and so on. Through these "overlaps," according to Lindars, the six chiastic sections form one whole unit continuing from start to finish (א to ת).

Anthony R. Ceresko also arrives to a similar conclusion. Developed from Dahood's observation of the inclusive elements in verses 1-2 and 21, Ceresko notices a unique chiastic arrangement of the words that have a common root.[62]

---

60. Ibid., 27.

61. Ibid., 28.

62. Anthony R. Ceresko, "The Function of Chiasmus in Hebrew Poetry," *CBQ* 40 (1978): 5-6.

verse 1 תהלה לדוד ארוממך אלוהי המלך ואברכה שמך לעולם ועד

verse 2 בכל־יום אברכך ואהללה שמך לעולם ועד

verse 21 תהלת יהוה ידבר־פי ויברך כל־בשר שם קדשו לעולם ועד

According to him, the identical roots (הלל, שם, ברך, עד, and עולם) in these verses are used repeatedly in a chiastic form to unify the acrostic psalm.

Lindars and Ceresko's chiastic symmetry supplements Liebreich and Magonet's literary division. Nonetheless, their chiastic literary structure does not underscore the linear progression of the theme, which Liebreich's literary division has beautifully captured. Therefore, we will revisit Liebreich's literary division in the following section with the help of Kimelman's new insights on positional features such as chiasm, juxtaposition, and *inclusion*, which support a linear progression in the psalm.[63]

Reuven Kimelman

Although Kimelman's literary structure is similar to that of Liebreich, his observations support a progressive movement in the psalm.[64] The progression is evident in the explication, intensification, or in the heightening of the theme, or the subject matter.

Prelude	: verses 1-2
Stanza I	: verses 3-6
Stanza II	: verses 7-9
Interlude	: verse 10
Stanza III	: verses 11-13
Stanza IV	: verses 14-20
Postlude	: verse 21

The subject matter is the "praise of YHWH," which is introduced in three stages in the psalm and each stage is marked by the word ברך "bless," which strategically appears at verses 1, 10, and 21, serving as prelude,

---

63. Reuven Kimelman, "Psalm 145: Theme, Structure, and Impact," *JBL* 113 (1994), 37-58.

64. Ibid., 35.

interlude, and postlude (see Liebreich's division above).[65] These stages show
a development ("progression").

Prelude (v. 1)	וּבָרְכָה שִׁמְךָ לְעוֹלָם וָעֶד	
Interlude (v. 10)	וַחֲסִידֶיךָ יְבָרְכוּכָה	
Postlude (v. 21)	וִיבָרֵךְ כָּל־בָּשָׂר שֵׁם קָדְשׁוֹ לְעוֹלָם וָעֶד	

The "prelude" starts ("I will bless your name forever and ever"), the interlude continues ("your faithful will bless you"[66]), and the postlude arrives at
the climax by way of achieving its ultimate goal ("all flesh shall bless his
holy name forever and ever"). Notice the progression in the subject (I =>
your saints=>all flesh) and the progress in the object of the sentence (your
name => your holy name).

According to Kimelman, Liebreich's literary division of the four stanzas
is based on *inclusion* and the thematic fields that show a progression from
one stanza to another.[67] He writes, "What is implicit in Stanza I and II
becomes explicit in Stanza III and IV."[68]

Stanza I	: verses 3-6	גָּדוֹל || גְּדֻלָּתְךָ	*Great* || *Greatness*
Stanza II	: verses 7-9	טוֹב || טוּבְךָ	*Good* || *Goodness*
Stanza III	: verses 11-13	מַלְכוּתְךָ || מַלְכוּתְךָ	*Kingship* || *Kingship*
Stanza IV	: verses 14-20	סוֹמֵךְ יהוה || שׁוֹמֵר יהוה	*Supports* || *Preserves*

Stanza I (vv. 3-6) is about God's greatness while Stanza II (vv. 7-9) is about
the God's abundant goodness. This is marked by the *inclusion* and the

65. Ibid., 40.

66. Few Medieval Hebrew manuscripts have second person suffix.

67. Kimelman sees the literary symmetry differently than Lindars and Magonet According
to him, all four stanzas reveal balance and symmetry structurally in their length. For
Stanzas I+II, before the interlude, constitute seven verses, while Stanzas III+IV contain
ten verses. However, when divided thematically, Stanza I + III constitute seven verses and
Stanzas II + IV make ten verses. Thus, the ratio 7:10 between the length of the psalm
before and after the interlude as well as the length of the psalm based on the theme retains
symmetry. Kimelman, "Psalm 145," 46.

68. Ibid., 41.

concentration of the root word גדול and טוב in the two stanzas respectively. Stanza I opens with the greatness of God and Stanza II closes with the goodness of God. Kimelman suggests that the two themes are in purposeful juxtaposition in order "to make a point that praise is generated by appreciating the link between divine greatness and goodness."[69] This juxtaposition is made more explicit in the following stanzas by mentioning that "God's goodness is an expression of his greatness."[70] Stanzas III (vv. 11-13) and IV (vv. 14-20) explain Stanzas I and II by making their thesis more specific and concrete. For example, in Stanza I, verse 4b has וגבורתיך יגידו ("and they will declare your mighty acts"), but in Stanza III verse 12a has להודיע| לבני האדם גבורתיו ("to declare his mighty acts to the sons of men"). The latter elucidates the former by adding the object "the sons of men." Again, in Stanza I, verse 5a has הדר כבוד הודך ("the glorious splendor of your majesty") but in Stanza III, verse 12 has וכבוד הדר מלכותו (and the glorious majesty of his Kingdom). The theme of glory and majesty is concretized by explicit mention of "his Kingdom." In fact, there is a chiastic pattern (הדר כבוד X כבוד הדר) between verses 5 and 12.[71] In this pattern, the latter explicates the former by adding the genitive phrase "of his Kingdom." We notice the *progression* in the explication.

In Stanza IV, there are seven verses, which clarify how the goodness of God mentioned in Stanza II is carried out. The psalmist informs us that YHWH supports and cares for all. Since he is the divine King, as introduced in Stanza III, the King's goodness is carried out through kingly protection. The King will protect the righteous and those who love him. The King will destroy all the wicked. Thus, the two stanzas in the first half of the psalm are interconnected with each other by way of juxtaposition, but in the second half, they are interconnected by explicating their corresponding themes in the previous stanzas in *progression*.

The linear progression of theme is also evident in the ascending order of some phrases.[72] For example, the compound phrase וגבורתיך ("and your

---

69. Ibid.

70. Ibid.

71. Such chiastic pattern can also be seen between verses 4b and 12a: להודיע | לבני האדם גבורתיו X וגבורתיך יגידו

72. Kimelman, "Psalm 145," 41-48.

might acts") in verse 4b exceeds the phrase וּלְגֻדְלָתוֹ ("and his greatness") in verse 3 because the former is plural while the latter is singular.[73] The former is most exclusively used for God in the Bible and it reappears twice (in verses 11 and 12) to describe the glorious grandeur of YHWH's Kingdom, while the latter does not appear at all. We also notice a gradual escalation in the theme of praise in the psalm.[74] The first stanza (vv. 3-6) informs of the inadequacy of an individual praising everyday. In verses 1-3, God is extolled (אֲרוֹמִמְךָ), blessed (אֲבָרְכֶךָ), praised (וַאֲהַלְלָה), and exceedingly praised (וּמְהֻלָּל מְאֹד). However, in verses 4-6, God's works are lauded (יְשַׁבַּח) from one generation to another, declared (יַגִּידוּ), narrated (אָשִׂיחָה), talked of (יֹאמְרוּ), and recounted (אֲסַפְּרֶנָּה). In this way, the psalmist explains the fact that YHWH's divine grandeur is limitless (אֵין חֵקֶר וְלִגְדֻלָּתוֹ). Hence, an individual praise cannot exhaust all the praise.

The progression in the psalm is evident in the heightening of the goodness of YHWH manifested in his abounding loving-kindness and forgiveness. In Stanza II (vv. 7-9) the theme of divine goodness envelopes the whole section in a liturgical form, echoing in verse 8 a text from Exod 34:6, but with some changes.[75]

Ps 145:8   חַנּוּן וְרַחוּם יְהוָה אֶרֶךְ אַפַּיִם וּגְדָל־חָסֶד

Exod 34:6   יְהוָה | יְהוָה אֵל רַחוּם וְחַנּוּן אֶרֶךְ אַפַּיִם וְרַב־חֶסֶד וֶאֱמֶת

In this reuse of the divine attributes, the psalmist purposefully reverses the order of רַחוּם וְחַנּוּן and replaces רַב־חֶסֶד with גְדָל־חָסֶד. Kimelman suggests that the reversal draws our attention to the theme of the stanza, and the replacement alludes to the sophisticated word play on Num 14:19 and Nah 1:3.

---

73. There are two typos in Kimelman's ascending order of language. In place of the first phrase וּתְלֹדוֹ (his greatness) it should be וְלִגְדֻלָּתוֹ, and in place of the phrase vocabulary וּגְדֻלֹתְךָ (and your mighty acts), it should be וּגְבוּרֹתֶיךָ. Kimelman also does not notice the fact that the LXX, the Syriac, and the Targum have the second phrase in singular form.

74. Kimelman, "Psalm 145," 43.

75. Ibid., 44.

Num 14:19   סְלַֽח־נָ֗א לַעֲוֺ֛ן הָעָ֥ם הַזֶּ֖ה כְּגֹ֣דֶל חַסְדֶּ֑ךָ

Nah 1:3   יְהֹוָ֗ה אֶ֤רֶךְ אַפַּ֙יִם֙ (וּגְדֹול־) [וּגְדָל־]כֹּ֔חַ וְנַקֵּ֖ה לֹ֣א יְנַקֶּ֑ה יְהֹוָ֗ה בְּסוּפָ֤ה

Ps 145:8   שַׁנּ֣וּן וְרַשׁ֑וּם יְהֹוָ֥ה אֶ֥רֶךְ אַ֝פַּ֗יִם וּגְדָל־חָֽסֶד׃

In Num 14:19, the "forgiveness of sin" is sought according to "YHWH's
abounding loving kindness," while in Nah 1:3, it is assured that although
YHWH is slow to anger, his "great power" (וגדל־[כח]) would not let the
guilty go unpunished. In Ps 145:8, the psalmist purposefully replaces כח
with חסד, substituting the vengeance context of Nahum with the context
of forgiveness from Num 14:19.[76] Thus, the psalmist heightens the goodness of God manifested in his abounding loving-kindness by alluding to
his forgiveness. YHWH is not only great (v. 3), but he also good (v. 9).
Additionally, we note intensification in the stanza at the semantic level.
Verse 7 begins with the third person plural subjects (ירננו, יביעו) but the
subjects in verse 9 are heightened by the double use of כל (טוב־יהוה לכל
על־כל־מעשיו ורחמיו).

The interlude (v. 10) provides a transition from stanza II (vv. 7-9) to
stanza III (vv. 11-13) by way of intensification. Its first colon (יודוך יהוה
כל־מעשיך) connects with the last colon of the previous verse 9 by sharing
the phrase כל־מעשיו / כל־מעשיך. But, its second colon continues the theme
of blessing from the prelude (vv. 1-2) by heightening the subject from singular (ואברכה) to plural (יברכוכה). At the same time, it also connects with
Stanza III by providing subjects (וחסידיך) for the two verbs (ידברו, יאמרו)
in verse 11.

In Stanza III (vv. 11-13), the psalmist brings about a heightened sense
of making YHWH's Kingship known to all humanity (להודיע | לבני האדם).
In contrast to Ps 106:8 (להודיע את־גבורתו), where there is no mention of
the audience, the psalmist does not limit himself to the nation of Israel but
includes all of humanity. Thus, Stanza III advances the praise of YHWH in
progression by mentioning כל־בשר ("all flesh") in the postlude.

In addition, three unique literary features in this stanza intensify the
theme of the "Kingship of YHWH." First, the reverse acrostic מ ל ך (King)

---

76. Ibid.

in verses 11, 12, and 13 signifies its centrality in the psalm.[77] According to Watson, this reverse acrostic implies a reversing the flow of time, which depicts eternity. The concept of eternity, however, is already made explicit by the two phrases כל־עלמים and בכל־דור ודור in verse 13. Second, there is anadiplosis of מלכותך ("your Kingdom") and מלכותו ("his Kingdom") as well as the triangular appearance of the root word מלך (King) in verses 11, 12 and 13.[78] This literary device catches the attention of the reader immediately. Lindars suggests that the poet is intentional in bringing emphasis to the theme through a triangular literary structure at the center of the psalm. Third, there is a chiastic structure in verses 11 and 12 that calls attention to the theme of sovereignty (גבורתך וכבוד הדר מלכותך; "glory of your Kingdom and his might").[79]

verse 11   כבוד מלכותך יאמרו וגבורתך ידברו

verse 12   להודיע|לבני האדם גבורתיו וכבוד הדר מלכותו[80]

The above two sets of nouns (מלכות + כבוד, and גבורה) repeat themselves in reverse order. In fact, the chiasm is also seen in the gender of the above nouns: [כבוד (masculine) + מלכותך (feminine)] + וגבורתך (feminine) X גבורתיו (feminine) + [כבוד (masculine) + מלכות (feminine)]. According to Berlin, these features mark these two verses as the pivotal point of the psalm.[82] Undoubtedly, the theme of YHWH's sovereign Kingship in the psalm is much more explicit than other YHWH Kingship psalms (Psalms 93, and 96-99) in the Psalter.

---

77. Watson points out the reverse root play of the root word מ ל ך (King). Watson, "Reversed Rootplay in Ps 145," 101-2.

78. B. Lindars, "The Structure of Psalm cxlv," *VT* 29 (1979), 26.

79. Watson, "Reversed Rootplay in Ps 145," 102; Berlin, "The Rhetoric of Psalm 145," 19; Kimelman, "Psalm 145," 45.

80. We notice that the chiastic structure is more explicit in the LXX as its Hebrew construction of verse 12 would have מלכותך and גבורתך.

81. We notice that the chiastic structure is more explicit in the LXX as its Hebrew construction of verse 12 would have גבורתך and מלכותך.

82. Berlin, "The Rhetoric of Psalm 145," 19.

In Stanza III, we notice the progression in verse 13 in the syntactical placement of the phrase בְּכָל־דּוֹר וָדוֹר ("through all generation") at the end of the sentence in contrast to the placement דּוֹר לְדוֹר ("one generation to another") in verse 4 at the beginning. It provides a visual sense of movement from "beginning to end."

In Stanza IV (vv. 14-20), the psalmist moves further in explicating how the goodness of YHWH is executed practically toward all humanity.

verse 16	לְכָל־שָׂי (all living)
verse 18	לְכָל־קֹרְאָיו (all who call him)
verse 19	יְרֵאָיו (all who fear him)
verse 20	וְאֵת־כָּל־אֹהֲבָיו (all who love him)

However, the goodness of YHWH reaches its climax in his final judgment, when YHWH will destroy all the wicked. Implicitly, the righteous will be vindicated. The climax will be marked by a universal praise (כָּל־בָּשָׂר) of YHWH.

Conclusion

The three major approaches (traditional, thematic, and rhetorical) to literary structure are not mutually exclusive.[83] It is possible to view the structure and movement at more than one level. In fact, the former benefits the latter in understanding the literary features. Undoubtly, recent literary divisions are more persuasive because of their in-depth and detailed considerations of the psalm's literary structure. In our observations, we found that the traditional form of literary division is too restrictive with its form-critical criteria, while the thematic literary division is arbitrary and perspectival, but the rhetorical approach is sensitive to the literary features and linguistics of the psalm. Since the psalm is acrostic in nature, the latter approach, with sensitivity to literary attributes, is appropriate. This approach pays more attention to the plausible poetic artistries of the poet that has shaped this psalm into a complex literary proposal.

---

83. J. Clinton McCann, *The Book of Psalms* (NIB 4; 12 vols.; Nashville: Abingdon, 1996), 1259.

Therefore, Liebreich, Lindars, and Kimelman's literary structure, which highlights the progressive change in the subject of ברך from an individual blessing to the community, and then all flesh blessing, deserves our attention. We will adapt their literary structure to highlight the progression of the themes in the internal structure of this psalm.[84] Notice the diagram on the next page, which captures the "progression" in the psalm. In the following diagram, the motif of individual blessing unfolds into the blessing of the community but it does not stop there.[85]

---

84. Barnabas Lindars, "The Structure of Psalm CXLV," *VT* 29 (1989): 23-30; Reuven Kimelman, "Psalm 145: Theme, Structure, and Impact," *JBL* 113 (1994): 35-58.

85. Later in the chapter we will discuss in detail the discourse meaning of ברך in the psalm.

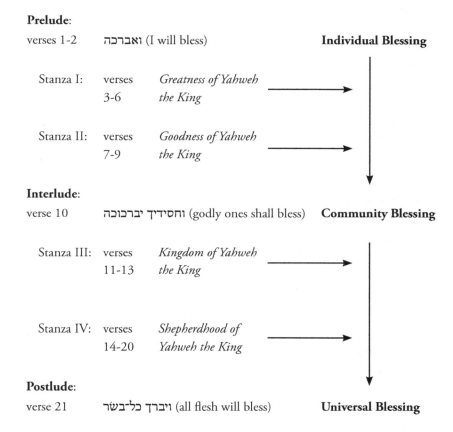

Prelude:

verses 1-2   ואברכה (I will bless)   **Individual Blessing**

Stanza I: verses   *Greatness of Yahweh*
             3-6   *the King*

Stanza II: verses   *Goodness of Yahweh*
             7-9   *the King*

Interlude:

verse 10   וחסידיך יברכוכה (godly ones shall bless)   **Community Blessing**

Stanza III: verses   *Kingdom of Yahweh*
             11-13   *the King*

Stanza IV: verses   *Shepherdhood of*
             14-20   *Yahweh the King*

Postlude:

verse 21   ויברך כל־בשׂר (all flesh will bless)   **Universal Blessing**

The experience of Yahweh's attributes (greatness, goodness, kingship, shepherdhood) is so contagious that it perpetuates from one generation to another until all humanity (כל־בשׂר) gives blessing. The above structure highlights the thematic development of "blessings" and the characteristics of Yahweh as King.

Finally, two observations are noteworthy. First, the centrality of the theme of the Kingdom of God in this psalm, which is commonly agreed upon in all three approaches. Second, the linear progression of the theme of praise and the reign of YHWH—from the individual to cosmic realm, which Liebreich and Kimelman's literary division has demonstrated. With these concluding observations, we will now proceed to the linguistic analysis of Psalm 145.

Linguistic Analysis

In this section, we will examine the lexical, syntagmatic, paradigmatic, semantic, and the pragmatic semantics of Psalm 145. We will focus on the
words and phrases that are significant literary markers in the psalm and
analyze their lexical, syntagmatic, and paradigmatic relations to uncover
the illocutionary and perlocutionary intentions in the discourse. We will
also consider the plausible pragmatics of the language system in the overall
setting or environment of the psalm.

The Anticipating Praise of David

The ultimate intent of the praise of David (תהלה לדוד) in the psalm is to
generate praise for YHWH perpetually (לעולם ועד) in all generations (בכל־
דור ודור) from all people (כל־בשׂר). Since human beings are God's creation,
their ultimate fulfillment rests in praising their Creator. Augustine in his
Confession quotes Ps 145:3 at the very beginning to recognize a human being's need to praise God. The word תהלה appears 29 times in the Psalter,
but as noticed earlier, Psalm 145 is the only psalm that has תהלה in its superscript.[86] The dictionary meaning of the word תהלה generally denotes a
praise or *song of praise*.[87] Kraus translates it as "song of praise" and "hymn."[88]
However, in the discourse of the psalm, what does the word תהלה mean in
the title תהלה לדוד. How does it differ from its feminine singular absolute
form תהלת in verse 21?[89] How does it connect with its verbal forms (אה־
ללה, imperfect; מהלל, participle) in verses 2 and 3?

In verses 1 and 2, the title phrase תהלה לדוד is immediately followed
by four syntagms with four first person imperfect verbs (אברכה, ארוממך,

---

86. תהלה occurs 29 times in the Psalter (Pss 9:15; 22:4, 26; 33:1; 34:2; 35:28; 40:4;
48:11; 51:17; 65:2; 66:2, 8; 71:6, 8, 14; 78:4; 79:13; 100:4; 102:22; 106:2, 12, 47; 109:1;
111:10; 119:171; 145:21; 147:1; 148:14; and 149:1). In contrast to Ps 145:1, Ps 142:1
has תפלה.

87. See Francis Brown et al., *Hebrew and English Lexicon: With an Appendix Containing
the Biblical Aramaic* (Peabody: Hendrickson Publishers, 1997), 239-40. See also Leslie C.
Allen, "hallel," *NIDOTTE* 1: 1035-38.

88. Hans-Joachim Kraus, *Psalms 1-59: A Continental Commentary* (trans. Hilton C.
Oswald; Minneapolis: Fortress, 1989), 26.

89. Hengstenberg suggests that the "return of תהלת in the concluding verse is a proof of
the originality of the superscription." Hengstenberg, *Commentary on the Psalms*, 535.

אברכך, and אהללה). In these two verses we notice two paradigmatic relations between the imperfect verbs (lexeme: AB‖BC; syntax: AB‖AB). We
also notice a grammatical parallelism between the second and the
fourth syntagm.

תהלה לדוד ארוממך אלוהי המלך וַאֲבָרְכָה שִׁמְךָ לְעוֹלָם וָעֶד:
בכל־יום אברכך וַאֲהַלְלָה שִׁמְךָ לְעוֹלָם וָעֶד:

The phonetic rhyming of the above bicolons adds aesthetic beauty; however, our concern here is the semantic relationship of these imperfect verbs.
We notice parallelism in the above bicolons, in which the intensification of
idea through the imperfect verbs is not merely synonymous but synthetic.
Liebreich claims it to be synonymous but that would mean a replication,
which the psalmist does not intend.[90] Since we have noticed that the over
all structure of the psalm supports a progressive development of theme, it
would be appropriate to suggest that the psalmist supplements the idea of
"extol" (רום) with "bless" (ברך) and "praise" (הלל).

The development of theme is also evident in the explication of the object of praise. The object of the verb ארוממך ("I will extol you") is אלוהי
המלך ("my god the king"), but the object of אברכה ("I will bless") and
אהללה ("I will praise") is שמך ("your name"). The psalmist draws our attention by introducing another object "your name" in parallel. For David,
therefore, praising his "God the King" is praising his "name." Similarly,
in verse 21, "praise of YHWH" is replaced by the blessing of "his holy
name." The new phrase "his holy name" supplements information about
the "name" of YHWH. Put differently, David's personal resolution to extol
(רום), bless (ברך), praise (הלל) his "God the King" involves paying homage
to YHWH's "name," which is "holy."

The praise of David in the psalm is both perpetual and consistent.
Notice the adverb "forever" (לעולם ועד) which follows the second imperfect
verb (אברכה) in verse 1. Likewise, an adverb "forever" (לעולם ועד) follows
the fourth imperfect verb (אהללה) in verse 2. However, an adverb "every
day" (בכל־יום) is also placed in front of the third imperfect verb (אברכך)

---

90. Liebreich, "Psalms 34 and 145," 188.

for an emphasis in verse 2. With these three phrases, the psalmist draws our attention to a changing pattern of adverbs—"forever" (לעולם ועד), "every day" (בכל־יום), and "forever" (לעולם ועד). We notice this emphasis also in verse 21 (לעולם ועד). Since the psalm in antiquity was primarily heard than read, this could not have gone unnoticed by the hearers. The emphasis is clearly on the time—how often and how long the praise will continue. In other words, the praise of David is consistent, on a daily basis, expanding perpetually forward, and continually.

The ultimate goal of David's praise (תהלה) is the cosmic praise of YHWH. This is evident in the use of the imperfect verbs. The psalmist switches from the first person singular imperfect verbs to third person imperfect verbs in verses 4-11.[91] He employs one singular (ישבח) and eleven plural third person imperfect verbs (יביעו, יספרו, יאמרו, ישיחו, ידברו, יגידו, ירננו, יודוך, יברכוכה, יאמרו, and ידברו) to describe the various ways through which the praise of YHWH's attributes may expand beyond his individual resolution. They all explicate different acts of proclamation with the a common ultimate purpose, which is summed up in verse 12: להודיע | לבני האדם גבורתך ("to make known to the sons of men his mighty acts").

Now let us examine the subjects of these verbs in the syntax. The occurrence of these verbs is interrupted by two hymnic bicolons (vv. 8 and 9), which places them into two groups. The subject of the first group of verbs is introduced in verse 4 as the people of one "generation" (דור), who will tell about YHWH's mighty acts to "another generation" (דור לדור). The subjects of the second group of verbs is introduced in verse 10 as "all that YHWH created" (כל־מעשיך) and the "godly ones" (חסיד) of YHWH. Thus, the praise expands from the psalmist to the godly ones of YHWH and then to all creation—*from one to all*. At the end in verse 21, the psalmist summarizes this movement—"*my* mouth will tell (ידבר) the praise of the Lord, and *all* flesh will praise (יברך) his holy name." The psalm begins as תהלה לדוד, but toward the end, it becomes a praise of YHWH (תהלת יהוה).

The title תהלה לדוד is programmatic. Most scholars agree that the extralinguistic context of the psalm is post-exilic. This poses the question: what

---

91. Two first person imperfect verbs (אשיחה and אספרנה) in verses 5-6 are changed to the third person plural imperfect in the LXX.

is the function of the title? Wilson has claimed that the function of the superscripts in Book V is editorially intended in order to present David modeling an example for the post-exilic community.[92] On the one hand, David is remembered as a historical example. On the other hand, David is democratized—"As David, so every man."[93] It is programmatic because placing the psalm of praise with its specific message in the mouth of David has great social, political, and theological ramification. In the absence of a political king, the post-exilic community of Israel is invited to join the historic David in praising YHWH, who has been their true King from the antiquity.

The Kingship of YHWH

The unique designation of God as "the King" by a king (תהלה לדוד) in the psalm is designed to present YHWH as the supreme King. Some translate it as "O King," others as "who art King," and still others "the King."[94] Earlier, we concluded that the most plausible translation in this context is "the King." In either way, the phrase המלך אלוהי is unique in the Psalter.[95] The phrase underscores the message—the Kingship of God, which is further emphasized in verses 11-13.[96] God is the reigning monarch.[97] Such an address not only acknowledges God's royal prerogative but also declares one's homage and absolute allegiance to his Kingship. Does this address represent the overall motif of the psalm to introduce YHWH as the supreme King?

In this section, we will consider the broad and narrow semantic field of the root word מלך to understand its connotation in the psalm. What does

---

92. Gerald Henry Wilson, *The Editing of the Hebrew Psalter* (Chico: Scholars Press, 1985), 172-73.

93. Ibid., 173.

94. See the footnote of verse 1 in the section "Translation." It is interesting to note that Kraus does not mention this psalm in the section on "The King in Worship" in his book *Theology of the Psalms*. See Hans-Joachim. Kraus, *Theology of the Psalms* (trans. Crim Keith; Minneapolis: Augsburg, 1986), 111-18.

95. Delitzsch writes, "If the poet is himself a king, the occasion for this appellation of God is all the more natural and the signification all the more pertinent. But even in the mouth of any other person it is significant." Delitzsch, *Biblical Commentary on the Psalms*, 388.

96. McCann suggest that the reverse acrostic observed in verses 11-13a is a poetic device to emphasize the message that God is king. McCann, *The Book of Psalms*, 1258-59.

97. Artur Weiser, *The Psalms: A Commentary* (Philadelphia: Westminster, 1962), 827.

the psalmist intend to communicate by placing God as "the King" in the mouth of David? The root word מלך, occurs 73 times in the Psalter (see a detailed analysis in appendix 4). Of the 73 occurrences, 47 times it refers to the human kings, while 18 times it qualifies יהוה but only 10 times it appears with אלוהים. Except for Ps 145:1, there are only six occasions when the word מלך appears with the definite article. In these six references, they designate a human being as the king or YHWH as the King, but not אלוהים.

the human king	יהוה הושיעה הַמֶלֶךְ יעננו ביום־קראנו	Ps 20:10
the human king	כי־הַמֶלֶךְ בטח ביהוה ובחסד עליון בל־ימוט	Ps 21:8
the human king	אין־הַמֶלֶךְ נושע ברב־חיל גבור לא־ינצל ברב־כח	Ps 33:16
the human king	חציך שנוני עמים תחתיך יפלו בלב אויבי הַמֶלֶךְ	Ps 45:6
the human king	ויתאו הַמֶלֶךְ יפיך כי־הוא אדניך והשתחוי־לו	Ps 45:12
the Lord the King	בחצצרות וקול שופר הריעו לפני	הַמֶלֶךְ יהוה	Ps 98:6

In other words, Psalm 145 is the only psalm in the Psalter which designates אלוהים as the "King" (מלך). This unique designation describes the specific motif of the psalm—"the praise of the Great King."[98]

The use of the first person "my" in the phrase "my God the King" is programmatic. The phrase "my god" with the root word מלך appears only on three occasions in the Psalter.

הקשיבה	לקול שועי מַלְכִּי וֵאלֹהָי כי־אליך אתפלל	Ps 5:3
ראו הליכותיך אלהים הליכות אֵלִי מַלְכִּי בקדש	Ps 68:25
גם־צפור	מצאה בית ודרור	קן לה	Ps 84:4
אשר־שתה אפרחיה את־מזבחותיך	
יהוה צבאות מַלְכִּי וֵאלֹהָי	

The first two psalms are Davidic and the third one is of the sons of Korah. In all three occurrences, the phrase "my God" appears with "my King" rather than "the King." Thus, Psalm 145 stands out as unique in combining the personal and particular prefixes to "God" and "King" respectively.

---

98. VanGemeren, "Psalms," 860.

The phrase "my God" underscores the testimonial nature of the psalm. It reveals how David understood, enjoyed, or experienced his relationship with YHWH. It represents the personal and intimate nature of his relationship with God. The second phrase "the King" highlights the specificity and the particular role of YHWH as the King in relation to David as the king. YHWH is not any other king but "the King" of kings. He is the King of king David, who is popularly recognized as an ideal king of Israel. Boice writes, "This is a significant statement from the mouth of Israel's king, for it acknowledges that although David may have been king of the elect nation of Israel, God is nevertheless the King of kings and therefore David's king too. And not only King of kings! He is the ultimate King of all creation and all persons."[99] The definite article draws the attention of the audience to what the psalmist is going to state about this king. For these reasons, some scholars claim the definite article to be a rhetorical literary device to distinguish the Kingship of YHWH. According to Alexander, it implies "the only true king, the king of kings, by whom they are put up and down, protected and punished."[100] In verse 3, the psalmist explicates המלך "the King" as גדול יהוה "the great Lord," whose greatness אין חקר "no one can fathom."[101] Then, in the rest of the psalm, he goes on to describe other attributes of YHWH (vv. 5-9), which can be implied as the attributes of the King. Thus, the unique syntagmatic construction אלוהי המלך is the motif of the psalm, which creates an expectation in the minds of the readers, sustains their interest in the King, who is the King of the king David, different from human kings (Ps 146:3), and whose kingdom is better than human kingdoms.

Despite the absence of the verb מלך being designated directly for YHWH, the continuity and progression of the motif of אלוהי המלך ("my God the King") in the psalm suggest a clearly implied theme of the Kingship of YHWH. The unity and continuity of the theme is framed by

99. James Montgomery Boice, *Psalms* (3 vols.; Grand Rapids: Baker, 1994), 1250.

100. Alexander, *The Psalms*, 293.

101. Leupold writes, "The opening statement concerns itself with the fact that the Lord is great and greatly deserving of praise. Yet for all that, the subject of God's greatness can never be sufficiently fathomed by any man; for that matter it is unsearchable." H. C. Leupold, *Exposition of the Psalms* (Grand Rapids: Baker, 1969), 976.

an *inclusion*. Notice the recurring word and phrase in verses 1 and 21 that form an *inclusion*.

ארוממך <u>אלוהי המלך ואברכה שמ</u>ך <u>לעולם ועד</u>:   verse 1

תהלת יהוה ידבר־פי <u>ויברך</u> כל־בשר <u>שמ</u> קדשו <u>לעולם ועד</u>   verse 21

The words and phrase ברך, שם, and לעולם ועד form *inclusion*. This implies that the phrase "my God the King." is in apposition with YHWH in verse 21. The divine name אלוהים in verse 1 is in parallel with the divine name יהוי in verse 21. These two verses surround the eight occurrences of YHWH in the psalm, placing YHWH in apposition to אלוהי המלך ("my God the King). At the same time, the central theme of "Kingdom" refers to יהוה, supporting the apposition of יהוה with אלוהים. Notice the phenomena in the following table:

verse 3	YHWH is great	גדול יהוה
verse 8	YHWH is merciful and compassionate	חנון ורחום יהוה
verse 9	YHWH is good	טוב־יהוה
verse 11-13	*Your, his, your Kingdom*	מלכותך, מלכותו, מלכותך
verse 13b	YHWH is faithful	נאמן יהוה
verse 14	YHWH sustains	סומך יהוה
verse 17	YHWH is righteous	צדיק יהוה
verse 18	YHWH is near	קרוב יהוה
verse 20	YHWH protects	שומר יהוה

In the table above, YHWH is the subject of all the attributes and actions. Even though, most psalms scholars do not classify Psalm 145 as a YHWH Kingship psalm, they recognize the Kingship of YHWH in these attributes and actions.[102] YHWH is presented here as the great (גדול), gracious (חנן), merciful (רחם), good (טוב), faithful (אמן), caring (סומך), righteous (צדיק), near (קרוב) and protecting (שומר) King. YHWH has all the

---

102. There are other YHWH kingship psalms, especially in Book IV, which thematically connect to Psalm 145. We will discuss this in chapter 5 in detail.

attributes of an ideal King. He has a Kingdom, which is superior to all human kingdoms (vv. 11-13). His Kingdom is glorious (כבוד) and mighty (גבור). All humanity will know about the glorious majesty of his Kingdom. YHWH's Kingdom is perpetual (כל־עלמים) and it continues through all generation (בכל־דור ודור).[103]

Frequent mention YHWH in Psalm 145 emphasizes YHWH as the superior King. The meaning of the Hebrew tetragrammaton YHWH has been explained in various ways by Hebrew scholars,[104] but our concern here is not merely the locution of the text, but its illocutionary meaning (what the communicator does in utterance), and perlocutionary meaning (what the communicator brings about by uttering) in Psalm 145. What does the psalmist intend to communicate? What is the semantic range of YHWH in the psalm? What does it connote? According to Chaim Pearl, YHWH is deliberately introduced as transcendent and omnipotent in the first half of the psalm (vv. 3, 4, 6, and 12) and then in the second half as immanent (vv. 8, 9, 14, 15, and 18) to balance the two natures of YHWH. Pearl writes:

---

103. Leslie notes the description of the eternal kingdom of God has great parallels with Daniel 4:3f (*For His dominion is an everlasting dominion and His kingdom endures from generation to generation*). See Elmer A. Leslie, *The Psalms: Translated and Interpreted in the Light of Hebrew Life and Worship* (New York: Abingdon, 1949), 53.

104. Terence Fretheim, "Yahweh," *NIDOTTE* 1: 1295-300.

The first half without the second would see God only as the omnipotent Creator; as a force which is remote from the world and unconcerned with the human condition. The second teaching without the first might reduce God merely to the figure of a benevolent father, ever ready to comply with even the petty wishes of His children. Such a view would reduce religious faith to a childish level and remove the dimension of awe, mystery, divine power and authority. Both concepts of God are therefore needed and together they offer a teaching for a mature and powerful personal faith.[105]

Pearl has rightly noted the locution in the text. However, the illocution and perlocution of the text imply that YHWH's introduction by the psalmist in Psalm 145 is more than just about balancing the transcendent and immanent attributes of YHWH for mature and powerful faith, but about introducing YHWH as the ultimate provider, protector, and judge of the universe. We noted earlier that the psalmist's primary intention is to introduce YHWH as the King. Therefore, all references to YHWH must be read in reference to this primary intention of the psalmist.

Furthermore, the psalmist emphasizes that YHWH is a King not because of his royal "actions," but because of his "attributes," which results in the royal "actions." The psalmist purposefully places the "attributes" of YHWH before he describes YHWH actions for such an emphasis. The following chart captures some of these syntactical arrangements, in which actions are subordinated to the attributes.

---

105. Pearle, "Psalm 145: Part I," 9.

YHWH as the KING

Verse	His Attributes	His Actions			
		Ruler	Provider	Protector	Judge
3	YHWH is great, His greatness				
4		your works your might			
5	glorious splendor of YHWH's majesty	wonderful works			
6		powerful, awesome works, great deeds			
7	abundant goodness righteousness				
8	gracious, compassionate, slow to anger, rich in love				
9		good to all	compassion on all		
11		glorious kingdom mighty			
12		glorious splendor mighty acts			
13		everlasting kingdom dominion through all			
13b	faithful loving				
14				upholds all, lifts up all	
15			give food on time		

16			satisfy the desires		
17	righteous, loving				
18				near to all	
19			fulfills the desires	saves	
20				watches over	destroys all wicked

Noteworthy in the above chart are the actions of YHWH as the ideal ruler, provider, protector, and judge. These actions of YHWH are under girded by his ideal "attributes." Human kings fall short in both the attributes and the actions (Ps 146:2). Thus, YHWH is the superior king.

Psalm 145 explicitly emphasizes that the Kingship of YHWH emanates from his "attributes" rather than his "actions." This is evident in its literary structure. Notice the five hymnic bicolons (vv. 3, 8, 9, 13, and 17),[106] which do not have any verbs. They are important literary markers to underscore the "attributes" of YHWH as well as the perpetual nature of YHWH's Kingship.

גדול יהוה ומהלל מאד ולגדלתו אין חקר:	verse 3
חנון ורחום יהוה ארך אפים וגדל־חסד:	verse 8
טוב־יהוה לכל ורחמיו על־כל־מעשׂיו:	verse 9
מלכותך מלכות כל־עלמים וממשלתך בכל־דור ודור:	verse 13
צדיק יהוה בכל־דרכיו וחסיד בכל־מעשׂיו:	verse 17

In verse 3, YHWH is introduced as great beyond human comprehension. In verse 8, YHWH is compassionate and merciful, slow to anger, and great in love. In verse 9, YHWH is good to all. Verse 13 has two parts. The first part is about his Kingdom, which is everlasting and continues through the next generations, but the second part describes YHWH is faithful and loving. In verse 17, YHWH is righteous in all his ways and loving in all his

---

106. Verse 3 has the verbal noun (participle) מהלל.

deeds. Notice the patterns formed by the syntactical constructions: גדול יהוה (v. 3), טוב־יהוה (v. 9), נאמן יהוה (13b) and צדיק יהוה (v. 17). Each of these verses ends with the hyperbole: אין חקר, על־כל־מעשיו, and בכל־מעשיו. It implies from the construction that the psalmist intends to emphasize the attributes of YHWH—the "attributes" and the "nature" of YHWH as the marker for the "actions" of YHWH. This is why the bicolons, which describe the "actions" of YHWH with the help of verbs and participles, are juxtaposed immediately after these hymnic sentences rather than before. Additionally, the hymnic verse 13 places YHWH's perpetual dominion and his Kingdom in between the two hymnic verses (vv. 9 and 17), which talks about his "attributes" and "nature." It may imply a connection between the "attributes" and the "nature" of YHWH and his perpetual Kingdom, which continues from generation to generation. The connection suggests that the royal "action" of YHWH's Kingdom emanates from his "attributes" and "nature." As is YHWH so are his Kingdom and dominion.

The Phenomena of the Blessing

The discourse meaning of the human blessing in the psalm connotes persuasive proclamation. The lexical semantic of the root word ברך is more than its dictionary meaning. The lexeme ברך, which appears four times [verses 1 (ואברכה), 2 (אברכך), 10 (יברכוכה) and 21 (ויברך)] in the psalm, is translated differently. Alexander translates it as "reverently praise."[107] The NIV translates it as "praise" (v. 1), "extol" (v. 10), and "praise" (v. 21), but the KJV, NAS and RSV retain "bless" throughout. Why does the NIV switch from one connotation to another? What does the word ברך actually mean in the psalm?

The dictionary meaning is inadequate in understanding the discourse meaning of the "blessing" in the psalm. The dictionary meaning of the root word ברך is explained with the help of two homonyms: (1) knee (Akkadian, Ugaritic, Aramaic, and Ethiopian); kneel, make kneel; (2) to bless (Ugaritic, Pheonician, Aramaic, Arabic, and Ethiopian).[108] In older etymological discussions, such as in BDB, the two were treated as originat-

107. Alexander, *The Psalms*, 293.
108. Michael L. Brown, "*brk*," *NIDOTTE* 1, 757-67.

ing from one root word.[109] It was assumed that the words "to kneel" and "to bless" are connected because one would receive the blessing or praise of the superior by bending down on one's knees. However, most scholars now reject this theory because in all ancient Semitic practices the deity is the giver rather than receiver of the blessings. How, then, should we translate it when a human being is the subject of the verb ברך?

In order to examine this, we will first examine its semantic domain in the Psalter and then in Psalm 145. In the Psalter, the root word ברך appears 76 times.[110] Of these, 54 times YHWH is the recipient of ברך, but only 22 times human beings are recipients. We will consider a few of these references to highlight the semantic fields of the word ברך elsewhere in the Psalter.

וַאֲבָרְכָה וֶת־יהוה בְּכָל־עֵת תָּמִיד תְּהִלָּתוֹ בְּפִי	Ps 34:2
בָּרְכוּ עַמִּים ׀ אֱלֹהֵינוּ וְהַשְׁמִיעוּ קוֹל תְּהִלָּתוֹ	Ps 66:8
בֹּאוּ נִשְׁתַּחֲוֶה וְנִכְרָעָה נִבְרְכָה לִפְנֵי־יהוה עֹשֵׂנוּ	Ps 95:6
שִׁירוּ לַיהוה בָּרְכוּ שְׁמוֹ בַּשְּׂרוּ מִיּוֹם־לְיוֹם יְשׁוּעָתוֹ	Ps 96:2
בֹּאוּ שְׁעָרָיו ׀ בְּתוֹדָה שְׁצֵרֹתָיו בִּתְהִלָּה הוֹדוּ־לוֹ בָּרְכוּ שְׁמוֹ	Ps 100:4
שְׂאוּ־יְדֵכֶם קֹדֶשׁ וּבָרְכוּ וֶת־יהוה	Ps 134:2

In the above references, ברך is used in parallel to different expressions. It is in parallel to a human proclamation of praise (תהלה; Ps 34:2), bowing down (שחה; Ps 95:6) before YHWH, kneeling down (כרע; Ps 95:6) before YHWH, singing (שיר; Ps 96:2) and proclaiming (בשר; Ps 96:2) YHWH's name and salvation, giving thanks (ידה; Ps 100:4) to him, and the lifting up (נשא; Ps 134:2) of hands in the temple. These are the semantic fields of ברך in a context when the subject of ברך is a human being. Now, let us examine it in Ps 145:1, 2, 10, and 21. Notice the parallelism and the chiasm in them.

---

109. Brown et al., *The Brown-Driver-Briggs*, 138.

110. The occurrences of ברך in the Psalter are: Pss 5:13; 10:3; 16:7; 18:47; 26:12; 28:6, 9; 29:11; 31:22; 34:2; 37:22; 41:14; 45:3; 49:19; 62:5; 63:5; 65:11; 66:8, 20; 67:2, 7, 8; 68:20, 27, 36; 72:15, 17, 18, 19; 89:53; 95:6; 96:2; 100:4; 103:1, 2, 21, 22; 104:1, 35; 106:48; 107:38; 109:24, 28; 112:2; 113:2; 115:12, 13, 15, 18; 118:26; 119:12; 124:6; 128:4, 5; 129:8; 132:15; 134:1, 2, 3; 135:19, 20, 21; 144:1; 145:1, 2, 10, 21; and 147:13.

verse 1	וַאֲרוֹמְמָךְ וֵלוֹהַי הַמֶּלֶךְ וַאֲבָרְכָה שִׁמְךָ לְעוֹלָם וָעֶד	ABA'B'[C]
verse 2	בְּכָל־יוֹם אֲבָרְכֶךָּ וַאֲהַלְלָה שִׁמְךָ לְעוֹלָם וָעֶד	ABB'[C]A'
verse 10	יוֹדוּךָ יְהוָה כָּל־מַעֲשֶׂיךָ וַחֲסִידֶיךָ יְבָרְכוּכָה	ABCC'[B]A'
verse 21	תְּהִלַּת יְהוָה יְדַבֶּר־פִּי וִיבָרֵךְ כָּל־בָּשָׂר שֵׁם קָדְשׁוֹ לְעוֹלָם וָעֶד	ABCB'C'A'[D]

In verse 1, ואברכה is used in parallel to ארוממך ("I will extol you") but in verse 2, אברכך ("I will bless you") is chiastically parallel to אהללה ("I will praise you"). Likewise, the phrase יברכוכה ("they will bless you") in verse 10 is also chiastically parallel to יודוך ("they will give thanks to you"), while in verse 21, the phrase ויברך כל־בשר (and all flesh will bless you) is chiastically parallel to ידבר־פי ("my mouth will proclaim"). The poet employs הלל, רום and ידה in parallel to ברך.[111] Other verbs such as יגידו ("they will declare") in verse 4, ידברו ("they will tell") and אשיחה ("I will meditate") in verse 5, יאמרו ("they will speak") and אספרנה ("I will recount") in verse 6, יביעו ("they will pour out") and ירננו ("they will sing joyfully") in verse 7, and יאמרו ("they will speak") and ידברו ("they will tell") in verse 11 are also parallel to ברך. In other words, the semantic domain of ברך in this psalm includes אמר ("speak"), הלל ("praise"), ידה ("give thanks"), נבע ("speak out loud"), נגד ("declare"), ספר ("recount"), רום ("extol"), רנן ("shout joyfully"), and שיח ("meditate"). We noticed earlier in Pss 34:2 and 66:8 that תהלה is also parallel to ברך. Thus, the lexeme ברך canot be translated merely as "to kneel" or "to bless." It also connotes extol, praise, declare, speak, tell, recount, meditate, shout joyfully, and give thanks. This broad semantic domain of ברך redefines the semantic domain of the title of the psalm as תהלה ("praise") as well. Probably, the title תהלה not only connotes the phenomena of "praise," but also a public declaration and persuasion with the intention that others may also "praise" YHWH.

The extra-linguistic context of the psalm implies a historical setting in which the psalmist saw the necessity of public proclamation of the message of the psalm—the Kingship of YHWH. The post-exilic community, surrounded by nations that had powerful kings, needed to be informed out loud that they have a King, greater than king David, who is more reliable and trustworthy. The hermeneutical underpinning of this proclamation

---

111. Liebreich, "Psalms 34 and 145," 188.

was primarily to give others their true spiritual identity in YHWH in a time of crisis.

The Language of Universalism and Particularism

Psalm 145 has both the language of universalism and particularism. On the one hand, it presents YHWH's reign as open ended and cosmic in nature, which includes all humanity. On the other hand, it mentions a people group with specific characteristics: the godly ones (חסיד; v. 10), the one who calls YHWH in truth (יקראו באמת; v. 18), the one who fears YHWH (יראיו; v. 19), and the one who loves (אהביו; v. 20). Buttenwieser claimed that Psalm 145 is about "the universal kingdom of God," marked by "broad universalism" only. There is no particularism in the psalm.[112] Briggs noted, "The universalism of the psalm is not the universalism of Isaiah 2, but the larger universalism of the Greek period."[113] This is probably because the particularism in the psalm is no longer defined on the basis of ethnicity or patriarchal descent, but by criteria through which all humanity can qualify. Let us examine this in the following paragraphs.

The unique language of universalism and particularism of the psalm is evident in its use of the lexeme כל. The lexeme כל appears 19 times (including the *nun* line) in the psalm, underscoring its significance. It occurs six times with a preposition ב (vv. 2, 13b, 13c, 13d, 17a, and 17b) in construct form, two times with the definite article ה and a preposition ל (vv. 9a and 18b) in absolute form, one time with the preposition על (v. 9b) in construct form, five times by itself in construct form (vv. 10, 13a, 20a, 20b, and 21), four times with a preposition ל (vv. 10, 13a, 20a, 20b, and 21) in construct form, and one time by itself (v. 15) in absolute form. Each of these references needs to be examined in their syntagmatic and paradigmatic context in order to know the semantic range of the lexeme כל in this psalm, as well as understand what do they semantically represent in each of these sentences.

In general, the lexical meaning of כל varies between *all, each, every, whole,* and *any*.[114] The semantic range of the lexeme כל in Psalm 145 is

---

112. Buttenwieser, *The Psalms*, 848.

113. Briggs et al., *A Critical and Exegetical Commentary on the Book of Psalms*, 526.

114. Brown et al., *The Brown-Driver-Briggs*, 483.

every, *all*, and *wholly*. Thirteen times it is used as an adjective (vv. 2, 10, 15, 13a, 13b, 13c, 13d, 16b, 17a, 17b, 20a, 20b, and 21) and six times as an object (vv. 9a, 9b, 14a, 14b, 18a, and 18b). The use of כל both as an adjective and as an object underscores the universal affectivity of the attributes of YHWH and his cosmic reign so that YHWH may receive universal praise.[115] First, the use of כל defines the attributes of YHWH [He is "faithful in *all* his promises" (v. 13c); "faithful in *all* his works" (v. 13d); "righteous in *all* his ways" (v. 17a), and "loving toward *all* he has made" (v. 17b)] to establish the impartial and universal availability of his goodness. Second, the use of כל qualifies YHWH's Kingdom ["your kingdom is an *everlasting* kingdom" (v. 13a) and "your dominion through *all* generation" (v. 13b)]. It emphasizes the continuity of YHWH's Kingdom in human history. Third, the use of כל underscores the universality of the recipients of his goodness ["the Lord is good to *all*" (v. 9a); "his compassion is upon *all*" (v. 9b); "the Lord upholds *all* those who fall" (v. 14a); "he lifts up *all*" (v. 14b); "*all* eyes wait upon you" (v. 15); "he satisfies the desires of *every one*" (v. 16b); "he is near to *all* (v. 18a)"; "to *all* who call him in truth" (v. 18b); and "the Lord watches over *all*" (v. 20)]. It claims the cosmic domain of YHWH's rule over all humanity. Fourth, the use of כל asserts the universal response ["*all* you have made will praise you" (v. 10); and "*all*-mankind will praise his Holy name" (v. 21)].

Since YHWH is righteous in *all* his ways, faithful in *all* his works, faithful in *all* his promises, and his dominion and the Kingdom is everlasting, there is hope for all. Even when the kings of the earth have failed, YHWH as the King will not fail. In his Kingdom, *all* are included. Therefore, YHWH deserves universal praise.

The use of כל, as a qualifier of the subject, stresses the cosmic nature of praise and expectations. In verses 10a ("*all* your creature will praise you") and 15 ("*all* eyes look up to you in hope"), the stress is on the involvement of *all* to praise YHWH or hope in YHWH for their nourishment. In the former case, verse 10b explicates *all creatures* as YHWH's *beloved/saints*, but in the latter, *all* may imply those who are *fallen* and *bowed down* (see in v.

---

115. According to Oesterley, the universalistic outlook was prominent among the Jews in post-exilic period, as it is evidenced in the book of Jonah. Oesterley, *The Psalms: Translated with Text-Critical and Exegetical Notes*, 572,

14). Finally, the psalmist, with the extensive use of the lexeme כל, undermines ethnic particularity. There is no language of covenant-based favor.
The emphasis, obviously, is on the favor available to "all his creatures" (vv.
9, 10, and 17), in contrast to his final judgment against "all the wicked"
(v. 20). As a result, at the end, the psalmist anticipates "all flesh" will praise
YHWH (v. 21).

As an object in a sentence, the lexeme כל highlights the universal domain of YHWH in which the particular people groups are defined with
criteria that are universally open-ended. The particular people groups can
be classified into three categories: (1) the common people ["the Lord is
good to *all*" (v. 9a), and "his mercies upon *all* his creatures" (v. 9b), "he
satisfies the desires of *all* living being" (v. 16b)]; (2) the needy people ["The
Lord sustains *all* those who fall" (v. 14a); "and he raises up *all* those who are
bowed down" (v. 14b)]; and (3) the virtuous people ["The Lord is near to
all who call upon him" (18a); "to *all* who call upon Him in truth" (v. 18b);
"The Lord protects *all* those who love him" (v. 20a)]. The first group is non-
specific and universal in nature. However, the second and the third groups
indicate certain specificity for the group through the qualifying clauses. In
the second group, we notice two types: "all those who fall" (הנפלים) and "all
who are bowed down" (הכפופים). The third group is presented as "the godly
ones who bless YHWH" (חסיד; v. 10), "the ones who call YHWH in truth"
(יקראו באמת; v. 18), "the one who fears YHWH" (יראיו; v. 19), and "the
ones who love Him" (אהביו; v. 20). It is noteworthy that these groups are
identified neither by their ethnic roots nor by their biological lineage. The
mention of an explicit covenant relationship is strikingly absent. Perhaps
the psalmist intends to exclude the hypocrites by emphasizing fear and
love, because "fear preserves love from degenerating into presumptuous fa-
miliarity; love prevents fear from beginning a servile and cringing dread."[116]
The new criteria call attention to a genuine individual relationship with
YHWH, which is available to all—Jews and Gentiles. This implies that the
particularism in this psalm is to be focused on moral and spiritual character, rather than covenant or ethnic identity—such an emphasis on moral
and spiritual character can be defined as *particularism of righteousness*.

---

116. Kirkpatrick, ed., *The Book of Psalms*, 817.

The language of particularism is placed in a context of the language of universalism in the psalm, suggesting a shift in the theological emphasis of the time. The purpose of the message in the psalm is not political but spiritual. The time is not for a nationalistic movement that might provoke a spirit of protest among the pious against the oppressing nations, but one that would provide comfort and hope in the existing circumstances. The comfort and hope rest in Israel's acknowledgment of YHWH as universal God and King whose reign is cosmic, supervening over all—YHWH is above all kings. He is the God of the Persians, Greeks, Romans, and Jews. Therefore, all should call on him in truth, all should fear him, and all should love him.

The Language of Hope

The language of Psalm 145 is forward looking—a language of hope. Although the psalm does have the lexeme for hope, the theme of hope is implicit in the language of the Kingdom of God, which is permanent, uninterrupted, and perpetual.[117] In one sense it is already actualized, in another sense, it is not yet there. Another generation is yet to come to continue the praise. Notice the phrase כל־עלמים (ever lasting) and ודור בכל־דור (through all generations) in verse 13 that underscore the last two nuances. The former connects verse 13 to verses 1, 2, and 21 and the latter connects to verse 4 (דור לדור).

Ps 145:1, 2, and 21 emphasizes the presence of the Kingdom as well as the perpetuity of its praise, while Ps 145:4 highlights the continuity of praise through generations. Leupold rightly states, "God's incomparable greatness in its broadest aspects is thought of as being the theme that shall occupy generations to come."[118] Estimating the value of the psalm, the Talmud claims, "Everyone who repeats the *Tehillah* of David thrice a day may be sure that he is a child of the world to come" (*Berakhot*, 4b).[119] There is a duality of time in the psalm. At one point, the psalmist is talking about the present reality of the Kingdom of God; at another, he anticipates its

---

117. John I. Durham, *Esther-Psalms* (ed. Clifton J. Allen; The Broadman Bible Commentary; 12 vols.; Nashville: Broadman, 1969), 455.

118. Leupold, *Exposition of the Psalms*, 976.

119. James Luther Mays, *Psalms* (Louisville: Westminster John Knox, 1994), 437.

perpetuity (לעולם ועד, דור ודור) and its fuller accomplishment in the future. We notice this in verse 13,

מלכותך מלכות כל־עלמים וממשלתך בכל־דור ודור

YHWH's Kingdom is not only a present reality, but also a continuing reality, which will pass through all generations to come.[120] Notice in the following verses:

דור לדור ישבח מעשיך וגבורתיך יגידו	verse 4
עיני־כל אליך ישברו ואתה נותן־להם את־אכלם בעתו:	verse 15
שומר יהוה את־כל־אהביו ואת כל־הרשעים ישמיד:	verse 20
ויברך כל־בשר שם קדשו לעולם ועד	verse 21

In verse 4, the phrase דור לדור implies that the third person imperfect verbs (ישבח and יגידו) are in non-perfective aspect.[121] In verse 15, the subject of the imperfect verb is ישברו ("they will hope"), which is plural—*the eyes of all will hope*. Likewise, in verse 20 the object of the imperfect verb ישמיד (he will destroy) is כל־הרשעים (all the wicked), which is generic. The wicked are present in every generation. They are destroyed and yet they are not yet fully destroyed, but YHWH, the King and the judge, will destroy them for sure. The future expectation in the language suggests for a language of hope—hope of vindication, protection and total deliverance. The righteous, the beloved of YHWH, those who fear and love YHWH, and those who call on YHWH in truth are provided "hope" through this expectation.

Finally, the language of hope in the psalm is also obvious in verse 21. The anticipation that "all flesh (כל־בשר) will bless YHWH" is an inclusive language. The psalmist anticipates "all-flesh" will join him. The individual act of praise will develop into community praise, and then into the praise

---

120. Commenting on verse 13, Alexander writes, "The meaning of the last clause is, they dominion still exists and shall exist in every successive generation." Notice also the aspect of the first person imperfect verbs in verses 1-2 (אברכך, אברכה, ארוממך, and אהללה), which are both non-perfective present and future. While the aspect of the third person imperfect verbs of verses 10 and 21 (ויברך and יברכוכה) are implied in the discourse as the non-perfective future—"it is so and will be so." Alexander, *The Psalms*, 293.

121. Ibid.

of all humanity.[122] Delitzsch writes, "The realization of this wish is the final goal of history."[123]

The continuity from the present to the future is also reflected in the literary features of the psalm. Notice the imperfect verbs that follow the hymnic bicolons (vv. 3, 8, 9, 13, and 17) and the cluster of participles (נאמן, סומך, זוקף, פותח, משביע, קרוב, and שומר) in the second half of the psalm. While the hymnic sentences describe the attributes of YHWH, the participles represent the habitual actions of YHWH.[124] Both habitual actions and the actions of YHWH represented by imperfect verbs are purposefully placed after the attributes of YHWH to signify that what YHWH "does" and "will do" emanates from who "YHWH is." The aspect of the third person imperfect verbs representing YHWH's actions in the discourse implies both non-perfective present and future actions—YHWH "is" and "will." Delitzsch rightly states, "God's Kingdom is a kingdom of all æons, and His dominion is manifested without exception and continually in all periods or generations."[125]

Therefore, the language of Psalm 145 is forward looking—a language of hopeful anticipation not only for the post-exilic community but also for those who will belong to the community of faith in the following generations until its full realization. This is why this language of hope, which carries the theme of the Kingdom of God as present reality as well as a future reality, finds continuity within the community of the New Testament.

Conclusion

Our discussions in this chapter lead us to make following seven conclusions. First, Psalm 145, as opposed to its traditional classification as a

---

122. According to Berlin, the general change and fluctuation from the first person verb to the third person is not random "but one that emphasizes the major purpose of the psalm: through the psalmist's praise everyone will come to praise God." Berlin, "The Rhetoric of Psalm 145," 21.

123. Delitzsch, *Biblical Commentary on the Psalms*, 392.

124. Alexander, *The Psalms*, 296.

125. Delitzsch, *Biblical Commentary on the Psalms*, 391.

hymn, combines more than one literary genre to communicate the message. Second, rhetorical critical analysis is more sensitive to the literary features and linguistics of the psalm than form-critical and thematic analysis. The traditional literary division is too restrictive with its form-critical criteria, while a thematic literary division is arbitrary. Since the psalm is acrostic and contains complex literary phenomena, rhetorical analysis enables the interpreter to notice certain literary features such as *key words*, *concentric structure*, *literary symmetry*, *chiasm*, *inclusion*, *linear progression of themes*, *acrostics* and *reverse root play*. These literary features unfurl the beautiful poetic artistries, which contains the message and the intent of the psalmist.

Third, the literary structure of Psalm 145 supports a linear development ("progression") of themes. It is evident in the explication and in the heightening of the subject matter in the psalm. For example, the theme of blessing develops by heightening the number of the participants—from individual blessing to community blessing, and then to universal blessing.

Fourth, the illocutionary intent of the psalm is to generate praise (תהלה) for YHWH perpetually (לעולם ועד) in all generations (בכל־דור ודור) from all people (כל־בשר). It is the only psalm, which has *inclusion* formed by the word "praise" (תהלת / תהלה). David is presented in the psalm as a "model" for the "godly ones" (חסיד) to praise YHWH and to influence others to join him in "praise."

Fifth, the unique address to God as "the King" by king David (תהלה לדוד) in the psalm is editorially intended to present YHWH as the supreme King. The psalm addresses the socio-historical context of Israel, in which human kings have failed to meet the ideal expectations. The Kingship of YHWH emanates from the very attributes of YHWH, whom Israel already knew through their history. YHWH is unique, superior to all, and his reign is perpetual in all generations. His "rule" is consistent with his "attributes."

Sixth, the central message of the psalm is the everlasting "Kingdom of God." In this Kingdom, YHWH's reign is cosmic and universal. It includes all humanity whom he created, yet YHWH's care for the godly ones (חסיד; v. 10), the one who calls YHWH in truth (יקראו באמת; v. 18), the one who fears YHWH (יראיו; v. 19), and the one who loves him (אהביו; v. 20) is assured in particular. The purpose of the message in the psalm is not political but spiritual. The hope of Israel rests in the acknowledgment of YHWH's everlasting universal Kingdom. YHWH is the present reigning King, whose dominion is cosmic and universal. He is the King of the Persians, Greeks, Romans, and Jews. There is no ethnic restriction. Therefore, all can call on him in truth, all can fear him, and all can love him.

Seventh, the language of Psalm 145 is a language of hope. The Kingdom of God is a present reality for the psalmist, yet it is not fully realized. The message of the "already and not yet" must be made known to all, giving hope to all, from generation to generation. The psalmist anticipates that the wicked will be destroyed and all humanity will receive salvation from YHWH. Finally, the climax will be reached when "all-flesh" (כל־בשׂר) joins him in "praise."

CHAPTER 4

The Last Davidic Psalm and the Final Hallel Psalms

Having analyzed the discourse meaning of the last Davidic psalm (Psalm 145) in the previous chapter, we will now proceed to investigate its placement in Book V. How does it connect with the final *hallel* psalms (Psalms 146-50)? How does the discourse meaning of Psalm 145 pave the way for the reading of the doxological psalms? How does it bond lexically, syntactically, thematically, and pragmatically with each of the final *hallel* psalms? Is there any theological motive for its placement before the final *hallel* psalms? To answer these questions we will first investigate the prevailing claims concerning the editorial purpose of Psalm 145 in Book V. Then, we will analyze the lexical and thematic relationship of Psalm 145 to the final *hallel* psalms to investigate probable editorial purpose(s) for the placement of the last Davidic psalm.

The Editorial Purpose

Wilson makes two significant claims concerning the purposeful placement of Psalm 145 in the Psalter. First, he claims that Psalm 145, along with Psalms 1, 73, 90, and 107, forms a "Final Wisdom Frame," which subsumes the "Royal Covenant Frame" (Psalms 2, 72, 89 and 144) in the Psalter.[1] According to him, the redactor(s) placed the "Final Wisdom

---

1. Gerald Henry Wilson, "Shaping the Psalter: A Consideration of Editorial Linkage in

Frame" around the "Royal Covenant Frame" to provide a sapiential reading to the final shape of the Psalter. Thus, the placement of Psalm 145 at
the end of the Psalter is editorially designed. Second, he claims that Psalm
145 is "the climax of the fifth Book of the Psalter."[2] In so being, Psalm 145
concludes the body of the Psalter proper; it "precipitates" the concluding
hallel psalms (Psalms 146-50), and it brings forth some of the major themes
of the Psalter.[3]

Traditionally, Psalm 145 has not been considered as the psalm that
forms the "Final Wisdom Frame" in the Psalter, nor it has not been seen as
the "climax" of the fifth book of the Psalter. Wilson's claims are primarily
based on observations made at the level of macro-structure of the Psalter.
His claims are deficient of a lexical, syntactical, semantic, thematic, and
pragmatic analysis. He did not consider the discourse meaning of Psalm
145 and its adjacent psalms (Psalms 138-44 and 146-50). In light of these
deficiencies, we will examine Wilson's two claims at the micro-level.

The Final Wisdom Frame

Wilson's claim concerning the placement of Psalm 145 in the "Final
Wisdom Frame" of the Psalter borders on being simplistic and overreach-
ing. As stated earlier, Wilson regards Psalm 145 along with Psalms 1, 73, 90
and 107 as constituting the "Final Wisdom Frame."[4] This frame subsumes
the "Royal Covenant Frame" (Psalms 2, 72, 89 and 144) to provide a sapiential perspective for understanding the final shape of the Psalter.[5]

---

the Book of Psalms," in *The Shape and Shaping of the Psalter* (ed. J. Clinton McCann;
JSOTSup 159, Sheffield: JSOT Press, 1993), 81.

2. Gerald Henry Wilson, *The Editing of the Hebrew Psalter* (Chico: Scholars Press, 1985),
225. See also Wilson, "Shaping the Psalter," 78-79; Gerald Henry Wilson, "King, Messiah,
and the Reign of God: Revisiting the Royal Psalms and the Shape of the Psalter," in *The
Book of Psalms: Composition and Reception* (ed. Peter W. Flint et al.; Leiden: Boston,
2005), 392.

3. Wilson, "King, Messiah," 392.

4. Wilson, "Shaping the Psalter," 80-81.

5. Ibid., 81.

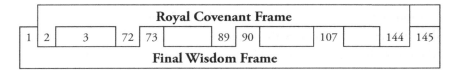

For him, the final shape of the Psalter is editorially bound by two distinct segments (Psalms 2-89 and 90-145). These segments represent two different periods of redaction. In the first segment of the Psalter, three royal psalms (Psalms 2, 72, and 89) have intentionally been placed at the seams in order to present "the Psalter as an exilic response to the loss of Davidic monarchy."[6] Psalm 2 initiates the royal Davidic covenant and advocates the nations to submit to the anointed one in Zion (Ps 2:12). Psalm 72, the Solomonic psalm, anticipates the continuation of the Davidic lineage through Solomon and the blessing of "all nations" through him (Ps 72:17). However, Psalm 89, at the end of the first segment (Psalms 2-89), presents an accusation against YHWH for failing to keep up his covenant promise and rejecting the Davidic kings and the kingdom (Ps 89:39-40). Thus, the "Royal Covenant Frame" of the first segment (Psalms 2-89) ends with a crisis and hopelessness, depicting the exilic state of despair. To this gloomy segment, according to Wilson, the sages editorially added the second segment (Psalms 90-150) to remind the readers the "foundational pre-monarchial faith of Israel" (Psalms 90, 105-106),[7] and to redirect them to trust YHWH, rather than human princes (Psalms 145-146).[8] In other words, the final redaction of the second segment (Psalms 90-150) is intended to shift the focus of the hope of Israel from the earthly Davidic king to the Kingship of YHWH.[9] In so doing, the placement of Psalm 145 and Psalm 1 in the final frame provides the "last word" on the wisdom perspective.[10]

---

6. Wilson, "King, Messiah," 391.

7. Richard J. Clifford does not see Psalm 90 in the same way as Wilson sees it. He explores the theology of the psalm in more detail. He comments, "Reflecting on God's history with this people [Israel], it [Psalm 90] insists that God live up to his promise made to their ancestors and bless these creatures of a moment with prosperity. . . . The poem can thus serve for God's community in every period of crisis and loss." Richard J. Clifford, "Psalm 90: Wisdom Meditation or Communal Lament?" in *The Book of Psalms: Composition and Reception* (ed. Peter W. Flint et al.; VTSup 99, Leiden: Boston, 2005), 205.

8. Wilson, "King, Messiah," 392-93.

9. Ibid., 392.

10. Wilson, "Shaping the Psalter," 81.

Additionally, Psalm 145, along with Psalm 107, forms an additional "wisdom frame" to emphasizes this sapiential reading of the Psalter.[11] While Wilson's claim is insightful, it fails to pay attention to the complexity of the composition of the Psalter.

In the so-called "Final Wisdom Frame," Psalms 1 and 145 have lexical and thematic correspondences; however, the wisdom language of the two psalms is distinct. Although the language of the "two ways" (the righteous and the wicked) in Psalm 1 is reiterated in Ps 145:19-20, it does not present similar image to make an *inclusion* or "frame." Notice the difference in the wisdom language of the two texts in reference.

Ps 1: 6   כי־יודע יהוה דרך צדיקים ודרך רשעים תאבד

For the Lord knows the way of the righteous,
but the way of the wicked will perish.

Ps 145:19-20   רצון־יראיו יעשׂה ואת־שׁועתם ישׁמע ויושׁיעם
שׁומר יהוה את־כל־אהביו ואת כל־הרשׁעים ישׁמיד

He will fulfill the desire of those who fear him,
He will also hear their cry and will save them
The Lord guards all those who love him,
but all the wicked, he will destroy

Apparently, Psalm 145 concludes the Psalter on a similar note as it begins in Psalm 1. There is some parallelism between the two ways of life and death, which might seemingly suggest the possibility of a "frame."[12] But this triggers questions. Does the part (Wilson only compares Ps 145:19-20 to Ps 1:6) represent the whole? Is the language of Psalm 145 similar to Psalm 1? Does the genre classification of the two psalms support a "The Final Wisdom Frame," which envelopes the other psalms? Our discourse analysis of the two psalms (Psalms 1 and 145) suggests otherwise. Although Psalm 145 revisits the theme of Ps 1:6, it would be inaccurate to suggest that they have a similar perspective and nuance on the language of wisdom.

---

11. Ibid., 79
12. Ibid., 80.

The language of the two ways of the righteous and wicked in two psalms differs. In Psalm 1, the righteous and wicked are recognized by their response to the "law of the Lord" (v. 2), their prospects (vv. 3-5), and the favor of YHWH upon them (v. 6). However, the language of Psalm 145 underscores the cosmic domain of YHWH, in which his goodness and greatness affects all humanity. Finally the wicked will be destroyed. However, the actual emphasis is on the cosmic domain of YHWH and his universal praise. Psalm 145, instead of duplicating the theme of the "two ways," develops it by placing the language of "two ways" in a new context—the context of the Kingdom of God. Hence, the relationship between the two psalms is of a "progression" rather than *inclusion* like "frame." For example, Psalm 1 also connects lexically with other psalms in Book I, as it links with Psalm 145. Notice the thematic pattern formed by the "blessing" formula in Book I.

אשרי־האיש אשר ׀ לא הלך	Ps 1:1
אשרי כל־חוסי בו	Ps 2:12
אשרי נשוי־פשע	Ps 32:1
אשרי אדם לא יחשב יהוה לו עון	Ps 32:2
אשרי הגוי אשר־יהוה אלהיו העם ׀	Ps 33:12
אשרי הגבר יחסה־בו	Ps 34:9
אשרי הגבר אשר־שם יהוה מבטחו	Ps 40:5
אשרי משכיל אל־דל	Ps 41:1

By using the "blessing" formula, Book I emphasizes the blessedness of a person in segregation from the wicked, in obedience to Torah, in taking refuge in YHWH, in forgiveness of sins, in trusting YHWH, and in being considerate toward the weak. Thus, Psalm 1 also has connections with psalms within Book I.

Wilson's second claim that Psalm 145 forms an additional wisdom frame with Psalm 107 also borders on overstatement. Although Wilson rightly observes that both psalms end with an explicit wisdom admonition (Ps 107:42-43 and Ps 145:20), he fails to notice their unique discourse meaning. To suggest a wisdom frame for the fifth book based on these two references is close to being simplistic. Notice the following two texts.

Ps 107:42-43   יראו ישרים וישמחו וכל־עולה קפצה פיה
מי־חכם וישמר־אלה וֹיתבוננו חסדי יהוה

The upright see it and they are glad;
and every wrongdoer covers his mouth
Who is wise, let him heed these things
and consider the steadfast love of the Lord.

Ps 145:19-20   רצון־יראיו יעשה ואת־שועתם ישמע ויושיעם
שומר יהוה את־כל־אהביו ואת כל־הרשעים ישמיד

He will fulfill the desire of those who fear him,
He will also hear their cry and will save them
The Lord guards all those who love him,
but all the wicked, he will destroy.

There are three observations that go against Wilson's claim. First, the
wisdom perspective in each psalm is different. Psalm 107 summons all wise
people (notice the rhetorical question מי, which may imply whoever) to
consider the "steadfast love" of the Lord. But the wisdom language in Ps
145:19-20 declares the final destruction of the wicked. After explicating
the categories of the beneficiaries of YHWH's help—*He* [YHWH] *fulfills
the desires of those who fear him, hears their cry, and saves them, and he guards
those who love him*—the judgment on the wicked is delivered. Thus, the
wisdom admonition in Psalms 145 differs from Psalm 107.

Second, Psalms 107 and 145 are not primarily wisdom psalms. Psalm
107 has two subgenres: an imperatival thanksgiving hymn (vv. 1-32) and
a general hymn that includes a wisdom element (vv. 33-43).[13] Psalm 145
is commonly regarded as a "praise hymn," but it is also a combination of
more than one genre.

Third, the imposition of a straightjacket frame undermines the diversity
of genre and different thematic patterns in the Psalter. For example, a study
on the theme of YHWH's consistent love ["his love endures forever," (־לעו י
לם חסדוכ) in Pss 100:4b-5; 106:1; 107:1; 117:2; 118:1-4, 29; and 136:1-2,
4-26] suggests a thematic pattern that runs outside Wilson's wisdom frame
of Psalms 107-145.

---

13. Leslie C. Allen, *Psalms 101-50* (WBC 21; Nashville: Nelson, 2002), 84.

Book IV

הודו־לו ברכו שמו	Ps 100:4b-5
כי־טוב יהוה לעולם חסדו ועד־דר ודר אמונתו	
הודו ליהוה קראו בשמו	Ps 105:1
הללויה | הודו ליהוה כי־טוב כי לעולם חסדו	Ps 106:1

Book V

הדו ליהוה כי־טוב כי לעולם חסדו	Ps 107:1
אודך בעמים | יהוה ואזמרך בל־אמים	Ps 108:4
הדו ליהוה כי־טוב כי לעולם חסדו	Ps 118:1
הדו ליהוה כי־טוב כי לעולם חסדו	Ps 118:29
הדו ליהוה כי־טוב כי לעולם חסדו	Ps 136:1
הדו לאלהי האלהים כי־טוב כי לעולם חסדו	Ps 136:2
הדו לאדני האדנים כי־טוב כי לעולם חסדו	Ps 136:3
הדו לאל השמים כי־טוב כי לעולם חסדו	Ps 136:26

An idea of a "frame" may undermine certain thematic patterns in the psalms, which may reveal significant information. We suggest that the placement of psalms at the seams with certain literary features and language (such as the wisdom content in Psalm 107 and 145) is editorially designed to effect transitions and thematic patterning, rather than forming an over-arching "frame" over the whole Psalter.

This is not to deny the prospect of the "Final Wisdom Frame" in the final shape of the Psalter. Wilson's claim concerning the movement from "Royal Covenantal" hopes to the "last word" of wisdom in the final shape of the Psalter is informative and insightful, but it requires an extensive lexical, syntactic, semantic, thematic, and pragmatic analysis of every royal and wisdom psalms in the Psalter, which is beyond the contour of this dissertation.

The Climax of Book V

According to Wilson, Psalm 145 is the "climax" of the fifth book in the Psalter because it performs three functions: it concludes the body of the Psalter proper; it brings forth some of the major themes of the Psalter;

and it "precipitates" the onset of the final *hallel* psalms (Psalms 146-50).[14] To suggest that Psalm 145 is the "climax" of the fifth book of the Psalter is an overstatement. The word "climax" may mean *peak, culmination,* or *pinnacle.* Is Psalm 145 the peak, the culmination, the pinnacle of the fifth book? Wilson makes statement without addressing these questions. One of the ways Wilson arrives at this conclusion is that he notices a tripartite division in the fifth book, which places Psalm 145 at the end of the fifth book.

The Tripartite Divisions

According to Wilson, the thematic patterns marked by the *hôdû* and *hallel* psalms in Book V suggest that it must end with Psalm 145 and not Psalm 150.[15] Wilson divides Book V into three major sections, ending the final section with Psalm 145. Each of these sections opens with a *hôdû* and closes with a *hallel* psalm. Zenger summarizes Wilson's argument into the following table.[16]

Section 1: 107-117			Section 2: 118-135				Section 3: 136-45	
107	108-10	111-17	118	119	120-34	135	136-7	138-45
hôdû	*David*	*hallel*	*hôdû*	*torah*	*Ascent*	*hallel*	*hôdû*	*David*

Wilson does not include the final *hallel* psalms (Psalms 146-50) in the table above because they are the doxology of the whole Psalter. He claims that the Section 3 concludes with Psalm 145, but he does not give convincing reasons.[17]

The tripartite division of Book V, based on the *hôdû* and *hallel* psalms, has three problems. First, the absence of the final *hallel* psalms in Section 3 creates asymmetry. Second, Psalm 137 does not fit into the category of the *hôdû* psalms. Third, Section 1 has eight *hallel* psalms (Psalms 111-17), but Section 2 has only one (Psalm 135). The long *torah* psalm (Psalm 119) and

---

14. Wilson, *The Editing*, 225-26; Wilson, "King, Messiah," 292.

15. Wilson, *The Editing*, 189-90.

16. See also Erich Zenger, "The Composition and Theology of the Fifth Book of Psalms, Psalms 107-145," *JSOT* 80 (1998): 83.

17. Wilson, *The Editing*, 189.

a big collection of the Ascent psalms (Psalms 120-34) in Section 2 raises more questions concerning this division.

Furthermore, other psalms scholars include the final *hallel* psalms in Section 3. Klaus Koch includes the final *hallel* psalms to show a symmetry in the tripartite division of Book V.[18] He looks at the tripartite divisions of Book V from different perspectives. For him, since the first two sections end with the *hallel* psalms, the third part must also end with the *hallel* psalms. He divides Book V into the following sections.

Part I	107-10: Psalms of David (107 as introductory psalm)
	111-118: Hallelujah- psalms
Part II	120-34: *hamma 'a lôt*- songs
	135-36: Halleluyah- psalms
Part III	138-45: Psalms of David
	146-50: Hallelujah- psalms

Koch excludes Psalms 119 and 137 as "post-compositional additions." He even goes on to suggest that the songs of ascents diachronically disrupt the close connection between Psalms 118 and 135, therefore, it is plausible that the original form of Book V did not contain them. He reads Psalms 107-18 and 135-50 as a coherent composition that might have been fixed prior to the writing of Chronicles.

Likewise, Reinhard Gregor Kratz also includes the *hallel* psalms (Psalms 146-50) as part of the third section (Psalms 136-50).[19] Unlike Wilson, who is concerned with the final shape of the Psalter, Kratz is primarily concerned with the theological concept of Book V. According to him, the theological idea of Book V was originally influenced by the historical work of the Chronicler. The redactors depoliticized its conception and transformed it for a universal and individual application. This redactional transformation of Book V allows the Psalter to culminate in a crescendo of *hallel* psalms,

---

18. Klaus Koch, "Der Psalter und seine Redaktionsgeschichte," in *Neue Wege der Psalmenforschung* (ed. K. Seybold and E. Zenger; Freiburg: Herders, 1995), 18. See also Zenger, "The Composition and Theology," 84.

19. Reinhard Gregor Kratz, "Die Tora Davids: Psalm 1 und die doxologische Funfteilung des Psalters," *ZTK* 93 (1996): 23-28.

first through individual praise in Ps 145:1-2 and then in universal praise in Ps 145:21. The praise is continued by an individual in Psalm 146, a community in Psalm 147, and finally by all creation in heaven and on earth in Psalms 148 and 150.[20]

Koch and Kratz's positions are insightful, but problematic because their theological interpretations of the fifth book and the final *hallel* psalms in relation to the historical works of the Chronicler are hypothetical.[21] It is also deficient of sufficient text-linguistic data to support their arguments for the place of Psalm 145 in the tripartite division of the fifth book.

The Gathering of the Major Themes

Wilson's assertion that Psalm 145 is the climax of the Psalter because it brings forth some the major themes of the Psalter borders on being simplistic.[22] Wilson mentions four major themes: (1)"the two ways" of the righteous and wicked (Ps 145:20; cf. Pss 1:6; 107:42); (2) the central theme of the fourth book—the Kingship of YHWH (Ps 145:1, 11-13; cf. Pss 93:1-3; 99:1-5; 102:12); (3) the "mighty acts" of YHWH (Ps 145:4-7; cf. Pss 92:5-9, 96:3-4); and (4) the "steadfast love" of YHWH (Ps 145:8-9, 13-20; cf. Pss 103:6-13; 107:4-9, 12).[23] In so doing, it concludes the body of the Psalter proper. Although Wilson's claim above is partly true, his conclusion is close to being simplistic and inadequate in textual data. In the following paragraphs, we will analyze each of the themes to provide text-linguistic data and suggest an improved view.

---

20. Ibid., 26.

21. Zenger, "The Composition and Theology," 88.

22. Wilson, "King, Messiah," 392.

23. Wilson, *The Editing*, 225-26. See also Wilson, "King, Messiah," 392-93.

The Two Ways of the Righteous and Wicked

As discussed earlier, the language of the "two ways" of the righteous and wicked in Pss 1:6 and 107:42 differs. Their different contexts provide a different nuance in the language of the "two ways." In Psalm 1, the language of the "two ways" of the righteous and wicked is more explicit. They are defined based on their response to the "law of the Lord" (v. 2), their prospects (vv. 3-5), and the favor of YHWH upon them (v. 6). However, the language in Ps 107:42 compares the response of the upright (יָשָׁר) and the wicked (עַוְלָה) after they see YHWH's mighty work. In fact, Psalm 107 does not use the Hebrew lexeme for "righteous" (צַדִּיק) and "wicked" (רָשָׁע).

Furthermore, in Psalm 145 the wicked are placed in contrast to those who call on him in truth (אֲשֶׁר יִקְרָאֻהוּ בֶאֱמֶת), those who fear him (יְרֵאָיו), and those who love him (אֹהֲבָיו). In verse 10, they are collectively addressed as the "godly ones" (חָסִיד) who bless YHWH. The Hebrew lexeme for "righteous" (צַדִּיק) occurs only once (v. 17), which qualifies YHWH. Although the psalmist anticipates the final destruction (hiphil imperfect, יַשְׁמִיד) of all "wicked" (רְשָׁעִים), it does not attempt to explicate the identity of the "wicked." It implies in the discourse that the "wicked" are those, who in contrast to the godly ones (חָסִיד), do not bless YHWH. Thus, the unique nuance of the language of the two ways in Psalm 145 supplements the theme of Psalm 1, and does not simply brings forth the same theme.

In addition, besides Psalm 145 there are two psalms in the collection of the final *hallel* psalms, which also uses the Hebrew lexeme for "wicked" (רָשָׁע).

שׁוֹמֵר יְהוָה אֶת־כָּל־אֹהֲבָיו וְאֵת כָּל־הָרְשָׁעִים יַשְׁמִיד   145:20

The Lord guards all those who love him, but all the *wicked*, he will destroy.

יְהוָה ׀ פֹּקֵחַ עִוְרִים יְהוָה זֹקֵף כְּפוּפִים יְהוָה אֹהֵב צַדִּיקִים   146:8-9[24]

יְהוָה ׀ שֹׁמֵר אֶת־גֵּרִים יָתוֹם וְאַלְמָנָה יְעוֹדֵד וְדֶרֶךְ רְשָׁעִים יְעַוֵּת

The Lord gives sight to the blind, the Lord lifts up those who are bowed down, the Lord loves the *righteous*.

The Lord watches over the alien and sustains the fatherless and the widow, but he frustrates the ways of the *wicked*

מְעוֹדֵד עֲנָוִים יְהוָה מַשְׁפִּיל רְשָׁעִים עֲדֵי־אָרֶץ   147:6[25]

The Lord sustains the humble but casts the *wicked* to the ground.

In the three references above, the wicked (רשעים) are not only contrasted with the righteous, but also the blind, bowed-down, alien, fatherless, widow, and humble. There are two possible interpretations of the above references. Either the identity of the "righteous" is explicated in contrast to the "wicked," or YHWH's concern not only includes the "righteous," but also those who are blind, bowed down, alien, fatherless, widow, and humble. In Ps 145:14, YHWH upholds (סמך) all those who fall (נפל) and lifts up all who are bowed down (כפף). The above two psalms (Psalms 146 and 147) supplement the theme of the two ways of the righteous and wicked in a significant way. Hence, Psalm 145 does not have the final say on the theme.

---

24. VanGemeren draws our attention to the hymnic style formed by the use of participles. He points out to the phrase "Maker of heaven and earth" in verse 6, which the psalmist explicates with the five-fold emphatic position of YHWH in verses 7-9. Willem A. VanGemeren, "Psalms," in *Psalms, Proverbs, Ecclesiastes, Song of Songs* (ed. Frank E. Gæbelein; EBC 5, Grand Rapids: Zondervan, 1991), 866. According to Allen, YHWH is presented with the "highest ideals of kingship." He is the source of wholeness, justice, vindication, food, freedom, and blessings. He adds, "The defenseless can find in Yahweh their royal champion." Allen, *Psalms 101-50*, 379.

25. Anderson translates the עָנָוִים as the "downtrodden" and connects the verse with Ps 34:2; 113:7; and 145:14. He see the event as the divine judgment of God. Bernhard W. Anderson, *The Book of Psalms* (NCBC; 2 vols.; Grand Rapids: Eerdmans, 1981), 945.

The Central Theme of the Fourth Book[26]

Psalm 145 does not simply bring froth the central theme of Book IV but it provides a new semantic and pragmatic nuance to the theme (the Kingship of YHWH; Ps 145:1, 11-13; cf. Pss 93:1-3; 99:1-5; 102:12).[27] In fact, it is not the last psalm in the Psalter that alludes to the theme of the Kingship of YHWH. Wilson's claim (Pss 93:1-3; 99:1-5; and 102:12) in this regard is close to being simplistic. In Ps 93:1-3, YHWH is projected as a king (מלך; v. 1; cf. Ps 145:1), robed in majesty (גאות), armed with strength (עז). His throne (כסא) is established (כון) from all eternity (מעולם; v. 2; cf. Ps 145:1-2). Under his care, the world is firmly established (כון).[28] He is mightier than all chaotic waters (vv. 3-4). The psalmist emphasizes YHWH's firm stability (כון), his control over the nature, his testimonies, and his majesty.

In Ps 99:2, YHWH is proclaimed as the Lord in Zion, who has dominion over all the nations.[29] Therefore, all nations must give thanks (ידה; v. 3; cf. Pss 97:12; 145:10) to his great and awesome name (שם; v. 3; Ps 145:1-2, 21). YHWH is holy (קדוש; verses 3, 5, and 9; cf. Isa 6:3).[30] He is

---

26. Scholars agree that the central theme of Book IV is the kingship of YHWH. A detailed discourse analysis of the YHWH Kinship psalms (Pss 93, 96-99) and other relevant psalms (Pss 95, 103) is presented in chapter 5.

27. Wilson, *The Editing*, 225-26.

28. According to Rowe, the verse refers to creation, yet there is no such lexical evidence. It may suggest YHWH's firm control and dominion over and against the chaotic forces that have the potential to destroy the world. Robert D. Rowe, *God's Kingdom and God's Son: The Background to Mark's Christology from Concepts of Kingship in the Psalms* (Leiden: Boston, 2002), 18. Davidson refers to the LXX heading of the psalm, which has "when the earth was inhabited" (εἰς τὴν ἡμέραν τοῦ προσαββάτου ὅτε κατῴκισται). See Robert M. A. Davidson, *The Vitality of Worship: A Commentary on the Book of Psalms* (Grand Rapids: Eerdmans, 1998), 309. Based on the LXX and *Tamid* 7.4, VanGemeren suggests that the psalm was sung before the Sabbath in the second-temple period. VanGemeren, "Psalms," 607.

29. Rowe suggests that Psalm 99 is more nationalistic than other enthronement psalms. In the psalm, YHWH's "enthronement in Zion 'upon the Cherubim' provokes a theophany that has world-wide effects, and his dominion over all the peoples is assured." Rowe, *God's Kingdom and God's Son*, 20-21.

30. VanGemeren points out the exegetical problem in the two refrains "He/The Lord is holy" (vv. 3, 5, and 9). He comments, "The nature of the King's rule is not different from his character. He is 'holy' (*qādôš*, v. 3), 'mighty' ('*ōz*, v. 4), and 'loves justice [*mišpāt*].' He is holy in his perfections and awe-inspiring in his glorious presence. The very revelation of this otherness ('holy') is the glory of the Great King." VanGemeren, "Psalms," 636. Mays thinks that the triple refrain indicates that "the entire psalm is meant to be an exposition of the holiness of the Lord. 'Holy' is the word for the numinous, the *mysterium tremendum* that belongs to deity as such." James Luther Mays, *Psalms* (Louisville: Westminster John Knox, 1994), 316.

the mighty (עז; v. 4) King and he loves justice (משפט; v. 4). He has established equity (מישר) and executed justice (משפט) and righteousness (צדקה) in Jacob (v. 4). Exalt (רום) YHWH and worship him (v. 5). YHWH has answered (ענה) the prayers of his people (v. 6). In the psalm, the Kingship of YHWH over all nations is proclaimed; however, the emphasis in the psalm is on his lordship over Zion and his righteous acts of work in Jacob. YHWH's redemptive work among his people Israel is a reason for the world to recognize YHWH as their King and give him thanks.

Wilson's reference to Ps 102:12 in the MT is a typo. Ps 102:12 is not directly connected to the theme of the Kingship of YHWH. The verse is about the ephemeral nature of human life (צל, עשב; v. 12). However, Ps 102:13 declares YHWH's throne (ישב) as eternal (עולם) continuing through all generation (לדר ודר). The emphasis placed in the phrase "but you" (ואתה; notice the waw disjunctive). The psalmist makes a comparison between ephemeral nature of human life and the eternal establishment of YHWH. In fact, Psalm 102 is not a YHWH Kingship psalm, but it is one of the seven penitential psalms (Pss 6; 32; 38; 51; 102; 130; 143). According to VanGemeren, Psalm 102 emphasizes the suffering and discipline that associates with sin (vv. 10, 23-24).[31]

In the previous chapter, we noted that the Kingship of YHWH is the central theme of Psalm 145. YHWH is the King who is good and great. His dominion is universal and everlasting through all generations. The semantic and pragmatic nuance of the theme of the Kingship of YHWH in Psalm 145 is unique. Not only does it emphasize the universal and everlasting nature of the Kingship of YHWH, but his providence, care, protection, and salvation to all he has made. In fact, Ps 145:1, 11-13 does not have many direct lexical connections with the texts that Wilson mentions in the fourth book (Pss 93:1-3; 99:1-5; 102:12). This does not suggest the absence of any thematic links between them. In fact, the phrase "the King" (המלך) with a definite article (ה), qualifying God, occurs only twice in the Psalter. The first one is in Book IV (Ps 98:6) and the second one is in Book V (Ps 145:1). Psalm 145 is the first psalm in Book V that alludes to the central

---

31. VanGemeren suggests the psalm is an individual lament, arising from an exilic situation, in which the godly and wicked lived together in exile. VanGemeren, "Psalms," 644.

theme of Book IV—with unique nuance. Wilson is right about the connection between Psalm 145 and the central theme of the fourth book, but the connection does more than just bringing it forth. It will become clearer in chapter 5 as we analyze Psalm 145 in relation to all other YHWH Kingship psalms in Book IV.

Additionally, Psalm 145 dos not conclude the theme of the Kingship of YHWH in the Psalter. Notice the two references in Pss 146:10 and 149:2.

146:10   יִמְלֹךְ יהוה | לְעוֹלָם אֱלֹהַיִךְ צִיּוֹן לְדֹר וָדֹר הַלְלוּ־יָהּ

The Lord reigns forever, your God, O Zion,
for all generations. Praise the Lord

149:2[32]   יִשְׂמַח יִשְׂרָאֵל בְּעֹשָׂיו בְּנֵי־צִיּוֹן יָגִילוּ בְמַלְכָּם

Let Israel rejoice in their Maker;
let the people of Zion be glad in their King.

The above two psalms allude to the theme of the Kingship of YHWH. Notice the lexemes מֶלֶךְ, לְעוֹלָם, and לְדֹר וָדֹר. To be precise, Psalm 149 concludes the theme of the Kingship of YHWH in the Psalter.

The "Mighty Acts" of YHWH

Although Ps 145:4-7 has thematic continuity with Pss 92:5-9 and 96:3-4 regarding the "mighty acts" of YHWH,[33] the illocutionary intent of each text is not the same. In Ps 92:5-9, the psalmist provides reasons for giving thanks to YHWH.[34] He is made glad (שׂמח; v. 5) by YHWH's works (פֹּעַל,

---

32. Kidner names Psalm 149 as a "Victory Celebration." He reads it as an eschatological event. VanGemeren also regards it as an eschatological hymn. However, Westermann reads it as a historical event that has already taken place. Derek Kidner, *Psalms 73-150: A Commentary on Books III-V of the Psalms* (London: Inter-Varsity Press, 1975), 489; VanGemeren, "Psalms," 875; Claus Westermann, *Praise and Lament in the Psalms* (trans. Keith R. Crim and Richard N. Soulen; Atlanta: John Knox, 1981), 90. Allen writes, "The psalm summarizes aspects of the covenant relationship and the hopes that grew there from." He adds, "Its nationalism is only the corollary of the particularism of the old covenant." Allen, *Psalms 101-50*, 401.

33. Wilson, *The Editing*, 225-26.

34. VanGemeren suggests that the mood in the Psalm is different from Psalm 90, hence the clause *ki* in verse 5 is affirmative "surely." VanGemeren, "Psalms," 604. Kraus, Tate, Anderson, and VanGemeren, translate it as "for." Kraus explains, "With the causative כִּי the real main theme begins as the conclusion to the introductory part of the verse (vv.

מעשׂה; v. 5), so he joyfully sings (רנן) about YHWH's works (מעשׂה). In verses 6-9, he describes YHWH's work as great (גדל; v. 6) and his thoughts as profound (עמק). The senseless humanity (אישׁ־בער; v. 7) and fools (כסיל; v. 7) do not understand his work.[35] They do not comprehend the fact that although the wicked (רשׁע; v. 8) and the evildoers (כל־פעלי און; v. 8) may flourish (צוץ), they are destined for an eternal destruction (שׁמד; v. 8). Put differently, in contrast to the psalmist, the wicked lack analytical ability to recognize YHWH's work. Instead of recognizing and praising YHWH's work, they are duped by their instant prosperity. They fail to foresee their doomed destiny. The illocutionary intent in the text is to differentiate the wicked and the righteous in their ability to recognize YHWH's works.

In Ps 96:3-4, the psalmist summons all the earth (כל־הארץ) to sing a new song (שׁיר חדשׁ; v. 1) to YHWH. The intent is to declare YHWH's glory (כבוד; v. 2) and marvelous deeds (פלא; v. 3) among all nations (בגוים / בכל־העמים; v. 3). They must declare because (notice the causal *ki*) YHWH is great (גדול; v. 4; cf. Pss 95:3; 99:2; 145:3; and 147:5) and most worthy of praise (v. 4, מהלל מאד). YHWH must be feared (v. 4, ירא) above all gods (על־כל־אלהים; v. 4). All the gods of the nations are idols (אלילים; v. 5), and YHWH has made (עשׂה; v. 5) the heavens (שׁמים; v. 5). Most scholars agree that the psalm has a polemic against idolatry similar to Isa 40:18-31; 41:21-24; 44:6-8.[36] The psalmist compares the greatness of YHWH with the gods of other nations. His illocutionary intent is to summon all the earth to praise YHWH because YHWH alone is the true God.

1-3). . . . The reason and cause for the song taken up in joy is the 'rule of Yahweh' (v. 4). Here the thought is neither of the works of creation nor of the deeds done by Yahweh in the history of Israel." Hans-Joachim Kraus, *Psalms 60-150: A Continental Commentary* (trans. Hilton C. Oswald; Minneapolis: Fortress, 1989), 228. See also Marvin E. Tate, *Psalms 51-100* (WBC 20; Dallas: Word Books, 1990), 460; Anderson, *The Book of Psalms*, 662.

35. VanGemeren points out two responses to the works of God in redemptive history: the response of the wicked (vv. 6-8) and the response of the wise (vv. 8-15). The phrase אישׁ־בער is the only occurrence in the Old Testament. According to VanGemeren, it is an expression for animal-like behavior. Tate translates it as "dunderhead." See VanGemeren, "Psalms," 604; Tate, *Psalms 51-100*, 460.

36. Delitzsch, Kraus, Anderson, and VanGemeren notice great similarities between the psalm and Isaiah 40-66. They suggest the possibility of its dependence on the Deutero-Isaiah. Franz Delitzsch, *Biblical Commentary on the Psalms* (trans. Francis Bolton; 3 vols.; Grand Rapids: Eerdmans, 1955), 90; Kraus, *Psalms 60-150*, 251-52; Anderson, *The Book of Psalms*, 681; VanGemeren, "Psalms," 620.

On the one hand, the lexical and thematic connections of Psalm 145 with Pss 92:5-9 and 96:3-4 show apparent thematic continuity. In Psalm 145, David praises YHWH, the King because YHWH is great (גדול; v. 3) and most worthy of praise (מהלל מאד; v. 3). YHWH's greatness no one can fathom. David declares that one generation will commend YHWH's "works and the mighty acts" (מעשׂה and גבורה; v. 4) to another. He describes YHWH's work as "wonderful" (פלא; v. 5), "awesome" (ירא; v. 6), "great" (גדול; v. 6), and "mighty" (גבורה; vv. 11-12). Additionally, lexical analysis on Psalm 145 in the Psalter shows that the lexeme מעשׂה occurs fifteen times in Book V (Pss. 107:22, 24; 111:2, 6f; 115:4; 118:17; 135:15; 138:8; 139:14; 143:5; 145:4, 9-10, and 17). It occurs two times at the beginning (Pss 107:22, 24; and four times at the end (Ps 145:4, 9-10, and 17) of Book V. Unlike Book IV, the subject of all these occurrences at the seams of Book V is YHWH.[37] Psalm 145 is the last psalm that uses the lexeme מעשׂה explicitly to describe the "might acts" of YHWH. These connections may demonstrate that Psalm 145 brings forth the themes from these references.

On the other hand, the connections between Psalm 145 and Pss 92:5-9; 96:3-4 show difference in the illocutionary intent of the theme. In Pss 92:5-9, the praise of YHWH is an intelligent act in contrast with the acts of senseless humans (אישׁ־בער; v. 7) and fools (כסיל; v. 7) who do not understand his work. The psalmist invokes the analytical ability of humans to give thanks to YHWH. In Ps 96:3-4 the motif of theme has a different socio-historical context. The praise of YHWH is invoked by comparing the greatness of YHWH with the idols of the nations. However, in Psalm 145, David invokes "thanksgiving" and "universal praise" for YHWH based on YHWH's compassion and goodness to all creation.

Therefore, we suggest that Psalm 145 does not simply bring forth the theme of the "mighty acts" of YHWH, but in fact, it provides a different nuance to the theme. The whole of the thematic patterns together paints a bigger picture. In fact, the thematic pattern does not conclude in Psalm 145 but flows into the final *hallel* psalms. In Ps 147:5, the theme of the

---

37. The lexeme מעשׂה occurs 12 times in Book IV (Pss 90:17; 92:5-6; 102:26; 103:22; 104:13, 24, 31; 106:13, 35, and 39). The subject at the beginning (Ps 90:17) and the end (Ps 106:35, 39) of the book is human being.

"mighty acts" of YHWH reappears with a different nuance. Notice its connection to Ps 145:3.

145:3   גדול יהוה ומהלל מאד ולגדלתו אין חקר

The Lord is great and he is to be praised highly;
and his greatness is unsearchable

147:5   גדול אדונינו ורב־כח לתבונתו אין מספר

Our Lord is great and mighty in power;
his understanding is infinite

In Ps 147:5, YHWH is described as great (גדול) with mighty power (רב־כח). The description follows the "actions" of YHWH in verse 3 ("he determines the number of the stars and calls them each by name"),[38] which differ from the actions of YHWH in Psalm 145. Similarly, in Ps 150:2, the psalmist exhorts the audience to praise YHWH for his גבורה, however the context described in verse 1 is different from Psalm 145. The psalmist mentions "sanctuary" and "heaven" ("Praise God in his sanctuary; praise him in his mighty heavens"). Hence, Psalms 147 and 150 adds new semantic, syntactic, and pragmatic context to the theme of YHWH's "might" (גבורה) and "greatness" (גדל).

The Steadfast Love of YHWH
Wilson claims that Ps 145:8-9, and 13-20 brings forth the theme of "steadfast love" (חסד) of YHWH from Pss 103:6-13; 107:4-9, 12.[39] To investigate this, we will first examine Wilson's references (Ps 145:8-9, 13-20; cf. Pss 103:6-13; and 107:4-9, 12) and then analyze other available data.

Let us revisit the discourse meaning of Ps 145:8-9. The hymnic sentences in these verses describe the attributes of YHWH. YHWH is gracious and compassionate. YHWH is slow to anger, but great in his "steadfast

---

38. Notice the preceding verses 2-4 and the following verses 6-9. In verses 2-4, YHWH builds up Jerusalem, gathers exiles, heals the broken-hearted, binds up wounds, determines the number of stars, and calls them each by name. In verses 6-9, YHWH sustains the humble and casts the wicked down. He covers the sky with clouds and supplies the earth with rain. He makes the grass grow on the hills, he provides food for the cattle and for the young ravens. Thus, the descriptions of the "acts" of YHWH are repeated on both sides of Ps 147:5.
39. Wilson, *The Editing*, 225-26.

love" (חסד). The language of the "steadfast love" (חסד) of YHWH in Psalm 145 is distinct in two ways.

First, it evokes the language of Exod 34:6 (יהוה אל רחום וחנון ארך אפים ורב־חסד ואמת; cf. Ps 145:8, חנון ורחום יהוה ארך אפים וגדל־חסד). In the Psalter, the language of Exodus is alluded to only six times (Pss 86:15, 103:8, 111:4, 112:4, and 116:5), but the references in Book V (Pss 111:4, 112:4, and 116:5) have a unique reversal of words. In these references, the Exodus imagery (Exod 34:6) is reversed from רחם וחנון to חנון ורחם, while the two occurrences in other books (Pss 86:15 and 103:8) are in the same order as in Exod 34:6 (רחם וחנון).[40] Furthermore, the clause ארך אפים ורב־חסד, which follows רחם וחנון in Exod 34:6, is retained in the psalms (Pss 86:15; 103:8) in Book III and Book IV, but in the psalms in Book V it is changed. Additionally, the phrase ורב־ח is changed to וגדל־חסד in Ps 145:8. As a result, the lexeme גדל in the phrase forms an *inclusion* (see verses 3 and 9) and highlights the theme of the "greatness" of YHWH.

Second, the language of the "steadfast love" (חסד) of YHWH in Psalm 145 is unique because it underlines the cosmic domain of YHWH's goodness and compassion. In verse 9, the compassion and goodness of YHWH are not limited, but extended to all He has *made*. This uniqueness is maintained in Ps 145:13-20. It begins with an emphasis on YHWH's identity as the *creator* and the *cosmic domain* of his action in verses 13 and 17—*and loving* (חסיד) *toward all he has made* (עשׂה). The cosmic domain of his action perpetuates eternally through all generations (vv. 11-13). YHWH's love and compassion is available to *all*, especially to those who fall and are bowed down (v. 14), those who call on him in truth (v. 18), those who fear him (v. 19), and those who love him (v. 20). The illocution of the language is to invite *all* humanity to receive the benefit of his goodness, resulting in universal praise (כל־בשׂר) for YHWH. Hence, the language of the "steadfast love" (חסד) of YHWH in Psalm 145 puts forward YHWH as the creator of all humanity, as the one who is compassionate and loving

---

40. The reason for the alternation in the phrase חנון ורחם in Book V (Pss 111:4, 112:4, and 116:5) is unknown. Kselman suggests that the acrostic arrangement of Psalm 145 is the reason; however, Ps 116 is not an acrostic psalm. The reversal of the exodus imagery may suggest some connection between these psalms in Book V and the language in 2 Chr 30:9; Neh 9:17, 31; Joel 2:13; and Jonah 4:2 because they all share the reversal in the same order. See John S. Kselman, "Psalm 77 and the Book of Exodus," *JANES* 15 (1983): 55.

to all. His domain of action is cosmic and universal. He is good to all and faithful to *all he has made.*

The language of the "steadfast love" (חסד) of YHWH in Ps 103:6-13 has a different nuance. Notice in the following text.

עשה צדקות יהוה ומשפטים לכל־עשוקים   103:6-13[41]

יודיע דרכיו למשה לבני ישראל עלילותיו
רחום וחנון יהוה ארך אפים ורב־חסד
לא־לנצח יריב ולא לעולם יטור
לא כחטאינו עשה לנו ולא כעונתינו גמל עלינו
כי כגבה שמים על־הארץ גבר חסדו על־יראיו
כרחק מזרח ממערב הרחיק ממנו את־פשעינו
כרחם אב על־בנים רחם יהוה על־יראיו

The Lord works righteousness
and justice for all the oppressed.
He made known his ways to Moses,
his deeds to the people of Israel:
The Lord is compassionate and gracious,
slow to anger, abounding in love.
He will not always accuse,
nor will he harbor his anger forever;
He does not treat us as our sins deserve
or repay us according to our iniquities.
For as high as the heavens are above the earth,
so great is his love for those who fear him;
As far as the east is from the west,
so far has he removed our transgressions from us.
As a father has compassion on his children,
so the Lord has compassion on those who fear him.

---

41. Although, the psalm proclaims the establishment of YHWH's throne (כסא) in heaven and his kingdom (מלכות) has dominion (משל) over all in verse 19, the psalm is not generally grouped with other YHWH kingship psalms (Pss 93, 96-100). In fact, it is one of the two Davidic psalms in Book IV. The other Davidic psalm is Psalm 101. Wilson purports that a 'Mosaic frame,' which provides an interpretive *entrée* to the book, binds the YHWH-*mālak* psalms and the two Davidic psalms together. David M. Howard Jr.'s work on Psalms 93-100 does not analyze the whole of Book IV. Wilson's claim remains to be tested. Wilson, "Shaping the Psalter," 75-76; David M. Howard, Jr., "The Structure of Psalms 93-100," (Ph.D. thesis, University of Michigan, 1986).

In the passage above, David exhorts himself (נפש; v. 1) to bless (ברך; v. 1) YHWH, because YHWH works (צדקה; v. 6) righteousness (צדקות) and justice (משפט) for the oppressed (עשק). In the past, YHWH has informed (ידע; v. 7) Moses and the people of Israel about his ways (דרך) and his deeds (עלילה). YHWH is compassionate and gracious (רחום וחנון; v. 8), slow to anger, abounding in love (חסד; cf. Exod 34:6, Ps 86:15). He will not always accuse (נצח; v. 9). He will not keep (נטר) his anger forever. He does not treat (גמל; v. 10) us as our sins deserve and his love (חסד; v. 11) is higher than the heavens. The greatness of YHWH's covenant love is emphasized in verses 12-18. The discourse in the psalm is primarily about covenant love (חסד) for the people of Israel. Notice, the lexeme חסד appears four times (vv. 4, 8, 11, and 17). In addition, David specifically refers to Moses and the sons of Israel ("make known his ways to Moses and his acts to the sons of Israel" (יודיע דרכיו למשה לבני ישראל עלילותיו) in verse 7. In contrast to Psalm 145, Psalm 103 specially refers to the person of David and history of Israel. Notice the participles in verses 3-5, which follow the personal exhortation of David. YHWH is the forgiver (סלח) of sins. He is the healer (רפא), the redeemer (גאל) of his life, the one who crowns (עטר) with love and compassion (חסד ורחמים), and the one who satisfies (שבע) the desire of youth. David knows these attributes of YHWH by his personal experience. These are the reasons why his soul (נפש; v. 1) must bless (ברך; v. 1) YHWH.

The language of the "steadfast love" (חסד) of YHWH in Psalm 107 is both close and open-ended. It alludes to Psalm 106, but it also resonates with Psalm 145. Wilson's claims that Psalm 145 brings forth the theme of the "steadfast love" of YHWH from Ps 107:4-9, 12 is not completely true. A discourse analysis of Psalm 107 reveals that the language of "steadfast love" (חסד) in the psalm has different illocutionary intent.[42] Although the theme of "steadfast love" (חסד) begins with a specific category, it broadens

---

42. Jorge Mejia observes, "This psalm [Psalm 107] presents itself now as the 're-reading' of a previous text with a different destination, as is the case with other Psalms (e.g. 131)." He adds, "This is note mere juxtapositioning of themes. It means that the four cases of danger have been seen as images of the new Exodus (as we have said for each). Thus, the new Exodus is seen as salvation, not just from the captivity of Babel, but from evil forces which threaten human existence, and from sin." See Jorge Mejia, "Some Observations on Psalm 107," *BTB* 5 (1975): 56, 66.

its scope by switching to generic and inclusive language.[43] For example, in Ps 107:2-3, the psalmist invokes the thanksgiving specifically from the post-exilic community (the redeemed of the Lord, גאולי יהוה), who are gathered (קבץ) from the four corners of the earth. Again in Ps 107:11, the first colon "for they had rebelled against the words of God" (כי־המרו אמרי־אל) clearly alludes to Ps 106:33 (for they rebelled against the Spirit of God; כי־המרו את־רוחו).

Nonetheless, unlike Psalm 106, the psalmist in Psalm 107 deliberately presents four typical situations of human sufferings [dangerous travel by land (vv. 4-9), imprisonment (vv. 10-16), illness (vv. 17-22), and dangerous travel by sea (vv. 23-32)] from which YHWH has delivered. At the end of each story of deliverance, the psalmist invokes thanksgiving for YHWH's "steadfast love" (חסד). It is important to note that each of these categories of suffering could be applied to the post-exilic community as well as others.[44] Consequently, the implied recipients of the "steadfast love" are not only the post-exilic community but also others who experienced YHWH's deliverance from human sufferings. This is reinforced by the use of a generic phrase "sons of men" (vv. 8, 15, 21, and 31; לבני אדם) in the refrain. This phrase forms an *inclusion* with Ps 145:12 (לבני האדם) in Book V.

In Ps 107:42-43, the psalmist mentions the response of three generic categories of people. The upright (ישר) see the "steadfast love" (חסד) of YHWH and rejoice, but the wicked (עולה) shut their mouths. The third group of people are wise (חכם), who are invited to consider the "steadfast love" (חסד) of YHWH. Unlike Psalm 106, these three categories of people come from all ethnic groups—both Jews and Gentiles. Thus, the discourse meaning of the "steadfast love" (חסד) of YHWH in Psalm 107, although it begins by relating to a particular group, broadens its influence universally

---

43. VanGemeren writes, "After an introductory invocation (vv. 1-3), the psalmist enumerates cases where the Lord delivered all kind of people in need (vv. 4-32) and concludes on hymnic praise of the Redeemer-God (vv. 33-42)." See VanGemeren, "Psalms," 681.

44. Mejia explains, "It should be further noted, regarding this section of Ps 107, that it was very easy to re-read it in the perspective of the new Exodus, when the Israelites traversed the desert coming out of Babel: then, they were really saved from hunger and thirst, because the desert bloomed under their feet, and they found their way to an 'inhabited city': Jerusalem (cf. Is 41:17-20; 43:18-21; 49:8-11)." See Mejia, "Some Observations on Psalm 107," 59.

to all humanity. The psalm gives us the foretaste of the theme, which finally finds its full development in Psalm 145.

Our discussions so far suggest that Psalm 145 has some continuity on the themes Wilson mentioned; however, thematic ideas in each psalm have distinct perspective in their unique literary context. Thus is will be inaccurate to suggest that Psalm 145 brings forth the aforementioned themes.

The Onset of the Final Hallel Psalms

Wilson argues that Psalm 145 ends Book V because Ps 145:21 "precipitates" and "motivates" the onset of the final *hallel* psalms (Psalms 146-50).[45] This is evident in their "dependence" and in the "significance of their arrangement."[46] Similar to the doxologies (Pss 41:14; 72:19; 89:53; and 106:48) of Books I-IV, Ps 145:21 is the doxology of Book V.

145:21   תהלת יהוה ידבר־פי ויברך כל־בשר שם קדשו לעולם ועד

My mouth will speak in praise of the Lord
Let every creature bless his holy name
for ever and ever

Wilson suggests that the final redactor(s) altered Ps 145:21 in the MT so that it may set into motion the final collection of הלל psalms (Psalms 146-50).[47] He compares the MT text of Psalm 145 with that of 11QPsᵃ. As discussed in the first chapter, unlike the MT, Psalm 145 is placed toward the middle of the scroll of 11QPsᵃ. The text of the 11QPsᵃ adds a refrain.

ברוך יהוה וברוך שמו לעולם ועד

Wilson claims that the similar phrases in Ps 145:1-2 and 21 are the reminiscent of the refrain in 11QPsᵃ.[48]

---

45. Wilson, *The Editing*, 225-26.
46. Ibid., 226.
47. Wilson, "Shaping the Psalter," 74. See also Wilson, *The Editing*, 266.
48. Wilson develops this idea from Sanders. James A. Sanders, *The Psalms Scroll of Qumran Cave 11 (11QPsᵃ)* (Oxford: Clarendon, 1965), 16.

145:1   ואברכה שמך לעולם ועד

145:2   ואהללה שמך לעולם ועד

145:21   ויברך כל־בשר שם קדשו לעולם ועד

He adds, "[If] such a 'doxology' or 'doxological refrain' ever had a place in MT150, it has purposefully altered to its present form in Ps 145:21 to provide the motivation for the final *hallel*."[49] This insight into the MT's connections with the 11QPs[a] may be accepted as plausible evidence for an editorial alteration of the MT; but it does not establish *why* the alteration might have been made in Ps 145:21. Furthermore, if the option of alteration was meant to provide a motivation for the final *hallel* psalms, why would the editor(s) prefer the lexeme ברך over הלל, while the latter would show better literary continuity.

We will now analyze the final *hallel* psalms' "dependence" on Ps 145:21 and the "significance" of their arrangement to investigate whether Psalm 145 is the "climax" of Book V.[50] Wilson asserts, "I have no doubt that this grouping [Psalms 146-50] functions as an *answer* [emphasis added] to the exhortation of David in Ps 145:21."[51] According to him, the anticipation of "praise" in Ps 145:21 results in a crescendo of "praise" responses.[52] In Psalm 146, the first response comes from David, who is cast in the first person. In Psalm 147, he is joined by Israel and Jerusalem (vv. 2, 12, 19-20). In Psalm 148, the horizon of response expands as the angels and the creation participate in the chorus (vv. 2-3, 11-12). In Psalm 149, Israel joins the praise response once again. Finally, the response reaches its climax in Ps 150:6 (כל הנשמה תהלל יה; "Let everything that has breath praise the Lord").[53] Thus , the final *hallel* psalms (Psalms 146-50) are dependent on Ps 145:21, because they are the collection of response anticipated in Ps 145:21. According to Wilson, the arrangement of the final *hallel* psalms

---

49. Wilson, *The Editing*, 226.

50. Ibid., 193-94.

51. Ibid., 193.

52. Mays also acknowledges that Ps 146 is "a response to the commitment to the lifelong praise at the end of Psalm 145." Mays, *Psalms*, 439.

53. Wilson writes, "Surely this is the reflex of 'all flesh' who David adjures in 145:21. Apparently this final chorus of praise has been carefully affixed in its position." Wilson, *The Editing*, 194.

has significance for the final shape of the Psalter. He proposes that Psalm 146 is the response of David himself. Hence, the statement in the Psalm 146 about the reliability of YHWH in contrast to the human kings makes sense.[54] Notice the text in Ps 146:3-5.

146:3-5   אל־תבטחו בנדיבים בבן־אדם | שאין לו תשועה

תצא רוחו ישב לאדמתו ביום ההוא אבדו עשתנתיו:

אשרי שאל יעקב בעזרו שברו על־יהוה אלהיו:

Do not put your trust in princes,
in the sons of men, who cannot save.
When their spirit departs, they return to the ground;
on that very day their plans come to nothing.
Blessed is he whose help is the God of Jacob,
whose hope is in the Lord his God,

David, the king himself, bows to the Kingship of YHWH and acknowledges the limitedness and the transient nature of human rulers. He puts his hope in the Lord and declares YHWH's dominion as eternal (Ps 146:10). In line with these themes, other final *hallel* psalms record the "praise" response of "all flesh," for YHWH is trustworthy (Ps 147:4-5, 15-18; 148:5-6) and YHWH is faithful to his people (Ps 147:2-3; 148:14, 149:4). YHWH will ultimately be victorious over all nations that oppress Israel (Ps 149:6-9). Since YHWH is the universal and cosmic King, Ps 150:6 finally re-affirms the theme of praise from "all-flesh" in Ps 145:21 by declaring, "Let everything that has breath praise the Lord."

Wilson's theory of the "dependence" of the final hallel psalms on Ps 145:21 and the "significance of the arrangement" of final *hallel* psalms has problems. First, it is not clear how the lexical and thematic connections (in the reference given by Wilson) prove the collection of the final *hallel* psalms to be a response (*answer*) to the anticipation built in the Ps 145:21. It might be agreeable to accept that one of the functions of Ps 145:21 is to

---

54. J. J. M. Roberts argues otherwise. He comments, "[T]he linked traditions of the imperial kingship of God, the choice of the Davidic line as the *human agent* [emphasis added] of divine rule, and the elevation of Zion/Jerusalem as the earthly seat of that divine rule lie at the very heart of later Christian theology." J. J. M. Roberts, "The Enthronement of Yhwh and David: The Abiding Theological Significance of the Kingship Language of the Psalms," *CBQ* 64 (2002): 686.

"precipitate" the final *hallel* psalms, but claiming the final *hallel* psalms as dependent on Ps 145:21 is exegetically questionable. Notice the connections in the references provided by Wilson.

145:21   תהלת יהוה ידבר־פי ויברך כל־בשׂר שם קדשׁו לעולם ועד

My mouth will speak in praise of the Lord.

Let every creature praise his holy name forever and ever.

146:1-2   הללו־יה הללי נפשׁי את־יהוה

אהללה יהוה בחיי אזמרה לאלהי בעודי

Praise the Lord. Praise the Lord, O my soul.

I will praise the Lord all my life;

I will sing praise to my God as long as I live.

147:1-2,   הללו יה | כי־טוב זמרה אלהינו כי־נעים נאוה תהלה

12, 19-20   בונה ירושׁל ם יהוה נדחי ישׂראל יכנס

שׁבחי ירושׁל ם את־יהוה הללי אלהיך צייון

מגיד (דברו) [דבריו] ליעקב חקיו ומשׁפטיו לישׂראל

לא עשׂה כן | לכל־גוי ומשׁפטים בל־ידעום הללו־יה

Praise the Lord.

How good it is to sing praises to our God,

how pleasant and fitting to praise him!

The Lord builds up Jerusalem;

he gathers the exiles of Israel.

Extol the Lord, O Jerusalem; praise your God, O Zion,

He has revealed his word to Jacob,

his laws and decrees to Israel.

He has done this for no other nation;

they do not know his laws. Praise the Lord

הללוהו כל־מלאכיו הללוהו כל־(צבאו) [צבאיו]   148:2-3,

הללוהו שמש וירח הללוהו כל־כוכבי אור   11-12

מלכי־ארץ וכל־לאמים שרים וכל־שפטי ארץ

בחורים וגם־בתולות זקנים עם־נערים

Praise him, all his angels,

Praise him, all his heavenly hosts.

Praise him, sun and moon,

Praise him, all you shining stars.

Kings of the earth and all peoples;

Princes and all judges of the earth;

Both young men and women;

Old men and children.

הללו יה | שירו ליהוה שיר חדש תהלתו בקהל חסידים   149:1-2

ישמח ישראל בעשיו בני־ציון יגילו במלכם

Praise the Lord. Sing to the Lord a new song,

his praise in the assembly of the saints.

Let Israel rejoice in their Maker;

let the people of Zion be glad in their King.

כל הנשמה תהלל יה הללו־יה   150:6

Let everything that has breath praise the Lord.

Praise the Lord.

Three observations stand against Wilson's claim. (1) David is already praising in Ps 145:1-2. The anticipation in Ps 145:21 is not for a response from David himself, but from all humanity (כל־בשר). (2) The anticipation of Ps 145:21 remains an anticipation in Ps 150:6. Notice the use of jussive in Ps 150:6 (תהלל), similar to Ps 145:21. Thus, Ps 150:6 is not an antiphonal response to Ps 145:21. It is not a closing statement but an open-ended anticipation of the "not yet." (3) The implicit intent in the final *hallel* psalms is to revisit Ps 145:21 by intensifying the "anticipation."[55] In so doing, instead of a response, the collection of the final *hallel* psalms saturates

---

55. VanGemeren rightly titles Ps 150:3-5 as "Praise the Lord with great intensity." See VanGemeren, "Psalms," 879.

the thematic pattern that explicates the theme of "praise" by giving more reasons for "praise" and by developing its horizon of influence. Thus, the anticipated response in Ps 145:21 is from all humanity (כל־בשׂר).

The liturgical reading of a single psalm or the Psalter as a whole anticipates a response from its audience. For this purpose, Book V, from Psalm 107 to Psalm 150, is compositionally arranged to affect motivation in a progressive manner. In this arrangement, the final *hallel* psalms are placed as a crescendo. Hence, the final *hallel* psalms cannot be limited to being a response (answer) to Ps 145:21. To be even more exegetically precise, we have argued in our discourse analysis of Ps 145:21 that "all flesh" cannot be interpreted as inanimate objects, but intelligent "human beings." Put differently, the anticipation of David in Ps 145:21 is praise from "human beings," (those who call on him in truth, who fear him, and those who love him). Therefore, it would be exegetically wrong to consider Ps 148:3 (כל־ כוכבי אור, שמש וירח) as a response to the anticipation in Ps 145:21.

Second, some psalms of the final *hallel* psalms (Psalms 146-50) have thematic connections with other psalms as well. This implies that the collection of the final *hallel* psalms, as the doxology of the whole Psalter, represents themes within and outside the confines of Ps 145:21. For example, Psalm 146 has two themes: "God of Jacob" and "God of Zion." These themes have no direct connection with Psalm 145, but rather with Pss 46:8, 12 and 9:12. Likewise, on the theme of "building Jerusalem," Ps 147:2 connects with Pss 122:3 and 51:20. On the theme of "celestial praise," Ps 148:4 connects to Ps 19:2. These thematic connections are synthetic in its development. Depending on the literary context of the final *hallel* psalms, some of these themes have their closure in the final *hallel* psalms.

Our discussions so far explicitly suggest that the thematic connections of the final *hallel* psalms are not limited to Ps 145:21. Hence, the collection of the final *hallel* psalms (Psalms 146-50) not only connects to the anticipation built in Ps 145:21, but also other psalms.

Third, Wilson's theory of significance of arrangement in the final *hallel* psalms, based on the assumption that Psalm 146 represents David himself, is hypothetical. Psalm 146 is not a Davidic psalm. Although, there are explicit lexical connections between Psalms 145 and 146,[56] following two distinct literary features set them apart. First, Psalm 145 is distinctly superscripted as Davidic psalm while Psalm 146 is not. Second, Psalm 146 has literary feature of opening and closing with imperative call to praise like all other *hallel* psalms. Thus, Wilson's suggestion for reading Psalm 146 as a response of David, is inaccurate. In fact, the illocution of the text in Psalm 146 is to draw our attention to YHWH by employing various themes, rather than featuring an image of David. It would be appropriate to explore exegetically the development of the thematic patterns based on lexical and thematic connections in the final *hallel* psalms, rather than seeking the continuity of a Davidic image.

The Final Hallel Psalms

The final *hallel* psalms (Psalms 146-50) share a unique literary feature of the "praise hymn," in which each psalm opens and concludes with an imperatival call to praise YHWH.[57] Each of the psalms uses the short form of YHWH (יה), which is not found in Davidic psalms (except for Pss 68:19, 122:4). Even in the body of the text the use of the lexeme הלל is frequent. For example, in Psalms 146, 147, and 149 the lexeme occurs three times each, while in Psalms 148 and 150, it occurs 12 and 13 times respectively. Hence, their genre is different from Psalm 145. Therefore, Psalm 145 cannot be grouped together with the final *hallel* psalms.[58] Nonetheless, Psalm 145 has dual literary features, which connect it to the adjacent psalms on both sides. One the one hand, it is the last Davidic. On the other hand, it

---

56. Notice Ps 145:1, cf. Ps 146:6, 10; Ps 145:12, cf. Ps 146:3; Ps 145:15, cf. Ps 146:7; Ps 145:17, cf. Ps 146:9; Ps 145:19, cf. Ps 146:6-7; and Ps 145:20, cf. Ps 146:6, 8, 9.

57. VanGemeren, "Psalms," 864.

58. Gunkel places Psalm 145 with Psalms 146-50 as a collection of hymns, while Westermann classifies Psalms 145-50 together as a collection of the psalms of descriptive praise. See Hermann Gunkel et al., *Introduction to Psalms: The Genres of the Religious Lyric of Israel* (trans. James D. Nogalski; Macon: Mercer University Press, 1998). 22; Claus Westermann, *The Psalms: Structure, Content and Message* (trans. Ralph D. Gehrke; Minneapolis: Augsburg, 1980), 81. A. F. Kirkpatrick also sees this psalm as the head of the series of the Psalms of praise. See A. F. Kirkpatrick, ed., *The Book of Psalms* (Cambridge Bible for Schools and Colleges; Cambridge: Cambridge University Press, 1902), 813.

has *inclusion* formed by "praise" (תהלת / תהלה). The psalm functions like *Janus* looking backward to Davidic groups of psalms, as well as forward to the final *hallel* psalms.

In the following paragraphs, we will investigate the lexical, syntactical, thematic, semantic, and pragmatic connections of each of the final *hallel* psalms (Psalms 146-50) with Psalm 145 in order to ascertain the placement of Psalm 145 before the final *hallel* psalms (Psalms 146-50) in the MT.

Psalm 146

Psalm 146 is the first psalm of the final *hallel* psalms. According to VanGemeren, the hymn describes "the many ways, in which the Lord, the Creator (vv. 5-6) and King (v. 10), sustains individuals who have faith in him, particularly the needy."[59] The hope of the needy does not rest (לו תשו־ עה) in the governance of the human kings but the Kingship of YHWH (v. 3).[60] According to Allen, verses 6-9 should be read in reference to verse 5, which mentions the people of Israel who are socially marginalized.[61] Put differently, the theme of creation in Psalm 146 must be placed in the context of the work of YHWH in the history of Israel. In the history of Israel, human rulers failed, but YHWH their creator and their King has always been reliable.

Psalm 146 connects to Psalm 145 lexically and thematically at various points. Lexical analysis of the two psalms shows numerous lexemes that are common to both psalms.[62] These lexemes contribute to the discourse

---

59. VanGemeren, "Psalms," 864.

60. Malchow suggests that the despair over human rulers developed through the history. He comments, "Once again the Judean kings did not measure up to expectation. They did not stop the rich in their oppression of the helpless. So Psalm 146 turns to God because he is the only one who will fulfill this function faithfully. . . . Psalm 146 helps people whose nation's past history has taught them to distrust human kings." Bruce V. Malchow, "God or King in Psalm 146," *TBT* 89 (1977): 1169-70.

61. Allen, *Psalms 101-50*, 379.

62. The common lexemes between the two psalms are: הלל (Ps 146:1-2. 10; cf. Ps 145:2-3); בן (Ps 146:3; cf. Ps 145:12); אדם (Ps 146:3; cf. Ps 145:12); אין (Ps 146:3; cf. Ps 145:3); יום (Ps 146:4; cf. Ps 145:2); עשה (Ps 146:6-7; cf. Ps 145:19); כל (Ps 146:6; cf. Ps 145: 2, 9, 10, 13, 14, 15, 16, 17 18, 20, and 21); שמר (Ps 146:6, 9; cf. Ps 145:20); אמת (Ps 146:6; cf. Ps 145:18); עולם (Ps 146:6, 10; cf. Ps 145:1); נתן (Ps 146:7; cf. Ps 145:15); זקף (Ps 146:8; cf. Ps 145:14); כפף (Ps 146:8; cf. Ps 145: 14); אהב (Ps 146:8; cf. Ps 145:20); צדיק (Ps 146:8; Ps 145:17); דרך (Ps 146:9; Ps 145:17); רשע (Ps 146:9; cf. Ps 145:20); מלך (Ps

meaning of the two psalms through their syntactic, paradigmatic, semantics, and pragmatic interactions. Comparison of the discourse meanings of the two psalms shows thematic continuity. Both psalms affirm that YHWH will rule through all generations (Ps 146:10; cf. Ps 145:4). In Ps 146:2, the psalmist echoes David's vow "I will bless you my God (אלוהים) the king" (Ps 145:1) with "I will sing praise to my God (אלוהים) as long as I live."[63] The two psalms together declare, "YHWH raises up those who are bent down" (כפף / זקף; Ps 146:8; cf. Ps 145: 14).[64] Both psalms affirm that YHWH gives (נתן; Ps 146:7; cf. Ps 145:15) food to the hungry. They together affirm the destruction of the wicked (רשע) (Ps 146:9; cf. Ps 145:20). Through the differences in their discourse meanings, the two psalms contribute in building a thematic pattern. Notice the thematic patterning in the two psalms:

(1) While both psalms develop the theme of זקף and כפף (Ps 146:8; cf. Ps 145:14) declaring YHWH raises (זקף) up all who are bent down (כפף), Ps 146:8 develops the theme with two rhemes: "YHWH opens the eyes of the blind" and "YHWH loves the righteous." Reading them together suggests that YHWH opens eyes for one to see before he raises them. He does not raise all who are bent down, but the righteous because he loves them.

(2) Likewise, both psalms affirm that YHWH gives (נתן; Ps 146:7; cf. Ps 145:15) food to the hungry, but in Ps 146:7 he does it because he upholds the cause of the oppressed (עשק). Thus, the latter psalm supplements the former.

(3) In Ps 145:20, David declares that YHWH watches over (שמר) those who love him. Ps 146:9 adds that YHWH keeps (שמר) faith and he watches over (שמר) strangers, orphans, and widows. Psalm 146 expands the idea of Ps 145:20.

(4) In Ps 145:1, David declares YHWH as my God (אלוהים) the King. But in Ps 146:10, he declares that YHWH, the God (אלוהים) of Zion (ציון) will rule forever and over all generations.

146:10; cf. Ps 145:1); and דור (Ps 146:10; cf. Ps 145:4).

63. Perhaps for this reason Wilson preferred to consider Psalm 146 as a Davidic psalm in continuation with Psalm 145. See Wilson, *The Editing*, 226-27.

64. Miller claims that these two are the only occurrences in the Old Testament and hence they are unique in their juxtapositioning. Patrick D Miller, "The End of the Psalter: A Response to Erich Zenger," *JSOT* 80 (1998): 108.

(5) In Ps 145:3, David declares the greatness of YHWH, which is un-searchable (אין חקר), but in Ps 146:3, the psalmist talks about the unreli-ability of human rulers, the sons of men (בבן־אדם), in whom there is no salvation (שאין לו תשעה). It establishes the fact that YHWH is the only Savior, who has no equal.

(6) In Ps 145:13f and 18, David declares YHWH is faithful in his words and he is near to those who call on him in truth (אמת). Ps 146:6 concludes YHWH is faithful (אמת) forever.

Psalm 145 has explicit thematic connections with Psalm 146.[65] These connections support their placement as adjacent psalms. However, the Davidic superscript of Psalm 145 and the literary feature of hallel in Psalm 146 justify their present order of placement.

Psalm 147

According to Allen, the psalm is an assortment of two interconnected themes: YHWH's power and control over nature and the patronage of the covenant people.[66] Schaefer divides the psalm into three sections: (1) the praise of God, the restorer of Israel, and caretaker of the stars (vv. 1-6); (2) nature, provided for by God who delights not in human exploits (vv. 7-11); (3) and God's power over nature and care for Zion and Israel (vv. 12-20).[67]

Psalm 147 connects with Psalm 145 lexically and thematically. Lexical analysis shows numerous shared lexemes.[68] These lexemes, through their

---

65. See the lexical and thematic comparison of Psalm 145 with Psalm 144 in the chapter 5.

66. Allen, *Psalms 101-50*, 385.

67. Konrad Schaefer, *Psalms* (ed. David W. Cotter; Collegeville: Liturgical Press, 2001), 341.

68. The common lexemes between Psalms 147 and 145 are: הלל (Ps 147:1, 12, and 20; cf. Ps 145:2); טוב (Ps 147:1; cf. Ps 145:7, 9); תהלה (Ps 147:1; cf. Ps 145:1); כל (Ps 147:4, 20; cf. Ps 145: 2, 9, 10, 13, 14, 15, 16, 17 18, 20, and 21); שם (Ps 147:4; cf. Ps 145:1); קרא (Ps 147:4, 9; cf. Ps 145:18); גדול (Ps 147:5; cf. Ps 145:3, 8); רב (Ps 147:5; cf. Ps 145:7); אין (Ps 147:5; cf. Ps 145:3); רשע (Ps 147:6; cf. Ps 145:20); עד (Ps 147:6, 15; cf. Ps 145:1); בן (Ps 147:9, 13; cf. Ps 145:12); נתן (Ps 147:9, 16; cf. Ps 145:15); גבורה (Ps 147:10; cf. Ps 145:4, 11-12); ירא (Ps 147:11; cf. Ps 145:6); חסד (Ps 147:11, cf. Ps 145:8); שבח (Ps 147:12; cf. Ps 145:4); ברך (Ps 147:13; cf. Ps 145:1); שבע (Ps 147:14; cf. Ps 145:16); דבר (Ps 147:15, 18, and 19; cf. Ps 145:5); נגד (Ps 147:19; cf. Ps 145:4); עשה (Ps 147:20; cf. Ps 145:19); כל (Ps 147:20; cf. Ps 145: 2, 9, 10, 13, 14, 15, 16, 17 18, and 21); and ידע (Ps 147:20; cf. Ps 145:12).

syntactical, paradigmatic, semantic, and pragmatic interactions, contribute to the discourse meaning of each psalm. Comparison of the discourse meaning of the two psalms shows some thematic continuity. Both psalms affirm that YHWH will deal with the wicked (רשׁע). In Ps 145:20, David tells us that the wicked (רשׁע) will be destroyed. In Ps 147:6, the psalmist informs us that YHWH will bring down the wicked (רשׁע) to the ground. On the other hand, the two psalms also connect with each other lexically through differences, forming thematic patterns that complement each other. Notice the following thematic patterns in the two psalms:

(1) Unlike Psalm 145, Psalm 146 has the language of particularism. In Ps 147:2, YHWH builds (בנה) up Jerusalem. He gathers (כנס) the exiles (נדח) of Israel. In verse 12, both Jerusalem and Zion are summoned to praise (שׁבח) YHWH.

(2) In Ps 145:3, 8, David proclaims, "Great (גדול) is the Lord (יהוה) and most worthy of praise; his greatness (גדולה) no one can fathom (אין חקר)." But in Ps 147:5, the psalmist uses different lexemes in the syntax, giving a new nuance to the declaration, "Great (גדול) is our Lord (אדון) and mighty in power (ורב־כח); his understanding (תבונה) has no limit (אין מספר)." The two psalms together enhance the understanding of the greatness of YHWH.

(3) Is Ps 145:4, one generation will commend (שׁבח) YHWH to another generation, but in Ps 147:12, the psalmist asks Jerusalem and Zion to commend (שׁבח, notice the imperative) YHWH.

(4) In Ps 145:12, all men will speak of the glory of YHWH's Kingdom and his power to make known (ידע) to all human beings YHWH's mighty deeds. In Ps 147:20, the psalmist informs us that YHWH has declared his word to Jacob and his ordinance to Israel, while other nations do not know (ידע) his ordinance. This clarifies why David is concerned about making YHWH's mighty deeds known to all human beings.

(5) In Ps 145:15, YHWH gives (נתן) food at the proper time to those who look to him. However in Ps 147:9, YHWH provides (נתן) food for the cattle and for the young ravens when they call. In other words, YHWH's care and provision is available to all of his creation.

(6) In Ps 145:16, YHWH opens his hand and satisfies (שׂבע) the desires of every living thing. But in Ps 147:14, YHWH grants peace to the people

of Jerusalem and Zion and satisfies (שׂבע) them with the finest of wheat. YHWH is the one who satisfies both Jews and Gentiles. YHWH is the satisfier of both Jerusalem and all living things.

(7) In Ps 145:19, YHWH "fulfills the desires of those who fear (ירא) him; he hears their cry and saves them." But in Ps 147: 11, YHWH "delights in those who fear (ירא) him, who put their hope (יחל) in his unfailing love (חסד)."

Thus, Psalm 147 brings forth the themes of Psalm 145 not only to show continuity (wicked will be destroyed), but also to provide a better perspective on the theme (YHWH provides food for the cattle too).[69] In addition, these themes find their mention in the context of the language of particularism, underscoring the fact that the people of Israel have not been forgotten. Since they suffered the feeling of rejection in Psalms 89 and 108, this implicit message in the editorial arrangement of the final *hallel* psalms is significant. YHWH builds Jerusalem. YHWH, who is good to all he has made—including his covenant people—is the ultimate help of all.

Psalm 148

Anderson names the psalm "Let the whole world praise YHWH."[70] VanGemeren divides the psalm into three sections: A. Call on heaven to praise YHWH (vv. 1-6); B. Call on earth to praise YHWH (vv. 7-12); and C. Rationale for praising YHWH (vv. 13-14).[71] The rationale for praise also occurs in verse 5 (notice the causal *ki*). YHWH must be praised because he is the creator, his name alone is exalted, and his splendor is high above all. Among its literary features, the psalm is unique in the use of the lexeme הלל, which occurs 12 times in 14 verses. It summons praises from all: heavens, high places, angels, heavenly hosts, sun, moon, stars, all earthly creatures over the land and the sea, all creations such as mountains and trees, all kings, nations young and old, men and women—a cosmic and universal

---

69. Miller also notices, "Psalms 146 and 147 continue in direct fashion the catalogue of descriptive praises that make up the body of Psalm 145, describing the Lord's care and provision in a series of participial phrases." Miller, "The End of the Psalter: A Response to Erich Zenger," 109.

70. Anderson, *The Book of Psalms*, 648.

71. VanGemeren, "Psalms," 871

praise. Put differently, the psalm explicates what David anticipated concerning the praise of YHWH in Psalm 145.

Psalm 148 connects with Psalm 145 lexically and thematically in various ways. It has many lexemes in common with Psalm 145.[72] These lexemes contribute to the discourse meaning of the psalm through their syntactic, paradigmatic, semantic, and pragmatic interactions. Comparisons of their discourse meanings reveal the following thematic patterns.

(1) Both psalms anticipate the cosmic and universal praise of YHWH. All will praise YHWH.

(2) In Ps 145:1, David exalts (רום) YHWH and praises (תהלה) him. In verse 10, David anticipates all godly ones (חסיד) will bless YHWH, but in Ps 148:14, YHWH will raise (רום) a horn, which is a praise (תהלה). He will raise praise for all his godly ones (חסיד), the sons of Israel, and the people close to the heart of YHWH.[73] The psalm clearly reaffirms that the people of Israel are still in YHWH's mind.

(3) In Ps 145:1, David the king praises the ultimate King YHWH, but in Ps 148:11, all the kings (מלך) of the earth and all nations, princes, and rulers are beckoned to praise YHWH.

(4) In Psalm 145, David praises YHWH because YHWH is great and good to all he has made. However, in Psalm 148, David praises YHWH for two different reasons (notice the causal clause *ki* in verses 5 and 13): (a) YHWH is the creator, he commanded and all were created; (b) YHWH's name *alone* is exalted. His majesty (הוד) is above the heaven and the earth.

Thus, the praise in Psalm 148 revisits the anticipation of praise for YHWH in Psalm 145. It summons all the kings of the earth to praise YHWH in response to David's anticipation of the universal praise. In YHWH's cosmic and universal praise all are included, especially the sons

---

72. The lexemes in the two psalms are: אשר (Ps 148:4; cf. Ps 145:18); על (Ps 148:4; cf. Ps 145:9); הלל (Ps 148:1-5, 7, 13-14; cf. Ps 145:2-3); כל (Ps 148: 2-3, 7, 9-11, 14; cf. Ps 145: 2, 9, 10, 13, 14, 15, 16, 17 18, 20, and 21); רום (Ps 148:4; cf. Ps 145:1); שם (Ps 148:5, 13; cf. Ps 145:1, 2, and 21); (Ps 148:6; cf. Ps 145:1, 2, 21); עד (Ps 148:6; cf. Ps 145:1, 2, and 21); נתן (Ps 148:6; cf. Ps 145:15); עשה (Ps 148:8; cf. Ps 145:19); דבר (Ps 148:8; cf. Ps 145:5); מלך (Ps 148:11; cf. Ps 145:1); הוד (Ps 148:13; cf. Ps 145:5); תהלה (Ps 148:14; cf. Ps 145:1); חסיד (Ps 148:14; cf. Ps 145:10); and בן (Ps 148:14; cf. Ps 145:12).

73. Anderson, depending on the LXX translation, prefers seeing Ps 148:14 as a future event. Anderson, *The Book of Psalms*, 951.

of Israel. In concluding, the psalmist gives a hope of "glory," which will be endowed by YHWH upon all who are involved in praising him.[74] This supplements the motivation for praise.

Psalm 149[75]

Westermann classifies the psalm as a "song of victory."[76] Brueggemann regards this as the "psalm of reorientation."[77] He acknowledges that development of the psalm is a bit unusual and surprising. It matches the content of Psalm 2 on the motif of defiance against the nations. Schaefer also agree with him. He believes that the human instrument is the "assembly of the faithful," who as a messianic community would achieve what was assigned to the Davidic king.[78] Eaton notices its connection with Ps 148:14. He sees the psalm looking forward to the full realization of YHWH's Kingdom across the world.[79] Lexically the psalm is unique because it has the highest occurrence of the lexeme חסיד in the final *hallel* psalms. It occurs three times (vv. 1, 5, and 9), forming an *inclusion*. It is also a unique psalm because it combines the two contrasting languages—battle and praise (v. 6).

Psalm 149 connects with Psalm 145 lexically as well as thematically. Lexical analysis reveals numerous common lexemes.[80] These lexemes form

---

74. VanGemeren interprets "horn" as endowment of "glory." See VanGemeren, "Psalms," 875.

75. Kidner, Allen and VanGemren consider the psalm to be an eschatological hymn. Kidner, *Psalm 73-150*, 489; Allen, *Psalms 101-50*, 397. VanGemeren, "Psalms," 875. According to Allen, the psalm "summarizes aspects of the covenant relationship and the hopes that grew there from." He adds, "Its nationalism is only the corollary of the particularism of the old covenant." Allen, *Psalms 101-50*, 401. For a structure analysis see Pierre Auffret, *Merveilles à nos yeux: Étude structurelle de vingt psaumes dont celui de 1 Ch 16:8-36* (New York: Walter de Gruyter, 1995), 277-81.

76. Westermann, *Praise and Lament*, 90-92.

77. Walter Brueggemann, *The Message of the Psalm* (Minneapolis: Augsberg, 1984), 165-67.

78. Schaefer, *Psalms*, 344-45.

79. J. H. Eaton, *The Psalms: A Historical and Spiritual Commentary with an Introduction and New Translation* (London: T & T Clark, 2003), 483.

80. Psalm 149 shares following lexemes with Psalm 145: הלל (Ps 149:1, 3, and 9; Ps 145:2, 3); תהלה (Ps 149:1; cf. Ps 145:1, 21); חסיד (Ps 149:1, 5, and 9; cf. Ps 145:10); עשה (Ps 149:2, 7, and 9); בן (Ps 149:2; cf. Ps 145:12); מלך (Ps 149:2, 8; cf. Ps 145:1); שם (Ps 149:3; cf. Ps 145:1, 2, and 21); כבוד (Ps 149:5; cf. Ps 145:5); רנן (Ps 149:5; cf. Ps 145:7); יד (Ps 149:6; cf. Ps 145:16); הדר (Ps 149:9; cf. Ps 145:5); כל (Ps 149:9; cf. Ps 145: 2, 9, 10, 13, 14, 15, 16, 17 18, 20, and 21).

the discourse meaning in each psalm through their syntactic, paradigmatic, semantic, and pragmatic interaction. Comparison of their discourse meanings exhibits the following thematic patterns:

(1) In 149:1, YHWH's praise (תהלה) is placed in parallelism with a "new song" (שיר חדש). The "new song" (שיר חדש) is to be sung in the assembly of the godly ones (חסיד). This alludes to David's desire to sing a "new song" (שיר חדש) in Ps 144:9. Although David does not mention the "new song" (שיר חדש) in Psalm 145, he anticipates that the godly ones (חסיד; v. 10) will join him in blessing YHWH.

(2) In Ps 145:1, 2, 21, David praises YHWH's name (שם), but he does not give us detail about the manner in which he will do it. In Ps 149:3, the psalmist tells us to praise YHWH's name (שם) by dancing (מחול) and by playing musical instruments (וכנור בתף). This additional perspective on how to praise YHWH's name (שם) is valuable, especially in a circle where "praise" is restricted to certain forms.

(3) In Ps 149:2, the word מלך is placed in parallel with עשה. The creator God is addressed as "the King." Israel and the people of Zion are asked to rejoice in this King. Then the godly ones (חסיד) are summoned to join. With praise in their mouths and a double-edged sword (חרב) in their hands, they are to inflict vengeance (נקמה) and punishment (תוכחה) against the nations (גוי). They are to bind (אסר) their kings (מלך) and nobles (כבד) with shackles. They will carry out the sentence, which YHWH has already written. The rebellious kings, who intend to break open the chains in Ps 2:3 will be shackled by the godly ones once again. This theme connects Psalm 149 with Psalm 2, forming an *inclusion* in the Psalter.

The psalmist declares that this event will bring the glory to all godly ones (חסיד). This verse also connects to Ps 148:14, where YHWH gives hope that he will endow "glory" upon his godly ones (חסיד). The psalm ends with a hope of victory for the godly ones (חסיד).

(4) In Ps 145:7, all people will celebrate the fame of YHWH's goodness and sing for joy (רנן) about YHWH' righteousness (צדקה); but in Ps 149:5, only the godly ones (חסיד) will sing for joy (רנן). They will sing for joy in their bed.

(5) The use of the lexeme עשה in the two psalms shows an interesting pattern. In Psalm 145 YHWH is the fulfiller (עשה) of the desire of those

who fear him. Likewise, in Ps 149:2, YHWH is the creator (עשה), but in Ps 149:7-9, the psalmist presents the godly ones (חסיד) as executer (עשה) of the justice for YHWH. According to the psalmist, YHWH will bestow "glory" upon the godly ones through this event. This implies that the godly ones (חסיד) are not pacifists, but warriors of God who are executors of the judgment of YHWH already written by him.[81]

Psalm 149 sobers the language of praise and universal goodness of YHWH by mentioning the role of the godly ones, who will execute YHWH's judgment against the wicked king. It brings the theme of worship and work together under one sovereign purpose and plan of YHWH, in which YHWH is the king who provides care, love, and justice to the nations through the godly ones.

Psalm 150

The psalm sounds like the concluding chorus of a grand finale—the peak of a crescendo of praise.[82] The repetition of the phrase "praise him" (הללוהו) eight times along with the names of eight musical instruments (נבל, שופר, כנור, תף, מן, עוגב, צלצל, and תרועה) sets this psalm apart in the whole Psalter. Brueggemann regards this as an "extravagant summons to praise" with an unreserved act of adoration, praise, gratitude, and awe.[83] Unlike other praise hymns, no reasons (absence of a causal clause ki) are mentioned in the psalm. Enough reasons have been given in the previous psalms in the Psalter. The illocutionary intent of the psalm is to burst forth the praise of YHWH at its climax. The placement of the psalm is perfect at the end of the Psalter.

---

81. According to Allen, the ending of the psalm has great parallels with the book of Revelation in the New Testament. He writes, "The psalm makes a closing statement in the Psalter like that of the book of Revelation in the NT when it pleads for the triumph of God's kingdom and the final overthrow of forces opposed to God and to the community of believers (Rev 19:1-8)." Allen, *Psalms 101-50*, 401.

82. Buttenwieser places Psalm 150 in the category of "didactic Psalms" alongside Psalms 1, 19, 37, 112, and 119, but he also regards this as doxology. Moses Buttenwieser, *The Psalms: Chronologically Treated with a New Translation* (Chicago: University of Chicago Press, 1938), 874. For a comprehensive structural analysis see Auffret, *Merveilles à nos yeux*, 284-86. Anderson regards the psalms as the concluding doxology of the whole Psalter. Bernhard W. Anderson, *Understanding the Old Testament* (4th ed.; Englewood Cliffs: Prentice-Hall, 1986), 545.

83. Brueggemann, *The Message*, 167.

VanGemeren divides the psalm into four sections, forming ABB´A´ pattern: A. Praise the Lord in heaven (v. 1); B. Praise the greatness of God (v. 2); B´. Praise the Lord with great intensity (vv. 3-5); A´. Praise the Lord on earth (v. 6).[84] VanGemeren rightly captures the emphasis on the intensity.

The psalm connects with Psalm 145 though numerous lexemes.[85] These lexemes contribute to the discourse meanings of the two psalms. Comparison of the discourse meaning of the two demonstrates the following thematic patterns.

(1) Both psalms praise YHWH for his might (גבורה) and his greatness (גדל; Ps 150:2; cf. Ps 145:4, 6).

(2) Both psalms anticipate universal praise. Notice the two phrases "all-flesh" (כל־בשׂר) and "all that has breath" (כל הנשׁמה; Ps 150:6; cf. Ps 145:21).

Thus, Psalm 150 gives final closure to Psalm 145 by affirming both the greatness of YHWH and the universal praise of YHWH.

Conclusion

In the discussions above, we noticed that Wilson's claims concerning the function of Ps 145:21 fail to capture the richness of the connections between Psalm 145 and the final *hallel* psalms.[86] Reading Psalm 145 in relation with the final *hallel* psalms compositionally enhances our understanding of some themes in four different ways. First, some themes are purposefully repeated for emphasis. For example, Psalm 146 reiterates the theme of YHWH's care for the weak—"YHWH raises up those who are bent down" (כפף / זקף; Ps 146:8; cf. Ps 145: 14). Second, other themes are explicated. Ps 147:9 explicates Ps 145:15 by informing us that YHWH feeds not only human beings, but also beasts. Ps 145:21 tells us that YHWH will destroy the wicked, but Ps 149:7-9 explains that the godly ones are the instrument in the hands of YHWH to execute his judgment. Third, other themes are

---

84. VanGemeren, "Psalms," 878.

85. The common lexemes between Psalms 150 and 145 are: הלל (Ps 150:1-6; cf. Ps 145:2); קדשׁ (Ps 150:1; cf. Ps 145:21); גבורה (Ps 150:2; cf. Ps 145:4); רב (Ps 150:2; cf. Ps 145:7); כל (Ps 150:2; cf. Ps 145:2, 9, 10, 13, 14, 15, 16, 17 18, 20, and 21); and ישׁמע (Ps 150:5; cf. Ps 145:19).

86. According to Siegfried Risse, Psalm 145 serves to prepare the way for the substance of praise in Psalms 146-50. Siegfried Risse, *Gut ist es, unserem Gott zu singen: Untersuchungen zu Psalm 147* (Altenberge: Oros Verlag, 1995), 199-216.

intensified. For example, the increased frequency of "Praise YHWH" in Psalms 148 and 150 suggests intensification. Fourth, there are themes that have no direct connections with Psalm 145, but they make sense when they are read in relation to the discourse of the Psalter. For example, the hope of Israel after the rejection in Psalm 89 apparently seems to be questionable. After reading the universal language of Psalm 145, one may wonder whether YHWH's "steadfast love" for all creation undermines his "steadfast love" for the people of Israel. Has YHWH rejected Israel (Psalms 89 and 108)? Psalms 146, 147, 148, and 149 tell us that Israel is part of his creation. YHWH builds Jerusalem. Allen rightly points out that "Psalm 145 sets out Yahweh's work in the realms of both the world and the covenant people."[87]

The Last Place

Considering the final *hallel* psalms as the doxology of the Psalter, we suggest that Psalm 145 is the last psalm of the fifth book of the Psalter, rather than the "climax" of the fifth book, or the Psalter proper. The following three textual evidences support this claim.

Inclusion-Like Feature
Psalm 145 forms both lexical and thematic *inclusion* with Psalm 107 in the fifth book, which suggests that Psalm 145 is the last psalm of the fifth book. Although the discourse meaning of Psalm 145 differs from Psalm 107, it shares a thematic concern that forms an *inclusion*. Notice the connection between Ps 107: 8, 15, 21, 31 and Ps 145:10.

107:8, 15. 21, 31   יודו ליהוה חסדו ונפלאותיו לבני אדם

Let them give thanks to the Lord
for his unfailing love and
his wonderful deeds for men,

---

87. Allen, *Psalms 101-50*, 77.

Ps 145:10   יודוך יהוה כל־מעשיך וחסידיך יברכוכה

All you have made shall give thanks to you,
O Lord, and your godly ones shall bless you.

Ps 145:12   להודיע | לבני האדם גבורתיו וכבוד הדר מלכותו

To declare your mighty acts to the sons of men
and the glorious majesty of your kingdom

Both psalms share universal language. It acknowledges YHWH's acts of
"steadfast love" for all men as well as anticipates thanksgiving from all men.
The phrase לבני האדם in Ps 145:12 alludes to the refrain לבני אדם in Ps 107:
8, 15, 21, and 31. Similarly the phrase יודוך יהוה in Ps 145:10 resonates to
the refrains in Ps 107:8, 15, 21, and 31 (יודו ליהוה). Both psalms introduce
YHWH as the savior (Ps 145:19, cf. Ps 107: 13, 19) of those who cry out
to him.

Lexical Features

A survey of the lexical connections of Psalm 145 in the Psalter tells us that
Psalm 145 is the last psalm for the following lexemes:

דוד	145:1
dna חקר מאד	145: 3
מעשה	145: 4
dna שׂיח פלא	145:5
עזז, אמר, dna ספר	145:6
זכר, נבע, dna צדקה	145:7
חנון, רחום, ארך, dna אף	145:8
רחמים dna מעשׂה	145:9
ידה	145:10
מלכות dna דבר	145:11
כבוד	145:12
ממשלה	145:13
סמך dna נפל	145:14
עין, אתה, אכל, dna עת	145:15

פתח, יד, ח, dna רצון	145:16
קרב	145:18
שועה dna ישע	145:19
שמד	145:20
פה dna בשר	145:21

These lexemes do not appear in the final *hallel* psalms. Since lexemes play a critical role in developing a theme, we suggest that thematic development based on these lexemes is final in Psalm 145.

Acrostic Feature

Psalm 145 is the last psalm of the fifth book because it combines a regular acrostic feature and the *inclusion* of "praise." Although Psalm 145 and the final hallel psalms connect with each other on the theme of the "praise" of YHWH, their distinct literary features clearly set them apart. Psalm 145 is one of the most regularly arranged acrostic psalms (א to ת). A number of scholars has made a remarkable observation concerning the "alphabetical thinking" in the Hebrew poetry.[88] Arguing from the same perspective, Anthony R. Ceresko claims that Psalm 150 has certain alphabetical features that support its placement as the last psalm in the Psalter.[89] Notice the bold alphabets in the text (MT).

---

88. Patrick W. Skehan was the first scholars to use the term "alphabetical thinking." He demonstrated the alphabetizing feature in the Song of Moses (Deut 32:1-43). The poem consists of 69 verses, which is equal to 3 times 23 Hebrew letters from א to ת. According to him, the word אלף in Deut 32:20 (איכה ירדף אחד אלף) indicates alphabetical thinking. He claims a similar feature in Psalms 74 and 94. Patrick W. Skehan, "Studies in Israelite Poetry and Wisdom," in *Catholic Biblical Quarterly Monograph Series* (CBQMS, Washington: Catholic Biblical Association, 1971), 75. Michael L. Barré also investigates alphabetical thinking in Psalms 1; 25; 37; 112; 119; Nah 1:2-9; Lamentations 1; 2; and 4. Michael L. Barré, "'Terminative' Terms in Hebrew Acrostics," in *Wisdom, You Are My Sister: Studies in Honor of Roland E. Murphy, O. Carm., on the Occasion of His Eightieth Birthday* (ed. Michael L. Barré; CBQMS, Washington, D.C.: Catholic Bible Association, 1997), 207-15. Victor Avigdor Hurowitz and Anthony R. Ceresko examines the alphabetizing in Psalm 34. See Victor Avigdor Hurowitz, "Additional Elements of Alphabetical Thinking in Psalm XXXIV," 52 (2002): 326-33; Anthony R. Ceresko, "The ABCs of Wisdom in Psalm XXXIV," *VT* 35 (1985): 99-104.

89. Anthony R. Ceresko, "Endings and Beginnings: Alphabetical Thinking and the Shaping of Psalms 106 and 150," *CBQ* 68 (2006): 42-44.

הללו יה | הללו־אל בקדשו הללוה ברקיע עזו   1

הללוהו בגבורתיו הללוהו כרב גדלו   2

הללוהו בתקע שופר הללוהו בנבל וכנור   3

הללוהו בתף ומחול הללוהו במנים ועוגב   4

הללוהו בצלצלי־שמע הללוהו בצלצלי תרועה   5

כל הנשמה תהלל יה הללו־יה   6

Ceresko draws our attention to a pattern of alphabetization (bold letters) in Psalm 150. He points out the Hebrew letter א in the phrase הללו־אל and ב in the phrase בקדשו and ברקיע in Ps 150:1. The use of divine name אל in the beginning instead of יה and the use of יה with the lexeme תהלל, which has letter ת at the end of the psalm in verse 6, are indicative of alphabetic thinking. The occurrence of תהלל יה in the final words of Psalm 150 is unique because it is the only occurrence (jussive form of הלל) in the whole Psalter. Thus, the opening with אל and the closing with תהלל יה in addition to other alphabetization in Psalm 150 support its placement as the last psalm in the Psalter.

Ceresko's argument is not very convincing. Alphabetical thinking alone could not be the only reason for the placement of Psalm 150 at the end of the Psalter, because there are other psalms, which have alphabetical thinking. We suggest Psalm 150 is the last psalm of the Psalter because it combines both alphabetical thinking and a distinct genre of "praise." Likewise, Psalm 145 also combines a very regular acrostic feature (א to ת) and the *inclusion* formed by "praise." This may be suggested a plausible reason for the placement of Psalm 145 as the last psalm in the fifth book.

Thematic Feature
Psalm 145 is the last psalm to use the Hebrew lexeme ידה. It is significant because ידה is the first lexeme in the fifth book. Notice all the occurrence of ידה in Book V.

הודו ליהוה כי־טוב כי לעולם חסדו   Ps 107:1

אודך בעמים | יהוה ואזמרך בל־אמים   Ps 108:4

הודו ליהוה כי־טוב כי לעולם חסדו   Ps 118:1

Ps 118:29	הודו ליהוה כי־טוב כי לעולם חסדו
Ps 136:1	הודו ליהוה כי־טוב כי לעולם חסדו
Ps 136:2	הודו לאלהי האלהים כי־טוב כי לעולם חסדו
Ps 136:3	הודו לאדני האדנים כי־טוב כי לעולם חסדו
Ps 136:26	הודו לאל השמים כי־טוב כי לעולם חסדו
Ps 138:1	לדוד ׀ אודך בכל־לבי נגד אלהים אזמרך
Ps 138:4	יודוך יהוה כל־מלכי־ארץ
Ps 145:10	יודוך יהוה כל־מעשיך וחסידיך יברכוכה

The use of ידה forms an *inclusion* in the fifth book. The first psalm com-
mands (notice the imperative) its audience to give thanks because YHWH's
"steadfast love" endures forever. To this imperatival statement David is first
to respond in the first Davidic psalm (Ps 108:4)—"I will give thanks (ידה)
to you, O Lord, among the peoples; and I will sing praises to you among
the nations." David continues in the first psalm of the second Davidic
group of psalms (Ps 138:1) with greater emphasis (*with all my heart*)—"I
will give you thanks *with all my heart*; I will sing praises to you before the
gods." First, he sings among the nations. Then, he sings before gods. In
Ps 138:4, he anticipates all the *kings of the earth* giving thanks to YHWH.
Finally, in Ps 145:10, he declares that all YHWH has made and all his saints
will give thanks to YHWH. In this thematic pattern, we notice an explicit
continuity of the theme of "thanksgiving" in the fabric of the fifth book.
Finally, the theme enlarges into a theme of "universal praise" and ends in
Psalm 145. Hence, concerning the theme of "thanksgiving" Psalm 145 is
the last psalm in the fifth book.

Doxological Features

Vincent claims that Psalm 145 is the concluding psalm of the fifth book because Ps 145:21 has remarkable connections with the doxologies of Books
I–IV.[90] He admits that Ps 145:21 does not use the phrase "God of Israel"
(אלהי ישראל) and "Amen" (אמן), but the use of the two phrases "blessing

---

90. M. A. Vincent, "The Shape of the Psalter: An Eschatological Dimension?" in *New
Heaven and New Earth Prophecy and the Millennium Essay in Honor of Anthony Gelston*
(Leiden: Brill, 1999), 61-82.

YHWH's holy name" and "forever" in all the doxologies are convincing evidence. Since Vincent observed the pattern in RSV, he failed to notice other important data in support of his argument. Notice the following doxologies and Ps 145:21 in the MT.

41:14	ברוך יהוה ׀ אלהי ישראל מהעולם ועד העולם
	אמן ׀ ואמן:
72:18-19	ברוך יהוה אלהים אלהי ישראל עשה נפלאות לבדו:
	וברוך שם כבודו לעולם וימלא כבודו את־כל הארץ
	אמן ׀ ואמן:
89:53	ברוך יהוה לעולם
	אמן ׀ ואמן:
106:48	ברוך־יהוה אלהי ישראל מן־העולם ׀ ועד העולם ואמר כל־העם
	אמן הללו־יה:
145:1	תהלה לדוד ארוממך אלוהי המלך ואברכה שמך לעולם ועד
145:2	בכל־יום אברכך ואהללה שמך לעולם ועד
145:10	יודוך יהוה כל־מעשיך וחסידיך יברכוכה:
145:21	תהלת יהוה ידבר־פי ויברך כל־בשר שם קדשו לעולם ועד

The use of lexeme for "blessing" (ברך) in the doxologies of Books I-III above is in passive form while in Psalm 145 it is imperfect. The connection that Vincent observed between Ps 145:21 and all the doxologies is also true for Ps 145:1 and 2 (YHWH is the implicit subject).

There are other striking features in Psalm 145 in comparison with the doxologies of Books I-IV that cannot be ignored. First, similar to Ps 145:1, 2, and 21, each of the doxology of Books I-IV (Pss 41:14; 72:18-19; 89:53, and 106:48) has YHWH as the object of the "blessing" (ברך) and the duration of the blessing is "forever" (לעולם).[91] Second, Psalm 145 is the only psalm which uses the Hebrew lexeme for "blessing" (ברך) four times (where

---

91. Patrick D. Miller also observes two striking features (ברך and לעולם) in Psalm 145 and suggests that the psalm is the concluding psalm in Book V. He writes, "So it is not quite accurate to say that Book V does not have a doxological ending like the other four books. Indeed it has one at the end of Psalm 145 that is very analogous to the ending of the other books and even seems to be a kind of *final* doxology, *le'ōlām wā'ed* three times in Psalm 145 and as the last words." Miller, "The End of the Psalter: A Response to Erich Zenger," 107.

YHWH is the object), two times with the phrase "forever" (לְעוֹלָם).[92] Third, the *inclusion* formed by the use of the Hebrew lexeme בְרךְ distinguishes the psalm as more closely connected to the language of the four doxological statements. Four, unlike Books I-IV, Book V does not have any doxology, nor does it have the closing word אמן. Fifth, the doxologies in Books I-III end with a double אמן, but the doxology of Book IV ends with the two lexemes אמן and הלל, indicating a shift in the language of doxology. Psalm 145 captures the shift by forming an *inclusion* of תהלת / תהלה (which is closely linked to the lexeme הלל) and paves the way to the final *hallel* psalms (Psalms 146-50).[93] These features suggest that Psalm 145 functions somewhat like a doxology in closing the fifth book in the Psalter.

Conclusion

Among several other findings in this chapter, five observations are note-worthy for our conclusion. First, a taxonomical classification of the psalms to provide an overarching structure for the editorial function and purpose of the Psalter may defy the literary richness of its composition. Wilson's "Final Wisdom Frame" for sapiential reading of the Psalter is one among such example. Second, Wilson's claims concerning the editorial placement of Psalm 145 are flimsy and lack exegetical data. At the macro-level, the placement of Psalm 145 in the "Final Wisdom Frame" and its function as the "climax" of the fifth book may seem insightful, but a micro-level analy-sis of the psalms exposes the discrepancy in his claims. Psalm 145 is not a wisdom psalm, but it is composed of multiple genres. It does not function as a "climax" (pinnacle) of the fifth book, but as the last psalm in the Psalter. Placed in the last position, it provides a transition between the closing of the fifth book and the initiation of the final *hallel* psalms.

Third, its literary features connect to its neighboring psalms on both sides. As the last Davidic psalm, it links with the Davidic group of psalms

---

92. Although the Hebrew lexeme בְרךְ occurs in Ps 147:3, the objects of the blessing are children and the phrase לְעוֹלָם is absent.

93. Anderson points out that in the later Jewish usage Psalms 145-50 were described as the Hallel hymns. Anderson, *The Book of Psalms*, 940.

(Psalms 138-44). At the same time, it has *inclusion* formed by "praise" (תהלת / תהלה), which links it to the group of final *hallel* psalms. The psalm functions like *Janus* looking backward to Davidic groups of psalms, as well as forward to the final *hallel* psalms.

Fourth, it is important to recognize the complex nature of the relationship between Psalm 145 and the collection of the final *hallel* psalms, and the richness of perspective their collective reading provides. Wilson's claim that the final *hallel* psalms are a response to Ps 145:21 is only one aspect of the observation. Numerous lexical and thematic connections between Psalm 145 and the final *hallel* psalms show other thematic continuity, patterns, and development that demands a "thick reading" of these psalms together. For example, in Ps 145:15, YHWH gives (נתן) food at the proper time to those who look to him, but in Ps 147:9, he also provides (נתן) food for the cattle and for the young ravens. In Psalm 145, YHWH will destroy the wicked, but in Psalm 149 the godly ones are the instrument in the hands of YHWH.

Finally, reading Psalm 145 in relation to the final *hallel* psalms suggests that Israel is part of the universal plan of YHWH. The hope of Israel is still effective. YHWH builds Jerusalem (Ps 147:2).

CHAPTER 5

David in the Kingdom of God

In the previous chapter, we established that the lexical and thematic connections between the last Davidic psalm (Psalm 145) and the final *hallel* psalms reveal numerous thematic patterns. These patterns enhance our understanding of the editorial arrangement of the last Davidic psalm in relation to the final *hallel* psalms in the Psalter. Nonetheless, the questions arise: why Psalm 145 is placed at the end of the last Davidic group of psalms in the MT. How does it connect to the two groups of Davidic psalms (Psalms 108-110 and 138-44) in Book V?[1] Why is king David depicted here addressing YHWH as the King? Apparently, the image of David at the beginning of the fifth book of the Psalter is sad. He is complaining of rejection (זנח; Ps 108:12) and crying for help (עזרה; Ps 108:13). However, at the end of the book he proclaims YHWH's faithfulness (אמן; Ps 145:13f) and his everlasting Kingdom (מלכות כל־עלמים; Ps 145:13). He is in the *presence* of the glorious King (הדר כבוד הודך; Ps 145:5). He proclaims YHWH's goodness and greatness, and anticipates "all-flesh" (כל־בשׂר; Ps 145:21) will praise him. What is the significance of this editorial arrangement? There are several possible approaches to investigate these questions. However, considering the limitation of this research, we will use two methods, which are the most relevant to the questions raised here. First, since Psalm 145 is a Davidic psalm, we will analyze the discourse meaning of each of the two Davidic groups of psalms (Psalms 108-10 and 138-44) in relation to Psalm 145. We will examine all thematic patterns emerging from this comparison

---

1. The question is raised only in relation with the two Davidic groups of psalm in the fifth book because most scholars agree that the four individual Davidic psalms in Book V are part of an earlier existing collection of the Ascent psalms.

to suggest reasons for the placement of this specific message in David's mouth and at the end of the Psalter. Second, we will investigate the possible illocutionary intent of the motif of the Kingdom of God in the psalms in relation to the YHWH Kingship psalms in Book IV. In chapter 3, we established that the theme of the Kingdom of God is central to Psalm 145. Most psalms scholars agree that Kingship of YHWH is the central theme of the Book IV.[2] One may wonder how Psalm 145 thematically connects to Book IV. Why is it placed at the end of the Davidic group of psalms in the fifth book instead in Book IV? Answering these questions will be the goal of this chapter.

The Davidic Psalms

Wilson claims the placement of the two Davidic groups of psalms (Psalms 108-10 and 138-45) at the beginning and end of Book V implies a purposeful editorial arrangement.[3] According to him, David in the first group of Davidic psalms is presented as the "wise man" who pays attention to the warning in Ps 107:39-42 and shows his absolute dependence on YHWH's steadfast love (חסד). He desires to sing the praises of YHWH among the nations (Ps 108:3), which becomes a "paradigm" of action to be followed both by the exilic community and the postexilic community living in hostility. David models for them an absolute reliance on YHWH, because the help of man is worthless (Ps 108:13; cf. Ps 146:3). Surrounded by his enemies, David does not despair but trusts YHWH. YHWH stands at the right hand of the needy (Ps 109:22, 31). He delivers David from those who condemn him to death (Ps 109:26-31). Thus, YHWH confirms David's trust with divine protection, dealing with his enemies (Ps 110:1). Likewise, in the second group of Davidic psalms, David models the paradigm of

---

2. Wilson claims Book IV is the center of the Psalter because of its language of the Kingdom of God. Mays also claims that the center of the Psalter is "The Lord reigns." See Gerald Henry Wilson, *The Editing of the Hebrew Psalter* (Chico: Scholars Press, 1985), 215; James Luther Mays, *The Lord Reigns: A Theological Handbook to the Psalms* (Louisville: Westminster John Knox, 1994), 12-22.

3. Wilson, *The Editing*, 221-22.

a bold witness of YHWH, especially for the exilic community. After the plaintive cry in Psalm 137 (How shall we sing YHWH's song in a foreign land?), David is presented bursting forth with praises "before the gods" and "toward your holy temple" (Ps 138:1-3). David represents the piety of Daniel, who even in exile turned his face toward the temple in Jerusalem on a daily basis to pray to YHWH. David praises YHWH in any land, because he anticipates all the kings of the earth will praise YHWH. All will sing that YHWH's glory is great (Ps 138:4-5).

Wilson's insight on David as a "paradigm" for the exilic and postexilic community is significant; however, it lacks a comprehensive discourse analysis of each psalm whose texts are linked. He selects the above texts arbitrarily and ignores the major portions of each psalm. It is not clear how the "paradigm" of David in Psalm 145 connects with the two groups of Davidic psalms to draw a story line of David and to suggest a purposeful placement of the Davidic psalms in the fifth book. In absence of a thorough discourse analysis of the "paradigm" of David in each Davidic psalm, Wilson's claims remain flimsy. Our intention is to compare the discourse analysis of each of these Davidic psalms and examine their relationships in order to suggest a purposeful placement of Psalm 145.

The Paradigm of David

The "paradigm" of David is a post-critical "intertextual reality" which has made its way into the study of the Davidic psalms and the psalms that mention David.[4] James L. Mays is one among the recent proponents of this approach. He argues:

> Yet simply to negate the notion of David of the Psalms because
> it is unhistorical or to eliminate texts like the psalms' titles (as
> the NEB does) because they are secondary dissolves the intra-
> textual context created for understanding the text and breaks

---

4. Childs was one among the earliest proponents for reading the Davidic titles in the context of the pietistic circle of Jews. He writes, "David's inner life was now unlocked to the reader, who was allowed to hear his intimate thoughts and reflections. It therefore seems most probable that the formation of the titles stemmed from a pietistic circle of Jews whose interest was particularly focused on the nurture of the spiritual life." Brevard S. Childs, "Psalm Titles and Midrashic Exegesis," *JSS* 16 (1971): 149.

the connection between texts and the church's continuous tradition about them.[5]

According to him, the "postcritical" approach accommodates historical,
literary, and canonical values. In his dissertation, Yohanna Katanacho also
argues the case for "intra-textual," literary, and theological significance of
the image of David in the Psalter.[6] In his literary review, he engages with the
thoughts of several scholars in discussions to make a case for building an
image of David based on the superscript in the psalms.[7] In his conclusion,
he suggests a "thick understanding" of the text, which incorporates insights
gained from both "pre-critical" and "post-critical" approaches, neither excluding the possibility of a historical David, nor editorial input. Neither of
the approaches by itself can address the "diverse spatiotemporal textual data
in the Psalter that reflects not only Davidic times but also postexilic times."[8]
Since the Davidic superscriptions have a compositional function in the
characterization of David, the editorial understanding of these superscriptions would require "a theological analysis of the various images of David as
well as the correspondences between these images."[9] With this assumption,

---

5. James Luther Mays, "The David of the Psalms," *Int* 40 (1986): 154.

6. Katanacho reviews literatures that provide a canonical portrait of David. His findings
suggest that each of the books of the Old Testament portray David in a specific way,
hence the portrayal of the David of the Psalter would pave the way for understanding the
canonical portrait of David. Yohanna Katanacho, "Investigating the Purposeful Placement
of Psalm 86," (Ph.D. thesis, Trinity International University, 2006), 170-86.

7. The study on the image of David has engaged many scholars in the last three decades.
See Mays, "The David of the Psalms," 143-55; P. Kyle McCarter, "The Historical David,"
Int 40 (1986): 117-29; Steven McKenzie, "Who Was King David?" *WW* 23 (2003):
357-64; Marti Steussy, "David, God, and the Word," *WW* 23 (2003): 365-73; Mark
Throntveit, "Was the Chronicler a Spin Doctor? David in the Books of Chronicles," 23
(2003): 374-81; Frederick Gaiser, "The David of Psalm 51: Reading Psalm 51 in Light of
Psalm 50," *WW* 23 (2003): 382-94; Tony Cartledge, "A House for God and a House for
David," *WW* 23 (2003): 395-402; Diane Jacobson, "And Then There Were the Women
in His Life: David and His Women," *WW* 23 (2003): 403-12; Ernst Waschke, "The
Significance of the David Tradition for the Emergence of Messianic Beliefs in the Old
Testament," *WW* 23 (2003): 413-20; J. Luyten, "David and the Psalms," in *The Psalms:
Prayers of Humanity, Prayers of Israel, Prayers of the Church* (ed. Lambert Leijssen; Leuven:
Abdij Keizerberg, 1990), 57-59.

8. Katanacho, "Placement of Psalm 86," 185.

9. Ibid., 186. Melody D. Knowles has described the portrait of David in Psalms 78, 89
and 132. She writes, "The significance of recognizing such flexibility in the rhetoric of
the topos lies, in part, in analyzing claims as to why particular motifs used in particular

we will move forward to investigate the "paradigm" of David in the two Davidic groups of psalms in Book V. Then we will compare each of them with the "paradigm" of David in Psalm 145 to understand its placement.

Psalm 108[10]

Psalm 108 is composed of two parts (vv. 1-5 and 6-13),[11] which are duplicates of the second half of other two psalms: Pss 57:8-12 and 60:7-14.[12] The former has the context of an individual lament, but the latter is introduced with a complaint against God's anger and rejection. Together in Psalm 108, they assume a new context for interpretation.[13] Anderson names the first part the "thanksgiving," while the second part the "Oracle of Hope" and the "Prayer for Help."[14] According to Allen, the vow of thanksgiving (vv. 2-4) is placed next to the remembrance of divine love (v. 5); while the prayer for God's deliverance (vv. 6-7) is placed before the divine oracle (vv. 11-12).[15] The questions concerning the implicit appeal for God's help (vv. 11-12) end in prayer (v. 13) and a proclamation of absolute trust in YHWH (v. 14).

---

psalms, and in more fully apprehending the scope of the Psalter." She concludes, "Although they [Psalms 78, 89, and 132] are shaped by their canonical proximity to other psalms that include the same topos, each of the three psalms contains a discrete version separately available for distinct liturgical purpose." Melody D. Knowles, "The Flexible Rhetoric of Retelling: The Choice of David in the Text of the Psalms," *CBQ* 67 (2005): 248-49.

10. Since a detailed textual critical analysis of each of the Davidic psalm (Psalm 108-10 and 138-44) is beyond the limit of this dissertation, the position advocated here is indebted to Leslie C. Allen and Willem A. VanGemeren. See Leslie C. Allen, *Psalms 101-50* (WBC 21; Nashville: Nelson, 2002); Willem A. VanGemeren, "Psalms," in *Psalms, Proverbs, Ecclesiastes, Song of Songs* (ed. Frank E. Gæbelein; EBC 5, Grand Rapids: Zondervan, 1991).

11. The new combination of earlier psalms illustrates the editorial activity and the "vitality of the older Scriptures" to address the new historical situation of the people of God. God's word is living, which speaks to a listening audience in a different contexts through different combinations and shape. Allen, *Psalms 101-50*, 96.

12. For a detailed structural analysis of Psalms 57, 60 and 108 see Pierre Auffret, *Voyez de vos yeux: étude structurelle de vingt psaumes dont le psaume 119* (VTSup 48; Leiden: Brill, 1993).

13. Allen, *Psalms 101-50*, 93-94. VanGemeren, "Psalms," 689.

14. Anderson divides the second part into two sections (vv. 8-10 and 11-14) but verse 7 in included in the first part. Bernhard W. Anderson, *The Book of Psalms* (NCBC; 2 vols.; Grand Rapids: Eerdmans, 1981a), 1: 443-45.

15. Allen, *Psalms 101-50*, 94.

In verses 2-4, David is a singer (אשירה ואזמרה) and a musician (הנבל
וכנור). He sings praises and thanksgiving (אודך). In verse 5, he explains the
reason for his praise (notice the causal *ki*): YHWH's steadfast love (חסד)
and faithfulness (אמת) is greater than the heavens. In verse 6, David desires to see God exalted (רום) above the cosmos (על־שמים) and over all the
earth (כל־הארץ).[16] In verse 7, he explains the purpose (notice למען): So that
God's beloved (ידיד) may have deliverance and his right hand may save
them (ישע). In verses 8-10, David hears God speaking in the sanctuary declaring his dominion throughout Shechem, the Valley of Succoth, Gilead,
Ephraim, Judah, Moab, Edom, and Philistia (vv. 8-10). It is good news of
hope for David. Perhaps, for this reason, he is confident (נכון לבי, v. 2) in
God.[17] He is confident that YHWH will give victory (באלהים נעשה־חיל, v.
14) and he will trample down (יבוס, v. 14) their enemy (צר, v. 14). Notice
that the "confidence of David" forms a thematic inclusion in the psalm.
The confidence is necessary because the situation of David and his people is
grim. In verse 12, they face rejection and abandonment (הלא־אלהים זנחתנו
ולא־תצא אלהים בצבאתינו). In the midst of the rejection, David anticipates
YHWH's cosmic exaltation and his dominion over all the earth. God's oracle must happen, because it would bring deliverance to David and to his
people.

Psalm 108 is connected to Psalm 145 lexically and thematically.[18] These
lexemes contribute in its syntactic, paradigmatic, semantic, and pragmatic context to formulate a discourse meaning unique to the psalms. A

---

16. Allen quotes J. Becker who points out how in these verses the whole is more than the
part. Verses 4 and 6 use the material from Psalm 60 with a new universal dimension. The
coming of different nationalities points to an eschatological relationship between Israel
and the nations. Ibid. See also Joachim Becker, *Israel deutet seine Psalmen* (Stuttgart: Verlag
Katholisches Bibelwerk, 1966), 65-67.

17. Allen asserts that the single appearance of "my heart is steadfast" in contrast to double
in Ps 57:8 represent haplography. Allen, *Psalms 101-50*, 93. Kraus prefers to read יהוה
instead of אלהים. Hans-Joachim Kraus, *Psalms 60-150: A Continental Commentary* (trans.
Hilton C. Oswald; Minneapolis: Fortress, 1989), 333.

18. The following lexemes occur in both the psalms: כבוד (Ps 108:2, 6, cf. Ps 145:5, 11
and 12); ידה (Ps 108:4, cf. Ps 145:10); גדול (Ps 108:5, cf. Ps 145:3, 6, and 8); חסד (Ps
108:5. cf. Ps 145:8); אמת (Ps 108:5, cf. Ps 145:18); רום (Ps 108:6, cf. Ps. 145:1); אלהים
(Ps 108: 2, 6, 8, 12, and 14. cf. Ps 145:1); כל (Ps 108:6, cf. Ps 145: 2, 9, 10, 13, 14, 15,
16, 17 18, 20, and 21); ישע (Ps 108:7, cf. Ps 145:19); דבר (Ps 108:8, Ps 145:5, 11, and
21); קדש (Ps 108:8, cf. Ps 145:21); אדם (Ps 108:13, cf. Ps 145:12); and עשה (Ps 108:14,
cf. Ps 145:19).

comparison of the discourse meaning in the two psalms shows some similarities: David is bold and confident. He praises YHWH. He desires to see YHWH exalted in the cosmos. In both psalms, the theme of thanksgiving (ידה) is explicit. However, the dissimilarities are also remarkable:

Psalm 108	Psalm 145
David *sings* and make music (vv. 1-2)	David *praises* everyday and forever (vv. 1-2)
David gives thanks (ידה) to YHWH among *nations* (v. 3)	All creation gives thanks (ידה) to YHWH (v. 10)
David alone praises among the nations and the people	One generation will tell it to another (v. 4)
David regards YHWH's steadfast love (חסד) and faithfulness (אמת) as greater than the heavens and skies (v. 5)	David regards YHWH to be gracious, and compassionate (ורחום חנון), slow to anger, and abounding in his steadfast love (חסד); He is faithful (אמן) in all his words (דבר) (vv. 8, 13f)
David desires to see YHWH exalted in the cosmos (v. 6)	David proclaims that YHWH's Kingdom is everlasting and his dominion continues through all generations. (v. 13)
David seeks the glory (כבוד) of YHWH over *all the earth* (v. 6)	All men will speak of the glorious (כבוד)splendor of YHWH's Kingdom and his power (v. 11)
David anticipates deliverance (ישע) of YHWH's beloved (ידיד) (v. 7)	David anticipates the salvation (ישע) of those who fear him (ירא) (v. 19)
David hears YHWH speak (דבר) (v. 8)	YHWH is silent

YHWH himself declares his dominion over other nations through an oracle (vv. 8-9)	David knows YHWH's dominion over all (v. 13)
David is lamenting from a situation of rejection (זנח) and abandonment (לא־תצא) (v. 12)	David praises throughout
He is waiting for help (עזרה) from YHWH (v. 13)	He anticipates YHWH's universal praise (v. 21)
David anticipates YHWH will trample (בוס) his enemies (צר) (v. 14)	David is confident that YHWH will destroy the wicked (v. 21)
David is concerned for his salvation as well as the salvation of YHWH's beloved (ידיד) (vv. 6, 13)	David is concerned with the proclamation of YHWH's Kingdom (vv. 11-13)

On the one hand, Psalm 145 echoes the themes of Psalm 108, forming an *inclusion* for Book V. On the other hand, they paint two different pictures of David. In Psalm 108, he is lamenting his rejection (זנח) and abandonment (ולא־תצא אלהים בצבאתינו). He is pleading for help (עזרה) and salvation (תשועה) for himself and for YHWH's 'beloveds' (ידיד). Human help to him is worthless (שוא). YHWH gives him an oracle, which brings hope, but the victory is still on the way. He hopes that YHWH will trample (בוס) his enemies (צר). It is implicit that the situation of David and his people in Psalm 145 is no longer grim. In fact, he is now concerned with the proclamation of YHWH's attributes and his universal praise. In Psalm 108, David alone gives thanks (ידה) to YHWH, but in Psalm 145 all creation is anticipated to give thanks (ידה). Comparison of the images of David in these two psalms suggests that the placement of Psalm 108 before Psalm 145 is fitting.

Psalm 109

Psalm 109 follows the pattern of an individual lament, but it also contains the aspects of a hymn of praise and a song of complaint. It is one of those imprecatory psalms,[19] which is difficult to interpret in light of the New Testament teachings (Mark 12:28-34; Matt 5:43-48; and Rom 12:17, 21) that we should love our enemies.[20] Because of its complex genre and difficult Hebrew text, scholars differ concerning its literary divisions.[21] Allen divides the psalm into two major halves: verses 1-19 and 20-31. Each half is subdivided into two strophes: 1-5 and 6-19, 20-25 and 26-31. For him, the stylistic features of the psalm reinforce the form and the meaning; however, they do not resolve the exegetical problem of the connection between verses 6-19 and 26-31.[22] VanGemeren divides the psalm into six thematic sections (vv. 1, 2-5, 6-15, 16-20, 21-29, and 30-31) in ABCB'C'A' pattern.[23]

According to Dahood, the David of Psalm 109 is an "aged person," but a very able poet.[24] His poetical ability is evident in the complex literary features. But for Brueggemann, the David of the psalm is a realist who enjoys freedom in the covenant bond of YHWH.[25]

---

19. Kraus names the psalm "Petition for deliverance from the curse of the enemies." According to him, the setting of the psalm is sanctuary. Kraus, *Psalms 60-150*, 339.

20. Martin J. Ward, "Psalm 109: David's Poem of Vengeance," *AUSS* 18 (1980): 163-68; Walter Brueggemann, *The Message of the Psalm* (Minneapolis: Augsberg, 1984), 81-89. Brueggemann thinks that the absence of the "steadfast-love" evokes the rage of the psalmist, because YHWH is the ultimate agent of justice. Walter Brueggemann, "Psalm 109: Three Times 'Steadfast Love'," *WW* 2 (2006): 144-54.

21. Dahood writes, "A perplexing Hebrew text makes it difficult to identify with certainty the dramatis personae and the sequence of action in this lament of an individual." See Mitchell Dahood, *Psalm III: 101-150* (AB 17A; 3 vols.; New York: Doubleday, 1970), 99.

22. Allen, *Psalms 101-50*, 101. Thijs Booij argues for the unity of the psalm and against the view that verses 6-19 to be a quotation of the adversaries against the psalmist. See Thijs Booij, "Psalm 109:6-19 as a Quotation: A Review of the Evidence," in *Give Ear to My Words: Psalms and Other Poetry in and Around the Hebrew Bible: Essays in Honour of Professor N.A. van Uchelen* (ed. Janet Dyk; Amsterdam: Kok Pharos, 1996), 91-106.

23. The six-fold structure has a reverse chiastic pattern that mirrors to each other in ABCB'C'A' pattern: A. Invocation to the God of Praise (v. 1); B. The Words and Acts of the Ungodly (vv. 2-5); C. Imprecation (vv. 6-15); B'. The Acts and Words of the Ungodly (vv. 16-20); C'. Prayer for God's Love and Judgment (vv. 21-29); A'. Benediction of the God of Praise (vv. 30-31). See VanGemeren, "Psalms," 689.

24. Dahood, *Psalm III*, 99.

25. Brueggemann writes, "On the one hand, this is, as elsewhere, faithful covenant speech, disciplined by the norms expectations of covenant. This inclination gives the psalm its overall shape. But alongside this, and not very well integrated into it, is a second kind

In verses 2-5, David is verbally abused by the wicked (רשע), deceitful men (מרמה), and liars (לשון שקר). He is hated (שנאה) and attacked (לחם). He has been treated unfairly. His goodness is returned with evil and hatred (רעה תחת טובה ושנאה תחת אהבתי). Therefore, David pleads for the vengeance of YHWH against his enemies. In verse 20, he anticipates the punishment of his adversaries from God (פעלת שטני מאת יהוה). In verse 21, he asks YHWH to deliver him for his name's (שם) sake and out of his "steadfast love" (חסד). He explains why YHWH must answer his prayers (notice the causal *ki* in verses 21-22, 31). He is confident of YHWH's deliverance because he is the poor and needy (אביון) and his heart is wounded (חלל). And YHWH stands (עמד) beside the needy (אביון) and saves (ישע) them. Nonetheless, amidst this gloomy situation, David is a man of praise (notice in verses 2 and 30, the inclusion formed by תהלה and הלל) as well as a man of prayer (תפלה, v. 4), who expresses his absolute dependence on YHWH for his vengeance.

Psalm 109 shares several lexemes with Psalm 145.[26] These lexemes contribute a unique discourse meaning in each psalm. A comparison of the discourse meaning in the two psalms shows some similarities. In both psalms, David starts and ends with "praise" (Ps 109:1, 30, cf. Ps 145: 1-2, 21). He uses his "mouth" to praise YHWH (Ps 109:30; cf. Ps 145:21). He remembers the steadfast love of YHWH (Ps 109: 21, 26; cf. Ps 145:8). He expects YHWH to deal with the wicked (Ps 109:6, 7; cf. Ps 145:20). At the same time, there are some differences in the thematic patterns of the two psalms.

---

of speech, not disciplined, not focused on Yahweh, not shaped by covenant—simply a *free, unrestrained speech of rage seeking vengeance*. . . . Thus the speech is an opportunity for realism that gives freedom of expression to those raw edges in our life that do not easily submit to the religious conviction we profess on good days." Brueggemann, *The Message*, 85.

26. The common lexemes are: תהלה (Ps 109:1; cf. Ps 145:1); פה (Ps 109:2, 30; cf. Ps 145:21); רשע (Ps 109:2, 6-7; cf. Ps 145:20); דבר (Ps 109:2-3; Ps 145:5, 11, 21); טוב (Ps 109:5, 21; Ps 145:7); על (Ps 109:2, 5, 6, 20; cf. Ps 145:9); יום (Ps 109:8; cf. Ps 145:2); בן (Ps 109:9-10; cf. Ps 145:12); דור (Ps 109:13; cf. Ps 145:4); שם (Ps. 109:13, 21; cf. Ps 145:1); ברך (Ps. 109:24, 28, cf. Ps 145:1); כל (Ps 109:11; cf. Ps 145:2, 9, 10, 13, 14, 15, 16, 17 18, 20, and 21); זכר (Ps 109:14-16; cf. Ps 145:7); חסד (Ps 109:12, 16, 21, 26; cf. Ps 145:8); אהב (Ps 109:17; cf. Ps 145:20); עשה (Ps 109:16, 21, 27; cf. Ps 145:19); בשר (Ps 109:24; cf. Ps 145:21); ישע (Ps 109:26, 31; cf. Ps 145:19); ידע (Ps 109:27; cf. Ps 145:12); יד (Ps 109:27. cf. Ps 145:16); ידה (Ps 109:30; cf. Ps 145:10); מאד (Ps 109:30; cf. Ps 145:3); רב (Ps 109:30; cf. Ps 145:7); and הלל (Ps 109:30; cf. Ps 145:1-3, 21).

Psalm 109	**Psalm 145**
David praises (הלל) YHWH with complain against the wicked (vv. 29-30)	David praises (הלל) YHWH with confidence (vv. 1-3, 21)
David elaborates the actions of the wicked (רשע) against him and their evil character (vv. 2-5, 16-18)	
David wishes his adversaries to have a difficult life (vv. 8-15)	David declares that YHWH is good to all, his compassion is over all he has made (v. 9)
David pleads and anticipates that YHWH will deal with the wicked (vv. 6-7, 15, 20)	David knows YHWH will destroy the wicked (v. 20)
David pleads with YHWH to deliver him for his *name's sake* and for the goodness of his *steadfast love* so that his adversaries will know that YHWH has done it (vv. 21, 26, 27)	All will make known the glorious Kingdom of YHWH and his power (vv. 11-13)
David is *poor and needy*, he is week and emaciated, he has become an object of scorn (vv. 22-25)	David is the announcer of YHWH's greatness and goodness Implicitly his situation is good (vv. 3-10)

Some themes exist in both psalms with similar semantics. These themes bind them together. On the other hand, the themes in which they differ complement each other building a fuller perspective. For example, David describes in detail the action and the character of the wicked in Psalm 108. This supplies a better understanding of the wicked in Psalm 145 who will be destroyed by YHWH. David in Psalm 108 is waiting for YHWH to act, but implicitly YHWH, in Psalm 145, is no longer silent. He is already a reigning great King whose goodness reaches to all he has made. David testifies to his mighty acts. David is no longer occupied with his troubled situation, but he is actively engaged in the proclamation of YHWH, anticipating universal praise for YHWH. The situation of David in Psalm 145 is improved from his situation described in Psalm 109.

Psalm 110

Traditionally, Psalm 110 is classified as the royal psalm.[27] It is one of the "most frequently quoted and alluded to in the NT."[28] Consensus on the historical critical issues concerning the psalm is not reached.[29] However, the literary analysis of the psalm has brought some consensus among scholars concerning its textual difficulties. The text in the *Biblia Hebraica Stuttegartensia* suggests numerous emendations in verses 3, 6 and 7. Willem van der Meer resolves these issues by determining the literary structure.[30] He analyzes the psalm in terms of two canticles [verses 1 -3 (except the superscript) and 4-7], each of which is subdivided into three strophes (vv.

---

27. Mowinckel classifies the following psalms as the royal psalms: Psalms 2; 18; 20; 21; 28; 45; 61; 63; 72; 89; 101: 110; and 132. Sigmund Mowinckel, *The Psalms in Israel's Worship* (New York: Abingdon, 1962), 47. A. Bnetzen and Johnson link this psalm with the New Year festival. Aage Bentzen, *King and Messiah* (London: Lutterworth Press, 1955), 23-25; Aubrey R. Johnson, *Sacral Kingship in Ancient Israel* (Cardiff: Wales, 1967), 130-32. For a detailed literary analysis see P Auffret, "Il est seigneneur sur les nations: Etude structurelle du psaume 110," *BN* 123 (2004): 65-73.

28. John Aloisi, "Who Is David's Lord? Another Look at Psalm 110:1," *DBSJ* 10 (2005): 103. See also David R. Anderson, *The King-Priest of Psalm 110 in Hebrews* (New York: Peter Lang, 2001), 87-113. Edward J. Kissane, "The Interpretation of Psalm 110," *ITQ* 21 (1954): 104-10.

29. Allen, *Psalms 101-50*, 111-12. See also Bentzen, *King and Messiah*; Johnson, *Sacral Kingship in Ancient Israel*; H. H. Rowley, "Melchizedek and Zadok," in *Festschrift für Alfred Bertholet zum 80 Geburtstag* (ed. Otto Eissfeldt Walter Baumgartner, Karl Elliger, and Leonhard Rost; Tübingen: Mohr, 1950). For a detail survey on the settings on the psalm. See Dwight Dongwan Kim, "Is Christ Sitting on the Davidic Throne? Peter's Use of Psalm 110:1 in His Pentecostal Speech Acts 2," (Th.D. thesis, Dallas Theological Seminary, 1993), 26-36; David Allan Jones, "A Theology of Psalm 110," (Th.M. thesis, Dallas Theological Seminary, 1981), 10-22.

30. Willem van der Meer, "Psalm 110: A Psalm of Rehabilitation," in *The Structural Analysis of Biblical and Canaanite Poetry* (ed. Willem van der Meer and Johannes C. de Moor; Sheffield: JSOT Press, 1988), 207-34.

1+2+3 and 4+5+6).[31] Except for Kraus, who claims three divisions (vv. 1-2, 3-4, and 5-7), most scholars agree with two divisions based on two oracles.[32]

The primary question of interpretation in the psalm is the identity of the "Lord" in verse 1—Who is David's Lord? Is he David, or his son Solomon, or the Messiah? Conservative psalms scholars argue for a messianic interpretation.[33] Since David is democratized in the psalm, our quest in the psalm is not historical, but an exegetical one: whether there is any pattern in the pedagogical image of David.

In the psalm, David assumes the role of a prophet. He narrates two oracles (vv. 1 and 4) from YHWH concerning his Lord (אדון). Both the oracles contain a promise for David's Lord. In the first promise, YHWH tells David's Lord to sit at his right hand until he subdues his enemies under him. YHWH will extend his dominion beyond Zion and he will rule over his enemies. He will have an army who will be willing to fight for him. In the first oracle, it is implied that David's Lord is a theocratic king, who will enjoy the favor of YHWH. He will have dominion beyond Zion and have a strong and willing army. In the second oracle (vv. 4-7), YHWH gives David an irrevocable oath for his Lord, the theocratic king. The king will assume the office of a priest (כהן) in the order of Melchizedek (מלכי־צדק).[34] YHWH will be at his right hand. He will judge the nations and crush the kings of all the earth (על־ארץ רבה). As a result, the king will quench his

---

31. van der Meer develops his approach by analyzing the work of Auffret and Kunz. He points out that Auffret's two sections division pays less attention to the literary aspect, while Kunz's method places too much emphasis on the masoretic accents. Ibid., 209-22, 30-33. See also P. Auffret, "Note sur la structure littéraire du Psaume," *Sem* 32 (1982): 83-88; L. Kunz, "Psalm 110 in masoretischer Darbietung," *TGl* 72 (1982): 331-35.

32. Kraus, *Psalms 60-150*, 346. Allen, *Psalms 101-50*, 113-14; VanGemeren, "Psalms," 697.

33. Aloisi comments, "The NT shows that Jesus and the apostles considered Psalm 110:1 to be a prophecy about the Messiah. Jewish leaders who interacted with Jesus on this subject and those who heard Peter's sermon on the Day of Pentecost also appear to have held this view." Aloisi, "Who Is David's Lord? Another Look at Psalm 110:1," 123. See also Derek Kidner, *Psalms 73-150: A Commentary on Books III-V of the Psalms* (London: Inter-Varsity Press, 1975), 392; Elliott E. Johnson, "Hermeneutical Principles and the Interpretation of Psalm 110," *BSac* 149 (1992): 428-37; Herbert W. Bateman IV, "Psalm 110:1 and the New Testament," *BSac* 149 (1992): 438-53.

34. Although the office of king and priest were a separate office, David and Solomon performed both roles. See VanGemeren, "Psalms," 699.

thirst from the brook and lift up his head in victory. Thus, the psalm is a psalm of hope for David and for the people of Zion.

Psalm 110 is connected to Psalm 145 both lexically and thematically. The lexical analysis shows that both psalms share very few lexemes.[35] These lexemes uniquely contribute to their syntactic, paradigmatic, semantic, and pragmatic meaning to provide the unique discourse meaning in the psalm. Comparisons of the discourse meaning in the two psalms demonstrate some similarities. In both psalms, David as a king talks about another King. He has a personal relationship with the King [Ps 110:1; cf. Ps 145:1 ("my" Lord/"my" God, the King)]; Both psalms talk about the rule of the coming King (Ps 110:2; cf. Ps 145:13), and about YHWH's judgment (Ps 110:5; cf. Ps 145:20). At the same time, a comparison of the discourse meaning of the two psalms reveals the dissimilarities between the two psalms.

Psalm 110	Psalm 145
YHWH tells David about his Lord (אדון), whose rule is not a present reality (v. 1)	YHWH is the reigning King (המלך) (v. 1)
YHWH will subdue (הדם) the enemies of David's Lord, (David's King is implied) (v. 1)	YHWH will destroy (שמד) all the wicked (כל־הרשעים) (v. 20)
Finally, YHWH will crush (מחץ) other kings; He will judge (דין) the nations (גוי), crushing the rulers of the whole earth—a universal judgment (vv. 5-6)	

---

35. The common lexemes in the two psalms are: עד (Ps 110:1; cf. Ps 145:1, 2, 21); יום (Ps 110:3, 5; cf. Ps 145:2); הדר (Ps 110:3; cf. Ps 145:5, 12); עולם (Ps 110:4; cf. Ps 145:1); רום (Ps 110:7; cf. Ps 145:1); אתה (Ps 110:4; cf. Ps 145:15); על (Ps 110:4-6; cf. Ps 145:9); and רב (Ps 110:6; cf. Ps 145:7).

YHWH will extend his mighty scepter (מטה) beyond Zion (מציון) (v. 2)	YHWH's Kingdom is cosmic (כל-בשר) and everlasting (כל-עלמים) (vv. 11-13)
YHWH is resolute to make the King in the order of Melchizedek, (מלכי-צדק), literally *king of righteousness* (v. 4)	YHWH is the King (המלך), who is righteous in all his ways (vv. 1, 17)
Implicitly the king will be victorious (רום) (v. 7)	All humanity (כל-בשר) will praise YHWH (v. 21)
The language of war and victory[36] (v. 3)	There is no language of war, rather YHWH's care to all he has made (עשה) (vv. 9-20)

Since the two psalms are placed at the end of the two Davidic groups, the above similarities and dissimilarities are significant. David, in both psalms, is talking about a "King" other than himself. In Psalm 110, the "King" will have ultimate dominion beyond Zion (universal) and all his adversaries will be destroyed.[37] In Psalm 145, YHWH is the reigning King and his Kingdom is cosmic and universal. Both underscores the cosmic judgment of YHWH that will include all [Ps 110:6 (גוים and על-ארץ רבה); cf. Ps 145: 20 (כל-הרשעים)]. Both anticipate the future with *hope* that YHWH will act.

At the same time, there are differences between them. Psalm 110 seems to be particularly concerned with the anticipation built into the first group

---

36. According to Allen, although the sole agency of victory is YHWH, the involvement of a human army in the holy war is not precluded. In verse 3, the emphasis is explicitly on the availability of the people (cf. Deut 20:4; 2 Sam 5:24). Allen, *Psalms 101-50*, 115.

37. Schaefer comments, "Psalm 110 portrays a messianic king who perfectly embodies power that derives from God, the divine representative who will come in the fullness of time to reign on earth. The apocalyptic movement saw the messianic victory over the nations as the climax of a drama played our in a universal context. The day of God's wrath was envisioned as the climax to world history." Konrad Schaefer, *Psalms* (ed. David W. Cotter; Collegeville: Liturgical Press, 2001), 274.

of Davidic psalms (Psalms 108-10), to which it is attached as the closing psalm. As we noted, Psalms 108 and 109 are lament psalms with the language of particularism—a concern for David and the people of Zion. To these specific concerns, Psalm 110 brings a hope—YHWH will help the king of Zion and he will destroy all his enemies. The language is explicitly particular, except for the hint that the *hope* is not limited to the boundaries of Zion, but it will go forth from Zion for *all*. It is more explicit only in Psalm 145—YHWH cares for all He has made. YHWH will enable the "king" of Psalm 110, but the ultimate King is YHWH himself who rules the cosmos. Thus, the situationality of Psalm 145 fits after the situationality of Psalm 110. The editorial arrangement reveals an extension of the covenant love of YHWH from David and Zion to all whom YHWH has made. Put differently, Psalm 145 is hope beyond the hope of Psalm 110. Therefore, reading Psalm 145 after Psalm 110 would be appropriate.

This is also shown by the significant connections between Psalm 145 and Psalms 111, 112 and 116, which follow Psalm 110. Notice the similarities between these psalms. They allude to the Exodus language (Exod 34:6)—*YHWH is gracious and compassionate* (חנון ורחום). As discussed in chapter 4, this is a unique alteration of the Exodus language (Exod 34:6) from רחם וחנון to חנון ורחם. The Psalter alludes to the language of Exodus only six times (Pss 86:15, 103:8, 111:4, 112:4, and 116:5), but the references in Book V (Pss 111:4, 112:4, and 116:5) have a special play of words. It reverses the Exodus imagery (Exod 34:6) from רחם וחנון to חנון ורחם, while the two occurrences in other books (Pss 86:15 and 103:8) are in the same order as in Exod 34:6 (רחם וחנון).[38] This unique alteration links Psalm 145 with Psalms 111, 112 and 116. Together these four psalms, like a quartet, sing in unison—*YHWH is gracious and compassionate* (חנון ורחום). Notice that all of them are placed after Psalm 110. Psalms 111 and 112 are part of the *hallel* psalms that follows Psalm 110 and close the first

---

38. It is not clear why the alternation חנון ורחם is made in Book V (Pss 111:4, 112:4, and 116:5). Acrostic arrangement may not be the reason because Psalm 116 is not an acrostic psalm. We can only speculate that the reversal of the Exodus imagery suggests some connection of the composition of Book V to the language in 2 Chr. 30:9; Neh 9:17, 31; Joel 2:13; and Jonah 4:2.

group of Davidic psalms. This unique relation confirms that the language of hope in Psalm 145 comes after the language of hope in Psalm 110.

Psalm 138

Psalm 138 is the first psalm of the second group of Davidic psalm in the fifth book. Noteworthy is the lonely superscript (לדוד),[39] which matches only Psalm 144 in Book V. Traditionally, the psalm is classified as an individual thanksgiving psalm.[40] Kirkpatrick, Anderson, and Mays regard it to be a communal thanksgiving.[41] Allen divides the psalm into three strophes: thanksgiving (vv. 1-3), YHWH's great praiseworthiness (4-6), and recurring of deliverance (vv. 7-8). According to him, the central strophe is bound together by the mentioning YHWH four times consecutively and the three occurrences of *ki* (twice temporal and once causal). The other two strophes surround the central strophe with the "motif of deliverance" from distress (vv. 3 and 7) and the "steadfast love" (vv. 2 and 8). He fails to notice the implicit confidence in verse 8. VanGemeren points out a movement in the grammatical structure of these strophes. He proposes both individual and communal elements in the psalms: A. Individual thanksgiving (vv. 1-3); B. Communal Thanksgiving (vv. 4-6); C. Confidence in the Lord's presence (vv. 7-8).[42]

---

39. Psalm 138 is one among seven Davidic psalms (Psalms 25, 26, 27, 35, 37, 103, 138), which has a single lonely phrase לדוד. The lonely superscript לדוד is mostly found in Book I. It is absent in Books II and III, once in Book IV and twice in Book V.

40. Allen, *Psalms 101-50*, 312; Hermann Gunkel et al., *Introduction to Psalms: The Genres of the Religious Lyric of Israel* (trans. James D. Nogalski; Macon: Mercer University Press, 1998), 199-221.

41. Kirkpatrick writes, "The tone and language of vv. 4-7 resemble cii. 15ff., and many passages in Is xl-lxvi where the hope of the conversation of the nations is connected with the Restoration of Israel from exile." See A. F. Kirkpatrick, ed., *The Book of Psalms* (Cambridge Bible for Schools and Colleges; Cambridge: Cambridge University Press, 1902), 782. Anderson sees many points of contacts with Isa 40-66. See Anderson, *The Book of Psalms*, 901. See also James Luther Mays, *Psalms* (Louisville: Westminster John Knox, 1994), 424.

42. VanGemeren suggests, "The structural elements move from the first person imperfect (vv. 1-2) to the cause of praise in the first person perfect (v. 3), to the summons to praise in the third person jussive (vv. 4-5), to the cause of communal praise (vv. 6-7), to finally an interchange between the third person and second person singular as a part of prayer to the Lord (vv. 7-8)." VanGemeren, "Psalms," 832-33.

In verses 1-3, David gives thanks (ידה) with all his heart (בכל-לבי).[43] He pledges to sing YHWH's praise (זמר) before all "gods" (אלהים). He resolves to bow down toward YHWH's holy temple and praise his name (שם) because of YHWH's steadfast love (חסד) and faithfulness (אמת). For YHWH has exalted his own name (שם) and word (אמרה) above all things. David acknowledges that YHWH answered (ענה) when he called (קרא). YHWH made him bold (רהב). In verses 4-6, David anticipates a universal singing and praising of YHWH—all kings of the earth (כל-מלכי-ארץ)—because YHWH's glory is great (כי גדול כבוד). Although YHWH is exalted (רום), he looks upon the lowly (שפל) and knows the proud (גבה) from afar. In verses 7-8, David is confident of YHWH's steadfast love (חסד). He is sure that YHWH will preserve (תחיני) and save (תושיעני) him. He will strike his foes (איב) with his hand. YHWH will not abandon the works (מעשה) of his hand, but he will fulfill (יגמר) the purpose for him.

Psalm 138 links with Psalm 145 through numerous lexemes.[44] These lexical connections, when examined at the semantic, syntactic, paradigmatic, and pragmatic levels, demonstrate some thematic similarities at the level of their discourse meaning. In both psalms, David sings praise to YHWH (Ps 138:1; cf. Ps 145:1-2). He praises YHWH's name (Ps 138:2; cf. Ps 145:1, 2, and 21). He anticipates *all the kings of the earth* will give thanks to YHWH (Ps 138:4; cf. Ps 145:10). He considers YHWH's steadfast love and his faithfulness (Ps 138:2, 8; cf. Ps 145:8, 13f).

---

43. Kraus regards the psalm as an individual song of thanksgiving sung in the cultic community, probably in the court of the temple. Weiser refers to the Septuagint, which mentions Zechariah, the singer, a simple member of the community. However, Kirkpatrick and Anderson consider the psalm as a communal thanksgiving song in which the singer represents the entire community to YHWH for restoring Israel from the Babylonian exile. See Kraus, *Psalms 60-150*, 506; Artur Weiser, *The Psalms: A Commentary* (Philadelphia: Westminster, 1962), 798; Kirkpatrick, ed., *The Book of Psalms*, 783; Anderson, *The Book of Psalms*, 901.

44. The common lexemes are: ידה (Ps 138:1-2; cf. Ps 145:10); כל (Ps 138:1, 2-4; cf. Ps 145:2, 9-10, 13-18, and 20-21); קדש (Ps 138:2; cf. Ps 145:21); שם (Ps 138:2; cf. Ps 145:1, 2, and 21); על (Ps 138:2, 7; cf. Ps 145:9); חסד (Ps 138:2, 8; cf. Ps 145:8); אמת (Ps 138:2; cf. Ps 145:18); יום (Ps 138:3; cf. Ps 145:2); קרא (Ps 138:3; cf. Ps 145:18); מלך (Ps 138:4; cf. Ps 145:1); שמע (Ps 138:4; cf. Ps 145:19); אמר (Ps 138:4; cf. Ps 145:6, 11); פה (Ps 138:4; cf. Ps 145:21); דרך (Ps 138:5; cf. Ps 145:17); גדול (Ps 138:5; cf. Ps 145:3, 8); כבוד (Ps 138:5; cf. Ps 145:5, 11-12); רום (Ps 138:6; cf. Ps 145:1); ידע (Ps 138:6; cf. Ps 145:12); יד (Ps 138:7, 8; cf. Ps 145:16); אף (Ps 138:7; cf. Ps 145:8); עולם (Ps 138:8; cf. Ps 145:1-2, 21); מעשה (Ps 138:8; cf. Ps 145:4); and כבוד (Ps 138:5; cf. Ps 145:5, 11-12).

On the other hand, the discourse meanings in the two psalms demonstrate some differences. Notice the differences in the following table.

Psalm 138	Psalm 145
David sings praises of YHWH before "gods" with *all his heart* (v. 1)	David sings praise *everyday* and forever (vv. 1-2)
David bows down toward the *holy temple* like Daniel (v. 2)	David is in *presence* of "my King"; the Kingdom of God is a present reality
David *called* and YHWH answered and he made him bold (v. 3)	YHWH is near to *all* who *call* on him in truth (v. 18)
All the *kings* of the earth praise YHWH when they hear YHWH speak (v. 4)	*All* will *give thanks* to YHWH because of YHWH's goodness and greatness (vv. 9-10)
David declares YHWH's *glory* great (v. 5)	David talks about the *glory* of YHWH's majesty and Kingdom (vv. 5, 11, and 12)
YHWH's protection and the salvation is personal to David (v. 7)	YHWH's act and salvation is for all he has made, all who call on him in truth, all those who fear him, and all those who love him (vv. 17-20)
YHWH strikes David's foes (v. 7)	YHWH will destroy all wicked (v. 20)
YHWH will fulfill his purpose for David (v. 8)	YHWH fulfills the desires of all those who fear him (v. 18)

On the one hand, the above similarities present a thematic continuity from Psalm 138 to Psalm 145, forming a thematic inclusion for the second group of Davidic psalms (Psalms 138-145). On the other hand, the dissimilarities in their discourse meaning set them apart complementarily. They complement each other either through developing the theme synthetically.

For example, in Ps 138:1, David gives thanks to YHWH and sings praise before all gods with all his heart (בכל־לבי), but in Psalm 145 David praises every day (בכל־יום) and forever (לעולם ועד). In the former, he sings before "gods," but in the latter, he expects one generation to proclaim YHWH's praise to another (v. 4). YHWH's steadfast love, his faithfulness, and his salvation begin with David in Psalm 138, but in Psalm 145 it expands to all he has made. In the former, David sees the glory of YHWH, but in the latter, he sees the glory of his majesty and his Kingdom. In the previous psalm, he is confident that YHWH will fulfill his promise, but in the final psalm, he sees that YHWH will fulfill the desires of all those who fear him. The thematic patterns in Psalm 145 show movement from individual to community, from particular to universal, and from exclusive to inclusive language. These patterns characterize Psalm 145 as the concluding psalm of the second group of Davidic psalms (Psalms 138-145).

Psalm 139

Traditionally, the psalm is regarded as a lament with hymnic features, but scholars differ on its genre classification.[45] VanGemeren suggests a combination of the component of hymn, thanksgiving, and lament.[46] Noticing the discontinuity of thought between verses 18 and 19, he divides the psalm into two parts: verses 1-18 and 19-24. The former contains thanksgiving for God's discernment, perception, and purpose for the individual. The latter is a prayer made during distress.[47] Siegfried Wagner argues for the motif of meditation (reflection), which brings together confession, prayer, and piety in the psalm.[48] Helen Schungel Strauman contests for a wisdom

---

45. According to Allen, the psalm exhibits a mixed form. Verses 19-24 read like an individual lament. Verses 21-22 assert innocence, but verses 7, 17, and 14 have hymnic features. Verses 13, and 15-16 talk about creation. The striking features are the absence of introduction and a subjectivity of treatment that breaks out of the form of the genre. Allen, *Psalms 101-50*, 323-24.

46. VanGemeren, "Psalms," 835.

47. VanGemeren further divides the two-part structure into four-fold expository outline: A. The Lord's discernment of individuals (vv. 1-6); B. The Lord's perception of individuals (vv. 7-12); C. The Lord's purpose of individuals (vv. 13-18); and D. Prayer for vindication (vv. 19-24). Ibid.

48. Wagner concludes, "In Ps CXXXIX begegnen Meditation (Reflektion), Bekenntnis und Gebet, offenbar Frömmigkeitsäußerungen des intellektuell regsamen Gottesfürchtigen

context.[49] Auffret divides the psalm into two parts (vv. 1b-16 and 17-24).[50] However, Montgomery, Würthwein, Wagner, and Allen divide the psalm into four strophes (vv. 1b-6, 7-12, 13-18, and 19-24).[51]

In verses 1-6, David articulates his overwhelming knowledge of God's intimate company in his private and inner life. According to him, God is not only omnipresent, but also omniscient about him. He is actively engaged through searching (חקר), knowing (ידע), discerning (בין), hemming (צור), and placing (שית) his hand upon David. Such a knowledge for David is too wonderful (פלאי) and too high (שׂגב). In verses 7-12, David underscores the same thought by explicating it synthetically. David does not know a place where God's presence would not abide with him. Whether it is heaven or "sheol," night, or day, everywhere God holds (אחז) his hand and leads (נחה) him. In verses 13-18, David explains how intimately YHWH knows him. God is David's originator (קנה) and the architect (סכך) of his shape in his mother's womb. He knew him even before he was formed. God controls David's life and destiny. He has ordained and numbered his days. God's thought is precious to David. In verses 19-24, David changes his tone from gratitude to imprecation. Godly thoughts are replaced with the thought of the wicked (רשע), bloodthirsty men (ואנשי דמים), malice (מזמה) and vanity (שוא), hate (שנא), and enemies (איב). David seeks the slaying (קטל) of the wicked, because they hate YHWH. He declares that YHWH's enemies are his own enemies. Nonetheless, he places himself under YHWH's scrutiny

---

in der spätnachexilischen jüdischen Gemeinde der sich bestimmten weisheitlichen Schulen angeschlossen haben mag." See Siegfried Wagner, "Zur Theologie Des Psalms CXXXIX," *VTSup* 29 (1978): 376.

49. Schüngel-Straumann writes, "Der Sitz im Leben ist die theologische Polemic innerhalb der Weisheit; der Dichter nimmt dafur aus theologischen Grunden die Form des individuellen Klagelieded in Anspruch." See Helen Schüngel-Straumann, "Zur Gattung und Theologie des 139," *BZ* 17 (1973): 51.

50. P. Auffret, "O Dieu, connais mon coeur: Étude structurelle du Psaume CXXXIX," *Sem* 47 (1997): 11-18.

51. James A. Montgomery, "Stanza-Formation in Hebrew Poetry," *JBL* 64 (1945): 383; Ernst Würthwein, "Erwängungen zu Ps 139," *VT* 7 (1957): 176-78; Wagner, "Zur Theologie Des Psalms CXXXIX," 359. Allen, *Psalms 101-50*, 321. For more information on Psalm 139, see Jan Holman, "The Structure of Psalm CXXXIX," *VT* 21 (1971): 298-99. For a comprehensive structural analysis of Psalm 139 see L. C. Allen, "Faith on Trial: An Analysis of Psalm 139," *VE* 10 (1977): 5-23. And for textual critical issues see Th. Booij, "Psalm CXXXIX," *VT* 55 (2005): 1-19.

(vv. 23-24). With his anxious zeal, he does not desire to walk on the path of offence (דרך־עצב), but he pleads with YHWH to lead him in the way everlasting (בדרך עולם). YHWH's ways are best and perfect.

Psalm 139 connects with Psalm 145 lexically and thematically in various ways. The lexical analysis shows numerous common lexemes.[52] These lexemes contribute in the syntactic, paradigmatic, semantic, and pragmatic meaning of the discourse in the two psalms. Comparison of the discourse meaning of the two psalms reveals few thematic similarities. In both psalms, David reflects on YHWH's wonderful work (Ps 139:14; cf. Ps 145:5). He expects YHWH to destroy the wicked (Ps 139:19; cf. Ps 145:20). At the same time, there are significant thematic differences, which provide clues for their placement in the Psalter.

Psalm 139	Psalm 145
David marvels at the intimate relationship and the care of YHWH he is favored with (vv. 1-5)	David praises the goodness and greatness of YHWH (vv. 1-3)
YHWH knows (ידע); David knows (ידע) fully well (vv. 1-2, 4, 14, and 23)	To make known (ידע) the goodness and greatness of YHWH to all human kind (v. 12)
David alone gives thanks (ידה) to YHWH (v. 14)	All that YHWH has made will give thanks (ידה) to him (v. 10)
Wicked are those who speak evil of YHWH; they hate YHWH and misuse his name (v. 20)	Wicked persons are not characterized (v. 20)

---

52. The common lexemes shared by the two psalms are: ידע (Ps 139:1-2, 4, 14, and 23; cf. Ps 145:12); אתה (Ps 139:2, 8, and 13; cf. Ps 145:15): אין (Ps 139:4; cf. Ps 145:3); כל (Ps 139:3-4; cf. Ps 145:2, 9-10, 13-18, and 20-21); על (Ps 139:5, 14, 16; cf. Ps 145:9); אמר (Ps 139:11, 20; cf. Ps 145:6); ידה (Ps 139:14; cf. Ps 145:10); ירא (Ps 139:14; cf. Ps 145:6. 19); פלא (Ps 139:14; cf. Ps 145:5): מעשׂה (Ps 139:14 cf. Ps 145:4, 9, 10, and 17); עין (Ps 139:16; cf. Ps 145:15); ספר (Ps 139:16, 18; cf. Ps 145:6); עולם (Ps 139:24; cf. Ps 145:1-2, 13, and 21).

David hates (שׂנא) those who hate YHWH (v. 21)	David declares YHWH's compassion (רחמים) for all he has made (v. 9)
David puts himself under the scrutiny of YHWH so that he will lead him in the way everlasting (בדרך עולם) (v. 24)	David pledges to praise YHWH everyday and forever; he acknowledges that YHWH's Kingdom is everlasting (vv. 1-2, 13)

In the similarities above, we notice the continuity of certain themes: (1) the relationship of David with YHWH, (2) YHWH's praise from the mouth of David, (3) YHWH's wonderful works, and (4) the ultimate destruction of the wicked. However, through the dissimilarities, Psalm 145 brings a new perspective on the image and the theology of David. David is no longer preoccupied with himself. His concern is YHWH's cosmic and universal praise, which includes others. In Ps 139:24, David wants YHWH to lead him in the everlasting way (Ps 139:24), but in Ps 145:13 he proclaims an everlasting Kingdom. In the former, the context of the wonderful works of YHWH is limited to himself, but in the latter, it is cosmic and universal. David is no longer under the scrutiny of YHWH, but is a bold worship leader, whose audience already knows the identity of the wicked and what they do. Hence, the descriptions of the actions of YHWH are numerous, but the descriptions of the actions of the wicked are none. These differences advocate the reading of Psalm 145 after Psalm 139.

Psalm 140

The psalm begins with an individual lament but ends with a confidence and hope in YHWH.[53] Eaton regard the psalm as a royal psalm because of the language of battle in the psalm [notice v. 3 (מלחמות) and v. 8 (ביום נשק)].[54] Steven J. L. Croft also suggests that this psalm is written for a king and the

---

53. According to VanGemeren, the psalmist has been falsely accused and so he turns to YHWH for his deliverance. YHWH is the righteous judge. The psalmist does not complain against God, but cries out for deliverance. The structure of the psalm vacillates between lament and confidence. VanGemeren, "Psalms," 841. Auffret presents an insightful structural analysis. Pierre Auffret, *Merveilles à nos yeux: Étude structurelle de vingt psaumes dont celui de 1 Ch 16:8-36* (New York: Walter de Gruyter, 1995), 202-17.

54. J. H. Eaton, *Kingship and the Psalms* (Naperville: Allenson, 1976), 63-64.

"wicked" (רשע) are either foreigners or the internal enemies of the king.[55] However, Allen thinks that the war motif in the psalm may also allude to "the hunting one as the metaphor for persecution."[56] Although Anderson notices the similarities with the royal psalm, he categorizes the psalm as a general petition for the judgment of YHWH.[57] He divides the psalm into three sections: A. General lamentation (vv. 1-5); B. Appeal to the righteous judge (vv. 6-11); and C. Confidence in God's coming justice (vv. 12-13). VanGemeren sees a chiastic structure in the pattern of ABA′B′: A. Prayer for Deliverance from evil (vv. 1-5); B. Confidence in God's deliverance (vv. 6-8); A′. Prayer for divine justice (vv. 9-11); B′. Confidence in God's deliverance (vv. 12-13).[58]

It is evident from the beginning of the psalm that David is in serious trouble. In verses 1-5, he cries out to YHWH for deliverance (חלץ) and protection (נצר) from evil (רע) and violent (חמס) men. David describes his adversaries as those who devise (חשב) evil plans (רעות) against him. They stir up (גור) war (מלחמות) continuously against him.[59] Their tongue is sharp (שנן) like a serpent (נחש). They have poison under their lips (עכ־שוב). They are wicked (רשע), violent (חמס), and proud (גאה). They set a trap and snare (פח and מוקש) for David. In verses 6-8, David expresses his confidence in YHWH. His plea for help to YHWH is established in the fact that YHWH is his personal God—"my God." YHWH is not a weak but a strong (עז) deliverer. He shields (סכך) David in the battle. David pleads with YHWH not to grant the desires of the wicked or make their evil plans succeed (פוק), lest they will become proud (רום).[60]

55. Steven J. L. Croft, *The Identity of the Individual in the Psalms* (JSOTSup 44; Sheffield: JSOT, 1987), 32, 124.

56. Allen, *Psalms 101-50*, 334. Moshe Greenberg suggests similar mythopoetic language in verse 12 (למדחפת) to be metaphorically associated with hunting. See Moshe Greenberg, "Two New Hunting Terms in Psalm 140:12," *HAR* 1 (1977): 149-53.

57. Anderson, *The Book of Psalms*, 913.

58. VanGemeren, "Psalms," 841.

59. BHS suggests the in יָגוּרוּ (qal; "attack") verse 2 to be amended as יְגָרוּ (piel; "stir up"). NIV has adopted the emendation.

60. Dahood translates יְרוּמוּ (qal; "they lift up") as vocative "O Exalted!" NIV translates it metaphorically in the context "they become proud." Allen translates "O God! Tear them away." It remains an exegetical crux. See Dahood, *Psalm III*, 303; Allen, *Psalms 101-50*, 333.

In verses 9-11, David prays for divine justice. He anxiously anticipates that YHWH will bring trouble upon his adversaries, by throwing them into the fire (אש), and hurling them into the miry pits (מהמר) so that they may never rise again. David does not expect them to be established in the land (ארץ), but to be hunted down (יצודנו למדחפת). David's imprecation is implicitly established in his understanding of YHWH's attributes. In verse 12; he declares YHWH is just—"the Lord secures justice for the poor (עני) and upholds the cause of the needy (אביון)." When justice is done, the righteous (צדיק) will praise YHWH's name and the upright (ישר) will live in YHWH's presence. It is implicit in the psalm that David identifies himself with poor, afflicted, needy, righteous, and upright people.

Psalm 140 connects with Psalm 145 lexically and thematically in various ways. A lexical analysis of the two psalms shows numerous lexemes that are common to both.[61] These lexemes, after syntactic, paradigmatic, semantic, and pragmatic analysis contribute meanings unique to the discourse of the psalm. Comparison of the discourse meaning of the two psalms demonstrates few similarities. David addresses YHWH as "my God" (Ps 140:7; cf. Ps 145:1). David acknowledges YHWH as the savior (Ps 140:8; cf. Ps 145:19), and YHWH is the ultimate help. However, it also shows some dissimilarity that may suggest the purposeful placement of Psalm 145. Notice the differences in the following table.

---

61. The common lexemes are: אדם (Ps 140:2; cf. Ps 145:12); כל (Ps 140:3; cf. Ps 145: 2, 9-10, 13-18, and 20-21); יום (Ps 140:3, 8; cf. Ps 145:2); שמר (Ps 140:5; cf. Ps 145:20); רשע (Ps 140:5, 9; cf. Ps 145:20); יד (Ps 140:5-6; Ps 145:16); אמר (Ps 140:7; cf. Ps 145:6, 11); נתן (Ps 140:9; Ps 145:15); רום (Ps 140:9; cf. Ps 145:1); על (Ps 140:11; cf. Ps 145:9); נפל (Ps 140:11; cf. Ps 145:14); עשה (Ps 140:13, cf. Ps 145:19); ידע (Ps 140:13; cf. Ps 145:12); צדיק (Ps 140:14; cf. Ps 145:17); ידה (Ps 140:14; cf. Ps 145:10):and שם (Ps 140:14; cf. Ps 145:1).

Psalm 140	**Psalm 145**
David pleads with confidence and hope that YHWH will deliver him (vv. 2-7)	David is implicitly delivered; he praises YHWH with the anticipation that all humanity will praise him (vv. 1-2, 21)
David is concerned with the men who are evil and proud (vv. 2-5)	David is concerned with YHWH's greatness and goodness (vv. 3-9)
David anticipates YHWH will be his deliverer (ישועה) (v. 8)	YHWH delivers (ישע) those who fear him (v. 19)
The righteous will give thanks (ידה) to YHWH's name (שם); David is one of the righteous who will give thanks (v. 14)	All YHWH has made will give thanks (ידה) and all human kind will bless his holy name (שם) (vv. 10, 21)
YHWH fulfills (עשׂה) justice (משפט) for the needy (עני / אבינים); Implicitly, David considers himself as poor and needy (v. 13)	YHWH fulfills (עשׂה) the desires of those who fear (ירא) him; David is one among them (v. 19)
David explains the activities of the wicked (vv. 3-6)	No description of the wicked (v. 20)
David prays to YHWH to guard (שמר) him (v. 4)	YHWH watches (שמר) all those who love him (v. 20)
David offers imprecatory prayers against the wicked (רשע) lest they exalt themselves (vv. 8-11)	YHWH is exalted and the wicked (רשע) will be destroyed (v. 20)

On the one hand, we notice the thematic continuity between the psalms. On the other hand, we observe certain thematic developments. Some themes are developed by adding new nuances to its meaning, while others are expanded in its application (from individual to community). For example, David anticipates that YHWH will be his deliverer (ישועה) in Ps

140:8, but in Ps 145:19 he declares that YHWH delivers (יֵשַׁע) those who fear him. David's concern in the final Davidic psalm extends beyond his personal salvation. He sees YHWH not only as a personal God, but also as a universal "King" who is good and compassionate to *all* he has made. In Psalm 140, he anticipates his personal deliverance, but in Psalm 145, he anticipates YHWH's universal praise. In the previous psalm, similar to other lament psalms (Psalms 109, 138 and 139), David explicates the activities of the wicked in detail, but in the final Davidic psalm, the descriptions are missing. This may be either to avoid the redundancy, or for an emphasis on "all inclusive praise." After having read Psalm 140, the sure destruction of the wicked in Psalm 145 becomes comprehensible as the just act of God. Chronologically, therefore, reading Psalm 140 before Psalm 145 is fitting.

Psalm 141

This psalm is an individual lament with an influence from the wisdom tradition.[62] Kraus assigns this psalm to the circle of Torah piety. However, the content of the psalm overwhelmingly upholds the lament spirit of Psalm 140. VanGemeren divides the psalm into four structural components: A. Prayer for deliverance (vv. 1-2); B. Prayer for Wisdom (vv. 3-5c); C. Prayer for vindication (vv. 5d-7); and D. Prayer for Deliverance and vindication (vv. 8-10).[63]

In verses 1-2, David calls upon (קרא) YHWH to hurry up (חוש). He pleads with him to hear (אזן) his voice (קול) and consider his prayer

---

62. Kraus regards the psalm to be of sapiential milieu, belonging to Torah piety, like Psalm 119. Allen accepts the presence of the wisdom element; however he also notices a situation of personal persecution in verses 8-10, which characterizes it also as an individual lament. VanGemeren suggests a mixed form: an individual lament, which includes the lament, confession of confidence, and imprecation. Kraus, *Psalms 60-150*, 527; Allen, *Psalms 101-50*, 341; VanGemeren, "Psalms," 846. For a detail structural analysis see Auffret, *Merveilles à nos yeux*, 218-35.

63. VanGemeren, "Psalms," 846. Allen informs that the structure of the psalm has been variously analyzed, largely on the basis of form-critical elements and motifs. A critical factor generally ignored is a stylistic pattern of repetition running through the psalm, notably לְפִי, " on/at my mouth," in verses 3, 7; the root שָׁמַר, "guard," in verses 3, 9; פְּעָלֵי עָוֶן, "evil-doers" in verses 4, 9; רְשָׁע(ים), "wicked," in verse 4, 10; and ע(ו)ד, "still, while," in verse 5, 10." Allen, *Psalms 101-50*, 342. Verses 5b-7 are considerd problematic, but Boij argues for its unity and clarity. See Thijs Booij, "Psalm 141: A Prayer for Discipline and Protection," *Bib* 86 (2005): 97-106.

(תפללה) like an incense offering (קטרת) and the lifting up of his hand like an evening sacrifice (מנחת־ערב). David's cry obviously underscores the urgency of time and his earnest desire for YHWH's quick attention. In verses 3-5c, David is aware of the subtle pressure of the evil within and without. Human beings, with their fallen nature, fail to resist the influence of the evil people in their speech and thought. They are often swayed by their companions. David requests that YHWH to set a guard (שמרה) over his mouth (פה) and watch over (נצר) his lips (שפה). He desires his heart (לב) not to be drawn to evil (רע) things, and not to participate in wicked (רשע) acts. He does not want to dine with the evildoers (פעלי־און). He would rather a righteous (צדיק) man strike (הלם) him in kindness (חסד), or rebuke (יכח) him. It would be like oil (שמן) on his head. In verses 5d-7, David switches his plea for help to a prayer of imprecation against the judges and the rulers (שפט), whose deeds are evil (רעה). He wants the wicked to face destruction at the mouth of the grave (שאול) so that they may know that his speech (אמר) was true. In verses 8-10, David turns back to his dire situation. His eyes are fixed on YHWH for a refuge (חסה). He is defenseless (ערה) against the snare (פח)/trap (מוקש) of the wicked and the evildoers. He pleads with YHWH to keep (שמר) him away from these traps. He wishes to pass by the traps safely, but expects those who set them to fall.

Psalm 141 links with Psalm 145 both lexically and thematically. Lexical analysis of the two psalms shows numerous shared lexemes.[64] These lexemes contribute to the discourse meaning in the psalm through their syntactic, paradigmatic, semantic, and pragmatic interactions. Comparisons of the discourse meaning of two psalms do not show many similarities, except for the fact that David speaks to YHWH (Ps 141:1; cf. Ps 145:3) in both psalms. However, they show numerous differences. Notice the differences in the following table:

---

64. The common lexemes between the two psalms are: קרא (Ps 141:1; cf. Ps 14518); פה (Ps 141:3; cf. Ps 145:21); על (Ps 141:3; cf. Ps 145:9); רשע (Ps 141:4; cf. Ps 145:20); דבר (Ps 141:4; Ps 145:5); שמע (Ps 141:6; cf. Ps 145:19); יד (Ps 141:6, 9; cf. Ps 145:16); אמר (Ps 141:6; cf. Ps 145:6); אל (Ps 141:4-5, 8; cf. Ps 145:15); את (Ps 141:4; cf. Ps 145:15); שמר (Ps 141:9; cf. Ps 145:20); נפל (Ps 141:10; cf. Ps 145:14); and עד (Ps 141:10; cf. Ps 145:1).

Psalm 141	**Psalm 145**
David prays (תפלה) to YHWH (v. 2)	David praises (תהלה) YHWH (v. 1)
David calls (קרא) upon YHWH (v. 1)	David exalts (רום) and blesses (ברך) YHWH, and proclaims that he is near to all who call (קרא) on him in truth (vv. 1, 18)
David pleads with YHWH to guard (שמרה) his mouth (פה) (v. 3)	David praises YHWH with his mouth (פה) (v. 21)
David pleads with YHWH to protect his heart from being tempted to evil, wicked things, and evil company (v. 4)	David praises YHWH's name everyday (v. 2)
David identifies the rulers (שפט) in the same cater gory as the evil doers (פעלי־און) (vv. 4-6)	David is silent about the social status of the wicked (v. 20)
David pleads with God to keep (שמר) him from the trap (v. 9)	YHWH keeps (שמר) all those who love him (v. 20)
David expects the wicked (רשע) to fall (נפל) in their own trap (v. 10)	David declares that YHWH will destroy (שמד) the wicked (רשע) (v. 20)

Comparison of the two images of David reveals remarkable changes. David moves from prayer (תפלה) to praise (תהלה); from restraining (שמרה) the mouth (פה) against evil to using the mouth (פה) for praise to YHWH; from expecting the wicked will fall (נפל) to being confident in their total destruction (שמד); from a detailed description of the wicked to an abrupt final judgment without explanation; and from an anticipation of YHWH's action against the wicked in particular to YHWH's action for all he has made. We suggest that these changes in the image of David are plausible reasons for the placement of Psalm 145 after Psalm 141.

Psalm 142

Psalm 142 is a prayer made in a cave. Allen elaborates on the difficulty about the historicity of the "cave."[65] Similar to Psalms 140 and 141, Psalm 142 is an individual lament.[66] Unique to this psalm is a plea for the deliverance from "prison" (מסגר). John Eaton suggests the "prison" may be a figure of speech for "suffering and danger."[67] Unlike Psalms 140-141, this psalm does not seek the punishment of enemies, but the company of the righteous (צדיק). Westermann divides the psalm into the following themes: an introductory cry for help, a lament concerning foes and self, a confession of trust, a petition in terms of hearing and saving, motifs for divine intervention, a vow of praise, and an assurance of being heard.[68] VanGemeren provides a broad expository classification: A. lament of the individual (vv. 1-2); B. loneliness in suffering (vv. 3-7a); A′ public thanksgiving (v. 7b).[69]

In verses 1-2, David offers a passionate prayer (תפלה). In his prayer, he cries aloud (זעק) by raising his voice (קול). He longs for mercy (חנן) from YHWH. He presents (שפך) his complaints (שיח) by telling (נגד) YHWH about his trouble (צרה). In verses 3-7a, David asserts that in the times when his spirit is faint (עטף) YHWH knows (ידע) David's way (נתיבה). But David also knows that the path (ארח) he is walking has hidden (טמן) snares (פח), laid by his adversaries. He asks YHWH to consider (נבט) his abandoned situation (ואין־לי מכיר) where he has no refuge and no one who cares

---

65. Allen explains the difficulty in establishing the historicity of the cave. He opts for the Childs' understanding on the process of historicization of the superscript in which the psalms are reading in light of the past to provide lessons for the present. He writes, "Here by means of inertextuality David is presented as a role model for the individual sufferer." Allen, *Psalms 101-50*, 348.

66. Eaton characterizes Psalm 142 a royal psalm and pre-exilic in its provenance. He sees some parallels with other royal psalms, especially with Ps 18:18, However, Croft does not see anything discreetly royal in the psalm. Eaton, *Kingship*, 85; Croft, *The Identity of the Individual*, 145. For structural analysis see Auffret, *Merveilles à nos yeux*, 236-48.

67. J. H. Eaton, *The Psalms: A Historical and Spiritual Commentary with an Introduction and New Translation* (London: T & T Clark, 2003), 466. Konrad Schaefer writes, "The prison is a metaphor for distress, like the trap, "the Pit" or Sheol (cf. Lam 3:7-9; Ps 88-6)." See Schaefer, *Psalms*, 332.

68. Claus Westermann, *Praise and Lament in the Psalms* (trans. Keith R. Crim and Richard N. Soulen; Atlanta: John Knox, 1981), 66-7.

69. VanGemeren, "Psalms," 849.

for him (אין דורש לנפשי). Even so, David declares that YHWH is his refuge (מחסה) and his portion (חלק) in the land of the living; but his confidence does not alter his low situation (דלל). The reality of a persecuting (רדף) adversary, who is too strong (אמץ) to overcome, compels David to cry (רנה) for deliverance (נצל). He pleads with YHWH to set him free (יצא) from his confinement and bondage (מסגר), so that, he may give thanks (ידה) to YHWH's name (שם). Then, the righteous (צדיק) will surround (כתר) him because of YHWH's generous dealing (גמל) with him.

Psalm 142 connects to Psalm 145 lexically and thematically on various points. Lexical analysis of the two psalms shows numerous shared lexemes.[70] Syntactic, paradigmatic, semantic, and pragmatic analyses of these lexemes help in understanding the unique discourse meaning of each psalm. Comparison of the discourse meanings of each psalm reveals some thematic similarities. In both of the psalms, David speaks to YHWH (Ps 142:1; cf. Ps 145:1-3). David recognizes that YHWH is the ultimate help (Ps 142: 6-7; cf. Ps 145:18-19). He desires to give thanks to YHWH (Ps 142:8; cf. Ps 145:10). This comparison also illustrates significant differences, which may suggest reason for the purposeful placement of Psalm 145. Notice the differences in the two psalms.

---

70. The common lexemes between the two psalms: על (Ps 142:4, 8; cf. Ps 145:9); ידע (Ps 142:4; cf. Ps 145:12); אין (Ps 142:5; cf. Ps 145:3); אמר (Ps 142:6; cf. Ps 145:6, 11); אתה (Ps 142:6; cf. Ps 14515); חי (Ps 142:6; cf. Ps 145:16); מאד (Ps 142:7; cf. Ps 145:3); ידה (Ps 142:8; cf. Ps 145:10); שם (Ps 142:8; cf. Ps 145:1, 2, and 21) and; צדיק (Ps 142:8; cf. Ps 145:17).

Psalm 142	**Psalm 145**
David will give thanks (ידה) to YHWH's name after he is set free from his suffering (v. 8)	David vows to praise (הלל / ברך) YHWH's name forever and ever; David proclaims that all humanity will give thanks (ידה) to YHWH (vv. 1-2, 10)
David's condition is very (מאד) low (v. 7)	YHWH is greatly (מאד) to be praised (v. 3)
David has no one (אין) (v. 5)	No one (אין) can fathom YHWH's greatness (v. 3)
David says (אמר) "You [YHWH] are my refuge" (v. 6)	All will tell (אמר) about the power of YHWH's awesome work and they will tell (אמר) of the glory of YHWH's Kingdom (vv. 6, 11)
YHWH knows (ידע) David's ways (v. 4)	David wants to make known (ידע) YHWH's mighty deeds to all men (v. 12)
YHWH is David's portion in the land of the living (חי) (v. 6)	YHWH fulfills the desire of every living (חי) thing (v. 16)

David of Psalm 142 is low and weak. He has no one who takes care of him, so he turns to YHWH for his refuge. His enemy is too strong to overcome. However, David of Psalm 145 is a worship leader, engaged in persuading others to praise YHWH. In this psalm, David is no longer low and weak, or seeking refuge, but he is already set free. Since he is set free, he resolves to praise YHWH everyday and forever (Ps 145-1-2). He proclaims that YHWH is *gracious and compassionate* (Ps 145:8). He asserts that YHWH *fulfills the desires of all those who fear him, he hears their cry and saves them* (Ps 145:19). The unanswered prayer in Psalm 142 seems to have been answered in the psalm. These differences give us compelling reasons to place Psalm 145 after Psalm 142.

Psalm 143

The genre of Psalm 143 is an individual lament.[71] According to Allen, it is the last psalm in the mini-lament collection of Psalms 140-143.[72] This psalm is also regarded as one of the seven penitential psalms in the Psalter.[73] Dahood and Eaton consider the psalm as royal because of its superscript, its proximity with Psalm 144, and its lexical links with the other royal psalms.[74] Brueggemann views the psalm as one that brings the external and internal dimensions of disorientation together.[75] Schaefer sees inclusion like structure in verses 1-3 and 11-12.[76] Notice the phrase "in your righteousness" (בצדקתך; verses 1 and 11); "your servant" (עבדך; verses 2 and 12); "enemy" (איב; verses 3 and 9); "my life" (נפשי; verses 3, 11, and 11) ; and the "divine name" (יהוה; verses 1 and 11). VanGemeren divides the psalm into two parts: Part I contains a prayer for God's righteousness (vv. 1-2) and a lament (vv. 3-6), while Part II contains petitions (vv. 7-11) and prayer for God's righteousness (v. 12).[77]

In verses 1-2, David pleads for YHWH's attention (notice the two imperatives of שמע / אזן) to his prayer (תפלה). He wants YHWH to answer (ענה) his prayer in his faithfulness (אמונה) and his righteousness (צדקה).[78] He requests YHWH not to bring judgment (משפט) on him [YHWH's servant (עבד) David], because no one can stand as righteous (צדק) before

---

71. Claus Westermann, *The Psalms: Structure, Content and Message* (trans. Ralph D. Gehrke; Minneapolis: Augsburg, 1980), 64, 181. See also Allen, *Psalms 101-50*, 352. Auffret presents a detail structural analysis in Auffret, *Merveilles à nos yeux*, 249-62.

72. According to Allen, Psalms 138 and 139 has been prefixed and Psalm 144 and 145 has been added to this mini collection. Allen, *Psalms 101-50*, 77.

73. Other penitential psalms are Psalms 6, 32, 38, 51, 102, and 130. In Christian tradition, these psalms represent seven rungs on the ladder of repentance. Psalm 143 is the last one against the last judgment. Ibid., 353; VanGemeren, "Psalms," 851. See also Norman Henry Snaith, *The Seven Psalms* (London: Epworth, 1964), 9-10.

74. Mitchell Dahood, *Psalm II: 51-100* (AB 17; 3 vols.; New York: Doubleday, 1968), 322; Eaton, *Kingship*, 64.

75. Brueggemann, *The Message*, 102-3.

76. Schaefer, *Psalms*, 333-34.

77. VanGemeren, "Psalms," 851.

78. According to VanGemeren, the faithfulness and righteousness of God are two qualities that "connote the absolute fidelity and perfection of God in keeping his covenant with his covenant children. The ground for answered prayer is the Lord's commitment to his people." Ibid.

YHWH. David is aware of his sin, which disqualifies him from YHWH's immediate attention. The basis for YHWH's answer to David's prayer is not David's righteousness, but YHWH's righteousness and faithfulness. In verses 3-6, David explains his pathetic condition. He is being pursued (רדף) by his enemies (איב), who are crushing (דכא) his life to the ground, making him sit (ישב) in the darkness (מחשך). He is like the one who has been dead (מות) for a long time (עולם), so his spirit is weak (עטף) and his heart is dismayed (שמם). Yet in midst of such a depressing moment, he remembers (זכר) the days (יום) of old. He meditates (הגה) and considers the work (פעל / מעשׂה) of YHWH's hand (יד). He spreads (פרשׂ) his hands (יד) with longing for YHWH. In verses 7-11, David repeats his request for a quick (מהר) answer from YHWH. Like others, David may go down into the pit (בור) if YHWH does not show up quickly, so he wants to hear (שמע) about YHWH's "steadfast love" (חסד) in the morning (בקר).[79] David has put his trust (בטח) in YHWH. He urges YHWH to teach (ידע) him the way (דרך) he should walk, teach (למד) him to do his will (רצון), and lead (נחה) him on level ground. YHWH must rescue (נצל) him from his enemies (איב), because he has hidden (כסה) himself in YHWH. David entreats YHWH to save (חיה) his life for his name's (שם) sake and in his righteousness (צדקה). He pleads with him to exterminate (צמת) and destroy (אבד) all of his enemies (צרר / איב) in his "steadfast love" (חסד), because David is his servant (עבד).

Psalm 143 links to Psalm 145 lexically and thematically in various ways. Lexical analysis of the two psalms shows numerous common lexemes.[80] These lexemes in their syntactic, paradigmatic, semantic, and

---

79. Brueggemann notices a remarkable connection between חסד and אמנה in the Psalm 143. He comments, "There is no need for confirmation, qualification, or any other augmentation. Such confidence is enough, and it is the only basis for such a prayer from the Pit. Note well: the basis is not in the one who prays, but in the one addressed." Brueggemann, *The Message*, 103.

80. The common lexemes in the two psalms are: שמע (Ps 143:1; cf. Ps 145:19); אמן (Ps 143:1; Ps 145:13f); צדקה (Ps 143:1, 11; cf. Ps 145:7); כל (Ps 143:2, 5, and 12; cf. Ps 145: 2, 9-10, 13-18, and 20-21); עולם (Ps 143:3; cf. Ps 145: 1, 2, and 21); זכר (Ps 143:5; cf. Ps 145:7); יום (Ps 143:5 cf. Ps 145:2); מעשׂה (Ps 143:5; cf. Ps 145:4, 9, 10, and 17); יד (Ps 143:5-6; cf. Ps 145:16); עשׂה (Ps 143:10; cf. Ps 145:19); חסד (Ps 143:8, 12; cf. 145:8); ידע (Ps 143:8; cf. Ps 145:12); דרך (Ps 143:8; cf. Ps 145:17); טוב (Ps 143:10; cf. Ps 145:7); and שם (Ps 143:11; cf. Ps 145:1).

pragmatic interaction contribute unique discourse meanings in each psalm. Comparison of the discourse meanings of the two psalms shows some similarity. In both psalms, David affirms that YHWH is good (טוב), righteous (צדקה; Ps 143:1; cf. Ps 14519), and faithful (אמן; Ps 143:1; cf. Ps 45:13f). On the other hand, it also shows some differences that hint about the purposeful placement of Psalm 145.

Psalm 143	**Psalm 145**
David pleads with YHWH to hear (שמע) his prayer (v. 1)	David declares that YHWH hears (שמע) the cry of those who fear him and he saves them (v. 19)
David asks YHWH to answer (ענה) him and save him in his righteousness (צדקה) (vv. 1, 11)	All will sing aloud YHWH's righteousness (צדקה) (v. 7)
David has been like a dead man for a long time (עולם) (v. 3)	David wants to praise YHWH forever (עולם) (vv. 1-2)
David will remember (זכר) the old days of YHWH's good deeds (v. 5)	All will celebrate the remembrance (זכר) of the abundant goodness of YHWH (v. 7)
David remembers the days (יום) of old to meditate on YHWH's work (v. 5)	David pledges to praise YHWH every day (יום) (v. 2)
David meditates on YHWH's work (מעשׂה) (v. 5)	YHWH's work (מעשׂה) will be proclaimed from generation to generation; YHWH is compassionate to all he has made (מעשׂה); All YHWH has made (מעשׂה) will give thanks (vv. 4, 9, 10 17)

David meditates on the work of YHWH's hands (יד) and he stretches out his hands (יד) to YHWH for an answer (vv. 5-6)

David declares that YHWH opens his hands (יד) and satisfies the desires of all living beings (v. 16)

David prays to YHWH to teach him to do (עשׂה) his will (v. 10)

YHWH fulfills (עשׂה) the desires of those who fear him (v. 19)

David acknowledges "you are my God" (אלוהים) (v. 10)

David declares you are my God (אלוהים), the King (המלך) (v. 1)

David desires to hear YHWH's steadfast love (חסד) in the morning; in his steadfast love (חסד) YHWH will destroy his adversaries (vv. 8, 12)

David declares that YHWH's steadfast love (חסד) is great (v. 8)

David asks YHWH to teach (יד) him the way (דרך) he should walk (v. 8)

All will speak about the glory and power of YHWH's Kingdom in order to make known (ידע) to all humanity YHWH's mighty deeds; YHWH is righteous in all his ways (דרך) (vv. 12, 17)

David pleads with YHWH to lead him with his good (טוב) Spirit (v. 10)

YHWH's goodness (טוב) is abundant and he is good to all (טוב) (v. 7)

David pleads with YHWH to save him for his name's (שׁם) sake (v. 11

David blesses YHWH's name (שׁם) and anticipates all humanity will bless YHWH's name (שׁם) (v. 1)

The placement of the image of David in Psalm 145 after the image of David in Psalm 143 shows a reasonable connection between the two psalms. David in Psalm 143 is lamenting. His enemies surround him. He is pleading with YHWH to preserve his life. He is still a student who wants to learn from YHWH the ways that he should walk. However, David of Psalm 145 declares that YHWH hears those who cry and saves those who fear him. He testifies that all the ways of YHWH are righteous. He blesses his name and anticipates all others will bless YHWH's name. It implies that David's personal experience of deliverance in YHWH has become the basis of his bold proclamation of YHWH's goodness and greatness to others in Psalm 145. The proclamation of Psalm 145 is therefore a testimonial declaration rather than a mere declamation. Hence, these reasonable connections suggest the placement of Psalm 145 after Psalm 143.

Psalm 144

Psalm 144 is a mix of genres. VanGemeren splits it into two sections: a royal lament (vv. 1-11) and a psalm of communal blessing (vv. 12-15).[81] The first section constitutes David's praise for YHWH's help and protection in a war (vv. 1-2), YHWH's care for transient human beings (vv. 3-4), David's prayer for YHWH's help against his foreign enemies (vv. 5-8), David's commitment to sing a new song (שיר חדש) to YHWH who delivers (vv. 9-10), and David's plea for deliverance from foreign enemies. The second section constitutes the enumeration of communal prosperity bestowed upon the people who belong to YHWH (vv. 12-15). The contrast between the two sections is problematic.[82] Raymond Tournay and Pierre Auffret argue for the unity of Psalm 144. They suggest that YHWH's deliverance should be understood as the basis of what happens in the second section.[83]

---

81. VanGemeren, "Psalms," 856. Allen also suggests the same, but he names the second section to be "a communal thanksgiving." According to him, in the first section the main petition (vv. 5-7) prefaces the hymnic praise of YHWH (vv. 1-2) and a reflection the human limitations (vv. 3-4) in order to arouse divine sympathy and intervention of YHWH in David's circumstances. See Allen, *Psalms 101-50*, 361. Allen, *Psalms 101-50*, 361. For structural analysis see Auffret, *Merveilles à nos yeux*, 262-76.

82. BHS emendation proposes "the blessing" formula אשרי in place of the particle interjection אשר. This emendation forms an *inclusion* with "the blessing" formula אשרי in verse 15. However, it fails to take into account the particle interjection אשר in verses 8 and 11. Furthermore, this emendation does not resolve the problem of connection between the two sections (vv. 1-11 and 12-15). Kraus prefers to read the particle interjection אשר in imperative form "Gib heil" (give salvation). See Kraus, *Psalms 60-150*, 540. J. H. Eaton translates the particle interjection אשר "in order that." See Eaton, *Kingship*, 127. Allen translates it as a prospective condition "when." See Allen, *Psalms 101-50*, 359-60.

83. Raymond Tournay, "Le Psaumé CXLIV. Structure et Interpretation," *RB* 91 (1984): 520; Auffret, *Merveilles à nos yeux*, 262-76. VanGemeren agrees with Tournay. See VanGemeren, "Psalms," 859. See also Hans Scharen, "An Exegetical and Theological Study of Psalm 144," (M.Th. thesis, Dallas Theological Seminary, 1984), 53.

In verses 1-2, David is introduced as the warrior king (קרב), who acknowledges YHWH as his rock (צור), loving God (חסד), fortress (מצודה),
deliverer (פלט), and shield (מגן). YHWH subdues (רדד) the people under
him. For the David of Psalm 144, human beings are transient but YHWH
is the Rock (צור; v. 1), who shows his power in a theophany and deliver
David from his enemies (vv. 3-8). In verses 9-10, David pledges to sing
a new song (שיר חדש) for YHWH who delivers David his servant (עבד)
from the deadly sword. Although David prays for his personal deliverance
(11), it implies in verses 12-14 that the prayer is made for the entire community whose prosperity and blessing would follow YHWH's deliverance.
David assumes the role of a priest to pray for the community and pro-
nounce blessings (v. 15). The blessing of David includes the people (העם),
who experiences such deliverance (שככה לו) and whose God is the Lord.
It is interesting to note that the double blessing (אשרי) does not specifically mention any ethnic people group, rather uses a language which is
inclusive and open ended. This connects the psalm with the language of
Psalm 145, providing a transition from the language of particularism to the
language of universalism. Wilson claims that this concluding phrase (אשרי)
provides an appropriate counter to the rebellious nation who stood against
YHWH in Ps 2:12 (אשרי).[84] In so being, it underscores throughout the
final admonition—*Blessed are all who take refuge* (חסה) *in him* (YHWH).
In other words, David of Psalm 144 puts his trust in YHWH for himself
and his people; he anticipates the people in general will put their trust in
YHWH—"Blessed are the people whose God is the Lord."

Psalm 144 connects with Psalm 145 lexically and thematically in various
ways. Lexical analysis reveals numerous shared lexemes in the two psalms.[85]
These lexemes through their syntactic, paradigmatic, semantic and pragmatic relations contribute unique meaning to each discourse. Comparison

---

84. Gerald Henry Wilson, "Shaping the Psalter: A Consideration of Editorial Linkage
in the Book of Psalms," in *The Shape and Shaping of the Psalter* (ed. J. Clinton McCann;
JSOTSup 159, Sheffield: JSOT Press, 1993), 80.

85. The common lexemes are: ברך (Ps 144:1; cf. Ps 145:1, 2, 10 and 21); יד (Ps 144:1,
7, 11; cf. Ps 145:16); חסד (Ps 144:2; cf. Ps 145:8); ידע (Ps 144:3; cf. Ps 145:12); בן (Ps
144:3; 7, 11-12 cf. Ps 145:12); (Ps 144:3-4; cf. Ps 145:12); יום (Ps 144:4; cf. Ps 145:2);
רב (Ps 144:7; cf. Ps 145:7); אשר (Ps 144:8, 11, 12; cf. Ps 145:18); נתן (Ps 144:10; cf. Ps
145:15); מלך (Ps 144:10; cf. Ps 145:1); and אין (Ps 144:14; cf. Ps 145:3).

of the discourse meanings of the two psalms shows some similarities. In both psalms, David speaks to YHWH (Ps 144:1; cf. Ps 145:1-2). He talks about the "blessing" of YHWH (ברך; Ps 144:1; cf. Ps 145: 1, 2, 10, 21), "the steadfast love" of YHWH" (חסד; Ps 144:2; cf. Ps 145:8), and YHWH as the "giver" (נתן; Ps 144:10; cf. Ps 145:15). These similarities reveal some thematic continuity between the two psalms. At the same time, the two psalms demonstrate some prominent differences. Notice the differences in the following table:

Psalm 144	Psalm 145
David says YHWH is the blessed one (ברך) (v. 1)	David will bless (ברך) YHWH every day and forever; all saints will bless (ברך) YHWH, and then all humanity will bless (ברך) YHWH (vv. 1, 2, 10, and 21)
David is warrior; notice the language of battle/war (v. 1)	David is a worship leader and a herald; notice the language of praise to the Kingship of YHWH (vv. 1-3)
YHWH subdues people under David (v. 2)	David himself is subdued under the Kingship of YHWH; YHWH is good and compassionate to all (vv. 1, 9)
David declares that men's days (יום) are brief (v. 4)	David wants to praise YHWH on a daily basis (יום); since one life is not enough, he expects one generation to tell the story of God to the next generation (vv. 2, 4)
David expects a temporal theophany of God against his enemies (vv. 5-6)	David declares YHWH's dominion, and his glorious Kingdom is everlasting (vv. 11-13)

David informs us that YHWH is thoughtful of sons (בן) of men; he pleads with YHWH to rescue him from the sons (בן) of the aliens (vv. 7, 11).

He anticipates the prosperity for the sons (בן) of Israel when YHWH will bring their deliverance (v. 12)

David pleads to YHWH to stretch out his hand (יד) and rescue him from the hand (יד) of aliens (vv. 7, 11)

David promises to sing a new song (שיר חדש) to God (v. 9)

David seeks the prosperity for his people (vv. 12-14)

David is a servant (v. 10)

David declares that all will speak of the glory of YHWH's Kingdom in order to make known the mighty deeds of YHWH to all the sons (בן) of humanity (v. 12)

David declares that YHWH opens his hand (יד) and satisfies the desires of living things (v. 16)

David sings every day (v. 2)

David anticipates universal providence for every living being (vv. 9, 13-17)

David is a priest and herald who praises YHWH's greatness/goodness (vv. 1-2, 21)

The above differences explain why Psalm 145 would appropriately be located after Psalm 144. The David of Psalm 144 is surrounded by aliens (בני נכר). The language of war and theophany, the mention of the human kings (Ps 144:10), and the cries for deliverance ["deliver me and rescue me" (vv. 7 and 11; פצני והצילני)] locate the psalm in a setting that precedes the language of Psalm 145. The ultimate goal in the former psalm is to obtain the deliverance, the prosperity, and the blessing for the people of God, in particular (אשרי העם שיהוה אלהיו). David is concerned with a present deliverance that would lead to a better future of post-exilic Israel. However, in the final Davidic psalm, David is no longer lamenting for deliverance. His ultimate goal is the universal praise of YHWH because his goodness and greatness encompass all he has made. YHWH will receive praise from all humanity. His dominion is cosmic and his Kingdom is eternal. The placement of Psalm 145 after Psalm 144 introduces an abrupt shift from the language of particularism to universalism, thus ending the fifth book of the Psalter on cosmic and universal note.

Conclusion

Comparison of the discourse meaning of the above ten Davidic psalms with Psalm 145 reveals numerous thematic patterns, movements, and developments that justify the placement of Psalm 145 as the last Davidic psalm in the fifth book. Providing a comprehensive observation on all possible patterns is a difficult task. No single overarching explanation would do justice to the complex inter-textual relations between these psalms. Nevertheless, at the expense of oversimplification, five observations are noteworthy.

(1) The reading of other Davidic psalms (Psalms 108-10 and 138-44) in relation to Psalm 145 provides a fuller picture of the reality of the Kingdom of God. Although YHWH is the present King and his Kingdom is a present reality, the dominion of "the evil one" in the present realm is also real. The wicked people are still around and people of God are not free from their attack. In such a context, other Davidic psalms (Psalms 108-10 and 138-44) provide a relevant "paradigm" of David. David models for us—a man of prayer, lament, and imprecation; a man who has been rejected and abandoned; and a man who is suffering and waiting for YHWH to intervene and deliver him from all the attacks. The "paradigm" of David in Psalm 145 would remain incomplete without the "paradigms" from the other Davidic psalms (Psalms 108-10 and 138-44).

(2) Psalm 145 provides a closure to the Davidic collections in the MT. The "closure" is evident in the image of David who is no longer lamenting, but praising. The image of David in the psalm, instead of lamenting, gives hope to others in the Kingship of YHWH.[86] In Psalm 108, David is rejected and abandoned. He is pleading to YHWH for help. In Psalm 109,

---

86. Berlin examines Psalms 137, 44, 69, and 78 to study the language of exilic and post-exilic community. She suggests that the religious state of mind of the exilic and post-exilic community captured the historical destruction of Jerusalem and the experience of exile in from of laments and complaints par excellence. The intent of the language was to provide the hope for the restoration in the God who is faithful to Israel. See Adele Berlin, "Psalms and the Literature of Exile: Psalms 137, 44, 69 and 78," in *The Book of Psalms: Composition and Reception* (ed. Peter W. Flint et al.; VTSup 99, Leiden: Boston, 2005), 64-86.

David is surrounded by his accusers. He is a man of prayers who offers an imprecatory prayer against his adversaries. He is poor and needy, someone who is fading away like evening shadow. Although lamenting is absent in Psalm 110, David is still waiting for his deliverance. It is only an affirmation of the oracle that he received in Psalm 108. The fulfillment is not yet on the horizon. However, there is hope for David at the end of Psalm 110. Thus, in Psalm 138 and partly in Psalm 139, he begins with the language of praise and confidence. But the reality of his troublesome situation takes over. David begins lamenting from Ps 139:19 and continues until the end of Psalm 144. He explicates every detail of the actions of the wicked and his various troublesome situations that justify his plea for deliverance from his foes. In all these laments, David becomes a "paradigm" for suffering humanity everywhere.

However, the final image of David is a "paradigm" for humanity to praise YHWH and stop lamenting. After several laments, Psalm 145 appears abruptly without any prayer, imprecation, complaint, or details of the wicked. In this psalm, David begins with blessing, exaltation, proclamation, and praise for the goodness and the greatness of YHWH. He ends the psalm with anticipation for the universal praise of YHWH. We do not know why David has stopped lamenting in Psalm 145, but we know that this arrangement provides a smooth transition to the final *hallel* psalms, ending the Psalter with "praise" for YHWH, rather than lament.

(3) Psalm 145 provides hope that includes all—hope for Zion and hope for all whom YHWH has made. There is no language of hope or lexeme to support this argument; however, the theme of the goodness of YHWH to all he has made and the implicit future expectations of David gives hope to all. The expectation in Psalm 108 and 110 still seems to be nationalistic—a human king (the return of the Davidide on the throne). However, Psalm 145 redefines Kingship of YHWH by extending the domain of his rule and providence to all creation. Not only the hope of Israel but also the hope of all humanity rests in YHWH, who is the great and mighty King over all. YHWH's covenant love toward his creation and his righteous attributes become overarching framework of which YHWH's covenant love for Zion becomes a part. The final hope in Psalm 145 broadens the nationalistic agenda of Psalm 110. It revives YHWH's ultimate intent for his creation

through the people of God. It alludes to YHWH's blessing to Abraham in whom the world will be blessed. It does not mention ethnic, historical, geographical, or religious particulars for inclusion, but all those who call on him in truth, those who fear him, and those who love him are included. The final hope in Psalm 145 is noted by the destruction of the wicked. YHWH assumes the role of a King as well as a judge on the final Day of Judgment. He will issue the final verdict on the wicked and execute them. Then, "all-flesh" will praise YHWH worldwide.

(4) Psalm 145 revives the theology of the Kingship of YHWH. Wilson noted that after the rejection of the Davidide king in Psalm 89, the sages placed Psalm 90 at the opening of Book IV, with the superscript ascribed to Moses, to revive the pre-monarchial concept of the Kingship of YHWH.[87] In similar way, Wilson's theory for the placement of Book IV after Psalm 89 may be applied to Psalm 145. The language of rejection in Psalm 108 (זנח) alludes to Psalm 89. But the language of Psalm 145 reminds the language of Book IV. In so doing, the kingship of David is overshadowed by the Kingship of YHWH. It revives the notion of the Kingship of YHWH for the context in which David is lamenting from a hostile environment.

(5) The placement of Psalm 145 redirects the theology of the Kingship of YHWH by bringing an emphasis on YHWH's providential care to all humanity. Using the language of Exodus, David informs us that YHWH is gracious and compassionate; slow to anger and abounding in his great love. YHWH is good to all he has made. He upholds those who fall, lifts up all who are bowed down. YHWH provides food on time to everyone who looks up to him. He opens his hands satisfies the desires of every living thing. These declarations redefines YHWH's cosmic domain in terms of his providential care to all creation. In contrast to all other Davidic psalms in the fifth book, the message of Psalm 145 shows a major shift in emphasis in theology of YHWH's love and providential care. It is simply profound for

---

87. Earlier in chapter 1, we mentioned that according to Wilson Book IV is the editorial "center" of the final form of the Psalter because it contains the answer to the problem of rejection posed in Psalm 89. The answer in the book is the four fold- messages: "(1) YHWH is the king; (2) He has been our 'refuge' in the past, long before the monarchy existed (i.e. in the Mosaic period); (3) He will continue to be our refuge now that the monarchy is gone; (4) Blessed are they that trust in him!" See Wilson, *The Editing*, 215.

its emphasis on YHWH's providential care to all humanity. The reading of this psalm will be received well in a public square.

This leads us to consider the YHWH Kingship psalms in Book IV and investigate how Psalm 145 relates to them.

YHWH Kingship Psalms in Book IV

The compositional arrangement of Book IV is unique.[88] It is the smallest book in the Psalter.[89] Out of the 17 psalms in the book, 13 psalms are without any superscript. The first psalm of the book (Psalm 90) is ascribed to Moses (למשה), which is followed by two major blocks of psalms—YHWH Kingship psalms (Psalms 93 and 96-99) and the Davidic psalms (Psalms 101 and 103/104).[90] The frequent occurrence of the phrase הוה מלך in the YHWH Kingship psalms is noticeable. The verbal form of the Hebrew word מלך (reign) occurs four times in Book IV (Pss 93:1; 96:10; 97:1 and 99:1) while there is only once in Book I (Ps 9:8), once in Book II (Ps 47:9, where the subject is אלהים not YHWH), once in Book V (Ps 146:10; with imperfect form), and not at all in Book III. Notice the pattern in the following table in comparison to other psalms.

---

88. David M. Howard's dissertation, *The Structure of Psalms 93-100*, presents an extensive linguistic and thematic analysis of Psalms 93-100. David M. Howard, Jr., "The Structure of Psalms 93-100," (Ph.D. thesis, University of Michigan, 1986). However, it fails to consider the editorial nature of the entire book. Wilson rightly comments, "The lack of attention to the broader context accounts for Howard's failure to understand the function of the positioning of Psalm 94, with its clear connections to the earlier complex of Psalms 90-92, between the initial YHWH-*malak* psalm (93) and the major collection for thee psalms in 95-99." See Gerald Henry Wilson, "Understanding the Purposeful Arrangement of Psalms in the Psalter: Pitfalls and Promise," in *The Shape and Shaping of the Psalter* (ed. J. Clinton McCann; JSOTSup 159, Sheffield: JSOT Press, 1993), 49-50.

89. Although Books III and IV have equal number of psalms (17), Book III has 367 verses, while Book IV constitutes of 323 verses only.

90. Wilson, "Shaping the Psalter," 75.

מלך אלהים על־גוים אלהים ישב | על־כסא קדשו	Ps 47:9
יהוה מלך גאות לבש	Ps 93:1
אמרו בגוים יהוה מלך אף־תכון תבל בל־תמוט	Ps 96:10
יהוה מלך תגל הארץ	Ps 97:1
יהוה מלך ירגזו עמים	Ps 99:1
ימלך יהוה | לעולם אלהיך ציון לדר ודר הללו־יה	Ps 146:10

Besides the features above, Book IV has two occurrences of the nominal form of the Hebrew word מלך (Pss 91:4 and 105:20), and a high concentration of royal language (Psalms 93 and 96-99). This feature of the language of YHWH Kingship psalms in Book IV connects Psalm 145 more closely.

Scholars vary on the list of YHWH Kingship psalms.[91] Robert D. Rowe points out that the reference to the language of the Kingship of YHWH is not only limited to the lexeme מלך, it is also expressed through the lexeme such as משל , כסא , ישב, דין, שפט, כבד, and גדל etc.[92] For our investigation,

---

91. Gunkel classified the enthronement songs (Psalm 47; 93; 96; 97; 98; and 99), which celebrate the enthronement of YHWH as the universal king. He regarded them as a special category of "hymns" composed to celebrate the enthronement of YHWH as the universal king. He suggested that these psalms were eschatological in nature and be dated as postexilic. Gunkel et al., *Introduction to Psalms*, 66-81. Mowinckel added Psalm 95. He writes, "There can be no doubt that Gunkel is wrong in excluding Ps 95 from the category of the 'enthronement' psalms 93; 96-99. Ps 95 has all the characteristics of others, *plus* something more: and this plus in fact opens the way to a deeper understanding of the enthronement psalms, and widens the number of psalms belonging in the same ideological connection." According to Mowinckel, the enthronement psalms had origin in the pre-exilic cult at the Jerusalem New Year festival, where YHWH was enthroned as the King. He translated יהוה מלך (Pss 93:1; 97:1; 99:1; and 96:10) as "YHWH becomes King." According to him, Psalms 47; 93; and 95-100 have themes of YHWH kingship. Mowinckel, *The Psalms in Israel's Worship*, 32, 106.

92. Robert D. Rowe identifies several psalms based on different lexemes. His data contains some error. The following list has been verified. In following references both YHWH and אלהים is the subject of מלך (Pss 5:2; 10:16; 22:28; 24:7-10; 29:10; 44:5; 47:3; 7-9; 93:1; 95:3; 96:10; 97:1; 98:6; 99:1; 103:19; 145:1, 11-13; 146:10; 149:2); משל (Pss 22:29; 59:14; 66:7; 89:9; and 103:19); ישב (Pss 2:4; 9:8, 12; 22:4; 29:10; 47:8; 55:19; 89:14; 99:1; 102; and 113:5); כסא (Pss 9:5, 8; 11:4; 45:7; 47:9; 89:15; 93:2; 97:2; and 103:19); דין (Pss 7:9; 9:9; 50:4; 72:2; 96:10; 110:6; 135:14; and 140:12); שפט (Pss 7:9, 12; 9:9, 12; 43:1; 58:1; 67:4; 75:8; 82:1-3, 8; 94:2; 96:13; and 98:9). The lexemes כבד and גדל are extensively used in the praise of YHWH. They are not often associated with the kingship language. Robert D. Rowe, *God's Kingdom and God's Son: The Background to Mark's Christology from Concepts of Kingship in the Psalms* (Leiden: Boston, 2002), 15.

we will consider Psalms 93, 95, 96, 97, 98, 99 and 103.[93] We will examine the discourse meaning of each psalm and then analyze their connections with Psalm 145.[94]

Psalm 93

In Psalm 93, YHWH is King (מלך; v. 1; cf. Ps 145:1), robed in majesty (גֵּאוּת), and armed with strength (עז).[95] His throne (כסא) is established (כון) from all eternity (מעולם; v. 2; cf. Ps 145:1-2). Under his care, the world is firmly established (כון).[96] He is mighty above all chaotic waters (vv. 3-4). He is a King whose testimonies (עדה) stand firm (אמן) and whose holiness (קדש) adorns his temple forevermore (v. 5). In contrast to Psalm 145, Psalm 93 emphasizes YHWH's firm stability (כון), his control over nature, his testimonies, and his majesty.

---

93. Traditionally, Psalms 95, 99 and 103 are not considered as the YHWH Kingship psalms. Since these psalms contain similar kingship language and some psalms scholars include them in their discussions, we will investigate them as well. Psalm 103 is the only psalm with Davidic superscript, which has the kingship language (v. 19). Its inclusion is therefore significant. Rowe includes Psalm 103. Ibid., 21. For a detailed lexical analysis of Psalm 103 in comparison with Psalm 145, see appendix 6.

94. A detailed textual critical analysis of each of the YHWH Kingship psalms (Psalms 93, 95, 96, 97, 98, 99 and 103) is not feasible within this dissertation, the position advocated here is indebted to Marvin E. Tate and Willem A. VanGemeren. Marvin E. Tate, *Psalms 51-100* (WBC 20; Dallas: Word Books, 1990); VanGemeren, "Psalms."

95. Weiser suggests that the psalm has its origin not in Israel but in Mesopotamia. The creation motif may probably be linked to a Babylonian source of the Enthronement Festival, where the celebration of the world's New Year marked the enthronement of the god Marduk as a symbol of victory over the power of chaos at the creation of the world. Weiser, *The Psalms*, 617. VanGemeren comments, "The canonical shape of the psalm in the MT bears no reminder of an original cultic situation.." VanGemeren, "Psalms," 607.

96. Rowe suggests the verse is referring to creation, but there is no such lexical evidence for it. The establishment of the world may refer to YHWH's firm control and dominion over and against the chaotic forces that has potential to destroy the world. Rowe, *God's Kingdom and God's Son*, 18. Davidson refers to the LXX heading of the psalm, which has "when the earth was inhabited" (εἰς τὴν ἡμέραν τοῦ προσαββάτου ὅτε κατῴκισται). He sees the psalm picking up the theme from Psalm 92. He sees several other connections with the language of the previous psalm. See Robert M. A. Davidson, *The Vitality of Worship: A Commentary on the Book of Psalms* (Grand Rapids: Eerdmans, 1998), 309. Based on the LXX and *Tamid* 7.4, VanGemeren suggests that the psalm was sung before the Sabbath in the second-temple period. VanGemeren, "Psalms," 607.

Psalm 95

Psalm 95 declares that YHWH is a great god (גדול; v. 3; cf. Pss 96:4; 99:2; 145:3; and 147:5) and a great King above all gods.[97] He is the rock of salvation (ישע; v. 1; cf. Pss 98:1; 145:19. Therefore, sing for joy, shout aloud, give thanks, and extol him (vv. 1-2). YHWH owns the depths of the earth, mountain peaks, seas, and the land (vv. 4-5). He is the creator, who made all of humanity.[98] Therefore, come and worship him. The psalm abruptly ends with a prophetic oracle in verses 8-11.[99] In comparison to Psalm 145, the psalm summons people to give thanks to YHWH by introducing who YHWH is in relation to other gods, creation, nature, and the humanity. He is the master who owns everything.

Psalm 96[100]

Ps 96:10 declares that YHWH reigns (יהוה מלך). At the beginning, all the earth (כל־הארץ) is summoned to sing a new song (שיר חדש; cf. Pss 33:3;

---

97. Kraus thinks that the older view that Psalm 95 would refer to a single occurrence (the dedication of the second temple) is ruled out. It refers to a regularly recurring cultic-liturgy. Kraus, *Psalms 60-150*, 246. Weiser quotes Mishnah, which regarded the psalm as a New Year psalm. For him, the psalm is a portion of a liturgy of the autumn festival in which YHWH is revealed as the Creator and the Lord of the universe (v. 4f), who "enters upon his reign as King (v. 3) and renews the covenant he made with his people." Weiser, *The Psalms*, 625. VanGemeren comments, "Though this psalm is not explicitly a psalm ascribing kingship to the Lord (Pss 93-100), its theme is nevertheless in harmony with the spirit of these psalms." VanGemeren, "Psalms," 616. For a detailed structural analysis see Marc Girad, "Analyse Structurelle du Psaume 95," *ScEs* 33 (1981): 179-89; P. Auffret, "Essai sur la structure littéraire du Psaume 95," *BN* 22 (1983): 47-69.

98. Anderson states, "The main themes of the Psalm are the kingship of Yahweh, his ownership of the world because he had created it, his care for the Covenant people, and the responsibilities of those who are in a Covenant relationship with him." Anderson, *The Book of Psalms*, 677.

99. Waltner names the psalm, "O that today you would listen!" According to him the hymn and the prophetic admonition is related to Psalm 50 and 81. He says, "The God of creation and of covenant expects the obedience that comes from hearing!" Wagner, "Zur Theologie Des Psalms CXXXIX," 463.

100. The psalm has its duplicate in 1 Chr 16:23-33. According to VanGemeren, this incorporation and the superscript of the LXX indicates the association of the psalm with "the glorious entry of the ark of the covenant into Jerusalem." The superscript in the LXX adds, "When the house was built after the Captivity. A song of David." (ὅτε ὁ οἶκος ᾠκοδομεῖτο μετὰ τὴν αἰχμαλωσίαν ᾠδὴ τῷ Δαυιδ). He admits that these traditions do not have bearing on the original life setting of the psalm. VanGemeren, "Psalms," 620. Delitzsch, Kraus, and Anderson notice great similarities between the psalm and Isaiah 40-66. They suggest the possibility of its dependence on the Deutero Isaiah. Franz

40:4; 96:1; 98:1; 144:9; and 149:1). The purpose of the new song is to proclaim his salvation (ישעה; v. 2), and to declare his glory (כבוד; v. 3) and marvelous deeds (פלא; v. 3) among all nations (בכל־העמים / בגוים; v. 3). YHWH is great (גדול; v. 4; cf. Pss 95:3; 99:2; 145:3; and 147:5) and he must be feared above all gods (על־כל־אלהים; v. 4). All the gods of the nations are idols (אלילים; v. 5).[101] YHWH is majestic and glorious. All the families (משפחות) of the nations must ascribe their loyalty to YHWH (v. 7). All should give the glory due to YHWH's name (v. 8; cf. Ps 145:1-2, 21).[102] All the earth (כל־הארץ) must worship and tremble before YHWH (v. 9). YHWH will come and judge (שפט / דין; Pss 96:10, 13; 98:9) the earth in righteousness and in truth (vv. 10-13).[103] In relation to Psalm 145, this psalm also talks about the greatness of God. It also anticipates universal praise (כל־הארץ). The idea of praising YHWH's name (שם) is similar.

Psalm 97

The Kingship of YHWH is the reason for the earth and the distant shore to be glad (שמח; Pss 96:11, 12; 98:7, 8).[104] YHWH will manifest his kingly power in the theophany (cf. Exod 19:16, 18; Judg 5:5; Ps 18:7-15; Hab

---

Delitzsch, *Biblical Commentary on the Psalms* (trans. Francis Bolton; 3 vols.; Grand Rapids: Eerdmans, 1955), 90; Kraus, *Psalms 60-150*, 251-52; Anderson, *The Book of Psalms*, 681.

101. Tate points out that the lexeme אלילים denotes "weak/insufficient/worthless" things. He refers to Job 13:4; Zech 11:7; Lev 19:4; 26:1; Isa 2:8; 18:20; 10:10, 11; 19:1-3; 31:7; and Ezek 30:13. He comments, "The original may have been 'gods,' used in MT a term of contempt. LXX uses δαιμονια, 'demons,' but the word can also mean 'gods.'" Tate, *Psalms 51-100*, 510.

102. Terrien comments, "The vision of peace and health (*shalom*) no longer results from Israel's self-centered ambition; it blooms from the junction of God's name and glory." Samuel L. Terrien, *The Psalms: Strophic Structure and Theological Commentary* (Grand Rapids: Eerdmans, 2003), 677.

103. Anderson names the psalm, "Yahweh is King and Judge." Anderson, *The Book of Psalms*, 680. Rowe suggests that verses 11-13 are clearly eschatological, because it refers to coming of YHWH. Rowe, *God's Kingdom and God's Son*, 19-20.

104. The LXX heading has "For David, when his land is established" (τῷ Δαυιδ ὅτε ἡ γῆ αὐτοῦ καθίσταται). Anderson suggests that the translator may have believed the psalm was adapted for celebrating the return from Babylonian exile. Anderson, *The Book of Psalms*, 686. Unlike Mowinckel, Kraus regards the phrase יהוה מלך is best described as "formula of obeisance." He states, "As the God who from primeval times has been enthroned and has ruled (cf. Ps 93:2), Yahweh is honored as king. In this obeisance all the world is to join." Kraus, *Psalms 60-150*, 258. For a details structural analysis see Auffret, *Merveilles à nos yeux*, 56-59.

3:3-5): clouds and thick darkness (עָנָן וַעֲרָפֶל) will surround him (v. 2); fire (אֵשׁ) will go forth and destroy his enemies (v. 3); lightening (בְרָק) will light up the world (v. 4); the earth (אֶרֶץ) will tremble (v. 4); and the mountains (הָרִים) will melt like wax (v. 5).[105] YHWH is the lord (עֶלְיוֹן / אָדוֹן) of all the earth (כָּל־הָאָרֶץ; verses 5 and 9) because his control and power is manifested in all of nature (vv. 3-5). He is above all gods (כָּל־אֱלֹהִים; v. 9). All the idol worshippers (עָבַד) will be put to shame (בּוֹשׁ) because all gods will worship (שָׁחָה) YHWH (vv. 7 and 9). Zion rejoices (שָׂמַח; v. 8) and the villages of Judah are glad (גִיל) because of YHWH's judgment (מִשְׁפָּט; v. 8). YHWH guards (שָׁמַר; v. 10; cf. 145:20) the lives of his faithful ones (חָסִיד) and delivers them from the hands of the wicked (רָשָׁע; v. 10). He sheds light (אוֹר) upon the righteous (צַדִּיק) and joy (שִׂמְחָה) in the upright heart (יָשָׁר; v. 11).[106] The faithful ones (חָסִיד) are expected to hate (שָׂנֵא) evil (v. 10) and the righteous (צַדִּיק) are summoned to rejoice and praise YHWH's holy name (קֹדֶשׁ; v. 12 cf. Ps 145:21). Similar to Psalm 145, this psalm also underscores the cosmic domain and universal praise of YHWH. The righteous will be delivered from the wicked.

Psalm 98

Psalm 98 is similar to Psalm 96. It begins with an admonition to sing a new song (שִׁיר חָדָשׁ; cf. Pss 33:3; 40:4; 96:1; 98:1; 144:9; and 149:1) and proclaims YHWH as the King (יהוה מֶלֶךְ / הַמֶּלֶךְ יהוה; Ps 96:10; cf. Ps 98:6) later in the text.[107] The psalmist exhorts the audience to praise YHWH for

---

105. According to Kraus, the psalm alludes to Deutero-Isaiah's prophetic reference. Similar to Psalm 96, the psalm has many connections to the message of Deutero-Isaiah, or Trito-Isaiah. He believes that the theophany has an eschatological-universal direction. However, Tate thinks that the verbs in verse 4-8 describe YHWH's past theophany activity rather than future. For him, the eschatological element in the kingship psalms is an implied element. See Kraus, *Psalms 60-150*, 257-58; Marvin E. Tate, *Psalms 51-100* (WBC 20; Waco: Word, 1983), 518.

106. According to Rowe, YHWH rewards with life and light to those who are faithful to his covenant. However, it is not explicit in the text. The absence of any specific reference to a covenant relationship may be intentional. Notice, the emphasis cast by the lexemes חָסִיד, צַדִּיק, and יָשָׁר. Rowe, *God's Kingdom and God's Son*, 20.

107. The LXX heading has "A Psalm of David" (ψαλμὸς τῷ Δαυιδ). Delitzsch notices that the psalm is the only psalm, which has a single superscript מִזְמוֹר in the MT. In *B. Aboda Zara*, 24b, it is called as מִזְמוֹר יָתוֹמָא (the orphan psalm). The Peshîtto Syriac has *De redemtione populi ex Ægypto*. However, he does agree that the "new song," refers to the song of Moses. Delitzsch, *Biblical Commentary on the Psalms*, 97. Tremper Longman

his historical work of salvation (ישועה; v. 1), his covenant love (חסד; v. 3), and his faithfulness (אמונה; v. 3) to the house of Israel (בית ישראל; v. 3). YHWH has revealed (גלה) his righteousness (צדקה; v. 2; cf. 145:7) by making known (ידע; v. 2; cf. Ps 145:12) his salvation to the nations (גוי; v. 2) and all the ends of the earth (כל־אפסי־ארץ; v. 3) have seen it.[108] All the earth (כל־הארץ; v. 4; cf. Pss 96:1, 9; 97:5, 9; 98:4; 100:1; and 108:6), all its inhabitants (ישב; v. 7), the sea (ים; v. 7; cf. Ps 96:11), the rivers (נהר; v. 8), and the mountains (הר; v. 8) are summoned to shout for joy and make music to YHWH the King. YHWH is coming and he will judge (שפט; v. 9; cf. Pss 94:2; 96:13) the world with righteousness (צדק; v. 8; cf. Ps 96:13) and equity (מישר; v. 8; cf. Pss 96:10; 99:4). Unlike Psalm 145, this psalm suggests a new song, which proclaims YHWH's historical work of redemption for Israel as a persuasive testimonial for the world. YHWH's righteousness is revealed in the redemptive history of Israel. Also, YHWH is projected as the coming judge.

Psalm 99

In Psalm 99, YHWH is proclaimed as the Lord in Zion, who has dominion over all the nations.[109] Therefore, all nations must give thanks (ידה; v. 3;

---

regards the psalm to be a victory song of a Divine Warrior who celebrated the return of YHWH, the commander of the heavenly hosts, leading Israel back home after the victorious holy war. Tremper Longman, "A Divine Warrior Victory Song," *JETS* 27 (1984): 267-68. However, Weiser and VanGemeren claim the historical situations in the psalm is "dehistoricized," assuming an eschatological dimension. They suggest that many saving events are "represented" as one event to provide an eschatological focus. Weiser, *The Psalms*, 637; VanGemeren, "Psalms," 627. Anderson attributes Psalms 96 and 98 to the same author. He interprets the salvation as the deliverance from exile. Since the psalm has many connections with Deutero-Isaiah, he believes that the poem might have inspired by the coming of Cyrus. Anderson, *The Book of Psalms*, 690-91. For a detail structural analysis see Auffret, *Merveilles à nos yeux*, 70-76.

108. Rowe presumes, "YHWH wants to extend to the whole world the righteous judgment and saving deeds he has worked for Israel." Rowe, *God's Kingdom and God's Son*, 20.

109. Anderson identifies the psalm as the last of the Enthronement Psalms. He places it in a cultic setting of the Feast of Tabernacles. The allusions to the Covenant may suggest an occasion for the renewal of the Covenant, which may be an important part of the great Autumnal Festival. Anderson, *The Book of Psalms*, 693. Rowe suggests that Psalm 99 is more nationalistic than other enthronement psalms. In the psalm, YHWH's "enthronement in Zion 'upon the Cherubim' provokes a theophany that has world-wide effects, and his dominion over all the peoples is assured." Rowe, *God's Kingdom and God's Son*, 20-21. Auffret provides a helpful structural analysis. See Auffret, *Merveilles à nos*

cf. Pss 97:12; 145:10) to his great and awesome name (שֵׁם; v. 3; Ps 145:1-2, 21). YHWH is holy (קָדוֹשׁ; verses 3, 5, and 9; cf. Isa 6:3).[110] He is the mighty (עֹז; v. 4) King and he loves justice (מִשְׁפָּט; v. 4). He has established equity (מֵישָׁר) and executed justice (מִשְׁפָּט) and righteousness (צְדָקָה) in Jacob (v. 4). Therefore, exalt (רוּם) YHWH and worshipped him (v. 5). YHWH has answered (עָנָה) the prayers of his people (v. 6). He spoke to them from the pillar of cloud. He punished them but he also forgave them. YHWH must be exalted. Similar to Psalm 145, this psalm declares the lordship of YHWH over all nations. All should give thanks to YHWH. His redemptive work among his people is a testimonial for the world to notice.

Psalm 103[111]

Psalm 103 is one of the two Davidic psalms in Book IV of the MT.[112] Both at the beginning and at the end of the psalm (see verses 1, 2 and 35) David exhorts himself (נֶפֶשׁ) to bless (בָּרַךְ) YHWH.[113] YHWH has been good to

---

yeux, 77-86.

110. VanGemeren points out the exegetical problem in the two refrains "He/The Lord is holy" (vv. 3, 5, and 9). He comments, "The nature of the King's rule is not different from his character. He is "holy" (*qādôš*, v. 3), "mighty" ('*ōz*, v. 4), and 'loves justice [*mišpāt*].' He is holy in his perfections and awe-inspiring in his glorious presence. The very revelation of this otherness ('holy') is the glory of the Great King." VanGemeren, "Psalms," 636. Mays thinks that the triple refrain indicates that "the entire psalm is meant to be an exposition of the holiness of the Lord. 'Holy' is the word for the numinous, the *mysterium tremendum* that belongs to deity as such." Mays, *Psalms*, 316.

111. Kraus, Weiser, Anderson, and VanGemeren claim that the psalm has the characteristics of the individual thanksgiving with strong hymnic features. However, Cüsemann and Eaton regard the psalm as an individual hymn because of its strong hymnic features. See Kraus, *Psalms 60-150*, 290; Weiser, *The Psalms*, 658; VanGemeren, "Psalms," 650. F. Crüsemann, *Studien zur Formgeschichte von Hymnus und Danklied in Israel* (WMANT 32; Neykirchen: Neukirchener, 1969), 298-304; J. H. Eaton, *Psalms: Introduction and Commentary* (London: S.C.M. Press, 1967), 246-47.

112. The other Davidic psalm is Psalm 101. Wilson purports that a 'Mosaic frame,' which provides an interpretive *entrée* to the book binds the YHWH-*mālak* psalms and the two Davidic psalms together. David M. Howard Jr.'s work on Psalms 93-100 does not analyze the whole Book IV. Wilson's claim remains to be litmus tested. Wilson, "Shaping the Psalter," 75-76; Howard, "The Structure of Psalms," 1-231.

113. Psalm 103 connects with Psalm 104 with the phrase "Praise the Lord, O my soul" (בָּרְכִי נַפְשִׁי אֶת־יהוה), which forms an inclusion in the both the psalms. This similarity has led some scholars (Gunkel, Kirkpatrick, and Schmidt) to suggest that same author composed them. Anderson, *The Book of Psalms*, 717. Psalm 104 shares numerous lexemes with Psalm 145 [בָּרַךְ (Ps 104:1, 35; cf. Ps 145:1), עָשָׂה (Ps 104:4, 19, 24; cf. Ps 145:19), כֹּל (Ps 104:11, 20, 24, 27; cf. Ps 145: 2, 9-10, 13-18, and 20-21), נָתַן (Ps 104:12, 27-28;

David (vv. 3-5). He forgave (סלח) his sins. He healed (רפא) him, redeemed (גאל) his life, and crowned (עטר) him with love and compassion (חסד ורח־מים). He satisfied (שבע) his desires and his youth has been renewed (חדש). Based on his personal testimonies, David goes on to say that YHWH works righteousness (צדקה) for all the oppressed (עשק; v. 6). YHWH is compassionate and gracious (רחום וחנון), slow to anger, abounding in love (חסד; cf. Exod 34:6, Ps 86:15; Ps 103:8). He will not always accuse (נצה; v. 9). He does not treat us (גמל; v. 10) as our sins deserve, but covenant-love (חסד; v. 11) is higher than the heavens. The greatness of YHWH's covenant-love (חסד)is emphasized in verses 12-18. The discourse in the psalm is primarily about the covenant-love (חסד) for the people of Israel. The lexeme חסד appears four times (vv. 4, 8, 11, and 17). In addition, David specifically refers to Moses and the sons of Israel ("He made known his ways to Moses and his acts to the sons of Israel," יודיע דרכיו למשה לבני ישראל עלילותיו) in verse 7. In Ps 103:19, David proclaims the establishment of YHWH's throne (כסא) in heaven, and his Kingdom (מלכות) has dominion (משל) over all. On the one hand, Psalm 103 has numerous common lexemes and some thematic continuity with Psalm 145. On the other hand, Psalm 103 is uniquely distinct from Psalm 145 with its explicit language of particularism, as mentioned above.[114] We will revisit the psalm later in this chapter.

Five prominent thematic patterns emerge from the YHWH Kingship psalms in Book IV.[115] At the expense of undermining the uniqueness of

---

cf. Ps 145:15), שם (Ps 104:17; cf. Ps 145:1), עד (Ps 104:23; cf. Ps 145:1), הלל (Ps 104:35; cf. Ps 145:2, 3), גדל (Ps 104:3; cf. Ps 145:3, 6, 8), מעשה (Ps 104:13; cf. Ps 145:4, 9, 10, 17), כבוד (Ps 104:31; cf. Ps 145:5, 11-12), טוב (Ps 104:28; cf. Ps 145:7, 9), אדם (Ps 104:14; cf. Ps 145:12), אכל (Ps 104:21, 27; cf. Ps 145:15), עת (Ps 104:27; cf. Ps 145:15), פותח (Ps 104:28; cf. Ps 145:16), יד (Ps 104:28; cf. Ps 145:16), עולם (Ps 104:31; cf. Ps 145:1), שיח (Ps 104:34; cf. Ps 145:5),רשע (Ps 104:35; cf. Ps 145:20)]. In Ps 104:27-28 and 145:15-16, the two psalms show close thematic continuity. However, the illocutionary intent of the discourse in Psalm 104 is to portray YHWH as the creator and sustainer of the world, while Psalm 145 presents YHWH not only as the creator and sustainer of all creation but also as the cosmic and universal king, who will receive "praise" from all that he has made.

114. For a detailed lexical analysis of Psalm 103 in comparison with Psalm 145, see appendix 6.

115. Scholars disagree on the eschatological theme in the YHWH Kingship psalms. Gunkel regarded the YHWH Kingship psalms as eschatological. Gunkel et al., *Introduction to Psalms*, 80-81. According to von Rad, the YHWH Kingship psalms such as Psalms 47, 93, 96, 97, and 99 "do not proclaim an eschatological event but a present

each theme in its discourse, we will discuss them broadly in order to understand the overarching frame of similarities and differences between the YHWH Kingship psalms and Psalm 145.[116]

First, YHWH is the King of all the earth. His throne (כסא) was established from eternity (Ps 93:2). He brought forth (חיל) the earth in the beginning (Pss 90:2; 102:26). He is the judge (שפט) of the earth (Pss 94:2; 96:13; 98:9). The depths (מחקר) of the earth are in his hands (Ps 95:4). All the earth must sing (שיר) a new song to YHWH (Ps 96:1). All the earth must worship (שחה; Ps 96:9) him and tremble (Pss 96:9; 97:4), and shake (Ps 99:1) before him. He is the Lord (אדון) of all the earth (Ps 97:5). He is the most high (עליון) over all the earth (Ps 97:9). His salvation (ישועה) is visible to all the ends of the earth (כל-אפסי-ארץ; Ps 98:3). Therefore, let the earth rejoice and be glad in the Kingship of YHWH (Pss 96:11; 97:1). Let the earth shout for joy (רוע) in the Kingship of YHWH (Pss 98:4; 100:1).

Second, YHWH is the King of all the nations.[117] He rules Zion and the surrounding towns of Judah (Ps 97:8), but he also rules over all nations (כל-העמים; Ps 99:2). He disciplines (יסר) the nations (גוים; Ps 94:10). All nations and all people must be told about the glory of YHWH (Ps 96:3). They must be informed that YHWH is the King (Ps 96:10). All the nations will fear the Lord (כל-מלכי הארץ) and all kings will revere his glory (Ps 102:16).

Third, YHWH is the King of all gods. His throne (כסא) is established in heaven and his Kingdom (מלכות) rules over all (Ps 103:19). He is the great King over all gods (Ps 95:3; ומלך גדול על-כל-אלהים). All gods bow down (שחה) to YHWH (Ps 97:7), because YHWH is exalted above all gods (Ps 97:9, על-כל-אלהים). The gods of all nations are just idols (אלילים; Pss 96:5; 97:7).

---

reality experienced in the cult." Gerhard von Rad, "*mlk* and *mlkt* in the OT," *TDNT* 1: 569.

116. May's brief exposition of the YHWH Kinship psalms in Book IV provides three outlines, namely YHWH is the King in the spheres of dominion, institution of his reign, and activities of his sovereignty. These classifications are too broad and topically misleading. Mays, *The Lord Reigns*, 14–15.

117. In fact, the theme alludes to Ps 47:3, 8-10, where the psalmist declares the Kingship of YHWH over all nations explicitly. His kingship is to be proclaimed among all the nations.

Fourth, YHWH is the King of all nature. His rule extends over every elements of nature. He has dominion over the mighty waters (מים רבים) of the seas (Ps 93:3-4). He holds the depths (מחקרי־ארץ) of the earth, and the mountain peaks (ותועפות הרים לו) belong to him (Ps 95:4). He made the sea (הים והוא עשהו), and formed the dry land (Ps 95:5, ויבשת ידיו יצרו). His power and might is manifested in nature (Ps 97:2-5): clouds and thick darkness (ענן וערפל) surround him; fire (אש) goes before him; lightening (ברק) lights up the world; and mountains (הרים) melt like wax. He is the lord of all creation (כל־הארץ). All creation will rejoice when the King comes to judge the world (Pss 96:11-13; 98:7-9).

Fifth, YHWH is the King who will come and judge the world with equity. He will pay back (שוב) what the proud deserve (Ps 94:2). He will judge the people with equity (ישר; Ps 96:10), in righteousness (צדק), and in truth (אמונה; Ps 96:13). Scholars disagree as to its future expectation.[118]

---

118. The idea of the coming judge suggests an eschatological theme. Gunkel regarded the YHWH Kingship psalms as eschatological. Gunkel et al., *Introduction to Psalms*, 80-81. According to von Rad, the YHWH Kingship psalms such as Psalms 47, 93, 96, 97, and 99 "do not proclaim an eschatological event but a present reality experienced in the cult." von Rad, "*mlk* and *mlkt* in the OT," 569. The debates on eschatological expectations in the Psalter have revolved around the usage of the two words "messiah" and "king." Some scholars contend that the "royal psalms" not merely represent the nostalgia or the witness of the glorious past, but also it acts like a "beacons to give direction to the hopes and expectations of a new king." See Walter Rose, "Messianic Expectations in the Old Testament," *IDS* 35 (2001): 284. Others, such as Norman Whybray and M. A. Vincent, are not enthusiastic about the eschatological interest in the Psalter. See Roger Norman Whybray, *Reading the Psalms as a Book* (JSOTSup 222; Sheffield: Sheffield Academic, 1996), 88-89; M. A. Vincent, "The Shape of the Psalter: An Eschatological Dimension?" in *New Heaven and New Earth Prophecy and the Millennium Essay in Honor of Anthony Gelston* (Leiden: Brill, 1999), 62. Geerhardus Vos asserts that it is "in the Psalter that the term Messiah enters into the eschatological vocabulary. This nomenclature of messianism does not have its seat in the prophets. The term Messiah, i.e. 'the Anointed,' is specifically proper to the Psalter." He also points out that the eschatological character of the Psalter is evidenced not only in the kingship language but also in other expressions, such as: (1) references to a new song (Pss 33:3; 96:1; 98:1; 144:9; 149:1), new things, new creation, or new name (cf. also Isa 42:9-10; 62:2; 65:17; 66:22; Rev 2:17; 21:5). These conceptions are all connected with the fulfillment of God's plan; (2) reference to "set time" (cf. Ps 75:2-[75:3, RV]; 102:14—[102:13]; and Hab. 2:3); (3) a definite fixed program and the implication that there is a plan organically linking the previous works of God with the present and future, eschatological events (Ps. 77:10ff; 138:8—"perfect that which concerneth me"; for not the work of thine own hand"); (4) reference to judgment being "written" (cf. Ps. 149:9) "Morning" in Psalms 46:5; 49:14; 130:6 (cf. 59:16; 112:4; 118:27; 143:8; Hos 6:3; Isa 17:14; 21:11-12) suggested the break (dawn) of the great day of Jehovah. See Geerhardus Vos, *The Eschatology of the Old Testament* (ed. James T. Dennison, Jr.; Philipsburg: Presbyterian and Reformed, 2001), 131, 40.

Broadly speaking, the theme of the universal Kingship of YHWH from Psalm 145 has a striking parallel in the YHWH Kingship psalms of Book IV. Put differently, Psalm 145 alludes to the YHWH Kingship psalms in Book IV by declaring the Kingship of YHWH over all humanity and over all the earth. Probably, the continuity of the theme in Psalm 145 is editorially intended to emphasize or revive certain theology in order to address the historical situation of the final redactor(s). This is also evidenced through the prominent difference in the thematic development. The specific elements of comparison of YHWH with other gods, YHWH's dominion over nature, and his coming as a judge (except for the destruction of the wicked) are absent in Psalm 145. In general, the illocutionary intent of the message of the YHWH Kingship psalms seems to be apologetic (Psalms 96 and 98) and nationalistic (Psalms 97, 98, 99 and 103), whereas Psalm 145 focuses on YHWH's compassionate goodness and greatness experienced by all humanity in his providential care and salvation.[119] Psalm 145 does not repeats some of the themes of the YHWH Kingship psalms. This may be for the following reasons: (1) the audience may already know them; (2) they are irrelevant to the new historical context; and (3) the necessary emphasis on the universal aspect of Kingdom of God theology, which invites all humanity to enjoy YHWH's love, care and protection. Our discussions so far suggest considering all of these reasons.

---

119. In addition, Psalm 145 differs significantly with the twelve psalms (Psalms 10; 24; 29; 47; 93; 95-99; 146; and 149) that has direct or indirect reference to YHWH Kingship theme. Psalm 145 uses YHWH as the subject more often than other psalms. The word YHWH appears only nine times (vv. 3, 8, 9 10, 14, 17, 18, 20, and 21), but it is implied 38 times within verses 3-21 (see appendix 5). The focus of the syntagmatic semantic in these verses is YHWH. Out of 22 bicolons (including *nun* bicolon), 18 bicolons in the nine verses describe attributes or the actions of YHWH. Four times YHWH is referred to as the third person "he" (vv. 19 and 20), four times as third person accusative "him" (vv. 18, 19, and 20), and eight times as the third person genitive "his" (vv. 3, 9, 12, 17, and 21). Then, sixteen times YHWH is referred to as second person genitive "your" (vv. 4, 10, 11, 12, 13, and 16) and four times he is referred to as second person "you" (vv. 10 and 15). Again, seven times YHWH is referred as the subject of the participles (מהלל in v. 3; סומך and זוקף in v. 14; נותן in v. 15; פותח in v. 16; and שומר in v. 20). In other words, the psalm is all about YHWH either as the subject or as the object in the syntax.

The Motif of the Kingdom of God

The motif of the Kingdom (מלכות) of God in Psalm 145 is unique. It is unique for its use of the Hebrew lexeme for "kingdom" (מלכות; Ps 145:11-13).[120] Out of 91 occurrences of מלכות in the Old Testament,[121] only seven times does it refer to YHWH's Kingdom (1 Chr 17:14; 28:5; Pss 45:7; 103:19; 145:11, 12, and 13) while all others times it refers to a human kingdom. It does not occur in the YHWH Kingship psalms (Psalms 47, 93, and 96-99). Five out of the seven references to YHWH's Kingdom (מלכות) appear in the Psalter and, most importantly, three appear in Psalm 145 in cluster form at the center of the psalm (vv. 11, מלכותך; 12, מלכותו; 13, מלכותך). Earlier in chapter 3, we discussed how some scholars, such as

---

120. Scholars differ on the theme of the Kingdom of God in the Old Testament. Some regard it as significant, others as a marginal. Some consider it as an early development while others see it as a late development. According to von Rad, reference to YHWH as the King is found only after the rise of the empirical monarchy. For him, the earliest references to the Kingdom of God are: Num 23:21; Deut 33:5; 1 Kgs 22:19, and Isa 6:5. von Rad, "*mlk* and *mlkt* in the OT*," But others include Exod 15:18; 1 Sam 12:12, Isa 24:23, and Isa 33:22. Martin K. Hopkins explores the idea of the Kingdom of God in the Old Testament extensively, except in Psalm 145. Martin K. Hopkins, *God's Kingdom in the Old Testament* (Chicago: H. Regnery, 1964). Hengstenberg equates the history of Israel as the history of the Kingdom of God. In his two volume works, he captures the significant events from Abraham to the return from the second exile. Ernst Wilhelm Hengstenberg, *History of the Kingdom of God Under the Old Testament* (2 vols.; Eugene: Wipf & Stock, 2005). In general, most scholars agree that the development of the motif is more explicit in the later writings such as Chronicles, the Psalters, and some Minor Prophets (Dan 7-12; Zech 14:16f, Obad 21, and Zeph 3:15, 1). Additionally, since the phrase "Kingdom of God" does not occur in the Old Testament at all, the opinion varies about the implicit motif in the other connected themes. In other words, the study of the motif is not limited to the study of the lexemes מלך and מלכות, but other lexemes such as ישב , כסא , משל , כבד , שפט , דין, and גדל etc. Sometimes the motif is intertwined with the language of creation and war. For a detailed discussion on the motif of the Kingdom of God and its development in the Old Testament see Martin J. Selman, "The Kingdom of God in the Old Testament," *TynBul* 40 (1989): 161-84; R. T. France, "Kingdom of God," in *Dictionary for Theological Interpretation of the Bible* (ed. Kevin J. Vanhoozer; Grand Rapids: Baker Academic, 2005), 420-22; Philip J. Nel, "*mlk*," *NIDOTTE* 2, 956-65.

121. The lexeme מלכות occurs 91 times in the Old Testament: Num 24:7; 1 Sam 20:31; 1 Kgs 2:12; 1 Chr 11:10; 12:24; 14:2; 17:11, 14; 22:10; 26:31; 28:5, 7; 29:25, 30; 2 Chr 1:1, 18; 2:11; 3:2; 7:18; 11:17; 12:1; 15:10, 19; 16:1, 12; 20:30; 29:19; 33:13; 35:19; 36:20, 22; Ezra 1:1; 4:5, 6a, 6b; 7:1; 8:1; Neh 9:35; 12:22; Esth 1:2, 4, 7, 9, 11, 14, 19f; 2:3, 16, 17; 3:6, 8; 4:14; 5:1, 3, 6; 6:8; 7:2; 8:15; 9:30; Pss 45:7; 103:19; 145:11, 12, 13; Eccl 4:14; Jer 10:7; 49:34; 52:31; and Dan 1:1, 20; 2:1; 8:1, 22, 23; 9:1; 10:13; 11:2, 4, 9, 17, 20, 21. Of them, 84 times it refers to the human kingdom while 7 times it refers to YHWH's Kingdom.

Watson, Lindars, and Kimelman, have observed literary phenomena that support the uniqueness and the centrality of the theme of מלכות in the psalm. We also discussed how the use of מלכות is unique in the psalm.

The three usages of מלכות in Psalm 145 are semantically different in comparison to the other four occurrences in the Old Testament. The other four occurrences of it in the Old Testament are 1 Chr 17:4; 28:5; Pss 45:7; and 103:19.

והעמדתיהו בביתי ובמלכותי עד־העולם וכסו יהיה נכון עד־עולם:	1 Chr 17:14
ומכל־בני כי רבים בנים נתן לי יהוה ויבחר בשלמה בני לשבת על־כסא מלכות יהוה על־ישראל:	1 Chr 28:5
כסאך אלהים עולם ועד שבט מישר שבט מלכותך:	Ps 45:7
יהוה בשמים הכין כסאו ומלכותו בכל משלה:	Ps 103:19
כבוד מלכותך יאמרו וגבורתך ידברו:	Ps 145:11
להודיע ׀ לבני האדם גבורתיו וכבוד הדר מלכותו:	Ps 145:12
מלכותך מלכות כל־עלמים וממשלתך בכל־דור ודור:	Ps 145:13

In 1 Chr 17:14, the lexeme מלכות is placed in the mouth of YHWH as "my kingdom" (במלכותי) along with "my house" (בביתי).[122] The context of the text is the prophet Nathan's speech to king David. Nathan is commissioned by YHWH in a vision (1 Chr 17:3, 7, and 15) to proclaim to David that he will not build the house for YHWH but rather one of his descendants will.[123] YHWH will establish throne of David's descendant forever (v. 12). YHWH will become his father and never take away his חסד love (v. 13) from him. He will cause David's descendant to stand (notice hiphil perfect of עמד), or settle him (NIV) in his "house" (בית) and in his "kingdom" (מלכות) forever (v. 14), establishing his throne for eternity. In verse 14, the word "house" (בית) and "kingdom" (מלכות) is used in parallelism. What does the phrase "my house and my kingdom" mean in this

---

122. However, the LXX translates it as "my house and his kingdom." At the same time, its parallel text in 1 Sam 7:16 has "your house and your kingdom," implying David's house and kingdom, but the LXX has "his house and his kingdom," implying the house and kingdom of David's descendents. It is beyond our purview to resolve whether this is a scribal error or pluriformity of the text.

123. Ironically, the prophet Nathan does not mention the name of the descendant, but historical implication suggests Solomon.

context? The key to understanding the phrase "my house and my kingdom" is in verse 13, where YHWH declares a relationship through which David's descendant becomes a member (a son) of the house of YHWH—through a relationship that lasts forever. The covenant relationship between YHWH and David's descendant is described with the metaphors of a 'father and son' relationship, which sets the context for understanding the phrase "my house and my kingdom." The phrase "my house and my kingdom" is a merismus, meaning "the whole frame of care, authority, and dominion" of YHWH as the father of the house. This is also evident in the use of the lexeme בית in first Chronicles chapter 17, where it switches its connotations from a "dwelling place" to "dynasty/family line."

verse 1	ויהי כאשר ישב דויד בביתו	dwelling place for the king
	הנה אנכי יושב בבית הארזים	dwelling place for the king (made up of Cedar)
verse 4	לא אתה תבנה־לי הבית לשבת:	dwelling place for God
verse 5	כי לא ישבתי בבית	dwelling place for God
verse 6	למה לא־בניתם לי בית ארזים:	dwelling place for God (made up of Cedar)
verse 10	ואגד לך ובית יבנה־לך יהוה	dynasty/family line
verse 12	הוא יבנה־לי בית וכננתי את־כסאו עד־עולם:	dwelling place for God
verse 14	והעמדתיהו בביתי ובמלכותי עד־העולם	dynasty/family line
verse 17	ותדבר על־בית־עבדך למרחוק	dynasty/family line
verse 23	אשר דברת על־עבדך ועל־ביתו	dynasty/family
verse 24	ובית־דויד עבדך נכון לפניך	dynasty/family
verse 25	גלית את־אזן עבדך לבנות לו בית	dynasty/family

In the above usages of בית in chapter 17, we notice that the emphasis shifts from the "dwelling place" to "dynasty" or "family line." The illocution and the perlocution of the text underline the concern for establishing a relationship, which YHWH wants to enjoy with the love and the authority of a father over David's house (David's dynasty). Therefore, the semantics of מלכות in 1 Chr 17:14 is particularly connotes the house of David.[124] Likewise, in 1 Chr 28:5 also the phrase "Kingdom of the Lord over Israel" (מלכות יהוהעל־ישראל) indicates particularism. The illocutionary intent of the text is limited to the house of David (Solomon) and to the boundaries of the nation of Israel.[125]

The context of מלכות in Ps 45:7 is uncertain because of the inherent problem in the text itself.[126] Most scholars agree that Psalm 45 is a royal wedding song, whose content is focused on the earthly king, who represents the divine king. Although the lexeme מלכות is used for the earthly kingdom, the emphasis is on the absence of any distinction between the earthly and divine.

The context of מלכות in Psalm 103 is the covenant love (חסד; verses 4, 8, 11, and 17) and the particular history of Israel (vv. 7-14), while the lexical semantic of מלכות in Psalm 145 emphasizes both the universal (all-inclusive) and the cosmic (all creation) aspect of the kingdom.[127] The psalmist's ultimate concern in Psalm 103 is limited to the covenant people of Israel. This contrast is made explicit in two ways: (i) The lexeme חסד appears four times (vv. 4, 8, 11, and 17) in Psalm 103, while only once in Psalm 145 (v. 8); (ii) The lexeme ידע in Ps 103:7 refers to Moses and the sons of Israel ("to make known his ways to Moses and his acts to sons of Israel," לבני ישראל עלילותיו יודיע דרכיו למשה) but in Ps 145:12 it is about all humanity ("to make known the acts of YHWH to all the sons of men," להודיע לבני האדם

---

124. Commenting on verse 14, Williamson writes, "This shift in focus from David to Solomon is crucial. Its effect is to throw the promise of an established dynasty forward on to him. . . . Consequently, the only legitimate kings are those whom he has **confirmed** and **established**." H. G. M. Williamson, *1 and 2 Chronicles* (NCB; Grand Rapids: Eerdmans, 1982), 136.

125. Roddy Braun comments, "God will build the house for David, i.e., will establish his dynasty, forever. More specifically, it is here that God's kingdom will be established (v 14), and it here that through David's seed (v 11), one of his sons, the throne would be established forever (v 14), i.e. through Solomon." Roddy Braun, *1 Chronicles* (WBC 14; Waco: Word Books, 1986), 200. Sara Japhet comments, "Sovereignty over Israel belongs to God, and it in this 'house' that Solomon's throne will be established." Sara Japhet, *I and II Chronicles: A Commentary* (OTL; Louisville: Westminster John Knox, 1993), 335.

126. Peter C. Craigie, *Psalms 1-50* (WBC 19; Waco: Word, 1983), 337.

127. This does not mean that Psalm 103 has no thematic connections with Psalm 145. In fact, Psalm 145 shows numerous thematic continuity when Psalm 103 and 104 read together. It is important to note that the themes assume different nuance in the new discourse setting of Psalm 145. For more details, see footnote number 113.

גבורתיו). Psalm 145 ends by anticipating that "all flesh" (כל־בשׂר) will bless, whereas Psalm 103 ends with a personal resolution—ברכי נפשׁי את־יהוה.

The lexical semantics of מלכות in Psalm 145 is uniquely inclusive, beyond any ethnic, geographical, or political boundaries, with the objective of obtaining the praise of YHWH from all humanity (כל־בשׂר).[128] Psalm 145 emphasizes the cosmic dominion of YHWH more frequently than Psalm 103. Psalm 145 mentions "all creation" four times (כל־ / כל־מעשׂיך מעשׂיו; verses 4, 9, 10, and 17), whereas Psalm 103 only one time (כל־מע־ שׂיו; v. 22). The mention of creation in Psalm 103 is more analogical than the symbolic of YHWH's dominion. Thus, we conclude here that the lexical semantics of מלכות in Psalm 145 is cosmic, beyond the house of David and the boundaries of the nation of Israel.

The theology of the Kingdom of God in Psalm 145 is presented by YHWH's dynamic actions, rather than dominion or reign of a geographical nature.[129] In comparison to the YHWH Kingship psalms (Psalms 47, 93, and 96-99), Psalm 145 is more explicit about YHWH's dynamic action instead of a mere declaration of his reign (הוה מלך). In Ps 145:11, the psalmist declares that all whom YHWH has made will not only declare his Kingship but also will tell the glory of YHWH's מלכות and גבו־ רה. In verse 12, the purpose of their telling is to make known (להודיע, the circumstantial infinitive) to all sons of men the glorious splendor of YHWH's "Kingdom and Might" (מלכות and גבורה). YHWH's reign in these two verses is cosmic, not limited to a particular political boundary. YHWH is the creator of the cosmos and his reign is cosmic. Earlier we

---

128. Scroggie comments, "Another characteristic of the Psalm [145] is its *universality*. This is more impressive when we remember the nationalistic outlook of the people of Israel (Jonah 4:1-2). If *generation* and *saints* in verses 4, 10, 13 could possibly be regarded as of Israel only, no such restriction can be attached to *men* (6), *all* (9) *sons of men* (12), and *all flesh* (21). The outlook reaches far beyond the boundaries of Israel and embraces all mankind, and in doing so it anticipates the outlook of the third Gospel of the Saviour of the World." W. Graham Scroggie, *The Psalms: Psalms I to CL* (Westwood: Fleming H. Revell, 1965), 106-07.

129. According to Oesterley, the kingdom in the psalm represents rule, or dominion "not connoting any thought of a land or area, the ordinary Jewish conception of the time." W. O. E. Oesterley, *The Psalms: Translated with Text-Critical and Exegetical Notes* (London: SPCK, 1939), 574.

discussed the chiasm in these two verses,[130] but we shall now examine the parallelism in them.

כבוד מלכותך יאמרו וגבורתך ידברו   verse 11

להודיע[131] | לבני האדם גבורתיו וכבוד הדר מלכות   verse 12

In the verses above, the glory of YHWH's Kingdom (מלכות) is in parallelism with his might (גבורה). This parallelism exists in chiasm. In parallelism, there are three possibilities: intensification by equivalence (synonymous), intensification by explication or addition (synthetic), and intensification through contrast (antithetic). The presence of chiasm and the intended emphasis on the מלכות cancels the plausibility of intensification through contrast (antithetic). Thus, the two phrases, "glory of YHWH's Kingdom" and "YHWH's might," are either equivalent ideas or one is the explication of the other. In both ways, the idea of מלכות in verses 11 and 12 is not a static geographical territory but a dynamic activity. It refers to the activities of YHWH that have been mentioned in previous verses. This is also evident in three lexical connections: (i) the noun גבורה connects verse 11 to verse 4 ("one generation will commend your works to another; they will tell of your mighty acts"); (ii) the verb (third person plural) אמר connects verse 11 to verse 6 ("they will tell of the power of your awesome works, and I will proclaim your great deeds"); (iii) the lexeme הדר connects verse 12 to verse 5 ("they will speak of the glorious splendor of your majesty, and I will meditate on your wonderful works"), where there is parallelism between YHWH's "wonderful works" and "the glorious splendor." Thus, the Kingdom of God is represented with "mighty acts," "awesome works," "great deeds," and "wonderful works." These are YHWH's dynamic actions witnessed in the cosmos.

The Kingdom of God in the psalm is characterized by an ideal governing *rule* of YHWH. Notice the parallelism between the phrases וממשלתך and מלכותך in verse 13. It is a synthetic parallelism where the idea is

---

130. See our discussions on Reuven Kimelman's literary structure on page 124-32.
131. We notice that the chiastic structure is more explicit in the LXX as its Hebrew construction of verse 12 would have גבורתך and מלכותך.

intensified by explication or addition. Using the lexeme מֹשֵל, the psalmist defines YHWH's Kingdom (מלכות) as a sphere of dominion in which certain actions of YHWH is executed. Although מֹשֵל does not have any direct lexical connection with rest of the psalm, the syntagmatic, semantic, and pragmatic connections imply that the actions of YHWH are the manifestations of YHWH's dominion (מֹשֵל; v. 13) in the human world. YHWH is the ultimate emperor, who rules the spheres of humankind. Notice the rule and the realm of YHWH's dominion in the following table.[132]

מֹשֵל of YHWH

Verse	Rule of מֹשֵל	Realm of מֹשֵל
13b	faithful, loving	all YHWH has made
14	upholds, lifts up	all who fall, bows down
15	gives food on time	eyes of all who look to YHWH
16	opens hand, satisfies the desires	every living thing
17	righteous, loving	all YHWH has made
18	near	all who call on YHWH, all who call him in truth
19	fulfills the desires, hears the cry, saves	who fear YHWH, who cry to YHWH
20	watches over	all who love YHWH
21	destroys	all the wicked

The psalmist describes how YHWH governs his Kingdom with certain actions (as listed in the second column above) and how the realm of his rule is over all, including the particular (who calls on YHWH in truth, who love him, and who fears him).

The concept of the cosmic מלכות of YHWH in Psalm 145 is the renewal of an ancient Old Testament prophetic belief. Prophet Jeremiah claimed YHWH is the cosmic King: "who should not revere you, O King of the nations? This is your due. Among all the wise men of the nations and in

---

132. See the discourse analysis in chapter 3.

all their kingdoms, there is no one like you" (Jer 10:7). In the same way, the prophet Isaiah presented YHWH as the cosmic ruler in Isa 2:2; 40:22; 43:9; 61:11; and 66:18, 20. The writer of 1 Chr 29:11 declares "Yours, O Lord, is the greatness and the power and the glory and the majesty and the splendor, for everything in heaven and earth is yours. Yours, O Lord, is the kingdom; you are exalted as head over all." Also in Ps 22:28, the psalmist proclaims the cosmic rule (מלכות) of YHWH ("for dominion belongs to the LORD and he rules over the nations"). Perhaps, the poet in Psalm 145 picks up a dormant theological thought and brings it to the forefront because of the prevailing historical situation.

The reality of the Kingdom of God is "already and not yet" in the psalm.[133] In one sense, the Kingdom of YHWH is already present; in another sense, it is yet to be accomplished. The notion of "already" is consistent with the psalm's plausible historical setting.[134] Since psalms scholars commonly agree to place this psalm in the post-exilic period, it is reasonable to assume that the psalmist composed such a psalm to help Israel consider YHWH as the King, who is better than all earthly kings are. DeClaissé-Walford states this more explicitly.

> The post-exilic Israelite community was vassal to one immense empire after another—the Persians, the Greeks, and the Romans. The people could not continue as a separate,

---

133. von Rad writes, "Some statements underline the timeless element in the kingly being of Yahweh as this embraces equally both past and future as well as present (Exod 15:18; 1 Sam 12:12; Ps 145:11-13; Ps 146:10)." von Rad, "*mlk* and *mlkt* in the OT*," 565-71. Vos purports eschatological and messianic content in the Psalter in general. He comments, "The universalism of the Psalter appears in the conversion of the nations to the service of Jehovah. This concept is approached; (1) through the kingship of Jehovah (Ps 97:1, 6); (2) through the prospect of universal peace (Ps 46:9); (3) through the principle of monotheism (Ps 78:82). All of these contain the germ of the working out of the doctrine of universalism." Vos, *The Eschatology of the Old Testament*, 143-44. Vos does not refer Psalm 145 in particular, but the other psalms contain the features that he describes. In addition, it also presents YHWH as the judge who will destroy the wicked. However, Oesterley denies any thing of eschatological nature in the psalms. He translates the imperfect ישמיד in habitual aspect "he destroyeth." Oesterley, *The Psalms: Translated with Text-Critical and Exegetical Notes*, 574-75.

134. John Carmody writes, "This psalm [Psalm 145] was sung by a community who expressed through it a very central conviction of their religious and national life." S. J. John Carmody, "The Theology of Psalm 145," *TBT* 43 (1969): 2978.

identifiable entity in the only form they had known—as a
nation with an independent king and court. The days of the
Davidic monarchy were gone forever. Therefore, the key to
survival was to transcend traditional ideas about the nation-
hood and recognize YHWH as king over the new "religious
nation" of Israel.[135]

Thus, it is plausible that the emphasis on the transcendence and omnipo-
tence of YHWH in Psalm 145 is primarily intended to call attention to
YHWH's immanence in the daily lives of Israel. YHWH, though invisible,
is indeed their King who is much more superior and competent than all
earthly kings they knew.

YHWH is not merely seated in the heavenly abode or in an innermost
room of the temple, but he is the one who is in the royal public court
actively engaged in Israel's daily social, economical, political, and spiritual
activities. This is why David calls him "my God, the King." Such an understanding of the YHWH Kingship is indicative of the unique historical
situation to which the psalm must have belonged.

The notion of the Kingdom of God as "not yet" is also consistent with
the historical reality of the post-exilic Israel. Although YHWH's domain
is supposed to be cosmic and his praise is supposed to be universal, it is
expressed as an anticipated event in the psalmist's real life experience —"all
the wicked he will destroy" and "all flesh will praise his holy name forever
and ever." There is no place for the wicked in the coming Kingdom, for the
King will destroy all of them (v. 20; cf. Ps 146:9). The future Kingdom,
without the wicked, is not a temporal but an eternal (v. 13; cf. Ps 146:10)
state. The identity of the "wicked" is generic, permeating across ethnic or
religious boundaries. This implies that YHWH will destroy all the wicked
irrespective of their ethnic and biological descent. Nevertheless "all flesh,"
all who are delivered by YHWH (v. 19), will praise YHWH. The praise of
YHWH in the new Kingdom will continue as an eternal event.[136] Thus, the

---

135. Nancy L. DeClaissé-Walford, *Reading from the Beginning: The Shaping of the Hebrew
Psalter* (Macon: Mercer University Press, 1997), 29.
136. James H. Waltner claims that the "emphasis of Psalm 145 on the glorious and
everlasting kingdom (vv. 11-13a) foreshadows the NT's proclamation of the kingdom of

notion of the Kingdom of God in the psalm is in one sense is "already" but in another sense, "not yet."

Conclusion

In this chapter, comparison of the discourse analysis of Psalm 145 with the two groups of Davidic psalms (Psalms 108-10 and 138-44) and the YHWH Kingship psalms in Book IV (Psalms 93, 95, 96, 97, 98, 99, and 103) can be summarized in the following five conclusions. First, the reading of ten Davidic psalms (Psalms 108-10 and 138-44) in relation to Psalm 145 provides a fuller perspective on the present realm of the Kingdom of God. Indeed, the Kingship of YHWH and his Kingdom are a present reality. However, the present dominion of "the evil one" is also real. Since the wicked people are still around, the people of God are not free from their attack. For such a situation, the image of David in the ten Davidic psalms (Psalms 108-10 and 138-44) is a model for us—a man of prayer, lament, and imprecation; a man who has been rejected and abandoned; and a man who is suffering and waiting for YHWH to intervene and deliver him from all the attacks. The image of David of Psalm 145 is supplemented by the images from the other ten Davidic psalms (Psalms 108-10 and 138-44) for our daily meditations.

Second, Psalm 145 presents a positive finish to the image of David in the MT. The end is evident by the last occurrence of lexeme דוד in the MT. This last occurrence presents a different image of David. David is no longer lamenting, but he is praising and proclaiming the Kingdom of God. In Psalm 108, we saw David as rejected and abandoned. He pleads to YHWH for help. In Psalm 109, David is a man of prayers who offers an imprecatory prayer against his enemies. In Psalm 110, David is still waiting for his deliverance. Although in Psalm 138, David praises with confidence, he soon begins lamenting in Ps 139:19 and continues until the end of Psalm 144.

God (Matt 6:33; Mark 1:15; Luke 4:43; John 3:2). James H. Waltner, *Psalms* (ed. Elmer A. Martens and Willard M. Swartley; Scottdale: Herald, 2006), 693. John's writing in Rev 11:15 ("The kingdom of the world has become the kingdom of our Lord and of his Messiah, and he will reign forever and ever") supports Waltner's claim.

However, in Psalm 145, David is no longer a "model" for rejection, abandonment, suffering, and complaining humanity, but he becomes a "model" for "praise" and "proclamation." It is obvious that the redactor(s) of the MT do(es) not want to close the Psalter with an image of David who laments and complains, but with an image of the one who "proclaims" the goodness of YHWH and his Kingdom.

Third, David of Psalm 145 provides hope that includes all—hope for Zion and hope for all whom YHWH has made. In Psalms 108 and 110, the hope is nationalistic—a human king (the return of a Davidic king on the throne)—but the hope in Psalm 145 is extended to all creation. This hope in Psalm 145 broadens on the nationalistic agenda of Psalms 110 and makes it universal and cosmic in its scope. It revives YHWH's ultimate intent for his creation through the people of God. Ultimately, the world will be freed from the wicked and be filled with the universal praise of YHWH.

Fourth, Psalm 145 revives the theology of the Kingship of YHWH. We noted that the language of rejection in Psalm 108 (זנח) alludes to Psalm 89, but the language of Psalm 145 alludes to the language of YHWH Kingship psalms in Book IV. Psalm 145 is the only psalm in Book V that uses the language of the Kingship of YHWH.

Fifth, Psalm 145 redirects the theology of the Kingship of YHWH by bringing an emphasis on YHWH's providential care to all humanity. On the one hand, the theme of the Kingship of YHWH in Psalm 145 is similar to the YHWH Kingship psalms of Book IV. They together proclaim the Kingship of YHWH over all humanity and over all the earth. YHWH is the deliverer and the coming judge. On the other hand, the language of the Kingship of YHWH in Psalm 145 is distinct from the language of Kingship of YHWH in Book IV. Psalm 145 uses the language of Exodus, declaring emphatically that YHWH is gracious and compassionate; slow to anger, and abounding in his great love. Such language does not occur in the YHWH Kingship psalms (Psalms 93, 96-100), except Ps 103:8. In addition, Psalm 145 declares that YHWH is good to all he has made. He upholds those who fall, lifts up all who are bowed down. YHWH provides food on time to everyone who looks up to him. He opens his hands and satisfies the desires of every living thing. Such language is absent in Book IV. The additions of such language in Psalm 145 suggest a new understanding of the theology of the Kingship of YHWH. The illocutionary intent of the message of the YHWH Kingship psalms in Book IV is apologetic (Psalms 96 and 98) and nationalistic (Psalms 97, 98, 99 and 103), whereas Psalm 145 focuses on YHWH's compassionate goodness, providential care, and salvation extended to all creation.

CHAPTER 6

Conclusion

In the 1989 Society of Biblical Literature meeting, James L. Mays posed a question regarding the validity of the compositional reading of the Psalter as a "useful third way."[1] His answer was "yes," but a modest one, because of the suspicion that the new method would abandon the traditional form-critical and cult-functional approaches to the Psalter. In an article, he explains his views concerning the relationship between the old and new approaches very well.

> Criticism is simply a procedure for clearing the mind to see what is there. The historical-critical question has been asked and much learned. It cannot be forgotten. The lesson has been, to sum it up in a rather presumptuous way, avoid genre-confusion; but it has been the broadening and the development of critical practice which has put tradition, literature, and canon in focus.[2]

The compositional reading of the psalms does not undermine the benefits received from reading the individual psalms in the older methods, but rather engages with them to make our understanding more comprehensive. Since numerous works are available in the older methods, the current psalms studies have begun to explore compositional critical analysis of the

---

1. J. Clinton McCann, preface to *The Shape and Shaping of the Psalter* (ed. J. Clinton McCann; JSOTSup 159, Sheffield: JSOT Press, 1993), 7.
2. James Luther Mays, "The David of the Psalms," *Int* 40 (1986): 144.

psalms. In line with the ongoing research, this dissertation was intended to supplement the reading of Psalm 145 in relation to the YHWH Kingship psalms in Book IV, the final *hallel* psalms, and the two groups of Davidic psalms in Book V.

Psalm 145 was considered for five reasons: (1) its placement in the MT is different from the LXX and the 11QPs[a]; (2) it is read in combination with Pss 84:5, 144:15, and 115:18 in the Talmudic tradition; (3) it reverses the Exodus imagery (Exod 34:6) from רחום וחנון to חנון ורחם, conforming to all the psalms in Book V (Pss 111:4, 112:4, 116:5), but not to the psalms in Book III (Ps 86:15) and Book IV (Ps 103:8) in the MT; (4) its unique thematic emphasis on the universal and eternal Kingdom of YHWH; and (5) the contextual relevance of its central theme in a polytheistic country like India.

In chapter 2, three types of methodological assumptions were stated: theological, hermeneutical, and exegetical. Under theological assumptions, we affirmed that the final shape of the Psalter is deeply imprinted with hermeneutical underpinnings from the community that shaped the text into its final form. The Psalter is not only encoded with historical information concerning the life situation of the individual psalms, but also the life settings of the editor and the community for whom it was compiled. Therefore, the hermeneutical question is not only what any individual psalm means to its reader, but also what it means in relation to other psalms. How does the editorial arrangement of Psalm 145 affect its theological message?

Regarding hermeneutical assumptions, we explained the issues involved with meaning. Meaning is more than just using the grammars and lexicons. In our discussion, we considered Vanhoozer's canonical linguistic approach, which draws our attention to discern meaning at more than one level. His method is sensitive to the final shape of the Psalter. The method commends "discourse analysis" as an appropriate hermeneutical tool both for individual psalms and for their compositional reading. It allows the psalms to speak to us at multiple levels in their own literary context (*Sitz in der Literatur*), rather than any hypothetical context.

Concerning exegetical assumptions, we stated five important conclusions. First, determining the date of the placement of Psalm 145 is a difficult task. In the absence of any historical data, we can only conjecture that the placement of Psalm 145 in the canon was sometime in the post-exilic period, and possibly before the time of the compilation of the LXX. Second, David is no longer a distant historical figure of remembrance but a "model" for all. He is democratized in the psalms for the readers to learn from his life. Third, in the compositional reading of the psalms, we notice "thematic patterning." Some themes are repeated but others are expanded by rhemes. Observation of this thematic patterning augments our theological understanding of the themes under considerations. Four, the acrostic structure of Psalm 145 is not only a mnemonic device but also a literary tool to communicate its message effectively. The message of the psalm is the universal kingdom of God and all-inclusive praise of YHWH. The acrostic and other literary features of the psalm facilitate the message. Five, broadly speaking, Psalm 145 has very few textual critical problems, except for the absence of a *nun* line in the MT. The illocutionary movement in the discourse favors the inclusion of a *nun* line.

In chapter 3, we noted that literary divisions of the psalm based on theological themes are arbitrary. The application of rhetorical literary criticism allowed different poetic and literary devices to show a progressive movement of the themes in the psalms, which earlier methods failed to capture. Analysis of key words, chiasm, literary symmetry, concentric structure, thematic progression, and other literary features in the psalm provided significant insight for the interpretation the psalm.

The literary structure of Psalm 145 shows a linear thematic development. The themes are developed either by explication or by heightening of the subject matter. For example, the theme of blessing is developed by heightening the number of the participants— from name (שֵׁם; v. 1) to holy name (שֵׁם קׇדְשׁוֹ; v. 21); from individual blessing (אֲבָרְכָה; v. 1) to community blessing (יְבָרְכוּכָה; v. 10), and then to universal blessing (יְבָרֵךְ; v. 21).

The central theme of Psalm 145 is the universal and cosmic kingdom of God. David in the psalm proclaims YHWH as the universal and ever-lasting King. He is good to all he has made. He is compassionate and his providential care is extended to all he has made. At the same time, he points out three groups of people to whom YHWH responds in particular: the godly ones (חׇסִיד; v. 10), the one who calls YHWH in truth (יִקְרׇאֻהוּ בֶאֱמֶת; v. 18), the one who fears YHWH (יְרֵאָיו; v. 19,), and the one who loves him (אהביו; v. 20). David anticipates YHWH will destroy all the wicked. He begins blessing YHWH individually, but he expects the community of the godly ones and then "all-flesh" to join him. David models the role of a priest and a herald.

In chapter 4, we argued against Wilson's claim concerning the purposeful placement of Psalm 145 in the "Final Wisdom Frame" and its function as the "climax" of the fifth book of the Psalter. Wilson's claim regarding the role of Psalm 145 in the "Final Wisdom Frame" is deficient of micro-level analysis. His claim undermines the complexities of the thematic patterns in the Psalter. Connected themes not only reveal continuity but also development. In other words, there are no duplicate psalms in the Psalter. Even the psalms that are repeated (Pss 57:8-12 and 60:7-14) assume different nuances in their new literary context.

In addition, the relationship of Psalm 145 to the final hallel psalms is much more complex than Wilson suggests. The detailed analysis of the discourse of the final *hallel* psalms and their comparison with Psalm 145 show multidimensional thematic patterning. Some themes of Psalm 145 find continuity in the final *hallel* psalms. For example, Pss 146:8 and 145:14 have continuity on the theme of "YHWH's raising those who are bent down" (כפף / זקף). But the theme of "praise" in Psalm 145 is intensified in Psalms 148 and 150 (notice the frequency of the phrase "praise YHWH"). Still other themes are explicated through thematic building. For example, Psalm 145 tells us that YHWH will destroy the wicked, but Psalm 149 informs us further that the godly ones will execute YHWH's judgment.

Furthermore, exegetical analysis does not support Psalm 145 as the "climax" of the fifth book; however, some exegetical data supports the placement of Psalm 145 as the last psalm in the Psalter. Five literary features support this claim. First, Psalm 145 forms an *inclusion* with Psalm 107 for the fifth book. Second, for some lexemes Psalm 145 is the last psalm in the Psalter. Third, Psalm 145 is the last acrostic psalm. Fourth, Psalm 145 is the last psalm for the theme of "thanksgiving" (ידה). Fifth, Psalm 145 has doxological features.

Placed as the last Davidic psalm in the fifth book, Psalm 145 has dual functions. With David in the superscript, it links with the Davidic group of psalms (Psalms 138-44), while with the *inclusion* formed by "praise"

(תהלה / תהלת), it links with the final *hallel* psalms. It functions like *Janus* looking backward to Davidic groups of psalms, as well as forward to the final *hallel* psalms. Thus, the literary features of Psalm 145 provide a transition between the closing of the fifth book and the initiation of the final *hallel* psalms.

In chapter 5, we analyzed the connections of Psalm 145 with the two groups of Davidic psalms (Psalm 108-10 and 138-44) and the YHWH Kingship psalms in Book IV. Our observations richly improved our understanding on the purposeful placement of Psalm 145 in the fifth book of the Psalter. The following five conclusions are noteworthy here. First, Psalm 145 provides only one aspect of the present reality of the Kingdom of God. Reading the psalm together with the ten Davidic psalms (Psalm 108-10 and 138-44) provides a wholistic understanding of the present reality of the Kingdom of God. Although YHWH is the reigning King, He cares, provides, and delivers; the fact is that the world is still under the active dominion of "the evil one." The wicked are still around and the people of God are not free from their attack. For the present, we need the image of David from other Davidic psalms (Psalms 108-10 and 138-44) to provide a model for us—a man of prayer, lament, and imprecation; a man who has been rejected and abandoned; and a man who is suffering and waiting for YHWH to intervene and deliver him from all the attacks.

Second, Psalm 145 declares a happy conclusion to the image of David in the MT. The end is evident by the last occurrence of lexeme דוד in the MT. However, the last occurrence associates with itself a unique image of David. David is no longer lamenting, but he is praising and proclaiming the Kingdom of God. Unlike Psalm 108, which began by projecting David as rejected and abandoned, Psalm 145 presents David as a "priest" and "herald" of the Kingdom of God. He provides hope that includes all—hope for Zion and hope for all whom YHWH has made. Ultimately, YHWH will destroy the wicked and "all-flesh" will join him in praising YHWH

Third, the designation of God as "King" is programmatic in the last Davidic psalm. In that, the redactor(s) are addressing a socio-historical context of post-exilic Israel. Four prominent messages emerge from its placement:

(1) YHWH is a superior king. He is the great king as well as the good king whose compassion, care, protection, and salvation are extended to all humanity—both Jews and Gentiles. It is also particular and specific because it is meant for those who call on him in truth, fear him, and love him.

(2) YHWH's kingdom is a present reality. His rule and dominion can intervene at anytime and anywhere, and in any historical reality. People of God must find comfort and assurance in the power and ability of this ultimate, great king, especially when no good king is to be found.

(4) The anticipation for YHWH's absolute rule and glory gives rise to a future hope. The expected destruction of the wicked, universal praise of YHWH, and the hope of salvation for all creation is handed down from generation to generation.

Fourth, Psalm 145 revives and redirects the theology of the Kingship of YHWH. It revives by alluding to the language of YHWH Kingship psalms in Book IV. Psalm 145 is the only psalm in Book V that uses this language. It also redirects the theology of the Kingship of YHWH by bringing forward an emphasis on YHWH's providential care to all creation. Although the theme of the Kingship of YHWH in Psalm 145 seems to be similar to the YHWH Kingship psalms of Book IV, it is distinct in its emphasis and illocutionary intent. These distinctions are noted in three aspects.

(1) Frequent comparison of YHWH with the idols of the surrounding nations suggests that the illocutionary intent of the message of the YHWH Kingship psalms in Book IV is apologetic and nationalistic, whereas Psalm 145 focuses on YHWH's compassionate goodness, providential care, and salvation extended to all creation. It is remarkable that the redactor(s) preferred to end the Psalter with Psalm 145, rather than the YHWH Kingship psalms of Book IV.

(2) Psalm 145 uses the language of Exodus, declaring emphatically that YHWH is gracious and compassionate; slow to anger, and abounding in his great love. This is absent in the YHWH Kingship psalms (Psalms 93, 96-100), except Ps 103:8.

(3) Psalm 145 declares that YHWH is good to all he has made. He upholds those who fall, lifts up all who are bowed down. YHWH provides food on time to everyone who looks up to him. He opens his hands and

satisfies the desires of every living thing. These emphases are absent in the language of Book IV.

The motif of the Kingdom of God in the last Davidic psalm has significant continuity with the motif of the Kingdom of God in the New Testament. In the New Testament, John the Baptist and Jesus Christ, the Son of David, appear proclaiming "the Kingdom of God" (Matt 3:2; 4:17; 4:23; 5:3; Mark 1:15; 3:2; 4:11; 10:15; etc.). Similar to Psalm 145, their message proclaimed good news for all humanity—Jews and Gentile. The goal was to reach out the whole "world."

Franz Delitzsch rightly observed continuity between of the post-exilic psalms and the New Testament. He wrote,

> [All] these post-exilic songs come much nearer to the spirit of the New Testament than the pre-exilic; for the New Testament, which is the intrinsic character of the Old Testament freed from its barriers and limitations, is in process of coming into being (*im Werden begriffen*) throughout the Old Testament, and the exile was one of the most important crises in this progressive process.[3]

We suggest that the spirit of the New Testament is greatly influenced by the post-exilic psalms. This is particularly true for Psalm 145. In the literary context of the Christian canon, its placement at the end of the Psalter brings it closer to the New Testament, binding them together on the theme of the universal Kingdom of God. Kraus rightly stated, "Psalm 145 is an important milestone on the way to the NT proclamation of the Kingdom of God."[4] James H. Waltner adds, "The emphasis of Psalm 145 on the glorious and everlasting kingdom (vv. 11-13a) foreshadows the NT's proclamation of the kingdom of God (Matt 6:33; Mark 1:15; Luke 4:43; John 3:3)."[5] Jesus did not explicitly quote Psalm 145; however, he referred his

---

3. Franz Delitzsch, *Biblical Commentary on the Psalms* (trans. Francis Bolton; 3 vols.; Grand Rapids: Eerdmans, 1955), 90.

4. Hans-Joachim Kraus, *Psalms 60-150: A Continental Commentary* (trans. Hilton C. Oswald; Minneapolis: Fortress, 1989), 549.

5. James H. Waltner, *Psalms* (ed. Elmer A. Martens and Willard M. Swartley; Scottdale:

teaching back to the Psalter (Luke 20:42; 24:44).[6] It would not be wrong to speculate that Jesus Christ and his audience knew Psalm 145. It is likely that their audience connected their proclamation to the theme of the Kingdom of God in Psalm 145. Even John's writing in Rev 11:15 has greater parallel to Psalm 145 than other psalms: "The kingdom of the world has become the kingdom of our Lord and of his Messiah, and he will reign forever and ever." The early Christian community saw Jesus Christ as the one who came not to destroy, but to fulfill the Torah and Prophets and provide the hope of salvation to all humanity. The Church today looks forward in anticipation for Jesus to return as the universal King.

These findings have important implications for correcting certain perceptions among people of other faiths in India who have regarded Christianity as the religion of the western nations, and the God of the Bible as the god of the Jews and the Europeans. The compositional reading of Psalm 145, which underscores the universal Kingdom of God, counters such false social, cultural, and religious bigotry. The churches in India are comprised of people who have embraced Christianity from diverse ethnic and religious backgrounds. The writer belongs to a community that has enjoyed a Buddhist heritage for more than two thousand years. The psalm provides a new perspective on the God of the Old Testament for his community. YHWH is the Creator God. Indeed, he is the God of Abraham and God of the Jews, but he is primarily the God of all humanity. He loves all that he has made. He provides care, love, protection, and salvation to all. He will destroy all the wicked. One day all humanity will praise him forever and ever. To that effect, the prophet Isaiah prophesied YHWH's claim—*before me every knee will bow; by me every tongue will swear*" (Isa 45:23f)—and Paul reiterated for the Church—*every tongue should confess that Jesus Christ is Lord, to the glory of God the Father* (Phil 2:11).

Herald, 2006), 693.

6. Craig A. Evans presents a detailed research on the connections between Jesus and the psalms. See Craig A. Evans, "Praise and Prophecy," in *The Book of Psalms: Composition and Reception* (ed. Peter W. Flint et al.; VTSup 99, Leiden: Boston, 2005), 551-79.

The Order of Qumran Psalms

[Gerald H. Wilson presents the new and unexpected order of the Masoretic Psalms in the 11QPsª with their superscripts and postscripts in the following table. The material between square brackets, [ ], is restored based on the MT and the space on the scroll, while the material within parentheses, ( ), is restored based on the MT alone.][1]

Psalm	Superscription	Postscript
101	[לדויד מזמור]	
102	[תפלה ל] עני כי יעטו [ף ולפני יהוה ישפוך שיחו]	
103	[לדויד]	
109	(למנצח לדויד מזמור)	
118	(הודו ליהוה כי טוב)	[הודו] ליהוה כי טוב
104	לדויד	הללויה
147	[?]	[הללויה]
105	הודו ליהוה כי טוב	(הללויה)
146	[?]	[הללויה]
148	No superscription	(הללויה)
[120]	(שיר המעלות)	
121	שיר המעלות	

---

1. Gerald Henry Wilson, "The Qumran Psalms Scroll (11QPsa) and the Canonical Psalter: Comparison of Editorial Shaping," *CBQ* 59 (1997): 450.

Psalm	Superscription	Postscript
122	שיר המעלות לדויד	
123	שיר לדויד למעלות	
124	(שיר המעלות לדויד)	
125	[שיר המעלות]	
126	שיר המעלות	
127	[שיר המעלות] לשלומוה	
128	(שיר המעלות)	
129	[שיר המעלות]	
130	שיר המעלות	
131	[שיר המעלות לדויד]	
119	No superscription	No postscript
135	No superscription	הללויה
136	הודו ליהוה כי טוב	No postscript
Catena	הודו ליהוה כי טוב	הודו ליהוה כי טוב
145	תפלה לדויד	זאת לזכור
154	?	?
Plea for Deliverance	?	?
139	(למנצח לדויד מזמור)	
137	No superscription	No postscript
138	לדויד	No postscript
Sir 51:13-20, 30	No superscription	No postscript
Apostrophe to Zion	No superscription	No postscript
93	הללויה	[?]
144	No superscription	No postscript
155	No superscription	[?]
142	(משכיל לדויד בהיות במערה תפלה)	No postscript
143	מזמור לדויד	[?]
149	[?]	הללויה

Psalm	Superscription	Postscript
150	No superscription	הללויה
Hymn to the Creator	No superscription	[?]
2 Sam 23:1-7	[?]	No postscript
David's composition	No superscription	No postscript
140	למנצח מזמור לדויד	[?]
134	(שיר המעלות)	No postscript
151A	הללויה לדויד בן ישי	No postscript
151B	תהלה גב[ו] רה ל[דו] יד משמשחו גביא אלוהימ	[?]

Canonization of the Psalter

[Wilson's three options for the canonization of the psalter[1]]

A. Direct-Sequential Linkage-[11QPs^a Prior]- Sanders

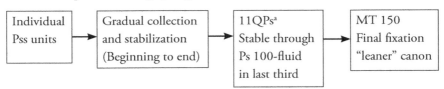

| Individual Pss units | Gradual collection and stabilization (Beginning to end) | 11QPs^a Stable through Ps 100-fluid in last third | MT 150 Final fixation "leaner" canon |

B. Parallel Collection

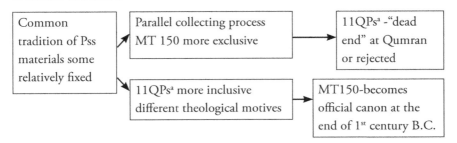

Common tradition of Pss materials some relatively fixed

Parallel collecting process MT 150 more exclusive

11QPs^a -"dead end" at Qumran or rejected

11QPs^a more inclusive different theological motives

MT150-becomes official canon at the end of 1st century B.C.

C. Library Edition-[MT150 prior-11QPs^a]—dependent Skehan

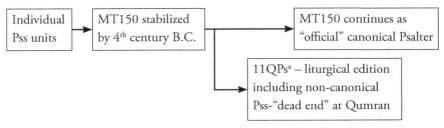

Individual Pss units

MT150 stabilized by 4th century B.C.

MT150 continues as "official" canonical Psalter

11QPs^a – liturgical edition including non-canonical Pss-"dead end" at Qumran

---

1. Gerald Henry Wilson, *The Editing of the Hebrew Psalter* (Chico: Scholars Press, 1985), 91-92.

Concentric Structure of Psalm 145[1]

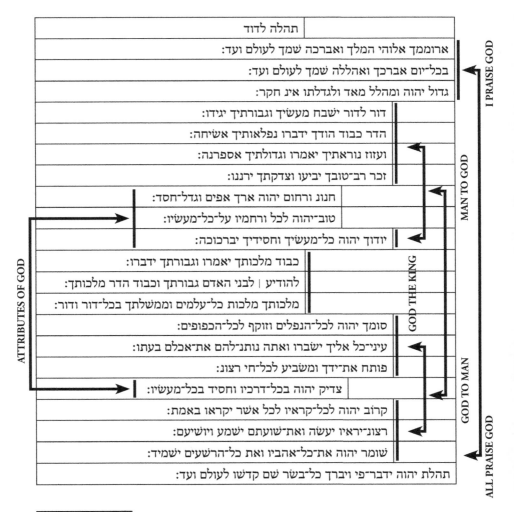

1. Jonathan Magonet, "Some Concentric Structure in Psalms," *HeyJ* 23 (1982): 366.

APPENDIX 4

Different Usage of מֶלֶךְ in the Psalter

[The lexeme occurs 73 times in the Psalter. Following are its different lexical usage. This table does not include the thematic and implied meaning, which is arbitrary.]

SL	Subject	Book I	Book II	Book III	Book IV	Book V
1	יהוה is the King (16 X)	10:16; 24:7, 8, 9, 10a, 10b; 29:10	47:3; 48:3		93:1; 95:3; 96:10; 97:1; 98:6; 99:1, 4	146:10; 149:2
2	אלהים the King (10X)	5:3	44:5; 45:6; 47:3, 7, 8, 9; 48:3,	68:25; 74:12		145:1
	God is King / Judge (שׁופט) (2X)		58:12	75:8	96:10; 99:4	
3	David king (5X)	2:6 (?); 18:51; 20:10 (?); 21:2, 8;	45:2, 6, 10, 12, 14, 15, 16 (?); 61:7; 63:12			144:10 (?)

257

4	Solomon is king (2X)			72: 1a, 1b;		
5	Other human king (36X)	2:2	45:2, 6, 10, 12, 14, 15, 16 (?); 48: 5; 61:7; 68:13, 15, 25, 30	68:30; 72:10a, 10b, 11; 76:13; 89:19, 28	102:16; 105:14, 20, 30	110:5; 119:46; 135:10, 11a, 11b; 136:17, 18, 19, 20; 138:4; 144:10
6	Human being is king +Judge	2:6; 2:10; 20:10;	33:16			148:11; 149: 8
7	My King +My God	5:3	44:5	68:25	84:4	

APPENDIX 5

The Use of YHWH in Psalm 145

Verses	YHWH (subject/object)	YHWH implied in the 3ms	YHWH implied in 2ms suffix	YHWH implied in the participle
3	יהוה (s)	ולגדלתו (his)		ומהלל
4			מעשׂיך (your) וגבורתיך (your)	
5			הודך (your) נפלאותיך (your)	
6			נוראתיך (your) וגדולתיך (your)	
7			טובך (your) וצדקתך (your)	
8	יהוה (s)			
9	יהוה (s)	ורחמיו (his) מעשׂיו (his)		
10	יהוה (o)		יודוך (you) מעשׂיך (your) וחסידיך (your)	
11			מלכותך (your) וגבורתך (your)	
12		BHS (his) BHS (his)	גבורתך (your) מלכותך (your)	
13			מלכותך (your) וממשׁלתך (your)	

| 14 | | | | סומך
וזוקף |
| 15 | | | אליך (you)
ואתה (you) | נותן |
| 16 | | | ידך (your) | פותח
ומשביע |
| 17 | יהוה (s) | דרכיו (his)
מעשׂיו (his) | | |
| 18 | יהוה (s) | קראיו (him)
יקראו (him) | | |
| 19 | | יראיו (him)
יעשׂה (he)
ישמע (he)
ויושיעם (he) | | |
| 20 | | אהביו (him)
ישמיד (he) | | שׁומר |
| 21 | יהוה (appo/o) | קדשׁו (his) | | |

Lexical Connections Between Psalms 103 and 145

Lexeme	Psalm 103	Psalm 145
לדוד	1	1
ברך	1, 2, 20, 21, 22 (2)	1, 2, 10, 21
יהוה	1, 2, 6, 8, 13, 17, 19, 20, 21, 22 (2)	3, 8, 9, 10, 14, 17, 18, 19, 20, 21
שם	1	1, 2, 21
קדש	1	21
חסד	4, 8, 11, 17	8
רחם	3	9
שבע	5	16
טוב	5	7, 9
עשה	6, 10, 18, 20, 21	19
צדקה	6, 17	7
ידע	7, 14	12
דרך	7	17
רחום	8	8
חנון	8	8
ארך	8	8
אף	8	8
עולם	9, 17 (2)	1, 2, 13, 21
ירא	11, 13, 17	6, 19

זכר	14, 18	7
שמר	18	20
מלכות	19	11, 12, 13 (2)
משל	19, 22	13
כל	1, 2, 3 (2), 6, 19, 21, 22 (2)	2, 9 (2), 10, 13 (2), 14(2), 15, 16, 17 (2), 18(2), 20(2), 21
דבר	20 (2)	5, 11, 21
רצון	21	16, 19
מעשיו	22	4, 9, 10, 17

Bibliography

Abegg, Martin G., Peter W. Flint, and Eugene Charles Ulrich, eds. *The Dead Sea Scrolls Bible: The Oldest Known Bible*. San Francisco: HarperSan Francisco, 1999.

Alexander, Joseph A. *The Psalms: Translated and Explained*. 3 vols. Philadelphia: Presbyterian Board of Publication, 1850.

Allen, Leslie C. "Faith on Trial: An Analysis of Psalm 139." *Vox Evangelica* 10 (1977): 5-23.

_____. הלל. Pages 1035-38 in vol. 1 of *New International Dictionary of Old Testament Theology and Exegesis*. Edited by Willem A. VanGemeren. 5 vols. Grand Rapids: Zondervan, 1997.

_____. *Psalms 101-50*. Word Biblical Commentary 21. Nashville: Nelson, 2002.

Aloisi, John. "Who is David's Lord? Another Look at Psalm 110:1." *Detroit Baptist Seminary Journal* 10 (2005): 103-23.

Alter, Robert. *The Art of Biblical Poetry*. New York: Basic Books, 1985.

Anderson, Bernhard W. *The Book of Psalms*. 2 vols. New Century Bible Commentary. Grand Rapids: Eerdmans, 1981.

_____. *The Living World of the Old Testament*. 4th ed. Silver Library. Harlow: Pearson, 2000.

_____. *Understanding the Old Testament*. 4th ed. Englewood Cliffs: Prentice-Hall, 1986.

Anderson, Bernhard W., and Steven Bishop. *Out of the Depths: The Psalms Speak for Us Today*. 3d ed. Louisville: Westminster John Knox, 2000.

Anderson, David R. *The King-Priest of Psalm 110 in Hebrews*. Studies in Biblical Literature. New York: Peter Lang, 2001.

Arens, Anton. *Die Psalmen im Gottesdienst des Alten Bundes: Eine Untersuchung zur Vorgeschichte des christlichen Psalmengesanges*. Trier: Paulinus, 1961

_____. "Hat der Psalter seinen 'Sitz im Leben' in der synagogalen Lesung des Pentateuch?" Pages 107-31 in *Les Psautiers, ses origines, ses problèmes littéraires, son influence.* Edited by Robert de Langhe. Louvain: Publication Universitaires, 1962.

Auffret, P. "Il est seignneur sur les nations: Etude structurelle du psaume 110." *Biblische Notizen* 123 (2004): 65-73.

_____. "Essai sur la structure littéraire du Psaume 95." *Biblische Notizen* 22 (1983): 47-61.

_____. "Essai sur la structure littéraire du Psaume 145." Pages 15-31 in *Melanges bibliques et orientaux. FS H Cazelles.* Edited by A. Caquot and M. Delcor. Neukirchen-Vluyn: Neukirchener, 1981.

_____. "Note sur la structure littéraire du Psaume." *Semitica* 32 (1982): 83-88.

_____. "O Dieu, connais mon coeur: Étude structurelle du Psaume CXXXIX." *Vetus Testamentum* 47 (1997): 1-22.

_____. *La sagesse a bâti sa maison: études de structures littéraires dans l'Ancien Testament et spécialement dans les psaumes.* Orbis biblicus et orientalis 49. Fribourg: Göttingen, 1982.

_____. *Merveilles à nos yeux: Étude structurelle de vingt psaumes dont celui de 1 Ch 16:8-36.* New York: Walter de Gruyter, 1995.

_____. "Note Sur La Structure Littéraire du Psaume CXXXVI." *Vetus Testamentum* 27 (1977): 1-22.

Baker, David W., and Bill T. Arnold. *The Face of Old Testament Studies: A Survey of Contemporary Approaches.* Grand Rapids: Baker Books, 1999.

Barr, James. *Comparative Philology and the Text of the Old Testament.* Oxford: Clarendon, 1968.

_____. *The Semantics of Biblical Language.* London: Oxford University Press, 1961.

Barré, Michael L. "'Terminative' Terms in Hebrew Acrostics." Pages 207-15 in *Wisdom, You Are My Sister: Studies in Honor of Roland E. Murphy, O. Carm., on the Occasion of His Eightieth Birthday.* Edited by Michael L. Barré. Catholic Bible Quarterly Monograph Series. Washington, D.C: Catholic Bible Association, 1997.

Barthélemy, Dominique, Adrian Schenker, and John Alexander Thompson. *Preliminary and Interim Report on the Hebrew Old Testament Text Project: Compte rendu préliminaire et provisoire sur le travail d'analyse textuelle de l'Ancien Testament hébreu.* Vol. 3. 2d rev. ed. New York: United Bible Societies, 1979.

Barton, John. "Intertextuality and the 'Final Form' of the Text." Pages 33-37 in *Congress Volume: Oslo 1998*. Edited by André Lamaire and Magne Sæbø. Supplement to Vetus Testamentum 80. Leiden: Brill, 2000.

Bateman IV, Herbert W. "Psalm 110:1 and the New Testament." *Bibliotheca sacra* 149 (1992): 438-53.

Becker, Joachim. *Israel deutet seine Psalmen*. Stuttgarter Bibelstudien 18. Stuttgart: Verlag Katholisches Bibelwerk, 1966.

_____. *Israel deutet seine Psalmen: Urform und Neuinterpretation in den Psalmen*. Stuttgarter Bibelstudien 18. Stuttgart: Verlag Katholisches Bibelwerk, 1967.

Bentzen, Aage. *King and Messiah*. London: Lutterworth Press, 1955.

Berlin, Adele. *The Dynamics of Biblical Parallelism*. Bloomington: Indiana University Press, 1985.

_____. "Psalms and the Literature of Exile: Psalms 137, 44, 69 and 78." Pages 64-86 in *The Book of Psalms: Composition and Reception*. Edited by Peter W. Flint, Patrick D. Miller, Aaron Brunell and Ryan Roberts. Supplements to Vetus Testamentum 99. Leiden: Boston, 2005.

_____. "The Rhetoric of Psalm 145." Pages 17-22 in *Biblical and Related Studies Presented to Samuel Iwry*. Edited by Ann Kort and Scott Morschauser. Winona Lake: Eisenbrauns, 1985.

Blackman, Aylward. "The Psalms in the Light of Egyptian Research." Pages 177-97 in *The Psalmists: Essays on Their Religious Experience and Teaching, Their Social Background, and Their Place in the Development of Hebrew Psalmody*. Edited by D. C. Simpson. London: Oxford University Press, 1926.

Boice, James Montgomery. *Psalms*. Vol. 3. Grand Rapids: Baker, 1994.

Booij, Thijs. "Psalm CXXXIX." *Vetus Testamentum* 55 (2005): 1-19.

_____. "Psalm 109:6-19 as a Quotation: A Review of the Evidence." Page 269 in *Give Ear to My Words: Psalms and Other Poetry in and Around the Hebrew Bible: Essays in Honour of Professor N.A. van Uchelen*. Edited by Janet Dyk. Societas Hebraica Amstelodamensis. Amsterdam: Kok Pharos, 1996.

_____. "Psalm 141: A Prayer for Discipline and Protection." *Biblica* 86 (2005): 97-106.

Braun, Roddy. *1 Chronicles*. Word Biblical Commentary 14. Waco: Word Books, 1986.

Brennan, Joseph P. "Some Hidden Harmonies in the Fifth Book of Psalms." Pages 126-58 in *Essays in Honor of Joseph P. Brennan*. Edited by Robert F. McNamara. New York: Saint Bernard's Seminary, 1976.

Briggs, Charles A., and Emilie Grace Briggs. *A Critical and Exegetical Commentary on the Book of Psalms*. Vol. II. The International Critical Commentary. Edinburgh: T. & T. Clark, 1906.

Brotzman, Ellis R. *Old Testament Textual Criticism: A Practical Introduction*. Grand Rapids: Baker Book, 2002.

Brown, Francis, S. R. Driver, Charles A. Briggs, Edward Robinson, James Strong, Wilhelm Gesenius, and Handwörterbuch Hebräisch-deutches. *Hebrew and English Lexicon: With an Appendix Containing the Biblical Aramaic*. Peabody: Hendrickson Publishers, 1997.

Brown, Michael L. "ברך." Pages 757-67 in vol. 1 of *The New International Dictionary of Old Testament Theology and Exegesis*. Edited by Willem A. VanGemeren. 5 vols. Grand Rapids: Zondervan Pub. House, 1997.

Brueggemann, Walter. *Abiding Astonishment: Psalms, Modernity, and the Making of History*. Literary Currents in Biblical Interpretation. Louisville: Westminster/John Knox, 1991.

_____. *The Message of the Psalm*. Minneapolis: Augsberg, 1984.

_____. *Praying the Psalms*. A Pace Book. Winona: Saint Mary, 1982.

_____. "Psalm 109: Three Times 'Steadfast Love'." *Word and World* 2 (2006): 144-54.

_____. *The Psalms and the Life of Faith*. Minneapolis: Fortress Press, 1995.

_____. "The Psalms in Theological Use: On Incommensurability." Pages 581-602 in *The Book of Psalms: Composition and Reception*. Edited by Peter W. Flint, Patrick D. Miller, Aaron Brunell and Ryan Roberts. Supplements to Vetus Testamentum 99. Leiden: Boston, 2005.

_____. "Response to James L. Mays, 'The Question of Context'." Pages 29-41 in *The Shape and Shaping of the Psalter*. Edited by J. Clinton McCann. Journal for the Study of the Old Testament: Supplement Series 159. Sheffield: JSOT Press, 1993.

Büchler, Adolf. "The Reading of the Law and Prophets in a Triennial Cycle." *Jewish Quarterly Review* 5 (1893): 420-68.

_____. "The Reading of the Law and Prophets in a Triennial Cycle." *Jewish Quarterly Review* 6 (1894): 1-73.

Buss, M. J. "Gunkel, Hermann (1862-1932)." Pages 487-91 in *Historical Handbook of Major Biblical Interpreters*. Edited by Donald McKim. Downers Grove: InterVarsity, 1998.

Buss, Martin. *Biblical Form Criticism in Its Context.* Edited by David Clines and
    Phillip Davis. Journal for the Study of the Old Testament: Supplement Series
    274. Sheffield: Sheffield Academic Press, 1999.

Buttenwieser, Moses. *The Psalms: Chronologically Treated with a New Translation.*
    Chicago: University of Chicago Press, 1938.

Buttrick, George Arthur. *The Interpreter's Bible: The Holy Scriptures in the King
    James and Revised Standard Versions with General Articles and Introduction,
    Exegesis, Exposition for Each Book of the Bible.* New York: Abingdon, 1951.

Calvin, John. *Commentary on the Book of Psalms.* Translated by James Anderson.
    Grand Rapids: Eerdmans, 1949.

Cartledge, Tony. "A House for God and a House for David." *Word and World* 23
    (2003): 395-02.

Ceresko, Anthony R. "The ABCs of Wisdom in Psalm XXXIV." *Vetus
    Testamentum* 35 (1985): 99-104.

_____. "Endings and Beginnings: Alphabetical Thinking and the Shaping
    of Psalms 106 and 150." *Catholic Biblical Quarterly* 68 (2006): 32-46.

_____. "The Function of Chiasmus in Hebrew Poetry." *The Catholic
    Biblical Quarterly* 40 (1978): 1-10.

Childs, Brevard S. *Introduction to the Old Testament as Scripture.* Philadelphia:
    Fortress, 1979.

_____. *Memory and Tradition in Israel.* Naperville: A.R. Allenson, 1962.

_____. "Psalm Titles and Midrashic Exegesis." *Journal of Semitic Studies*
    16 (1971): 137-50.

_____. "Reflections on the Modern Study of the Psalms." Pages 377-88
    in *Magnalia Dei: The Mighty Acts of God: Essays on the Bible and Archaeology
    in Memory of G. Ernest Wright.* Edited by George Ernest Wright, Frank
    Moore Cross, Werner E. Lemke, and Patrick D. Miller. Garden City:
    Doubleday, 1976.

_____. "Response to Reviews of Introduction to the Old Testament as
    Scripture." *Journal for the Study of the Old Testament* 16 (1980).

Chinitz, Jacob. "Psalm 145: Its Two Faces." *The Jewish Bible Quarterly* 24 (1996):
    229-32.

Christensen, Duane L. *Deuteronomy 21:10-34:12.* Word Biblical Commentary
    6B. Nashville: Thomas Nelson, 2002.

Clements, R. E., and Edward Ball. *In Search of True Wisdom: Essays in Old
    Testament Interpretation in Honour of Ronald E. Clements.* Sheffield: Sheffield
    Academic, 1999.

Clements, Ronald. "Mowinckel, Sigmund." Pages 505-10 in *Historical Handbook of Major Biblical Interpreters*. Edited by Donald McKim. Downers Grove: InterVarsity, 1998.

Clifford, Richard J. "Psalm 90: Wisdom Meditation or Communal Lement?" Pages 190-205 in *The Book of Psalms: Composition and Reception*. Edited by Peter W. Flint, Patrick D. Miller, Aaron Brunell and Ryan Roberts. Supplements to Vetus Testamentum 99. Leiden: Boston, 2005.

_____. *Psalms 73-150*. Abingdon Old Testament Commentaries. Nashville: Abingdon Press, 2003.

Clines, David. "Psalm Research 1955: I. The Psalms and the Cult." *Tyndale Bulletin* 18 (1967): 103-26.

_____. "Psalm Research 1955: II. The Psalms and the Cult." *Tyndale Bulletin* 20 (1969): 105-25.

Cotterell, Peter. "Linguistics, Meaning, Semantics, and Discourse Analysis." Pages 134-60 in vol. 1 of *New International Dictionary of Old Testament Theology and Exegesis*. Edited by Willem A. VanGemeren. 5 vols. Grand Rapids: Zondervan, 1997.

Cotterell, Peter, and Max Turner. *Linguistics and Biblical Interpretation*. Downers Grove: InterVarsity, 1989.

Craigie, Peter C. *Psalms 1-50*. Word Biblical Commentary 19. Waco: Word, 1983.

Craigie, Peter C., and Marvin E. Tate. *Psalms 1-50*. 2d ed. Word Biblical Commentary 19. Nashville: Thomas Nelson Publishers, 2004.

Crenshaw, James. Introduction to *The Psalms in Israel's Worship*, by Sigmund Mowinckel. Grand Rapids: Eerdmans, 2004.

Croft, Steven J. L. *The Identity of the Individual in the Psalms*. Journal for the Study of the Old Testament: Supplement Series 44. Sheffield: JSOT Press, 1987.

Crüsemann, F. *Studien zur Formgeschichte von Hymnus und Danklied in Israel*. Wissenschaftliche Monographien zum Alten und Neuen 32. Neykirchen: Neukirchener, 1969.

_____. *Studien zur Formgeschichte von Hymnus und Danklied in Israel*. Wissenschaftliche Monographien zum Alten und Neuen Testament. Neukirchen: Neukirchener, 1969.

Dahood, Mitchell. *Psalm II: 51-100*. The Anchor Bible 17. New York: Doubleday, 1968.

_____. *Psalm III: 101-150*. The Anchor Bible 17A. New York: Doubleday, 1970.

Davidson, Robert M. A. *The Vitality of Worship: A Commentary on the Book of Psalms.* Grand Rapids: Eerdmans, 1998.

De Beaugrande, Robert, and Wolfgang U. Dressler. *Introduction to Text Linguistics.* Longman Linguistics Library. London: Longman, 1981.

De Wette, Wilhelm, and Theodore Parker. *A Critical and Historical Introduction to the Canonical Scriptures of the Old Testament.* Translated by Theodore Parker. Vol. II. 2d ed. Boston: Little, Brown, and Company, 1858.

De Witt, John. *The Psalms: A New Translation with Introductory Essay and Notes.* New York: Anson D. F. Randolph, 1891.

DeClaissé-Walford, Nancy L. "An Intertextual Reading of Psalms 22, 23, and 24." Pages 139-52 in *The Book of Psalms: Composition and Reception.* Edited by Peter W. Flint, Patrick D. Miller, Aaron Brunell and Ryan Roberts. Supplements to Vetus Testamentum 99. Leiden: Boston, 2005.

_____. *Introduction to the Psalms: A Song from Ancient Israel.* St. Louis: Chalice Press, 2004.

_____. *Reading from the Beginning: The Shaping of the Hebrew Psalter.* Macon: Mercer University Press, 1997.

Delitzsch, Franz. *Biblical Commentary on the Psalms.* Translated by Francis Bolton. Vol. III. Grand Rapids: Eerdmans, 1955.

Dibelius, Martin. *Die Formgeschichte des Evangeliums.* Tübingen: Mohr, 1919.

_____. *From Tradition to Gospel.* Translated by Bertram Lee Woolf. London: Ivor Nicholson and Watson, 1934.

Dickson, David. *A Commentary on the Psalms.* The Geneva Series. Edinburgh: Banner of Truth, 1985.

Driver, Godfrey. "The Psalms in the Light of Babylonian Research." Pages 109-75 in *The Psalmists: Essays on Their Religious Experience and Teaching, Their Social Background, and Their Place in the Development of Hebrew Psalmody.* Edited by D. C. Simpson. London: Oxford University Press, 1926.

Durham, John I. *Esther-Psalms.* Edited by Clifton J. Allen. The Broadman Bible Commentary 4. Nashville: Broadman, 1969.

Eaton, J. H. *Kingship and the Psalms.* Studies in Biblical Theology. Naperville: Allenson, 1976.

_____. "The Psalms and Israelite Worship." Pages 238-73 in *Tradition and Interpretation: Essays by Members of the Society for Old Testament Study.* Edited by George Anderson. Oxford: Clarendon, 1979.

_____. *The Psalms: A Historical and Spiritual Commentary with an Introduction and New Translation.* London: T & T Clark, 2003.

_____. *Psalms: Introduction and Commentary.* Torch Bible
        Commentaries. London: S.C.M. Press, 1967.
Evans, Craig A. "Praise and Prophecy." Pages 551-79 in *The Book of Psalms:
        Composition and Reception.* Edited by Peter W. Flint, Patrick D. Miller,
        Aaron Brunell and Ryan Roberts. Supplements to Vetus Testamentum, 99.
        Leiden: Boston, 2005.
Firth, David G. "The Teaching of the Psalms." Pages 159-74 in *Interpreting the
        Psalms: Issues and Approaches.* Edited by David G. Firth and Philip Johnston.
        Downers Grove: InterVarsity, 2005.
Firth, David G., and Philip Johnston, eds. *Interpreting the Psalms: Issues and
        Approaches.* Downers Grove: InterVarsity, 2005.
Fishbane, Michael. "Types of Biblical Intertextuality." Pages 38-52 in *Congress
        Volume: Oslo 1998.* Edited by André Lamaire and Magne Sæbø. Supplements
        to Vetus Testamentum 80. Leiden: Boston, 2000.
_____. *Biblical Interpretation in Ancient Israel.* Oxford: Clarendon,
        1985.
Flint, P. W. *The Dead Sea Scrolls and the Book of Psalms.* Studies on the Texts of
        the Desert of Judah 17. Leiden: Brill, 1997.
Flint, Peter W., Patrick D. Miller, Aaron Brunell, and Ryan Roberts, eds.
        The Book of Psalms: Composition and Reception. Supplements to Vetus
        Testamentum 99. Leiden: Boston, 2005.
Fokkelman, J. P. *Reading Biblical Poetry: An Introductory Guide.* Louisville:
        Westminster John Knox Press, 2001.
France, R. T. "Kingdom of God." Pages 420-22 in *Dictionary for Theological
        Interpretation of the Bible.* Edited by Kevin J. Vanhoozer. Grand Rapids:
        Baker Academic, 2005.
Fretheim, Terence. "יהוה." Pages 1295-300 in vol. 1 of *New International
        Dictionary of Old Testament Theology and Exegesis.* Edited by Willem A.
        VanGemeren. 5 vols. Grand Rapids: Zondervan, 1997.
Gaiser, Frederick. "The David of Psalm 51: Reading Psalm 51 in Light of Psalm
        50." *Word and World* 23 (2003): 382-94.
Gerstenberger, Erhard S. "Der Psalter als Buch und als Sammlung." Pages 3-13
        in *Neue Wege der Psalmenforschung: für Walter Beyerlin.* Edited by Klaus
        Seybold, Erich Zenger and Walter Beyerlin. Herders Biblische Studien 1.
        Freiburg: Herder, 1994.
Gillingham, S. E. *The Poems and Psalms of the Hebrew Bible.* Oxford Bible Series.
        Oxford [England]: Oxford University Press, 1994.

Gillmayer-Bucher, Susanne. "The Psalm Headings. A Canonical Relectur of the Psalms." Pages 247-54 in *The Biblical Canons.* Edited by J. M. Auwers and H. J. Jonge. Bibliotheca ephemeridum theologicarum lovaniensium 163. Leuven: Leuven University Press, 2003.

Girad, Marc. "Analyse Structurelle du Psaume 95." *Science et esprit* 33 (1981): 179-89.

Goldsworthy, G. "Kingdom of God." Pages 615-20 in *New Dictionary of Biblical Theology.* Edited by T. Desmond Rosner Brian S. Alexander, D. A. Carson, Graeme Goldsworthy. Leicester: Inter-Varsity Press: Downers Grove, 2000.

Goshen-Gottstein, Moshe H. "The Psalms Scroll (11QPsa): A Problem of Canon and Text." *Textus* 5 (1966): 22-33.

Gottwald, Norman. *Studies in the Book of Lamentation.* Chicago: Alec R. Allenson, 1954.

Goulder, M. D. *The Prayers of David (Psalms 51-72).* Journal for the Study of the Old Testament: Supplement Series 102. London: New York, 2004.

_____. *The Psalms of Asaph and the Pentateuch.* Journal for the Study of the Old Testament: Supplement Series 233. Sheffield: Sheffield Academic Press, 1996.

_____. *The Psalms of the Return (Book V, Psalms 107-150): Studies in the Psalter IV.* Journal for the Study of the Old Testament: Supplement Series 258. Sheffield, Eng.: Sheffield Academic Press, 1998.

_____. *The Psalms of the Sons of Korah.* Journal for the Study of the Old Testament: Supplement Series 20. Sheffield: JSOT Press, 1982.

_____. "The Social Setting of the Book II of the Psalter." Pages xx, 680 p. in *The Book of Psalms: Composition and Reception.* Edited by Peter W. Flint, Patrick D. Miller, Aaron Brunell and Ryan Roberts. Leiden: Boston, 2005.

Grant, Jamie A. "The Psalms and the King." Pages 101-18. in *Interpreting the Psalms: Issues and Approaches.* Edited by David G Firth and Philip Johnston. Downers Grove: InterVarsity, 2005.

Gray, John. "The Hebrew Conception of the Kingship of God: Its Origin and Development." *Vetus Testamentum* 6 (1956): 268-85.

Greenberg, Moshe. "Two New Hunting Terms in Psalm 140:12." *Hebrew Annual Review* 1 (1977): 149-53.

Groom, Susan Anne. *Linguistic Analysis of Biblical Hebrew.* Carlisle: Waynesboro, 2003.

Guber, Mayer. *Rashi's Commentary on Psalms (Book I-III): With English Translation, Introduction, and Notes.* Edited by Bruce Chilton Jacob Neusner,

Fascing Darrell, William Green, Sara Mandell, and James Strange. South Florida Studies in the History of Judaism 161. Atlanta: Scholars, 1998.

Guilding, Aileen. "Some Obscured Rubrics and Lectionary Allusion in the Psalter." *Journal of Theological Studies* 3 (1952): 41-55.

Gunkel, Hermann. *Die Psalmen.* Handkommentar zum Alten Testament. Göttingen: Vandenhoeck & Ruprecht, 1926.

_____. *Die Psalmen.* Göttingen: Vandenhoeck & Ruprecht, 1926.

_____. *Einleitung in Die Psalmen: Die Gattungen der Religiösen Lyrik Israels.* Göttingen: Vandenhoeck and Ruprecht, 1933.

_____. *The Psalms: A Form-Critical Introduction.* Translated by Thomas M. Horner. Philadelphia: Fortress Press, 1967.

Gunkel, Hermann, and Joachim Begrich. *Introduction to Psalms: The Genres of the Religious Lyric of Israel.* Translated by James D. Nogalski. Macon: Mercer University Press, 1998.

Gunkel, Hermann, and B. E. S. *Israel and Babylon the Influence of Babylon on the Religion of Israel: A Reply to Delitzsch).* ATLA Monograph Preservation Program. Philadelphia: John Jos, 1904.

Gzella, Holger. "New Ways in Textual Criticism." *Ephemerides theologicae lovanienses* 81 (2005): 387-23.

Haller, Von Max. "Ein Jahrzehnt Psalmenforschung." *Theologische Rundschau* 1 (1929): 377-402.

Halliday, M. A. K. *An Introduction to Functional Grammar.* 2d ed. London: Edward Arnold, 1992.

_____. *Language as Social Semiotic: The Social Interpretation of Language and Meaning.* Baltimore: University Park Press, 1978.

Halliday, M. A. K., and Gunther R. Kress. *System and Function in Language: Selected Papers.* London: Oxford University Press, 1976.

Harman, Allan M. *Commentary on the Psalms.* Fearn: Mentor, 1998.

Hayes, John Haralson. *An Introduction to Old Testament Study.* Nashville: Abingdon, 1979.

Haynes, Stephen R., and Steven L. McKenzie. *To Each Its Own Meaning: An Introduction to Biblical Criticisms and Their Applications.* Rev. ed. Louisville: Westminster John Knox, 1999.

Hengstenberg, Ernst Wilhelm. *Commentary on the Psalms.* Vol. III. Cherry Hill: Mack Publishing, 1845.

_____. *Commentary on the Psalms.* 2 vols. Edinburgh: T & T Clark, 1846, 1876.

_____. *History of the Kingdom of God Under the Old Testament*. 2 vols. Eugene: Wipf & Stock, 2005.

Holladay, William. *The Psalms through Three Thousand Years: Prayerbook of a Cloud of Witnesses*. Minneapolis: Fortress, 1993.

Holm-Nielsen, S. "The Importance of Late Jewish Psalmody for the Understanding of Old Testament Psalmodic Tradition." *Studia theologica* 14 (1960): 1-53.

Holman, Jan. "The Structure of Psalm CXXXIX." *Vetus Testamentum* 21 (1971): 298-310.

Hopkins, Martin K. *God's Kingdom in the Old Testament*. Chicago: H. Regnery, 1964.

Hossfeld, Frank-Lothar, and Erich Zenger. *Psalmen 51-100*. Herders theologischer Kommentar zum Alten Testament. Freiburg im Breisgau: Herder, 2000.

_____. *Psalms 2: A Commentary on Psalms 51-100*. Edited by Klaus Baltzer. Translated by Linda M. Maloney. Hermeneia. Minneapolis: Fortress, 2005.

House, Paul R. *Beyond Form Criticism: Essays in Old Testament Literary Criticism*. Sources for Biblical and Theological Study 2. Winona Lake: Eisenbrauns, 1992.

_____. *Old Testament Theology*. Downers Grove: InterVarsity, 1998.

Howard, David M., Jr. "Editorial Activity in the Psalter: A State-of-the-Field Survey." Pages 52-70 in *The Shape and Shaping of the Psalter*. Edited by J. Clinton McCann. Journal for the Study of the Old Testament: Supplement Series 159. Sheffield: JSOT Press, 1993.

_____. "The Psalms and Current Study." Pages 23-40 in *Interpreting the Psalms: Issues and Approaches*. Edited by David G. Firth and Philip Johnston. Downers Grove: InterVarsity, 2005.

_____. "Recent Trends in Psalm Study." Pages 329-68 in *The Face of Old Testament Studies: A Survey of Contemporary Approaches*. Edited by David W. Baker and Bill T. Arnold. Grand Rapids: Baker, 1999.

_____. "The Structure of Psalms 93-100." Ph.D. diss., University of Michigan, 1986.

_____. *The Structure of Psalms 93-100*. Biblical and Judaic Studies from the University of California. Winona Lake: Eisenbrauns, 1997.

Hurowitz, Victor Avigdor. "Additional Elements of Alphabetical Thinking in Psalm XXXIV." *Vetus Testamentum* 52 (2002): 326-33.

Jacobson, Diane. "And Then There Were the Women in His Life: David and His Women." *Word and World* 23 (2003): 403-12.

Japhet, Sara. *I and II Chronicles: A Commentary.* The Old Testament Library. Louisville: Westminster John Knox, 1993.

John Carmody, S. J. "The Theology of Psalm 145." *The Bible Today* 43 (1969): 2972-79.

Johnson, A. R. "The Psalms." Pages 162-209 in *The Old Testament and Modern Study: A Generation of Discovery and Research; Essays by Members of The Society for Old Testament Study.* Edited by Harold Rowley. Oxford: Clarendon, 1951.

Johnson, Aubrey R. *Sacral Kingship in Ancient Israel.* Cardiff: Wales, 1967.

Johnson, Elliott E. "Hermeneutical Principles and the Interpretation of Psalm 110." *Bibliotheca sacra* 149 (1992): 428-37.

Jones, David Allan. "A Theology of Psalm 110." Th.M. thesis, Dallas Theological Seminary, 1981.

Jonker, Louis C., ed. *Revisiting the Psalm Headings: Second Temple Levitical Propaganda?* Edited by Dirk J. Human and Cas J. A. Vos. Psalms and Liturgy. New York: T & T Clark, 2004.

Katanacho, Yohanna. "Investigating the Purposeful Placement of Psalm 86." Ph.D. diss., Trinity International University, 2006.

Kidner, Derek. *Psalms 73-150: A Commentary on Books III-V of the Psalms.* The Tyndale Old Testament Commentaries. London: Inter-Varsity Press, 1975.

Kim, Dwight Dongwan. "Is Christ Sitting on the Davidic Throne? Peter's Use of Psalm 110:1 in His Pentecostal Speech Acts 2." Th.D. diss., Dallas Theological Seminary, 1993.

Kimelman, Reuven. "Psalm 145: Theme, Structure, and Impact." *Journal of Biblical Literature* 113 (1994): 37-58.

King, E. J. "The Influence of the Triennial Cycle Upon the Psalter." *Journal of Theological Studies* 5 (1903): 203-13.

Kirkpatrick, A. F., ed. *The Book of Psalms.* Cambridge Bible for Schools and Colleges. Cambridge: Cambridge University Press, 1902.

Kissane, Edward J. "The Interpretation of Psalm 110." *Irish Theological Quarterly* 21 (1954): 103-14.

Kittel, Gerhard, Gerhard Friedrich, and Geoffrey William Bromiley, eds. *Theological Dictionary of the New Testament.* Grand Rapids: Eerdmans, 1985.

Klein, William., Craig L. Blomberg, and Robert L. Hubbard. *Introduction to Biblical Interpretation.* Dallas: Word Publishing, 1993.

Knowles, Melody D. "The Flexible Rhetoric of Retelling: The Choice of David in the Text of the Psalms." *Catholic Biblical Quarterly* 67 (2005): 236-49.

Koch, Klaus. "Der Psalter und seine Redaktionsgeschichte." Pages 243-77 in *Neue Wege der Psalmenforschung*. Edited by K. Seybold and E. Zenger. 2 ed. Herders Biblische Studien 1. Freiburg: Herders, 1995.

Kratz, Reinhard Gregor. "Die Tora Davids: Psalm 1 und die doxologische Funfteilung des Psalters." *Zeitschrift fur Theologie und Kirche* 93 (1996): 1-34.

Kraus, Hans-Joachim. *Psalms 1-59: A Continental Commentary*. Translated by Hilton C. Oswald. Minneapolis: Fortress, 1989.

_____. *Psalms 60-150: A Continental Commentary*. Translated by Hilton C. Oswald. Minneapolis: Fortress, 1989.

_____. *Theology of the Psalms*. Translated by Crim Keith. Minneapolis: Augsburg, 1986.

Kselman, John S. "Psalm 77 and the Book of Exodus." *The Journal of the Ancient Near Eastern Society* 15 (1983): 51-58.

Kugel, J. *The Idea of Biblical Poetry*. New Haven: Yale University Press, 1981.

Kuntz, J. Kenneth. "Engaging the Psalms: Gains and Trends in Recent Research." *Currents in Research: Biblical Studies* 2 (1994): 77-106.

Kunz, L. "Psalm 110 in masoretischer Darbietung." *Theologie und Glaube* 72 (1982): 331-35.

Leech, Geoffrey. *Semantics*. Harmondsworth: Penguin Books, 1974.

Lemaire, André, and Magne Sæbø, eds. *Congress Volume: Oslo 1998*. Supplements to Vetus Testamentum 80. Leiden: Boston, 2000.

Leslie, Elmer A. *The Psalms: Translated and Interpreted in the Light of Hebrew Life and Worship*. New York: Abingdon, 1949.

Leupold, H. C. *Exposition of the Psalms*. Grand Rapids: Baker, 1969.

Liebreich, Leon J. "Psalms 34 and 145 in the Light Their Key Words." *Hebrew Annual College Annual* 27 (1956): 181-92.

Limburg, James. *Psalms*. Edited by Patrick D. Miller and David L. Bartlett. Westminster Bible Companion. Louisville: Westminster John Knox, 2000.

Lindars, Barnabas. "The Structure of Psalm CXLV." *Vetus Testamentum* 29 (1989): 23-30.

Lindbeck, George A. "Postcritical Canonical Interpretation: Three Modes of Retrieval." Pages 26-51 in *Theological Exegesis: Essays in Honor of Brevard Childs*. Edited by K.G. McCreight. Grand Rapids: Eerdmans, 1999.

Lohfink, Norbert, and Erich Zenger. *The God of Israel and the Nations: Studies in Isaiah and the Psalms*. Collegeville, Minn.: Liturgical Press, 2000.

Longman, Tremper. "A Divine Warrior Victory Song." *Journal of the Evangelical Theological Society* 27 (1984): 167-74.

Low, Roy Kong. "An Exegetical and Theological Study of Psalm 145." Th.M. thesis, Dallas Theological Seminary, 1984.

Lucas, Ernest C. *Exploring the Old Testament: A Guide to the Psalms and Wisdom Literature.* Downers Grove: Inter Varsity Press, 2003.

Lutz, Luise. *Zum Tema 'Thema': Einfüruing in die Thema-Rhema-Theorie.* Hamburg: Hamburger Buchagentur, 1981.

Luyten, J. "David and the Psalms." Pages 57-59 in *The Psalms: Prayers of Humanity, Prayers of Israel, Prayers of the Church.* Edited by Lambert Leijssen. Leuven: Abdij Keizerberg, 1990.

Magonet, Jonathan. "Some Concentric Structure in Psalms." *Heythrop Journal* 23 (1982): 365-76.

Malchow, Bruce V. "God or King in Psalm 146." *The Bible Today* 89 (1977): 1166-70.

Mays, James Luther. "The David of the Psalms." *Interpretation* 40 (1986): 143-55.

——————. *The Lord Reigns: A Theological Handbook to the Psalms.* Louisville: Westminster John Knox, 1994.

——————. "Past, Present, and Prospect in Psalm Study." Pages 147-56 in *Old Testament Interpretation: Past, Present, and Future: Essays in Honor of Gene M. Tucker.* Edited by Gene M. Tucker, James Luther Mays, David L. Petersen and Kent Harold Richards. Nashville: Abingdon, 1995.

——————. *Psalms.* Interpretation: A Bible Commentary for Teaching and Preaching. Louisville: Westminster John Knox, 1994.

——————. "The Question of Context in Psalm Interpretation." Pages 14-20 in *The Shape and Shaping of the Psalter.* Edited by J. Clinton McCann. Journal for the Study of the Old Testament: Supplement Series 159. Sheffield: JSOT Press, 1993.

Mays, James Luther, and Donald G. Miller. *The Hermeneutical Quest: Essays in Honor of James Luther Mays on His Sixty-Fifth Birthday.* Princeton Theological Monographs Series 4. Allison Park: Pickwick, 1986.

McCann, J. Clinton. "The Book of Psalms." Pages 641-1280 in *The New Interpreter's Bible: Volume IV.* Nashville: Abingdon, 1996.

——————. "The Books I-III and the Editorial Purpose of the Psalter." Pages 93-107 in *The Shape and Shaping of the Psalter.* Edited by J. Clinton McCann. Sheffield: JSOT Press, 1993.

_____. Preface to *The Shape and Shaping of the Psalter*. Edited by J. Clinton McCann. Journal for the Study of the Old Testament: Supplement Series 159. Sheffield: JSOT Press, 1993a.

_____. *A Theological Introduction to the Book of Psalms: The Psalms as Torah*. Nashville: Abingdon, 1993.

_____, ed. *The Shape and Shaping of the Psalter*. Journal for the Study of the Old Testament: Supplement Series 159. Sheffield: JSOT Press, 1993b.

_____. "The Psalms as Instruction." *Interpretation* 46 (1992): 117-28.

McCann, J. Clinton, and James C. Howell. *Preaching the Psalms*. Nashville: Abingdon, 2001.

McCarter, P. Kyle. "The Historical David." *Interpretation* 40 (1986): 117-29.

_____. *Textual Criticism: Recovering the Text of the Hebrew Bible*. Guides to Biblical Scholarship. Philadelphia: Fortress, 1986.

McKenzie, Steven. "Who Was King David?" *Word and World* 23 (2003): 357-64.

McNamara, Martin. *The Psalm in the Early Irish Church*. Edited by Phillip Davis David Clines, and John Jarick. Journal for the Study of the Old Testament: Supplement Series 155. Sheffield: Sheffield Academic Press, 2000.

Meer, Willem van der. "Psalm 110: A Psalm of Rehabilitation." Pages 207-34 in *The Structural Analysis of Biblical and Canaanite Poetry*. Edited by Willem van der Meer and Johannes C. de Moor. Sheffield: JSOT Press, 1988.

Mejia, Jorge. "Some Observations on Psalm 107." *Biblical Theology Bulletin* 5 (1975): 55-56.

Millard, Matthias. *Die Komposition des Psalters: Ein formgeschichtlicher Ansatz*. Forschungen zum Alten Testament 9. Tübingen: Mohr, 1994.

Miller, Patrick D. "The End of the Psalter: A Response to Erich Zenger." *Journal for the Study of the Old Testament* 80 (1998): 103-10.

_____. "The Beginning of the Psalter." Pages 83-92 in *The Shape and Shaping of the Psalter*. Edited by J. Clinton McCann. Journal for the Study of the Old Testament: Supplement Series 159. Sheffield: JSOT Press, 1993.

Miller, Patrick D. and Peter W. Flint. "Introduction and Overview of Psalms Scholarship in this Volume." Pages 1-8 in *The Book of Psalms: Composition and Reception*. Edited by Peter W. Flint, Patrick D. Miller, Aaron Brunell, and Ryan Roberts. Leiden: Boston, 2005.

Montgomery, James A. "Stanza-Formation in Hebrew Poetry." *Journal of Biblical Literature* 64 (1945): 379-84.

Mowinckel, Sigmund. *The Psalms in Israel's worship*. New York: Abingdon Press, 1962.

_____. *The Psalms in Israel's Worship*. Translated by D. R. Ap-Thomas. 2 vols. Grand Rapids: Eerdmans, 2004.

Muilenburg, James. "Form Criticism and Beyond." Pages 27-44 in *Hearing and Speaking the Word: Selections from the Works of James Muilenburg*. Edited by Thomas F. Best. Chico: Scholars Press, 1984.

Munch, P. A. "Die alphabetische Akrostichie in der judischen Psalmendichtung." *Zeitschrift der deutschen morgenlandischen Gesellschaft* 90 (1936): 703-10.

Murphy, Roland E. "Reflections on Contextual Interpretation of Psalms." Pages 21-28 in *The Shape and Shaping of the Psalter*. Edited by J. Clinton McCann. Journal for the Study of the Old Testament: Supplement Series 159. Sheffield: JSOT Press, 1993.

Neale, J. M., and Richard Frederick Littledale. *A Commentary on the Psalms: From Primitive and Mediaeval Writers and from the Various Office-Books and Hymns of the Roman, Mozarabic, Ambrosian, Gallican, Greek, Coptic, Armenian, and Syriac Rites*. Vol. 4. 2d ed. London: Joseph Masters, 1976.

Nel, Philip J. "מלך." Pages 956-65 in vol. 2 of *New International Dictionary of Old Testament Theology and Exegesis*. Edited by Willem A. VanGemeren. 5 vols. Grand Rapids: Zondervan, 1997.

Oesterley, W. O. E. *The Psalms: Translated with Text-Critical and Exegetical Notes*. Vol. 2. London: SPCK, 1939.

Ogden, C. K., and I. A. Richards. *The Meaning of Meaning*. 8th ed. London: Routledge, 1946.

Pearle, Chaim. "The Theology of Psalm 145: Part I." *The Jewish Bible Quarterly* 20/1 (1991): 3-10.

_____. "The Theology of Psalm 145: Part II." *The Jewish Bible Quarterly* 20/2 (1991/92): 73-78.

Perdue, Leo G. *The Collapse of History: Reconstructing Old Testament Theology*. Overtures to Biblical Theology. Minneapolis: Fortress, 1994.

Pietersma, Albert. "Septuagint Exegesis and Superscriptions of the Greek Psalter." Pages 443-75 in *The Book of Psalms: Composition and Reception*. Edited by Peter W. Flint, Patrick D. Miller, Aaron Brunell and Ryan Roberts. Supplements to Vetus Testamentum. Leiden: Boston, 2005.

Prinsloo, W. S. "Psalm 145: Loof Jahweh Van A tot Z." *In die Skriflig* 25 (1991): 457-70.

Rendtorff, Rolf. "The Psalms of David: David in the Psalms." Pages 53-64 in *The Book of Psalms: Composition and Reception*. Edited by Peter W. Flint, Patrick D. Miller, Aaron Brunell and Ryan Roberts. Supplements to Vetus Testamentum 29. Leiden: Boston, 2005.

Risse, Siegfried. *Gut ist es, unserem Gott zu singen: Untersuchungen zu Psalm 147.* Münsteraner theologische Abhandlungen 37. Altenberge: Oros Verlag, 1995.

Roberts, J. J. M. "The Enthronement of Yhwh And David: The Abiding Theological Significance of the Kingship Language of the Psalms." *Catholic Biblical Quarterly* 64 (2002): 675-86.

_____. "Mowinckel's Enthronement Festival: A Review." Pages 97-115 in *The Book of Psalms: Composition and Reception.* Edited by Peter W. Flint, Patrick D. Miller, Aaron Brunell and Ryan Roberts. Supplements to Vetus Testamentum 99. Leiden: Boston, 2005.

Rose, Walter. "Messianic Expectations in the Old Testament." *In die Skriflig* 35 (2001): 284-90.

Rowe, Robert D. *God's Kingdom and God's Son: The Background to Mark's Christology from Concepts of Kingship in the Psalms.* Arbeiten zur Geschichte des antiken Judentums und des Urchristentums. Leiden: Boston, 2002.

Rowley, H. H. "Melchizedek and Zadok." Pages 461-72 in *Festschrift für Alfred Bertholet zum 80 Geburtstag.* Edited by Otto Eissfeldt Walter Baumgartner, Karl Elliger, and Leonhard Rost. Tübingen: Mohr, 1950.

Sanders, James A. *Canon and Community: A Guide to Canonical Criticism.* Guides to Biblical Scholarship. Philadelphia: Fortress, 1984.

_____. *From Sacred Story to Sacred Text: Canon as Paradigm.* Philadelphia: Fortress, 1987.

_____. *The Dead Sea Psalms Scroll.* Ithaca: Cornell University Press, 1967.

_____. *From Sacred Story to Sacred Text: Canon as Paradigm.* Philadelphia: Fortress, 1987.

_____. *The Psalms Scroll of Qumran Cave 11 (11QPs^a).* Discoveries in the Judaean Desert of Jordan 4. Oxford: Clarendon, 1965.

Schaefer, Konrad. *Psalms.* Edited by Cotter David W. Berit Olam: Studies in Hebrew Narrative and Poetry. Collegeville: Liturgical Press, 2001.

Scharen, Hans. "An Exegetical and Theological Study of Psalm 144." M.Th. thesis, Dallas Theological Seminary, 1984.

Schüngel-Straumann, Helen. "Zur Gattung und Theologie des 139." *Biblische Zeitschrift* 17 (1973): 39-51.

Scroggie, W. Graham. *The Psalms: Psalms I to CL.* Westwood: Fleming H. Revell, 1965.

Sellers, Ovid. "The Status and Progress of Research Concerning the Psalms." Pages 129-43 in *The Study of the Bible Today and Tomorrow.* Chicago: University of Chicago Press, 1947.

Selman, Martin J. "The Kingdom of God in the Old Testament." *Tyndale Bulletin* 40 (1989): 161-84.

Sheppard, Gerald T. *Wisdom as a Hermeneutical Construct: A Study in the Sapientializing of the Old Testament.* Beiheft zur Zeitschrift für die alttestamentliche Wissenschaft 151. Berlin: de Gruyter, 1980.

Simon, Uriel. *Four Approaches to the Book of Psalms: From Saadiah Gaon to Abraham Ibn Ezra.* SUNY Series in Judaica. Albany: State University of New York Press, 1991.

Skehan, Patrick W. "Studies in Israelite Poetry and Wisdom." Pages 75-95 in *Catholic Biblical Quarterly Monograph Series.* Washington: Catholic Biblical Association, 1971.

Snaith, Norman Henry. *The Seven Psalms.* London: Epworth, 1964.

Stamm, Johann. "Ein Vierteljahrhudert Psalmenforschung." *Theologische Rundschau* 23 (1955): 1-62.

Steussy, Marti. "David, God, and the Word." *Word and World* 23 (2003): 365-73.

Sweeney, Marvin A., and Ehud Ben Zvi, eds. *The Changing Face of Form Criticism for the Twenty-First Century.* Grand Rapids: Eerdmans, 2003.

Tate, Marvin E. *Psalms 51-100.* 2d ed. Word Biblical Commentary 20. Waco: Word, 1983.

_____. *Psalms 51-100.* Word Biblical Commentary 20. Dallas: Word Books, 1990.

Terrien, Samuel L. *The Psalms: Strophic Structure and Theological Commentary.* The Eerdmans Critical Commentary. Grand Rapids: Eerdmans, 2003.

Theodoret, Bishop of Cyrus. *Theodoret of Cyrus: Commentary on the Psalms, Psalm 1-72.* Edited by Elizabeth Clark Thomas Halton, Joseph Lienhard, Frank Mantello, Kathleen McVey, Robert Sider, Michael Slauser, Cynthia White, Robin Young, and David McGonagle. Translated by Robert Hill. The Fathers of the Church: A New Translation 102. Washington, D. C.: Catholic University of America, 2000.

Throntveit, Mark. "Was the Chronicler a Spin Doctor? David in the Books of Chronicles." *Word and World* 23 (2003): 374-81.

Tournay, Raymond. "Le Psaumé CXLIV. Structure et Interpretation." *Revue biblique* 91 (1984): 520-30.

Tov, Emanuel. "Criteria for Evaluating Textual Readings: The Limitations of Textual Rules." *Harvard Theological Review* 75 (1983): 429-48.

_____. *Textual Criticism of the Hebrew Bible.* 2d rev. ed. Minneapolis: Fortress, 2001.

Ulrich, Eugene Charles. *The Dead Sea Scrolls and the Origins of the Bible*. Studies
in the Dead Sea scrolls and Related Literature. Grand Rapids: Leiden, 1999.

VanGemeren, Willem A. *Guide to Old Testament Exegesis*. Jackson, Miss:
Reformed Theological Seminary, 1984.

_____. "Psalms." Pages 1-880 in *Psalms, Proverbs, Ecclesiastes, Song of
Songs*. Edited by Frank E. Gæbelein. The Expositor's Bible Commentary 5.
Grand Rapids: Zondervan, 1991.

Vanhoozer, Kevin J. *The Drama of Doctrine: A Canonical-Linguistic Approach to
Christian Theology*. Louisville: Westminster John Knox, 2005.

_____. "Exegesis and Hermeneutics." Pages 52-64 in *New Dictionary
of Biblical Theology*. Edited by T. Desmond Alexander and Brian S. Rosner.
Downers Grove: Inter-Varsity Press, 2000.

_____. *First Theology: God, Scripture, and Hermeneutics*. Downers Grove:
InterVarsity, 2002.

_____. *Is There a Meaning in This Text? The Bible, the Reader, and the
Morality of Literary Knowledge*. Grand Rapids: Zondervan, 1998.

_____. "Language, Literature, Hermeneutics, and Biblical Theology:
What's Theological About a Theological Dictionary?" Pages 15-50 in vol.
1 of *New International Dictionary of Old Testament Theology and Exegesis*.
Edited by Willem A. VanGemeren. 5 vols. Grand Rapids: Zondervan Pub.
House, 1997.

Vincent, M. A. "The Shape of the Psalter: An Eschatological Dimension?" Pages
61-82 in *New Heaven and New Earth Prophecy and the Millennium Essay in
Honor of Anthony Gelston*. Leiden: Brill, 1999.

von Rad, Gerhard. "מלך and מלכות in the OT." Pages 565-71 in vol. 1 of
Theological Dictionary of the New Testament. Edited by Gerhard Kittel.
Translated by Bromiley Geoffrey William and Gerhard Friedrich. Grand
Rapids: Eerdmans, 1964.

Vos, Geerhardus. *The Eschatology of the Old Testament*. Edited by James T.
Dennison, Jr. Philipsburg: Presbyterian and Reformed, 2001.

Wagner, Siegfried. "Zur Theologie Des Psalms CXXXIX." *Supplements to Vetus
Testamentum* 29 (1978): 357-76.

Waltner, James H. *Psalms*. Edited by Elmer A Martens A. and Willard M.
Swartley. Believers Church Bible Commentary. Scottdale: Herald, 2006.

Ward, Martin J. "Psalm 109: David's Poem of Vengeance." *Andrews University
Seminary Studies* 18 (1980): 163-68.

Waschke, Ernst. "The Significance of the David Tradition for the Emergence of
Messianic Beliefs in the Old Testament." *Word and World* 23 (2003): 413-20.

Watson, W. G. E. "Reversed Rootplay in Ps 145." *Revue biblique* 62 (1981): 101-102.

Weiser, Artur. *The Psalms: A Commentary.* The Old Testament Library. Philadelphia: Westminster, 1962.

Wellhousen, Julius. *The Book of Psalms: A New English Translation with Explanatory Notes and Appendix on the Music of the Ancient Hebrews.* Edited by Paul Haupt and Horace Furness. Translated by John Taylor Horace Furness, and J. A. Paterson. The Sacred Books of the Old and New Testaments 14. New York: Dodd, Mead, 1898.

Westermann, Claus. *Praise and Lament in the Psalms.* Translated by Keith R. Crim and Richard N. Soulen. Atlanta: John Knox, 1981.

_____. *The Psalms: Structure, Content, and Message.* Translated by Ralph D. Gehrke. Minneapolis: Augsburg, 1980.

Whybray, Roger Norman. *Reading the Psalms as a Book.* Journal for the Study of the Old Testament: Supplement Series 222. Sheffield: Sheffield Academic, 1996.

Williamson, H. G. M. *1 and 2 Chronicles.* New Century Bible Commentary. Grand Rapids: Eerdmans, 1982.

Wilson, Gerald H. "The Qumran Psalms Manuscripts and the Consecutive Arrangement of Psalms in the Hebrew Psalter." *Catholic Biblical Quarterly* 45 (1983): 377-88.

_____. *The Editing of the Hebrew Psalter.* Chico: Scholars Press, 1985.

_____. "Evidence of Editorial Division in the Hebrew Psalter." *Vetus Testamentum* 3 (1984): 337-52.

_____. "A First Century C. E. Date for the Closing of the Book of Psalms?" *The Jewish Bible Quarterly* 28 (2000): 102-10.

_____. "King, Messiah, and the Reign of God: Revisiting the Royal Psalms and the Shape of the Psalter." Pages 391-406 in *The Book of Psalms: Composition and Reception.* Edited by Peter W. Flint, Patrick D. Miller, Aaron Brunell, and Ryan Roberts. Leiden: Boston, 2005.

_____. *Psalms: From Biblical Text to Contemporary Life.* The NIV Application Commentary. Grand Rapids: Zondervan, 2002.

_____. "The Qumran Psalms Scroll (11QPsa) and the Canonical Psalter: Comparison of Editorial Shaping." *Catholic Biblical Quarterly* 59 (1997): 448-64.

_____. "The Qumran Psalms Scroll Reconsidered: Analysis of the Debate." *Catholic Biblical Quarterly* 47 (1985): 624-42.

_____. "The Shape of the Book of Psalms." *Interpretation* 46 (1992): 129-42.

_____. "Shaping the Psalter: A Consideration of Editorial Linkage in the Book of Psalms." Pages 72-82 in *The Shape and Shaping of the Psalter*. Edited by J. Clinton McCann. Journal for the Study of the Old Testament: Supplement Series 159. Sheffield: JSOT Press, 1993.

_____. "The Structure of the Psalter." Pages 159-74 in *Interpreting the Psalms: Issues and Approaches*. Edited by David G. Firth and Philip Johnston. Downers Grove: InterVarsity, 2005.

_____. "Understanding the Purposeful Arrangement of Psalms in the Psalter: Pitfalls and Promise." Pages 42-51 in *The Shape and Shaping of the Psalter*. Edited by J. Clinton McCann. Journal for the Study of the Old Testament: Supplement Series 159. Sheffield: JSOT Press, 1993.

_____. "The Use of 'Untitled' Psalms in the Hebrew Psalter." *Zeitschrift für Die alttestamentliche Wissenschaft* 97 (1985): 404-13.

_____. "The Use of Royal Psalms at the 'Seams' of the Hebrew Psalter." *Journal for the Study of the Old Testament* 35 (1986): 85-94.

Würthwein, Ernst. "Erwängungen zu Ps 139." *Vetus Testamentum* 7 (1957): 165-82.

_____. *The Text of the Old Testament: An Introduction to the Biblia Hebraica*. Translated by Erroll F. Rhodes. Grand Rapids: Eerdmans, 1995.

Zenger, Erich. "The Composition and Theology of the Fifth Book of Psalms, Psalms 107-145." *Journal for the Study of the Old Testament* 80 (1998): 77-102.

_____. "New Approaches to the Study of the Psalms." *Proceedings of the Irish Biblical Association* 17 (1994a): 37-54.